TEACHERS
OF
YOUNG
CHILDREN

Robert D. Hess
STANFORD UNIVERSITY

Doreen J. Croft
DE ANZA COLLEGE

with the assistance of
Anne Kirby

TEACHERS OF YOUNG CHILDREN

HOUGHTON MIFFLIN COMPANY
BOSTON
New York
Atlanta
Geneva, Illinois
Dallas
Palo Alto

Copyright © 1972 by Houghton Mifflin Company. All rights reserved. No part of this work may be reproduced or transmitted in any form or by any means, electronic or mechanical, including photocopying and recording, or by any information storage or retrieval system, without permission in writing from the publisher.

Printed in the U.S.A.
Library of Congress Catalog Card Number: 74-166473
ISBN: 0-395-11225-7

To Allison Davis and Paul Hanna
and to
Karen and Colleen Croft
Jared, Alyssa, Devin and Bradley Hess

EDITOR'S INTRODUCTION

For the young person who is contemplating a career in the field of early childhood education, these are times of extraordinary opportunity. Probably no other branch of education is currently receiving more attention, not only from educators and behavioral scientists but also from state and national political leaders. Prompted by an impressive array of data concerning the beneficial influence on young children of well-conceived educational experiences, legislators, (including school board members) have given ever more enthusiastic support to programs of day care, nursery education, kindergarten, where it has previously not existed, and improved services in the lower elementary years. Some of these programs, spurred by a nagging awareness that some children, especially the poor, suffer terrible and lasting disadvantages because of circumstances beyond their control, are deliberately compensatory in nature and spirit. Others are in response to the growing desire of young mothers to launch or continue their careers outside the home, thus creating the need for appropriate child-care services. Still others perpetuate and build upon established traditions of early education that are an important part of the American dream of fulfillment (at least in part) through schooling. Nearly all are influenced in some way by one or another of the presumably exemplary models that have been developed by various theorists, particularly in recent years.

Within the expanding literature that both responds to the need for better educational service to the young and stimulates its further development, this textbook and *its companion handbook* will almost certainly earn solid recognition. Both are authentic, well-documented, readable, and geared to the needs of the young and relatively inexperienced teacher. Both are grounded in developmental theory, and yet rich in ideas of immediate and practical application. The handbook, of course, is by definition the more explicitly practical of the two volumes; but the basic text also contains a great deal of practical help for the teacher whose concern is with "what" and "how" as well as "why." Some readers, in fact, will probably value these books primarily because the authors obviously have a rich and comprehensive awareness of classroom situations and have addressed themselves with remarkable skill to the problems and questions that figure most prominently in the daily, workaday lives of classroom teachers.

Textbooks in this field rarely succeed to the extent these authors have, in integrating psychological research and theory on child development with early education theory and practice. Given the fluid state of research and theory, there are serious difficulties both in making logical connections and in deriving suggestions for teacher behavior. That these difficulties have been so skillfully overcome, and that the material is conveyed so clearly to the reader, are accomplishments that the most mature critics should particularly appreciate. In fact, although the target readership is the collegiate pre-professional group, the solid scholarship in this volume will probably appeal to graduate students and veteran teachers as well.

The authors have been remarkably effective in their summaries of recent work in the field, perhaps especially those dealing with language and with social development. They are also very effective in maintaining an objective and balanced view while examining the numerous controversies which stir so many emotions among the early-childhood experts. Quite likely the strongest feature of the book is the skill and the thoroughness with which is presented what educators and others have learned over the past ten or fifteen years about the so-called "disadvantaged child." There is not, to my knowledge, any single published volume which contains a more thorough or up-to-date discussion of this problem as it affects young children and of the various alternative strategies that may be considered for coping with it. The material showing how parents, community workers, aides, and other non-professional personnel can be involved in the early education process is particularly though not exclusively geared to such strategies.

A consulting editor inevitably betrays his own bias, and limitations, in his work with authors and in his evaluation of their performance. I confess to being an eclectic in this field, for example, and therefore I rejoice that Hess and Croft have chosen an eclectic approach. I am primarily a practitioner, to cite another bias, and I therefore appreciate the down-to-earth, yet solidly-based, proposals that abound in this book. I have a strong conviction that early childhood is that branch of educational activity where the chips these days are the bluest, and it excites me to have in hand a book that seems especially capable of guiding our work with young children. My expectation is that many prospective and inservice teachers will find in the chapters that follow the help that they need and want.

Robert H. Anderson

Harvard University

PREFACE

The spotlight in early education is shifting from the child to the teacher. During the past decade of rapid change, children—especially those from low-income families—have held the center of the stage. This concentration upon the need to prepare children cognitively for school has produced a wealth of research results, new materials, innovative programs and new teaching techniques. There has probably been no period in the history of early education that has produced such an outpouring of new resources.

These new ideas and materials are effective only to the extent that they are properly used. The teacher is obviously the key person in the process. Without her touch and skill, the most sophisticated curriculum will be limp and boring. It is her philosophy and technique that count.

This book is thus oriented toward the teacher. The complexity of early education demands that she be even more professional than ever before. The days of the nursery school teacher as a "glorified baby sitter" (if indeed they ever existed) have disappeared.

Working directly in classrooms with young children is only one of her many roles. She has other audiences to which she must relate if her work with children is to be most effective: these include colleagues organized to exert influence upon the field through local, state and national associations, parents of the children in her class, and a community which wants to have a part in making decisions about the education of its children.

The teacher is often observed by researchers and evaluators, who with their reports and lectures, are often in a position to influence policy and availability of public funds. She must know about her competition—the corporation nursery schools, franchises, child development centers, "drop in" schools run by colleges, and mobile units which cover wide rural areas—and also keep up with the new programs and techniques urged upon her by colleagues and others.

Through it all, she keeps an eye on her own career. What are the implications of the new laws on credentialing, what's happening to salary levels, what new courses are being offered and how can she get the course credit she needs for advancement?

And, always, there is the ultimate question—how can she do a more effective job with the children in her class?

The teacher entering the field of early education can look forward to an exciting and successful career if she is willing to take the time and get the training needed to become a real "pro." We hope this book will help her take the first big step.

RDH
DJC

Palo Alto, California

ACKNOWLEDGMENTS

This book grew out of the ideas, encouragement, work and expert knowledge of many people. Paul Hanna first suggested the idea and helped us recognize the potential importance of a book of this kind. One of the central themes—the effect of society, culture and institutions upon education and cognitive development—came from the work and writing of Allison Davis.

Our decision to collaborate stemmed from the hope that our diverse backgrounds in the field of early education, representing both academic and practical experience, complemented each other and might provide a useful and interesting balance. Bill MacDonald of Houghton Mifflin Company helped stimulate our initial interest in the project and offered other kinds of encouragement. In the preliminary stages of the book, Cathy Caldwell gave us valuable advice and information about writing and publishing matters. We are sorry that illness forced her to withdraw from more active participation.

Anne Kirby played a starring role in this production. Not only did she help us put our ideas and materials into a working draft of the manuscript, but she lent a support that went far beyond her obligation. Her husband, Robert Van Valkenburgh, suffered with good humor the disruption that the months of work brought to his household and to his own company, The Altoan Press; he gave us technical advice, ran off copies of chapters, bound working copies of manuscript and helped in more other ways than than we can recount. These two generous people have our unlimited gratitude.

Others also played crucial roles. Mrs. Lyn Sharpe did the many sorts of things that only an efficient, helpful, bright secretary can do—looking up especially elusive references, typing or retyping sections on short notice so that they might make the morning mail, retyping the bibliography and checking its accuracy, and in general making things more pleasant.

Jan Miller did most of the typing of the manuscript, setting standards of quality, speed and conscientiousness that even exceeded our expectations. Stan Wilson supplied useful editorial help. Romayne Ponleithner compiled the index and counselled us on the details of manuscript preparation and proofreading. Karen Croft checked items, xeroxed, ordered things, made lists and helped with details. Colleen Croft gave us her indulgence.

Advice and counsel from colleagues was freely given and gratefully received. Especially helpful were Constance Kamii and Courtney Cazden, to whose work we often referred and who provided many helpful suggestions for our sections on cognitive and language development. Robert Anderson, our series editor, not only offered useful hints and criticisms as we proceeded but passed along comments from his wife, a professional in early education, who graciously took time to read sections of the manuscript. Herb Zimiles reviewed a near final draft and provided an especially detailed and constructive evaluation. Richard Mansfield, attorney at law in Palo Alto, and Birt Harvey, clinical professor of pediatrics at Stanford University, gave us expert and essential technical information on issues of law and health. Mrs. Estelle Wyman, of the California State Department of Social Welfare, provided useful comments on the early chapters.

Many others helped us orient our writing toward the real world of early education. Directors of nursery schools permitted us to take pictures and talk with their staff members. Parents gave permission for the use of photographs of their children. The central figures, the children themselves, cooperated and even staged some of the more difficult scenes. ("Like, man, who ever heard of a teacher who *asked* you to start a fight?") Mel Malinowski, a young and talented photographer of children's play, worked under enormous time pressure to record some of these scenes. We wish we had discovered him sooner. Our gratitude as well goes to Bob Overstreet for letting us use pictures from his outstanding collection of candid photos of children.

We are also in debt to: Dorothy Hamlin, Director of the nursery school at De Anza College, and Ann Smith and Helen Pillsbury, staff members at Greenmeadow Nursery School, all of whom gave us their support and cooperation; and the students in our classes, who suffered through expositions of some of the ideas, and read and commented (too gently, we fear) on specific chapters.

All of these people have made the book better than it would otherwise have been. This is to let them know that we will not forget their contributions.

CONTENTS

	Editor's Introduction	vii
	Preface	ix
	Acknowledgments	x
Chapter 1	**Early Education as a Career**	**1**
	The Motivation to Teach Young Children	1
	The Importance of Early Experience: Can Education Make a Difference?	3
	Social Relevance of Early Education	15
	Career Opportunities	20
Chapter 2	**Schools and Systems of Early Education**	**27**
	The Structure of Responsibility	27
	Patterns of Professional Training	40
	Dimensions which Differentiate Schools	44
	The Impact of the Physical Environment	49
Chapter 3	**School and Family: Partners or Competitors?**	**72**
	The Rationale for Parent Involvement	72
	Getting Parents Involved	80
	Parents as Teachers	91
Chapter 4	**Social Opportunity and Educational Achievement**	**104**
	The Nature of the Problem	104
	The Sources of Inequality	115
	The Disadvantaged Experience	121
	Differences in Educational Achievement	126
Chapter 5	**Programs Are Tools, Not Religions**	**134**
	Head Start Brings a New Era	134
	Approaches to Educational Intervention	144
	The Growth of Programs of Early Education	147
	Some Illustrative Programs	150
	Underlying Assumptions of Programs	160
	Issues that Differentiate Programs	161

Chapter 6	**Growth of Language and Cognitive Abilities**	**172**
	Growth of Language Abilities	172
	Growth of Cognitive Abilities	184
	Activities for Achieving Cognitive Goals	187
Chapter 7	**Social Concepts and Behavior**	**200**
	Growth of Self-Knowledge	200
	Concepts of Social Relationships	207
	Patterns of Social Behavior	211
	Regulating Behavior and Developing Social Competence	220
Chapter 8	**The Versatility of the Arts in a Preschool Program**	**229**
	The Place of the Arts in the Curriculum	229
	The Arts as Development of Artistic Capabilities	234
	Relationship of the Arts to Cognitive, Affective and Social Development	257
Chapter 9	**Crisis in the Preschool**	**264**
	Crisis Doesn't Mean Failure	264
	The Major Areas of Crisis	271
Chapter 10	**The Challenge of Evaluation**	**291**
	The Inevitability of Evaluation	291
	The Purpose of Evaluation	312
	Diagnosing Progress and Setting Goals	316
	Index	317

CHAPTER 1

EARLY EDUCATION AS A CAREER

THE MOTIVATION TO TEACH YOUNG CHILDREN

Assume for a moment that you have recently been hired as a teacher of preschool children. It's your first day on the job. Although you don't yet know which of the children is LeRoy, David, Cordelia or Mary, you recall most of their names from a list given you. You're a bit anxious but nonetheless you feel prepared.

While the children enter the room you spend the first moments helping them take off and hang up coats and sweaters and showing them where to get a drink, where to wash their hands and go to the bathroom—in general, getting them used to their new surroundings. When the head teacher is called to the office phone you are left alone with the children. During the time she's gone:

> Two boys begin to fight over a truck.
> A thumb sucker stands rubbing his genitals.
> One child starts crying, "Mama, Maamaa, Mamamamam, aaAAaa . . ." her sobs turning into gigantic hiccups.
> The block builders create a structure dangerously high.
> Arms outstretched, a boy zooms around the room with appropriate sound effects.
> Two children sit passively on small chairs.
> What will you do? First? Next?
> Why?

There are many responses to these situations, some of them effective and constructive, some less useful and less likely to help you cope with the nursery school scene depicted above. Although a teacher is not often called upon to deal with so many minor crises all at once, she is frequently in the midst of situations which demand immediate action. The preschool classroom is a constantly changing, challenging scene.

As a teacher in such a classroom, you will have two major resources to rely on in dealing with incidents and in providing conditions in which young children can learn. One of these is your training—what you've been taught about the behavior of children, your knowledge about research and new developments in the field, your mastery of techniques and procedures of the daily curriculum, including ways to stimulate enthusiasm, cool a fight, soothe hurt feelings or get children to listen to a song, story or lesson. The other resource is what you as an individual bring to your work. Although your training may be identical to that of another teacher, each of you will function quite differently because of dissimilarities in background, values, and attitudes. The unique way that you combine your personal life experiences and your training will emerge under stress. There will be times, perhaps more often than you expect, when

Vietnam Vet Chooses Career as Nursery School Teacher

Donald Ryerson, recently returned from two years in Vietnam, is the only male in a class of 31 students taking Education #110-A at Northern State College.

"Being with so many gals is really great," Ryerson conceded, "but it's not why I took the course." Then he explained that he had had a lot of time to think of the world situation while in Vietnam.

"It seemed to me that mankind's only salvation lies in young children," he said, "and I want to have something to do with them."

Ryerson estimated that it will take two to four years to complete his work for a standard teaching credential with specialization in early childhood education.

"It will be worth it," he said, "if it means I can help bring peace for the next generation."

FIGURE 1-1

the pressures of the situation are such that you haven't time to recall what the textbook said or what a teaching supervisor did. You'll be on your own!

Why are you thinking of going into the field of early education? Your motivations reflect your experience and personality, and are relevant both to your training and to your future success as a professional. Your reasons for wanting to become a teacher reveal something of the image you have of what being a teacher will mean and of the rewards and gratifications you will get from working with young children. What are your reasons? What will they mean on the job?

Perhaps you've been told, "You're certainly good with kids!" Or, you realize you enjoy children and are much more comfortable with them than with adults. Maybe you've read a news account such as the one shown in Figure 1–1 and agree with the veteran's reasoning. However, there will be many days on the job when "love for little children" or feelings of idealism will not be enough. Your ingenuity and talents will be taxed to the utmost and nothing will seem to work; or the children may present no difficulties, but the demands of teachers, parents and administrators will make life seemingly impossible.

You may think of yourself as a preschool teacher because you want to help children from low-income or minority neighborhoods get a better start in life. Perhaps you believe that what they need is more tender loving care and personal attention which you assume they haven't had. You may be surprised and hurt to discover that they are not as grateful as you inwardly hoped, and that they don't all want to be like you and your friends. They and their families may have ideas quite different from yours about what to expect from school and from life and you find you can't "help".

Perhaps you are a housewife who is ready to extend your career beyond home and family by capitalizing on the experience you have had with your own children. You may find, however, that during years of child-rearing you have developed a unique style for dealing with children and that the varied demands of a preschool group call for more flexible approaches. Your style may be difficult to change, requiring relearning, rather than relying on familiar ways of handling children.

The expectations that brought you to this class are important and it is useful to try to recognize and examine them. They have provided the initial motivation for your training. They will be a source of satisfaction and occasionally of disappointment. This is the initial phase of your preparation, however, and with growing experience you may find that your ideas about early education will change and your motivations will be somewhat different than those you brought to this class.

The knowledge now at hand about children and about techniques of teaching make it possible to develop skills to be a successful teacher. This does not mean that there is only one cluster of talents that make for effective teaching. Competence with young children involves a dynamic set of processes which go far beyond the question of whether your personal characteristics match a set of criteria on some "ideal teacher" list. Good teachers are successful in their own unique ways, combining ingenuity and experience with professional training.

Success in a nursery school is no more accidental than success in any field. Just as it is possible to learn to perform delicate operations, or defend clients in court, it is possible to learn skills and strategies that will help you deal effectively with preschoolers. You will be competing in an increasingly complicated field. New programs, alternative methods of teaching, knowledge about early education, and growth and development of preschool children have increased enormously because of new research and experience of the past few years. It will take hard work and serious study to become an effective professional, and a continuing effort is necessary to keep up with the field.

A real professional in early education is not merely a "glorified baby sitter." There is a body of knowledge and concepts and a range of skills to be mastered. The more professional you become, the more you can contribute to the field and the more gratification you will get from your work. While it is important that you want to work with young children and feel a genuine warmth and attraction for them, this is not enough. The thing that counts most is willingness to learn both about yourself and your profession.

THE IMPORTANCE OF EARLY EXPERIENCE: CAN EDUCATION MAKE A DIFFERENCE?

Since it takes a great deal of time and effort to become a competent professional in early education, it is important to consider whether you and other teachers will be

FIGURE 1–2

John Amos Comenius (1592–1670), Czech educator who wrote first text using pictures for teaching children.

Jean Jacques Rousseau (1712–1778), French philosopher who believed education should start at birth and continue through 25th year.

Johann H. Pestalozzi (1746–1827), Swiss educational reformer who emphasized use of objects at early age to develop powers of observation and reasoning.

able to have a significant effect upon young children. This is an ancient question and one on which evidence is still accumulating. Early education is the concern of a broad spectrum of educators, sociologists, psychologists, philosophers, physiologists, biologists—in short, of men and women of many professions. It is a field which has been expanded by the contributions of scholars of many disciplines.

Plato, as long ago as the third century B.C. argued that children be removed from their parents at an early age and transferred to institutional care and training. Leading thinkers of the 17th, 18th and 19th centuries advocated that education begin early for the benefit of society in order to avoid serious social problems (Figure 1–2).

Concern about early learning and development is reflected in studies and programs involving thousands of children all over the world. Much of the inquiry and discussion in early education is concentrated in the following general areas:

1. Are there periods for learning which are especially critical?
2. What is the influence upon behavior of genetic endowment compared with environmental factors?
3. What is the effect of formal education on the behavior of young children?

Subjects for these studies have included both humans and animals. Children have been observed in institutions, laboratory circumstances, cooperative nurseries, and in "compensatory" programs such as Head Start and Follow Through. The significance of studies on animals is limited, of course, by the fact that in experiments with animals, we are not certain that under identical circumstances (difficult to achieve at best) humans would react in similar ways. Nonetheless, they provide a body of knowledge which helps shape new research questions and reach more sophisticated generalizations about relationships between behavior and environment.

Research with animals provides a great deal of *specific* information that cannot be obtained from studies on humans. The conditions of experience can be changed and manipulated for animals in ways that would not be reasonable for young children

Robert Owen (1771–1858), Welsh socialist who believed that character is determined by environment.

Frederick Froebel (1782–1852), German educator who devised a system of educational games for children and founded the kindergarten.

John Locke (1632–1704), English philosopher who theorized that understanding is derived from one's own experience of the external and social world.

and much more detailed knowledge can be accumulated. It is more difficult to discover the effects of different kinds of experience upon humans and we must summarize and extrapolate from natural situations, such as children in foster homes, institutions and the like. Work with animals thus offers explicit information which suggests ways to conceptualize the impact of experience upon the human young.

One of the significant conclusions to come from these studies is that what is learned first stays longest and is the most difficult behavior to extinguish. Studies of language show that first learnings serve as a filter through which subsequent experiences are understood and interpreted. Because they are novel experiences, whatever we learn first is likely to make the greatest impression on us. Also, once we learn something and establish patterns of behavior, it is more difficult to learn to do the same thing in another way.

Critical Periods of Learning

The significance of early experience in certain species is illustrated by the concepts of *imprinting* and *critical periods*. An influence which takes place only during a specific and brief period very early in the life of an organism was given the name of *imprinting* by Konrad Lorenz (1935). His work verified earlier research such as the study by Heinroth (1910), who found that graylag geese, which have been cared for by humans during incubation, and then reared by them in isolation for the brief period of rapid development right after hatching, will thereafter follow human beings (or whatever they see first upon emerging from the egg) rather than their own kind. This behavior continues even through adult life, including the mating periods. Lorenz (1937) conducted similar experiments with geese, bitterns, and other birds and many, though not all, species became imprinted.

Imprinting apparently results in a learned behavior, not an instinctive one, and is virtually irreversible. Scott's work (1963) offers a dramatic example. A sheep that he had kept in his house and bottle-fed for its first ten days of life still wandered in a field by itself even after three years, while the balance of the flock stayed together. Other studies indicated that the young animals became imprinted upon an entire species or type, not just on a single person or object. Ducks that had been imprinted upon a moving decoy would follow any similar mechanical device in preference to another duck. Imprinting also occurs in mammals such as the alpaca and deer (E. Hess, 1962).

Closely allied to the concept of imprinting is the notion of *critical periods*. This refers to a belief that organisms are particularly vulnerable to change during periods of rapid growth. If this is true, it follows that what we experience (learn) at certain times is likely to have much greater impact than what is learned at other times. Imprinting takes place in very early life and during a relatively short time span—as little as ten minutes in the case of ducklings. Critical periods occur when an organism is undergoing relatively rapid change, as, for example, during the preschool years.

A series of experiments with dogs in a variety of environments led Scott to conclude that for all dogs there is a critical period for the formation of primary social attachments. In one experiment he isolated a dog and her pups in a one-acre field surrounded by a high board fence. Food and water were supplied only through a hole in the fence. No human contact was made with the pups except that as they reached different ages they were individually released and cared for in the laboratory for a week, then returned to the enclosure.

Scott (1969, p.47) reported:

> Puppies removed during the first five weeks of life behaved like any normal puppy making immediate contact with people as soon as they were old enough to walk efficiently. At seven weeks, puppies began to be shy, and puppies removed at fourteen weeks had become essentially wild animals, so fearful that they could be tamed only by confinement and forced contact, together with hand feeding. My wife and I took one of these wild puppies home and tried to make a house dog out of it. Eventually it became a fairly satisfactory pet, but it was always shy with strange people, and if there were any choice between consorting with a dog and one of its human masters, it always chose a dog.

Results of the Harlows' work with monkeys (1962) at the primate laboratory at the University of Wisconsin agree with Scott's conclusions. Monkeys that were isolated from their mothers at birth and kept apart for six months to a year were irreversibly damaged both socially and psychologically. The Harlows' research suggests that the first year is a critical period for the growth and development of young monkeys.

The evidence for specific environmental influences upon behavior of a number of species in early stages of growth is impressive and convincing. We have less information about comparable specific effects in human development although Scott (1963) argues that something similar to imprinting occurs in humans during the first six months of life. A great deal of controversy exists about the ways and extent of the impact of early experiences upon human behavior. Early events apparently do have significant influences but they apply in different ways to different areas of behavior. Also, the connection between the environmental stimulus and the resulting behavior is probably more diffuse and may be less permanent.

Experimental methods of the kind used with animals are, of course, often not appropriate with humans. Thus, information about effects of early experience on children typically comes from natural or unplanned situations which enable researchers to examine the effects of unusual or vastly dissimilar early life conditions.

One such pseudo-experimental situation exists in orphanages or similar institutions. Children who grow up in such circumstances have often been compared with children from more typical family settings.

In a comparison of the development of infants raised in a nursing home with children brought up in an orphanage, Spitz (1945) found something suggesting critical periods of development. He noted that those in the orphanage were dull, fearful, had impaired physical growth and skills, and showed little initiative. Both groups of children had had comparable medical care, food, and housing facilities. Genetic factors apparently did not account for the differences in behavior. It was observed, however, that the children in the nursing home had received both direct and indirect human contact; those in the orphanage had undergone marked social and sensory deprivation during the same period. Thus, at a time of relatively rapid growth, that is, during a critical period, one group was exposed and vulnerable to positive influences on development, the other to negative influences. The subsequent desirable and undesirable results appeared to be the outcome of these different treatments.

Even this glimpse of the evidence about critical periods suggests that it is a concept important to the development of patterns of behavior in children. Knowledge about the processes which may create critical periods (or something similar) in humans is incomplete and fragmentary. It is of increasing relevance, however, as programs of early learning become more deliberately planned, and as they are more likely to be administered through massive programs of day care, pre-packaged programs for cognitive stimulation, computer-based instruction, and mass media.

There has been a marked increase in research on these issues in the past few years and our knowledge about the effects of early experience in human development is likely to expand rapidly. Teachers and other professionals in the early education field will find it essential to keep informed about new developments that will help them be aware of the kinds of experiences that are most likely to affect development. They will then be in a better position to provide a learning environment for children that helps them develop their resources most effectively.

Influence of Genetic Endowment and Environmental Factors

The extent to which behavior is determined by genetic endowment—that is, by factors present at birth—and how much it is shaped by environmental influences is still being debated. The interest in this question has been heightened by Jensen's (1969) arguments about genetic contributions to intelligence. Perhaps a more useful approach to this old problem is that inherited and learned behaviors are constantly interacting from conception onward. The growth of an organism is dependent both on its innate capabilities and potential and on the modification of these factors through interaction with its environment. Therefore, it is useful to go beyond the question of which of the two factors contributes the most to a particular behavior. In the search for an explanation of anything so complex as human intelligence, it is also helpful to question *in what manner* genetic and environmental factors contribute to the specific behavior under observation. It is true that both influences are constantly present, but the amount of influence of each varies with the characteristic.

Physical features such as the color of skin and eyes, the quality of nails and hair, are almost wholly products of genetic endowment and are changed little if any by environment. A study of Hopi children made by Dennis and Dennis (1940) presents an instance of the predominance of a genetic factor over environment. They observed that children who are swaddled and carried on their mothers' backs learn to walk at about the same ages as children whose arms and legs are free. Genetic factors also influence behavior often thought to be social in nature. Twins reared from birth in separate environments show first social smiling at nearly identical times (Freedman, 1965). This suggests the primacy of genetic influence over situational factors for this particular behavior.

The examples given earlier of the effects of imprinting and critical periods indicate the potential influence of social contexts on certain behaviors at a very early age. In addition to effects upon specific human behaviors, environmental elements have been shown to influence general features and behaviors such as physical growth and social development. At one time it was thought that the final shape and height of body structure was genetically set at birth. Children were destined to be tall or short, fat or thin by virtue of the general characteristics of the families into which they were born. However, the overall increase in height and weight during the last several decades for the average populations of several countries, including the United States, shows strong influence of environmental factors on human growth.

There is evidence that experience not only changes behavior but actually modifies biological structure itself. Rosenzweig and his associates (1962) working with rats found that with enrichment of environment, chemical and anatomical changes took place in the brain. In addition, they found noticeable improvement in the ability to solve certain problems. Krech (1966) took the opposite direction by depriving rats of the stimulation of an enriched environment. His results mirrored those of Lindsley, in that isolation produced underdeveloped, restless organisms. Casler (1961) in his studies concluded that unless an environment encourages sensory exploration, poor physical growth and reduced mental growth can be expected.

Studies by Kugelmass, Poull, and Samuel (1944) of undernourished children over two years of age show that restoration of proper diet was accompanied by IQ gains of as much as 18 points. The physical development of young children who have recovered from chronic malnutrition is apparently less than that of children of the same age and race who have not been nutritionally deprived.

Evidence is available which indicates that malnutrition also interferes with the central nervous system. Another consequence of malnutrition in young children is apathy. Malnourished children show much less response to stimulation than well-nourished children. David Glass (1968, p. 49) notes:

> Apathy can provoke apathy and contribute to a cumulative pattern of reduced adult-child interaction. This has consequences for learning, for maturation, for interpersonal relations, and so on—the end result being significant risk of backwardness in more complex learning.

Psychological factors of the environment may affect physical growth. Widdowson (1951) worked with children of four to 14 years of age in two German orphanages. He noticed that although the kinds and amounts of food given to the children were equal, the average gain in weight of one group was very nearly three times that of the other over a six-month period. However, switching supervisors of the two institutions reversed the trend. By the end of the next six months, the children who had gained the most weight now lost their lead even though they were given amounts of food greater than the other group. Since the most obvious difference between the two situations was the harsh tactics used by the supervisor of the institution in which children lost weight, Widdowson concluded that fear in children made the difference in growth.

Some of the most striking evidence that environmental factors influence the total development of human organisms can be found in two studies by Harold Skeels (1966). His original work, which took place in the early 1930's, was followed up thirty years later with startling results. Initially an experimental group of thirteen children, all under three years of age and all considered unsuited for adoption, were transferred from an orphanage to become "house guests" in an institution for mentally retarded girls and women ages eighteen to fifty. Tests showed that the ten girls and three boys had no gross physical handicaps but that their development was seriously retarded. IQ's ranged from 35 to 89.

No special program or training was planned for the experimental group in their new environment other than fitting into the routines of the inmates. One, or at most two, children were placed in each ward. From the first, the attendants and older girls became fond of the children, gave them gifts, and saw that they had privileges and outside experiences as well as constant attention and stimulation.

As they grew old enough, the children attended the institution's regular kindergarten, spent time with orphanage children their own age on the playground, went to movies, and had opportunities to participate in school programs, group singing, and chapel services. Each child had an older girl or adult who figuratively "adopted" him or her, thus setting up a close one-to-one relationship. The personal interest shown the younger child and his activities and achievements was a unique feature of the experimental setting.

Once the data had been analyzed, a contrast group of matching composition (except slightly higher in intelligence scores) was observed and tested on the same factors over a similar period of time. This group, however, remained in the original cottage environment of the regular orphanage.

The thirteen children of the experimental group were observed from six months to four and one-half years. Final tests for mental development showed an IQ change of anywhere from +7 to +58 points. None had failed to show some gain. The contrast group, however, in an experimental period of not quite two years to three and one-half years, showed only one child with a gain in IQ (2 points) and negative change ranging from −8 to −45 points. In his original report Skeels (1966, p.17) stated:

> The contrast between the richly stimulating, individually oriented experience of the children in the experimental group and the depersonalizing, mass handling, and affectionless existence in the children's home can hardly be emphasized enough.

In a follow-up study of adult achievement, Skeels (1966) sought to determine what happened to the two groups of children when they became adults. By extraordinary effort he succeeded in locating all subjects from both the experimental and contrast groups. A summary of his findings appears in Table 1–1.

Skeels (1966, p. 56) pointed out that his was a pioneering study, involving only a

DATA	EXPERIMENTAL GROUP	CONTRAST GROUP
Survival	All 13 reached adulthood, 11 in adoptive homes.	One subject died in the institution age 15. None had been adopted.
Occupational Level	All self-supportive; none were wards of any institution or exhibited delinquent behavior, economic dependency, or need for psychiatric or agency support.	4 were institutionalized and without occupation. Others worked as dishwashers, part-time cafeteria help, or gardeners. One became a typesetter.
Marital Status	8 of 10 girls married, 1 boy. Nine had children. 1 divorce. None of the children showed any sign of abnormality or organic pathology. As a group they were considered well developed and attractive.	1 married, 1 divorced—latter had a child that tested mentally retarded. Married man, however, had 4 normal, fine children.
Education	Mean grade completed: 12.8. One male had B.A. degree—4 others up to 2½ years of college—these figures compare favorably with 1960 census for similar aged adults in U.S. as whole.	Only one educated beyond 8th grade—he had one semester of college. Median: 3rd grade.

TABLE 1-1 ADULT STATUS OF SKEELS' RESEARCH GROUPS
adapted from H. M. Skeels, "Adult Status of Children with Contrasting Early Life Experiences," *Monographs of the Society for Research in Child Development,* 1966, *31,* No. 3, Serial No. 105, pp. 32, 39, and 40.

few subjects, and that it would therefore "be presumptuous to attempt to identify the specific influences that produced the changes observed." However, this contrast in outcome between the children who were in a deprived, unresponsive environment and those who experienced enriched environmental opportunities is one of the most significant studies of the effect of early environmental experience.

The highly complex traits that make up human intelligence result from the interaction of vast numbers of gene combinations and environmental conditions. Behavior of this type is not easily related to particular contributory elements. Nonetheless, one of the factors that seemed to be critical in the development of the children in Skeels' study was the close emotional relationship they had with older girls and women.

Other studies have shown that children's behavior is shaped by their reaction to adults, through imitation and identification. Bandura, Ross and Ross (1963a) conducted experiments designed to determine the extent to which aggression can be transmitted to children watching aggressive behavior of adult models on filmed sequences. Preschoolers who watched physical and verbal aggression directed toward a life-sized inflated plastic doll exhibited aggressive behavior when frustrated that almost doubled that of the control group who saw only subdued and inhibited behaviors by models. Furthermore, the inhibited behaviors were themselves imitated.

Bandura and his associates (1963b) also had a group of preschoolers watching a television-projected film in which aggressive behavior was rewarded (an adult model was able to get another's possessions by domineering means). Another group watched the same situation but the aggressive model was punished by the adult whose possessions he sought to take. A third group of children saw neither film.

Although the children who saw aggression rewarded said they disapproved of the actions of the aggressive model, they imitated his behavior by almost identical acts. Those who saw aggression punished failed to imitate the aggression and behaved very much like the group who had had no exposure to the models. Subsequently, the latter two groups of children were encouraged by the offer of rewards for imitating the model's aggressive behavior. The previous differences in performance were then eliminated as those who had not originally displayed aggressive behavior learned to exhibit it to the same degree as the first group. The girls, who had been most critical of the model, acquired as much imitative aggression as the boys.

These experimental modifications of behavior are significant in that they reveal some of the processes through which behavior in a specific situation can be altered by patterns of stimuli in the environment. These situations are of short duration, of course, but it is reasonable to assume that where the patterns in the environment are more stable, the resulting behavior on the part of children is likely to persist over longer periods of time.

Effects of Formal Education on Behavior of Young Children

In addition to examining the transmission of behavior through models, i.e., evaluations of the changes which can be produced in a controlled experimental laboratory situation, researchers have also been concerned with the effects of formal and more diffuse educational programs on young children. Since there seem to be optimum times for learning, i.e., critical periods, even in humans, and evidence shows that these are most likely to occur in early life, questions of what shall be taught young children, how, and by whom, are issues of increasing significance.

Acquisition of motor and intellectual skills is linked to the levels of maturation of an organism. A child cannot be taught to talk before a certain stage of motor development, nor taught to reason logically without first reaching the necessary level of maturation. He is not simply a miniature adult but has his own patterns of physical and mental growth. In recent years the work of behavioral scientists and technologists has demonstrated that quite young children can be taught a variety of specific skills. For example, they can learn to read, to spell by punching keys on a typewriter, and to memorize more complex poems earlier than had been thought possible for children of their age. Sometimes, however, there is little enduring advantage; such skills are eventually acquired by other children and apparent gains level off.

Many persons feel that formal instruction implies an academic pressure which emphasizes only right answers, and correct ways. They believe that such an instructional environment can only result in harm to young children who need to explore and find out for themselves what the world has to offer and what it demands. However, the work of Benjamin Bloom (1964) and J. McV. Hunt (1961) among others supports the view that early education *of some kind* is desirable since children's ability to learn and their actual achievement are both influenced by early experience.

One example of the effects of early intervention is the "early training" project conducted by Susan Gray and her associates (Klaus and Gray, 1968). Their program involved preschoolers, with subsequent follow-up through the primary grades. Their subjects were sixty-two children of disadvantaged parents who lived in a small Tennessee town, and a control group in a similar town some distance away. The experimental group of preschoolers was given classroom instruction for ten weeks during each of two (or three) successive summers. The children and their families received home visits and instruction between the summer sessions.

The program provided specific experiences designed to "develop attitudes conducive to school achievement . . . and to enhance certain intellectual abilities" (p.1). Short term IQ gains were significant, but testing at the end of first grade showed little difference in IQ gains between the experimental and control groups. Subsequent implementation of the program, however, and testing in reading readiness, language, and personality characteristics favored the experimental children, although once again not all gains held more than two years.

In addition to the changes effected in the program's subjects, Klaus and Gray found evidence that benefits accrued to both the families and the total community of the experimental group. These findings appear especially significant when it is realized that program contacts represented only about 2 percent of the average waking hours of a child from birth to six years. Their research suggests that the question is not whether programs of early intervention should be used, but how such programs can be made as effective as possible.

One of the earliest prekindergarten programs for educationally disadvantaged children was that of the New York State Education Department under the direction of Louis T. DiLorenzo (1969). This study, which predated Head Start, involved eight New York school districts and approximately 1800 children whose parents were willing to have them in half-day classes. Begun in 1965 with three "waves" of preschoolers, it continued through 1969 with as much follow-up as possible into kindergarten, first and second grades.

From the beginning the program was designed "to assess the immediate educational goals which were the objectives of the program." The evaluation was concentrated on measurement of the following:

Capacity to learn
Self-concept
Language Development
Physical Growth

Although broader goals were originally contemplated, the final selection was limited to the four listed above because they were felt to have the greatest priority in terms of school readiness. Some of the other questions raised were: whether the effectiveness of the prekindergarten programs differed according to the sex, race, or socio-economic status of the children; whether some types of programs were more effective than others; and whether there were carry-over effects in readiness and achievement as the child progressed through the grades. Programs were categorized as "cognitively oriented" if they emphasized teaching of specific school-related skills and as "traditional" if the emphasis was on the total development of the child.

Individual pretesting and posttesting of the children constituted the basic data of the study together with reports and ratings by teachers, program directors, and teams of observers. Additional data were collected through parent or guardian interviews.

The findings showed that the disadvantaged child in the cognitively oriented experimental group out-performed disadvantaged children from a control group on ratings of both intelligence and language. This was not true of children in the more traditional programs. Neither cognitive nor nursery education programs significantly improved self-concept or physical development above that of the control group. In his report (1969, p. 0–3) DiLorenzo states:

> The cognitive programs were able to close some of the gap between disadvantaged and nondisadvantaged children. However, the difference that remained exceeded the difference overcome. In the most successful district, the rate of improvement achieved would have required two years of kindergarten at the same rate of progress to completely close the cognitive gap.

The work of Gray and DiLorenzo indicates that significant short-term effects result from early intervention programs at the preschool level. Some generalized effects on later school achievement have also been noted, especially where parents have been involved. However, much remains to be learned and many research scholars are cautious about results until more can be determined about long-term effects.

There are a number of reports indicating that an initial acceleration in the rate of development does not continue after the first year of formal schooling, whether that year is kindergarten or first grade. Those who were not in the program often caught up with those who were. Despite the many explanations offered for this situation (usually suggesting that the quality of the preschool training is not maintained in the public schools), none fully accounts for the leveling off that takes place. Nor has there been a definitive statement that tells what kinds of programs of early education offer the most lasting effects upon achievement.

James O. Miller, (1969a, p. 6), then Director of the National Laboratory on Early Childhood Education, proposed these generalizations about short-term intervention:

1. Where limited intervention objectives in the psychomotor and cognitive areas are clearly delineated and intervention techniques are specifically designed to accomplish those objectives, significant gains can be obtained over a short intervention period.
2. Such gains can be obtained over the chronological age range from neonate through early school years.
3. Little evidence is available concerning the longevity of obtained effects or the effect of specific gains on more complex skills.

Continuing research is needed to adequately assess both the immediate and long-range effects of early education and of the relative impact on different types of curricula. The problems of setting up evaluative studies are severe and attempts to conduct such research occasionally meet opposition from various groups. Despite the lack of final evidence, however, there is a persistent belief in the value of early programs of education and child care and it seems probable that more programs will appear. The recent success of the TV series *Sesame Street* will undoubtedly encourage optimism and confidence in programs of early intervention.

SOCIAL RELEVANCE OF EARLY EDUCATION

Maintaining the System

The teacher is concerned not only with her influence upon individual children but also with her role in a broader professional context. She has a sense of her impact and influence on a much larger audience.

Early education extends beyond a teacher and her own class of young children. As part of a professional association, her involvement can effect changes which have consequences for the family, the community and the larger society.

Every society decides for itself which persons and institutions have responsibility for training its young. In the United States, the training of children has traditionally been left to the discretion of parents alone until the child reaches legal school age (generally at six). Outside persons or agencies, however well-qualified, are rarely permitted to interfere with, much less take over, this responsibility. Even when the parents' decisions may clearly be to the child's disadvantage, social workers, ministers, psychologists, teachers or other professionals, as well as neighbors and friends, who might wish to interfere, have neither custom nor law on their side. Unless the life or safety of a child is clearly at stake, the parents have both the right and the responsibility to train their children as they choose. The interest and concern of anyone outside the family circle is usually considered at best "meddling in affairs that are none of your business."

Once the child reaches school—and by school is meant first grade, since few states require kindergarten attendance or make nursery or play school mandatory—the burden of socialization is shared. The school typically is not only given the right to decide what learning will be required of students and who will teach the subjects prescribed, but it is expected to exercise that right. Traditionally, however, responsibility for transmission of moral, social, and emotional values was assigned to the family. The school reinforced these family standards. In turn, the family supported the schools. Throughout our country's history, school and home thus complemented one another in the task of socialization.

A society's survival is dependent on its ability to socialize, or train, its young. Typically, the young are trained in ways that tend to perpetuate the values and norms of the culture and society into which they are born or in which they live. Political systems and other institutions of a nation are no more stable than socialization makes them. Unless young people have been brought up to hold values, attitudes and beliefs similar to those of the dominant sector of adults in their society, it is unlikely that they will maintain the ways and stability of the social community. In the past, reliance has been upon training in the home and education in the schools to insure allegiance to societal norms. There is some question whether this model is still appropriate.

Education During Times of Social Change

There are severe social cleavages in this country which raise new questions about the role of education. These lines of conflict and division are: *first,* between racial and ethnic groups, especially between whites and the "third world" members of the society: *second,* between the poor and the middle-class groups; and *third,* between a generation which was encouraged to value achievement, growth, industrial development and expansion and a younger generation which, threatened by the consequences of war, overpopulation, pollution, and waste of natural resources, is reconsidering those values. In the midst of such profound conflict and change, it seems hardly appropriate to perpetuate patterns of behavior that have created these national crises. In such times the value of education to society lies in its capability to help prepare the young for the task of dealing with these new and emerging issues.

Today the teacher of young children has a social responsibility not faced by school or home in the past. She is called on to help prepare children for life in a world of technology where rapid change is a dominant feature. She is asked to help even very young children select, interpret, and evaluate information from media virtually unknown to their fathers and mothers, grandfathers and grandmothers. Television, radio, movies, and pictorial journalism constantly bombard children with enormous amounts of information and stimuli. Children need to know how to select and deal with what they are seeing and hearing from these sources. What is real and what is unreal? Is the funeral of a King or a Kennedy the same or different from a funeral in a cartoon or movie? How is the killing and maiming witnessed in some of our more lurid gangster programs better or worse than the everyday life of our soldiers in Vietnam? If it's commendatory for a man to walk on the moon, what's wrong with a boy exploring a nearby creek or quarry?

The need to teach children to relate to the new technological features of their world, and to relate to machines without suffering loss of their own humanity, is only one of many important new areas of learning in a changing society. Perhaps even more critical is the need to teach children attitudes and techniques which will help them protect an environment from the consequences of an excessive number of people in relation to the physical resources available. In a sense, the education of the young now must include attitudes and skills for survival. While much of the learning about the functional relation of man to his environment comes during and after formal schooling, it is possible to begin to instill as early as preschool an awareness of the importance of protecting the environment from man.

Early Education as Social Opportunity

One general line along which changes are taking place is the area of improved educational opportunities for the poor and the minority groups in the United States. Institutions involved in early education are being asked to assume more of this responsibility than in the past. In part, this has come about through a recognition that there is a need for greater effort to be invested in teaching at all levels, and a conviction that schooling in early years will be particularly effective in increasing opportunities for children from low-income homes. In effect, though not usually intentionally, this also implies a dissatisfaction with the family as the agent for early education of poor children. Some programs are designed to change parental behavior toward their children (see chapter 3). This seems to support the assumption that the family as a socializing agent, especially in poor communities, has not done as well as was expected, and a number of writers place the blame of early failure in school on the family.

There is a great deal of dissatisfaction and disagreement with this accusation, however, especially among ethnic groups who feel that such an attitude denigrates the cultural contributions that the ethnic family makes. Consequently, attempts are underway to develop programs which will recognize and utilize the resources of the various cultural backgrounds from which children come.

The widespread growth of compensatory educational programs represents a change in the responsibilities for socializing young children, and professionals in early educational settings are often part of these efforts. While the need for improving educational experience is evident, it should also be recognized that the school is taking on a role which is different in several basic ways from its traditional function.

Education as Intervention

Education, whether carried on by the family, the school, or some other agency, is a type of intervention in that it changes the lives of individuals. It is an attempt to help the child (no matter what his social stratum) to become a competent adult. Traditionally the school has supported the family in this molding process and their joint venture is intended to prepare the child to maintain the values of the society.

The process is much more complex than this simple summary suggests, however, especially in eras of social, economic, political, and scientific change. Conditions have so altered educational needs that they have forced changes in the values of adults responsible for the training of young children—values more suited to contemporary circumstances. Children are now being socialized for change. This means that the school no longer only supports the family's values and patterns of behavior, especially in poor and minority communities. It also introduces new ideas and attitudes.

When a teacher attempts to teach children within the traditional conception of socialization, children are encouraged to develop into adults very much like their parents. When she seeks to promote behavior different from that of the parents (an assumption basic to compensatory education as we know it in such programs as Head Start), society is faced with some profound implications.

If compensatory education lives up to its intent, children will grow to be *unlike* their parents. They will acquire values and patterns of behavior not patterned after those of their own immediate communities. The consequences both to the child and to society of this shift in traditional responsibility for socialization are to some degree unknown. But we do know it will create stresses for the child and his family as well as for certain parts of the society.

One of the more obvious consequences is a competition that is created between family and school. Actually there is potential competition whenever someone other than the family works with preschool children. Because the teacher is responsible for working with quite young children, some barely out of infancy, she necessarily fulfills the role of mother as well as teacher. Helping a child with his clothing, attending to his toilet needs, providing comfort as well as band-aids and ointment when he's physically hurt—these and many other highly personal attentions are now part of her daily relationship with the children to whom she is also teaching cognitive and learning skills.

In middle-class communities, the goals of a teacher are likely to be consistent with those of the home. Within the scope of early childhood education in a compensatory program, however, the teacher may try to "unteach" certain patterns learned at home by not reinforcing them at school. She will also provide experiences not likely to be given children in their homes. She may try to teach them what she regards as "good manners," or try to change their televiewing habits, or suggest an early bedtime and other patterns of activity that are not equally valued in their own homes. And she will probably reinforce these same new behaviors.

When she engages in such activities she assumes still another role—that of an "expert" who knows better than the parent what to do. Until quite recently, parents would not permit this, at least not insofar as teachers of young children were concerned. Personality development and morality training were primarily the responsibility of the family with, in some cases, an assist from the church. But rarely if ever were they left up to the school or the teacher. Even though this responsibility is seemingly relinquished when a child enters first grade, schools are still expected to support the "basic values" established by the family, while taking care not to tamper with them.

However, in any early education program (not just in a compensatory system), the teacher necessarily will be transmitting values and attitudes at a highly critical time in the life of children. From this standpoint she may actually be in direct competition with the family. This will be especially true if there is a difference between what the family teaches and what she advocates. Even if the difference is not very marked, the teacher takes over a large part of the mother's role. In a federal or state program, she is, in effect, an agent of the government with the additional authority that this implies.

A program that places the mother in a subordinate position for any reason is likely to encourage either dependence on and compliance with the teacher and school, or frustration and even rebellion. In a middle-class community mothers often feel that they, too, are experts and if they disagree with the teacher, they are likely to confront her. If they can't out-talk her, they can deal with the situation in other ways.

But mothers in low-income areas, on the lowest rung of the socio-economic ladder, find it difficult to match the teacher's expertise and advantage in education, experience, and language. In a dozen ways, even without meaning to, the teacher can put them down. The impact of what the teacher does, in her contact with the family as well as with the child, can be significant in an early education compensatory program.

The Teacher as Community Adviser

Viewing the trend to educate children at ever younger ages, some people have voiced concern that the process is being turned over to the educational system in its present form. These people are not satisfied with what the schools are doing now at elementary and secondary levels. They dislike the idea of giving an educational system which they consider to have failed a chance to extend its influence by setting up a preschool program.

As our way of life becomes more complex, as more and more women join the work force, industry as well as government is becoming concerned with the problem of child care. Who will make administrative decisions? What programs will be offered? How will they be selected and tried out?

Schools are receiving large amounts of money and great authority to spend their own funds. They are expected to select personnel and curricula appropriate to the children in their care. Because early education is a new addition to many public schools, they will need assistance in making judgments in these areas. As a teacher you will have an important role in both the lives of young children and in the community.

CAREER OPPORTUNITIES

Let us assume that you are strongly motivated to work with young children and are convinced you can develop the competence to affect the children in the communities in which you may work. You have made the decision to teach. What are the opportunities for a career in this field?

Public Commitment to Early Education

Within the last two decades a great deal of attention has been given the impact that early experience has upon the development of young children. As long ago as 1950, the White House Conference approved of early education in the form of kindergarten and nursery schools as a "desirable supplement to home life," a recommendation repeated and expanded by the conference of 1970. But parents and school districts were relatively slow to translate these recommendations into schools, and job opportunities were scarce.

(Percent of 3-5 Population)

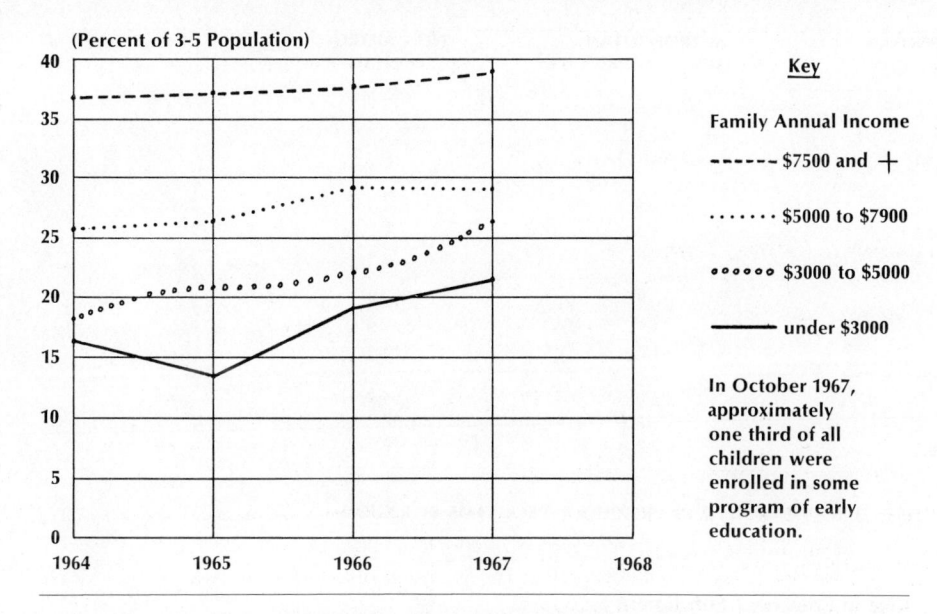

Key

Family Annual Income

------ $7500 and +

.... $5000 to $7900

○○○○○ $3000 to $5000

——— under $3000

In October 1967, approximately one third of all children were enrolled in some program of early education.

FIGURE 1-3 PRESCHOOL AND KINDERGARTEN ENROLLMENT 1964–1967
adapted from Miller, J. O., Document No. 70706-N-F0-U-09 Nat. Lab. on E.C. Ed. (1969b), pp. 9–10.

By 1960 the Educational Policies Commission of the National Education Association recommended that all children aged four or over have the opportunity to go to school at public expense. Yet as James O. Miller (1969b, p.3) points out:

> The year 1965 must stand as a landmark year in early childhood education. The administration's investment in the war on poverty created Head Start. Head Start was a singular commitment to young children at the federal level. While there had been other federally sponsored programs for day care, they had not been directed toward serving the needs of young children per se, but were instituted to provide child care for women employed in critical war and defense industries during the 40's. Support for preprimary education had come mainly from middle class and upper middle class parents concerned with developing social and group experiences for their children. Other private programs existed providing day care for children of working mothers. A number of universities had nursery school facilities associated with minor training programs. These facilities also served the research interests of professionals concerned with child development during the early years. It is fair to say that no national commitment nor universal interest in the field was evident prior to 1965.

The period following 1965 was one of rapid growth and change for the field of early education, with a dramatic increase in career opportunities as a result of the expansion of both research and innovative programs. Early learning and education acquired a degree of attraction, visibility, and salience for educators and behavioral scientists that they had not known before. This rise in interest was undoubtedly a consequence of the commitment at the national level to early education and especially to early education as a route to greater opportunity for children from poor and minority families. Large increases in federal funds for both experimental and operational purposes also intensified interest.

CHILDREN	METROPOLITAN CENTRAL CITY	METROPOLITAN OUTSIDE CENTRAL CITY	NON METROPOLITAN
Total 3–5	36.6	35.5	24.1
White	36.5	35.3	25.3
Nonwhite	37.0	38.3	16.9
Total 3's	9.0	7.7	4.5
White	9.0	7.2	4.2
Nonwhite	8.8	13.6	6.4
Total 4's	26.8	26.3	12.4
White	24.7	25.1	11.9
Nonwhite	31.6	41.7	15.4
Total 5's	72.1	72.0	54.2
White	73.6	72.8	58.2
Nonwhite	68.7	62.0	29.1

TABLE 1–2 PERCENT OF CHILDREN 3 TO 5 ENROLLED IN PRESCHOOL PROGRAMS BY REGION—OCTOBER, 1967
adapted from Miller, J. O., Document No. 70706-N-F0-U-09 Nat. Lab. on E.C. Ed. (1969b).

Rise in Preschool Enrollment

Growth in the field was not uniform in all directions, but it followed some of the national concerns and the guidelines upon which Head Start and similar programs were built. Much greater emphasis was given to programs for disadvantaged children, defined as coming from low-income homes and from minority families. For a number of reasons there was also greater allocation of funds to urban areas. This pattern of growth is indicated by the data in Figure 1–3 which gives enrollment statistics.

As of October 1967, the data were by age level as follows:

1 of every 23 three-year-olds was in a preschool program.
1 of every 4.7 four-year-olds was in a preschool program.
2 of every 3 five-year-olds were in a preschool program.

These figures and those charted in Table 1–2 need little elaboration. During the years 1964-1967 the total number of children between the ages of three and five remained approximately the same—about twelve million. The sharp increase in enrollment of preschoolers from families of lower income, and the disproportionate percentages of nonwhites enrolled in programs for three- and four-year-olds clearly suggests financial support from governmental sources. For the most part, these differences are a result of Head Start and other programs funded by federal, state, and local agencies together with some private organizations.

However, families from high income levels enroll a much larger proportion of children than do families from any other group. Thus programs of early education do not yet reach enough of those most in need. If there were equal proportions of enrollment in low-income areas, 800,000 additional children would be in preschool programs of some kind at this time.

Federally sponsored groups are concentrated in metropolitan areas where the density of population makes them more readily accessible to larger numbers of children. The percentages of white and nonwhite children enrolled in preschool programs in metropolitan central city areas, metropolitan areas outside the central city, and non-metropolitan areas are given in Table 1–2.

FACILITY	AGES SERVED	DESCRIPTION
Day Care Center	2–16	Eligibility generally based on economic need. Hours usually from 7 a.m. to 6 p.m. Full time and part time staff. Older children provided "home base" when not in school.
Head Start and other Compensatory Programs	4–6	Summer and year-round programs supported by federal, state, and/or local funds. Provide schooling for children considered culturally disadvantaged. Half-day sessions with hot meals. Trained staff and aides who are usually from local area, volunteers and parent assistants.
Kindergarten	5–6	Program geared to needs of children prior to entering first grade. Some public, others private. Generally headed by credentialled teacher with assistants.
Laboratory/Demonstration School	2–5	Primarily intended to train teachers and used as a facility for research. Commonly located on a school campus. Student teachers from sponsoring institution of higher learning work under supervision of teachers from school faculty.
Nursery School	2½–5	Usually half-day sessions though many schools have programs both mornings and afternoons. Most often privately owned or financed as a cooperative. Some under adult education program for local school district. Head teacher usually credentialled and has assistants, aides and volunteers to help.
Parent Cooperative	2½–5	Formed by parents to provide program for children and instruction for themselves. Parents participate regularly along with trained teachers. Some night meetings with fathers and mothers.
Play School	2–6	Private facilities in homes, churches, and other locations where owners are licensed (in some states) to take children for supervised play in small groups. Can be half or whole day.

TABLE 1–3 KINDS OF SCHOOLS USING PERSONNEL TRAINED IN EARLY CHILDHOOD EDUCATION

Again figures tell a clear story. Metropolitan areas have the highest percentage of enrollment; the fewest children are enrolled in programs in rural areas. In both white and nonwhite categories, more five-year-olds are in early childhood education programs because of state aid and local school district support for kindergarten programs. However, at this time, only slightly more than half of the states provide aid at any preschool level, and for several years California was the only state that gave aid for day care programs.

The Range of Early Educational Programs

The number and variety of programs for preschoolers are increasing. This means, of course, broader opportunities for employment. A brief description of some of the programs and a summary of their staff needs are given in Table 1–3.

In addition to those facilities provided for preschoolers who will eventually attend public schools at the appropriate age level, some states and communities provide centers with special facilities for children with specific physical or learning disabilities such as blindness, deafness, crippling, retardation, aphasia, and autism. Such centers are staffed by trained personnel although some also use volunteers and aides. These centers are both publicly and privately sponsored.

More and more child care facilities are being established by industry to serve the needs of their employees, especially by organizations that hire large numbers of women. They find that women who are relieved of the worry of providing adequate care for their children tend to be more reliable employees. At present, the care is often safekeeping and playtime interspersed with meals and rest periods. Gradually, perhaps, management will also become interested in offering educational experiences for young children.

Institutions such as hospitals and universities are beginning to provide care or facilities for children of both their professionald and their service staffs. Their responsibility frequently extends from early infancy beyond preschool ages. Directors of these programs, like industrial leaders, are seeking help in designing environments and programs that are best for children. Such new and emerging institutions are particularly in need of professional advice and information.

In recent years the federal government has set up parent-child centers in various areas of the United States. These programs require that parents participate and help in determining policies affecting their preschool children. Parent-child centers operate in conjunction with nearby research facilities such as colleges and universities. They are staffed by both professionals and parents. Another government sponsored program is Follow Through. It is federally funded and provides an extension of early intervention programs such as Head Start to determine their effectiveness in the primary grades. Follow Through is staffed by trained teachers, aides, assistants, and volunteers.

Despite all these encouraging trends, of twelve million preschoolers, only 10 percent of the third who come from poor families are being served by programs of early education. In addition, at present there are approximately only 110,000 places in day care programs to meet the following needs:

1. All-day care for roughly one million children up to six years of age from poor families

2. Provision for the 38,000 children estimated to receive no care at all while their mothers work, and probably double that number who are left in the care of children under sixteen

Pending federal and local legislation is expected to remedy at least some of these needs by allocating funds for day care centers. Especially significant from the standpoint of career opportunities is the fact that provisions have been introduced in federally sponsored programs that make it mandatory for supervisors to be trained in child growth and development.

Where Will You Work?

Where you decide to work may well be determined by the opportunities made available through funding and legislation. As more facilities are provided for young children, and as the need for trained personnel increases, you will want to examine the advantages and constraints of the program in which you choose to work. The information you will need is generally available from local boards of education, departments of social welfare, newspaper ads, and visits to schools and early education associations. If certification is required (as it most certainly will be if you decide to work within a public school system that has made provision for educating children at kindergarten and earlier), this information is available from hiring agencies and the school districts themselves.

You may gain some perspective on the importance of salary if you stop to answer these questions:

What am I likely to be doing ten years from now?
What do I *want* to be doing ten years from now?

Considered in these terms, a comparatively low-paying job for a year or two may provide just the experience needed for the kind of work you really want later on. Also, many jobs involving education of young children are especially satisfying in that they offer opportunities to serve society and bring about change. Most important, working with young children may be a start toward the realization of many of the hopes you have for a better world.

REFERENCES

Bandura, A., Ross, D., and Ross, S. Imitation of film-mediated aggressive models. *Journal of Abnormal and Social Psychology,* 1963a, 66, No. 1, 3–11.

Bandura, A., Ross, D., and Ross, S. Vicarious reinforcement and imitative learning. *Journal of Abnormal and Social Psychology,* 1963b, 67, No. 6, 601–607.

Bloom, B. S. *Stability and change in human characteristics.* New York: John Wiley and Sons, Inc., 1964.

Casler, L. Maternal deprivation: a critical review of the literature. *Monographs of the Society for Research in Child Development,* 1961, 26, No. 2, Serial No. 80.

Dennis, W., and Dennis, M. G. The effect of cradling practices upon the onset of walking in Hopi children. *Journal of Genetic Psychology,* 1940, 56, 77–86.

DiLorenzo, L. T. Prekindergarten programs for educationally disadvantaged children. *Final Report Project No. 3040,* Albany, New York: New York State Education Department, Office of Research and Evaluation, December 1969.

Freedman, D. An ethological approach to the genetical study of human behavior. In S. G. Vandenberg (Ed.), *Methods and goals in human behavior genetics.* New York: Academic Press, 1965, 141–161.

Glass, D. C. (Ed.) *Environmental influences.* Proceedings of a conference under the auspices of Russell Sage Foundation and Rockefeller University. New York: Rockefeller University Press, 1968.

Harlow, H. F., and Harlow, M. Social deprivation in monkeys. *Scientific American,* 1962, 207, No. 5, 136–146.

Heinroth, O. Beitrage zur biologie, namentlich ethologie and psychologie der anatiden. *Verhl. 5 International Ornothologie Kongr.,* 1910, 589–702.

Hess, E. Ethology: an approach toward the complete analysis of behavior. In R. Brown, E. Galanter, E. Hess, and G. Mandler, (Eds.), *New directions in psychology.* New York: Holt, Rinehart and Winston, 1962.

Hunt, J. McV. *Intelligence and experience.* New York: Ronald Press Co., 1961.

Jensen, A. R. How much can we boost IQ and scholastic achievement? *Harvard Educational Review,* 1969, *39,* No. 1, 1–123.

Klaus, R. A., and Gray, S. W. The early training project for disadvantaged children: a report after five years. *Monographs of the Society for Research in Child Development,* 1968, *33,* No. 4, Serial No. 120.

Krech, D., Rosenzweig, M. R., and Bennet, E. L. Environmental impoverishment, social isolation and changes in brain chemistry and anatomy. *Physiology and Behavior,* 1966, *1,* 99–104.

Kugelmass, I. M., Poull, L. E., and Samuel, E. L. Nutritional improvement of child mentality. *American Journal of the Medical Sciences,* 1944, *208,* 631–633.

Lorenz, K. Z. Imprinting. In R. C. Bomey and R. C. Teevan (Eds.), *Instinct.* Princeton, N.J.: D. Van Nostrand, 1961.

Miller, J. O. *Review of selected intervention research with young children.* Urbana, Ill.: ERIC Clearinghouse on Early Childhood Education, College of Education, University of Illinois, 1969a.

Miller, J. O. *The National Laboratory – a critical period of initiative.* Document No. 70706-N-F0-U-09, Urbana, Ill.: National Laboratory on Early Childhood Education, 1969b.

Rosenzweig, M. R. et al. Effects of environmental complexity and training on brain chemistry and anatomy: a replication and extension. *Journal of Comparative Physiological Psychology,* 1962, *55,* No. 4, 429–437.

Scott, J. P. The process of primary socialization in canine and human infants. *Monographs of the Society for Research in Child Development,* 1963, *28,* No. 1, Serial No. 85.

Scott, J. P. A time to learn. *Psychology Today,* March 1969, *2,* No. 10, 46f.

Skeels, H. M. Adult status of children with contrasting early life experiences. *Monographs of the Society for Research in Child Development,* 1966, *31,* No. 3, Serial No. 105.

Spitz, R. A. Hospitalism: an inquiry into the genesis of psychiatric conditions in early childhood. In *The Psychoanalytic Study of the Child, 1* (3rd ed.), New York: International University Press, 1945, pp. 53–74.

Widdowson, E. M. Mental contentment and physical growth. *The Lancet,* 1951, *1,* 1316–1318.

CHAPTER 2

SCHOOLS AND SYSTEMS OF EDUCATION

THE STRUCTURE OF RESPONSIBILITY

A popular image of a school is one of a classroom teacher instructing a group of students. However, schools are also complex social organizations consisting of a variety of roles encompassing specific duties, responsibilities and privileges. The potential complexity of the school as an educational system is suggested by the organizational pattern of a children's center within a large school district (Figure 2–1).

Although many early educational units are much smaller in size, they have some of the principles, problems, and advantages of more elaborate organizations. Administrative services are intended to facilitate teaching functions, and the definition and implementation of roles have a direct impact on a teacher's effectiveness. This influence is not easily evident in an efficient school where the administrative network is designed to support the teacher, but it is all too obvious when unnecessary red tape or administrative ineptness interrupt, burden, or frustrate the teacher.

Success in teaching is often closely tied to an understanding of the structure of the school, an ability to adjust to or change the system, and a capacity to develop one's own zone of influence and effectiveness. Every complex human social organization has two structures—one visible and explicit, the other unseen and implicit. Even in relatively simple organizations, such as a preschool with half a dozen staff members, there is a complex arrangement of formal expectations and informal understandings that help people relate to one another.

The formal expectations of how people in an organization carry out preassigned tasks is the more obvious and more easily learned part of the network of human interaction. The informal system, unstated but equally important, includes more subtle relationships resulting from the ways people work with and regard one another. Both formal and informal structures are crucial in the operation of an organization, and both must be understood for effective performance.

A new teacher may be given a list of prescribed duties such as the following.

8:30 a.m.	Mix paints and prepare art materials for the day
9:00 a.m.	Greet children at the door
9:20 a.m.	Supervise indoor play areas
10:00 a.m.	Serve juice
10:20 a.m.	Read stories

Since so many spontaneous factors go into teaching, the many ways her tasks could be carried out are not entirely specified. If it *were* possible to anticipate how each teacher might follow formal expectations, the instructions would possibly contain these or similar additions:

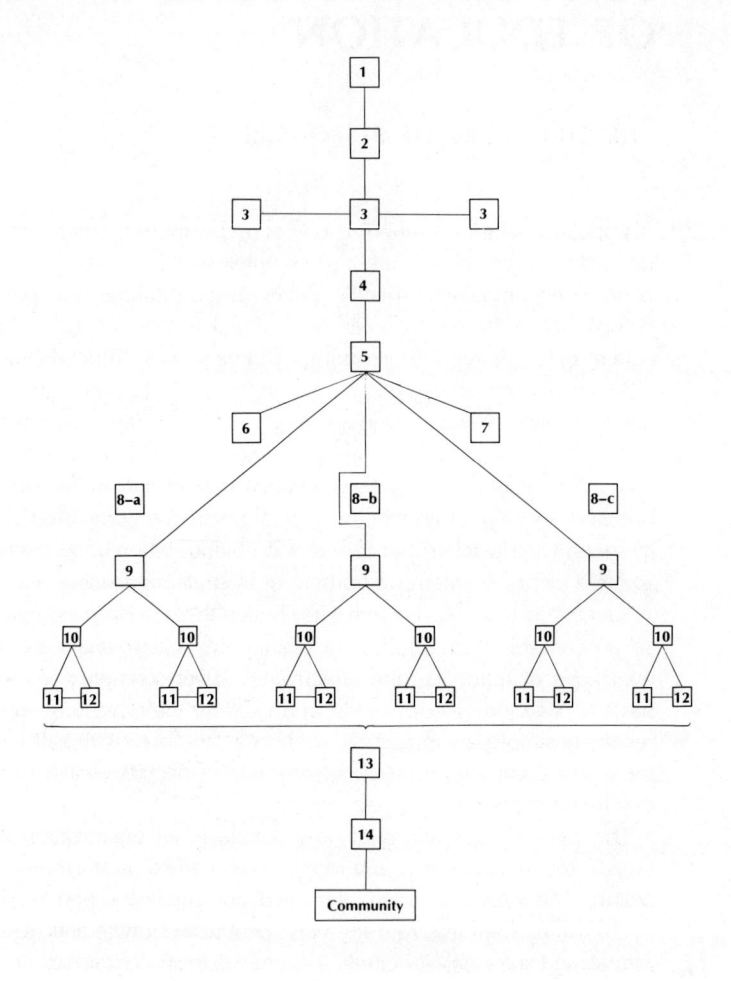

1. Trustees	**8–b.**	Children's Center B
2. Superintendent	**8–c.**	Children's Center C
3. Assistant Superintendents	**9.**	Center Coordinators
4. Director	**10.**	Classroom Directors
5. Administrative Assistant	**11.**	Assistant Teachers
6. Secretary	**12.**	Aides
7. Clerk-Receptionist	**13.**	Parent Advisory Committee
8–a. Children's Center A	**14.**	Parents' Organization

FIGURE 2–1 ORGANIZATIONAL STRUCTURE OF A CHILDREN'S CENTER

8:30 a.m.	Mix paints
	Compare notes on staff impressions of a particularly difficult child
9:00 a.m.	Greet children
	As children are brought to school chat with some of the mothers, especially Colleen's.
9:20 a.m.	Supervise indoor play areas
	When Debbie's mother comes to help, ask about the sister who's in junior high
10:00 a.m.	Serve juice . . .

However casual such extensions of a formal role may seem, they can increase the value of a teacher's contribution to the school. For example, when greeting children at the door, a teacher recalled that just the day before Colleen F.'s mother had been surprisingly abrupt. She wondered whether the behavior indicated dissatisfaction with the school or its staff. Therefore she made it a point to engage Mrs. F. in conversation. She complimented her on her dress and they talked about the details of how it was made. The mother seemed friendly and glad to talk. Nothing was said about Colleen, but the teacher felt that by taking time for conversation at this level, she was making it possible to have more directed discussions later. Also, when the conversation ended she felt that Mrs. F.'s abruptness had not been caused by anything at school.

The informal structure of a school system is not openly defined and can be learned only by participating in the system itself. The use of titles, the right to rearrange the chairs and tables in a room, the deference paid supervisors and visitors, the shared understandings of unspecified behaviors, many of which depend solely on the personalities of the people involved—all of these go to make up the informal structure of an organization. Although designated as "informal," the expectations are not necessarily friendly and flexible. On the contrary, they can be quite harsh and even rigid, as many a teacher realizes when she finds herself subtly ostracized because of something she did. The reactions of others in the organization may be as binding as any written rule.

Both formal and informal aspects of the matrix of roles and duties affect all members of an organization. A sensitive person utilizes this knowledge to express some of her own views about the organization. For example, the director of a school made it a point to share the assigned duties of all her staff members. She relieved an aide by helping change the children who had dirtied their clothes; she occasionally took over cleaning the easels; sometimes she read stories and supervised group activities. In this way she was communicating that she understood what it was like to be in the position of her teachers. Without any verbal statement she was letting them know she would

OWNER/BOARD	DIRECTOR	TEACHER	ASSISTANT TEACHER
Overall legal responsibility and financial management	Hires, trains, directs staff	In charge of and responsible for smooth running of daily program	Teaches and works directly with children under supervision of teacher
Selects site and/or buildings	Confers with parents and leads discussion groups	Sets atmosphere of school and classroom	Assists teacher in preparation of materials – often prepares all materials for a special project
Sets policy for school as a whole	Coordinates work of school with community agencies	Determines duties and responsibilities of other teachers	Helps plan daily activities
Chooses director	Has charge of public relations and publicity	Maintains discipline of staff and students	Contributes to observation and evaluation of children
Decides on enrollment, staff size, salary scale, fees, and school year	Responsible for record keeping – health, employment, personal data, testing	Usually determines schedule and curriculum	Supervises and works with aides and often with volunteers
Provides for maintenance of buildings, grounds, and equipment	Selects and purchases most equipment and material	Assists with parent meetings and conferences	Fills in for teacher upon request
	May or may not teach	Responsible for seeing that materials are on hand and ready as needed	May relieve teacher of responsibility for specific activities of daily schedule or special activities such as field trips
	May or may not direct research	Teaches and works directly with children	
		Serves as model for on-job training	
		Has charge of teacher evaluation	

TABLE 2-1 SUMMARY OF DUTIES AND RESPONSIBILITIES WITHIN A PRESCHOOL PROGRAM

not permit her formal role to interfere with the sharing of human qualities, and that as far as she was concerned, recognizing feelings was as important as stressing roles.

As with any organization composed of human beings, the way a school functions is a matter of how well people understand and carry out their roles. Even though tasks may be well-defined, not everyone sees them from the same perspective. Understanding viewpoints other than your own can help you see how your role complements and supports those that others play.

Table 2-1 presents a summary of the duties and responsibilities associated with some of the roles in a preschool program. The larger and more complex the school, the more specialized each of the roles becomes. Conversely, the smaller the organization, the more one person tends to assume the duties and responsibilities of several roles. For example, child care for a group of children in a private home may be handled by the owner who is also director, teacher, nurse, treasurer, and in charge of maintenance.

How do those involved in preschool education think of themselves and their roles? Examples of what people have to say about themselves and their work follow. Although each person speaks as a unique individual, he also expresses a perception of the school as a system which comes from the particular place he occupies in it.

An Assistant Teacher's Concerns

Today was Monday—the first day in another week of kids and school at the Oak Street Community Center. Barbara D. walked briskly along, thinking about the day ahead. After two years of being a teacher—well, assistant teacher—but why did the teacher always have to introduce her as "our assistant teacher"?—it seemed that on many days she did as much teaching as Mrs. J. In fact, it seemed to Barbara that more and more Mrs. J. was being called to the office to talk to a parent or to see somebody about fixing something. Thank goodness Barbara could be with the kids most of the time—they were really great. Sometime it might be nice to talk more with parents, though. She'd certainly like to see what kind of mother prissy Eleanor had. Did that woman go around putting everything in its place all the time, too? But today was Monday and that meant having to think about all the materials that needed readying for the week's art projects and science projects and cooking projects and whatever good old Mrs. J. had decided they were going to do. Did all teachers insist on having materials arranged a week ahead? Not that anything ever went wrong—Mrs. J. was just great that way—she really kept things moving. And she was getting a lot better about letting people make suggestions, though Barbara wished she wouldn't interfere with discipline so much . . . like the time last Friday when Mrs. J. found Johnny sitting at a table and suggested he go outside even though the aide had told him to stay right where he was until she called him. But Barbara had to admit she probably wouldn't be able to do as well when she got to be a head teacher.

She knew that no matter how much work she had to face today, at least she hadn't called in sick as she had done twice last year. She still felt guilty every time she thought about that. She had known she wasn't really sick. The first time it was because she felt so ashamed for slapping Maxie when he spit at her. The worst part was that no one had said a word to criticize her. It was almost as though they had known exactly how she felt and that it would never happen again. She hadn't had nerve enough to bring it up herself and Maxie did get better about following group rules. The other time was only four or five weeks later. By then she was getting along pretty well with the kids but finding herself angrier and angrier because she always seemed to be the one who had to clean up the paint jars. It was such a small thing she didn't want to mention it to Mrs. J. —well, actually there had never been a chance because everyone was too busy to have meetings for anything but announcements or planning for a special project. And besides, they were so nice to each other—it was just that you never could be really sure how they felt about you. Barbara still considered that the paint job should be taken care of by the aide. Wasn't that what aides were for? Facing her feelings again she knew the same answer. She'd just been jealous because the aide was so popular with the kids . . .

this year it was better, though. Besides, it was a different aide, one that was much more helpful and didn't always have to be told what to do. Barbara hated supervising anyone else, even though she knew that she was expected to work with aides and volunteers who came to help with the regular program.

Then she remembered. This week, in fact this morning, a new volunteer was coming—a man. She knew his name was Tom and that he was going to be at school for two or three weeks. It was her job to see he had a chance to be with the children as much as possible, especially outdoors. Did that mean no chores? What was so special about him besides the fact he was a man? Why shouldn't he take his turn with everything? Barbara knew these answers, too. She could still hear Mrs. J. explaining, "We need volunteers, especially men. And we want Tom to enjoy his work and to know how important we think it is to give children a chance to interact with him. I know you'll do your best to see they are together as much as possible."

Barbara knew she'd follow Mrs. J.'s instructions. But wouldn't it be great if Tom turned out to be someone with whom she too could interact?

What is expected of an assistant teacher depends in large measure, of course, on the kind of school in which she works. It also depends on how long she's worked there. In some programs she will assume most of the tasks and duties of the teacher but without ultimate responsibility or authority. Many are in charge of a group of children, supervise the work of aides and volunteers, often deal with parents, and generally make choices and decisions on their own.

Even though a teacher may direct the overall program, once a general notion of what needs to be done has been established, an assistant often functions relatively independently. Others in this role serve as assistants. They work within sight of the teacher, are held responsible for most of the housekeeping chores such as mixing paint, seeing that children are properly clothed, and getting out and putting away supplies. As far as direct contact with children is concerned, they usually work with small groups for a short period of time at the suggestion of the teacher.

Whether assistant teachers are on their own or under constant supervision, their concerns about themselves and their work are surprisingly similar. They wonder if they are doing a good job, they wonder what the staff and parents and children think about them, and they wonder whether they might find greater opportunity and satisfaction in another school.

A Teacher's Perspective

Mrs. E. is a teacher in a large private nursery school. She is a tall, vivacious woman in her mid-forties who has been teaching nearly a dozen years. The school employs four

HEALTH HISTORY	FAMILY AND SOCIAL HISTORY	IDENTIFICATION AND EMERGENCY
Immunizations, by kind and date	Marital status of parents	Names, addresses and home and business phones of parents
Allergies, especially in regard to food	Names and relationship of other members in the household	Whom to call in case of emergency if parent can't be reached
Physical conditions requiring special attention at school	Where is child cared for and by whom when not in school?	Names of persons authorized to take child from the nursery school

TABLE 2–2 EXAMPLES OF THE TYPE OF RECORDS JUDGED "MOST USEFUL" BY NURSERY SCHOOL TEACHERS

other women like her, each with an assistant and a helper (aide). She has twenty-four children as her direct responsiblity.

Except for hiring (and firing), which is done by the school's owner largely on her recommendation, she works as autonomously as a teacher in a smaller school. She plans her own curriculum and day-to-day procedures. Once a week she and the three other teachers meet with the director and with the owner of the school to go over mutual concerns. The following dialogue tells something about how Mrs. E. views her role as a teacher:

Q. Mrs. E., how would you define your role as a teacher?
A. That isn't easy to answer. I guess I see myself mostly as someone who plans for individual children and then sees that the plans are carried out.
Q. How do you do this?
A. Well, I know pretty well how the owner and director feel about the children and it's up to me to work out a program that satisfies what they want to achieve. Of course I agree with their philosophy or I would never have taken employment with them.
Q. Do you work directly with children?
A. Oh, yes, indeed. Every day. All of the staff shares equally in teaching and observing the children. Perhaps I don't have as many of the housekeeping chores, but I'm responsible, and during school hours I'm with the children as much as anyone.
Q. You say, "During school hours." Does this mean you have school-related work at other times?
A. Well, I spend a good many hours keeping up reports and records,[1] talking with parents formally and informally, and . . .
Q. Are you the only person who has contact with parents?
A. Yes, I guess I am. Of course, if a parent is visiting we don't expect the assistant or any member of the staff to be rude or to ignore our visitor. But I am the only one who discusses the children's work with them.
Q. Who purchases equipment and supplies?
A. I do—or at least I make up lists of things I feel are needed and throughout the year I can draw on a general fund up to any amount that has been budgeted.

---

[1] Table 2–2 describes some of the kinds of information Mrs. E. and many teachers keep on file. Such records make readily available both background and experiential information.

If I'm lucky I'll have an assistant with an eye for inexpensive or junk materials and she'll make suggestions or bring things in. But purchases are up to me.

Q. How does your staff know what you expect them to do?

A. Do you mean do we have lists of duties, staff training sessions, and that kind of thing?

Q. Something like that.

A. Well, first of all, the owner rarely hires anyone who hasn't some experience and training. But training goes on all the time—especially with new staff. Once they are hired and we talk over the general purposes of the school and perhaps discuss the few specific rules such as "No running with juice," "No throwing sand," and so on, they are pretty much on their own. But they are expected to watch how things are done and to ask questions. And all of us feel free to offer suggestions to one another. If I see a situation being handled improperly, we stay a few minutes after school and go over it. Of course I would never speak critically to an assistant or helper in front of the children!

Q. What do you consider your most important function?

A. As far as staff is concerned, or the children?

Q. Both, or either.

A. Well, as far as staff is concerned, I think it's important to see that they know whether they are doing a good job or not and to help them realize how important they are in the lives of the children. As far as the children are concerned, I think I try hardest to provide a responsible environment for all their needs. By this I mean I want every child to develop both skills and concepts.

Q. One more question. Suppose at the end of a year you were to say to yourself, "This has been a good year." What would you mean?

A. Now, that's easier to answer. It's a good year when the children have made progress. That is, when their curiosity has grown, they're interested in many activities and are eager to go on.

The Viewpoint of an Aide

Private schools, such as the one for which Mrs. E. works, frequently hire aides. Those who fill this role are often high school girls fond of children, housewives who want to work part-time, young men and women interested in careers in social service or recreational work, and students seeking experience in the field of preschool education. They tie shoes, take children to the toilet, mop up spilled juice, and do a variety of other essential tasks. Many also spend time helping teach and are given responsibility for specific activities such as rhythms, dramatic play, and supervising the use of equipment. Their close relationship with the children can be an important source of feedback for teachers working out activities to meet individual needs.

Compensatory programs use aides in much the same way but often with an important difference. Under guidelines set by state and federal agencies, these aides often must be hired from applicants who already live in the target area and know the families and children whom the program serves. Their familiarity with the neighborhood and the people make them a valuable liaison resource.

Glancing up from the stack of applications which lay on the desk before her, the program coordinator called "Marlena, Marlena García?"

Hearing her name, a slender, dark-haired teenage girl hesitantly crossed the room with a small boy at her side. As she reached the desk she pulled him slightly behind her and waited quietly.

The woman spoke again. "Are you Marlena García?"

"Sí, señora." The child stepped forward and answered, too. "Me llamo José." Then proudly added, "José Castillo."

The coordinator, busy with her papers, took no notice. "You applied for work as an aide in the Community Day Center?" she asked.

"Sí, señora, I need work bad." Marlena waited, unconsciously stroking the child's black hair while the woman returned to the application form she held.

Name: *Marlena García*
Address: *160 Bonita Street*   Phone: *no*
Age: *18*, Citizenship: *Mexican-American* Married: *yes*
Education: *1½ years high school* Children: *1 dead*
Experience: *none*

"How far do you live from here?"

"¿Perdón?"

Not sure whether the girl hadn't heard or hadn't understood, the coordinator spoke louder. "Do you live near here?"

"Aaahh. Sí. Sí. Vivo en la calle Bonita. It is near. Two blocks—three."

"Good. Can you work full time?"

Again Marlena stood in doubt. "¿Perdón—what you mean please?"

The coordinator drew a breath and sought to explain in Spanish. "Puedo—puedes trabajar todos—todo día?"

"Oh, sí, sí, señora." Eyes aglow Marlena pulled the boy closer daring to hug him delightedly. Then she turned to answer the coordinator. "Puedo trabajar las horas que tú quieres, señora." At ease now in her own language and with hands and eyes explaining and emphasizing, Marlena told the woman that she could work many hours "anytime they wanted her," that she was a good worker and loved "los niños" very, very much. Hugging José, who returned her affection with a warm smile, she explained that she needed work because her husband was laid off his job and . . .

She was interrupted. "How long have you lived . . ." Remembering, the coordinator tried again. "Cuanto tiempo tienes . . . viviendo . . . en la calle Bonita?"

Marlena hesitated. Did it really matter how long? Truthfully she replied, "Maybe a year en la calle Bonita, señora."

The coordinator considered. Here was a girl eager to work. One who could certainly help with the children, one who knew the neighborhood and was sufficiently bilingual to serve as interpreter. But would she be able to get the parents to listen to her? Had she lived in the area long enough to know the families she would be asked to deal with?

José began shifting from foot to foot, tugging at Marlena's skirt. "Vámonos, Marlena, estoy cansado."

This time the coordinator noticed him. "Is he yours?" she asked.

"Oh, no, señora. Es mi hermano."

"You have other brothers and sisters? They live here?"

"Sí, Señora. Two brother. Four sister." Marlena smiled proudly. "Todo mi familia. I live with them until I marry and go to calle Bonita."

Now the coordinator was smiling, too. "Can you come to work tomorrow?" she asked. "We really need your help."

"Si, señora."

Volunteers: An Important Resource

Just as aides are an important resource in many preschool programs, so too are volunteers. Those with special interests or talents often enrich a preschool program by visiting briefly and sharing what they know or do best. Others are involved as aides; they contribute their time and abilities on a day-to-day basis. One such volunteer is Karen, a tall blond girl in her late twenties who works in a Head Start program.

During convalescence from a serious accident, Karen had looked for work that she felt she could handle on a part-time basis. "I love children," she explains, "and though I had never had any experience or training, I decided helping out two or three days a week would be just about right for me."

The first few days were difficult because it took her a while to become accustomed to the continuous activity and high noise level of the children. By watching the teacher and her assistant closely, however, and by listening to their explanations, she soon came to feel a more efficient part of the school and is now working the same schedule as the teacher and assistant—five mornings a week.

At first the teacher would find moments to tell Karen specifically what she wanted her to do and how to go about the various tasks assigned her. "The assistant teacher was very helpful, too," Karen recalls. "I always felt they expected me to ask about anything I didn't know."

Every morning when she first comes to school Karen looks at the schedule the teacher has posted for the day. "That way I know what special things are planned," she says. "Some days I'm at the clay table, or maybe I help with a holiday craft. But since the assistant comes an hour early and puts all the materials out, all I do is look them over so I know what they are."

She greatly admires the way the teachers are trying to help the children and says she's glad to do what they want her to. She remembers an occasion when one of the mothers volunteered to come in and sing for the children and then to teach them a new song. "Of course we told her how much we appreciated her coming, and talked with the children about how nice it was for people to volunteer to help. . . ." In recounting the experience she laughed. "By the time the mother came I had become so involved with the children that I found it impossible to remember I was a volunteer too, and I don't think they did. At least no one mentioned it."

Because she has become so interested in preschool education, after the year's work is up she plans to take courses and perhaps get a degree in nursery education. According to Karen, that will be time enough for her to make some of the changes she's thought about.

"I'd have the children out more on field trips, for instance," she suggests. But she doesn't think it important enough to mention yet. Her satisfaction comes from seeing a child accomplish something they've worked on together. "The day five-year-old Shirley wrote her name and realized she could do so again and again," Karen said, "I don't know who was proudest!"

Like many volunteers, Karen finds gratification in working with children. Her lack of training in a particular field has not meant she is unable to be effective. Through her willingness to learn and her efforts to interact with children and staff, she has found she can contribute a great deal to what she considers "proper education" for children.

Unlike Karen, but like the mother who sang for the children and then taught them a new song, many volunteers come only occasionally for special purposes. Some are highly skilled, such as doctors and dentists and artists; others bring knowledge of different cultures and languages; many are willing to share job skills or hobbies. Some come into the classroom and interact with the children; a few prefer to help by building or repairing equipment.

Like many busy men, a children's dentist in the San Francisco Bay area looks forward to the annual invitation he receives to visit a cooperative nursery. He puts on a bright Hawaiian shirt, brings a huge set of teeth, an oversize toothbrush, some free samples of tooth paste, and sugarless gum. His simple, clear explanations about healthy teeth keep a large group of three-to-fives and their parents entranced. He obviously enjoys having the children tell him what they eat, and he tells them that if they eat the same foods that a rabbit does, they will have good, strong, healthy teeth.

He demonstrates how and when to brush teeth. The children swarm around him to touch the things he has brought and they respond with exclamations of joy when he hands out the sugarless gum. Parents have many questions to ask and he seems pleased to be able to talk with them about their children's health. He is a very busy man yet he willingly spends two hours or more at the school whenever he is invited. Preparing his presentation, ordering the samples, and adjusting appointments takes additional time, but he puts aside work that pays him in money for the feeling he has of contributing to his community. Mostly he likes *being appreciated,* and the poster the children made for him is prominently displayed in his waiting room.

Many potential volunteers will never let a teacher know they have a special interest or talent; it will be up to the teacher and her staff to find out what resources of this kind are available. In whatever capacity volunteers serve, they need to be relied on and appreciated as individuals.

Administrators: The Supporting Roles

Teachers, assistant teachers, aides, and volunteers in a preschool program are generally in direct contact with children. Important roles are also filled by people who may rarely interact with preschoolers. This is not because they prefer isolation, but rather because their duties and responsibilities often keep them too busy to be at school in the classroom.

Mrs. C., director of an all-day program involving some eighty-five children and half a dozen teachers backed up by assistants, aides, and volunteers, is one such person.

"I spend so much time on the phone finding staff and then interviewing and scheduling them that I have little time for much else," she says in a tone of regret. "I'd like it much better if I could just pop into a classroom when I have a minute or two. But if I go out, that always seems to be the time when I'm most needed right here."

The program she administers involves a great deal of record keeping, frequent budget crises, and many parent conferences. She says she's lucky to get to see the teachers, much less the children. "We can't seem to find a time when it's convenient for us to get together," she explains. "But my door is always open to the staff members, literally as well as figuratively, and they know it."

Mrs. S., chairman of the Board of Directors of a parent co-op, feels more fortunate. "I'd probably never get over to the school except, thank goodness, I'm a parent, too. That means I'm obligated to help with the children one morning a week."

In her role as Board Chairman she feels her concerns are not only those of a director but also those of an owner. With one exception. "I'll bet I get more phone calls from people wanting to know why the grass is cut so short, or which fathers were supposed to repair the tree house," she explains. "That's because in a parent co-op *everyone* feels he's running the whole show!"

Like most directors and owners, Mrs. S. keeps in close touch with the person in charge of the school program itself. "I'll miss those phone calls when I'm no longer chairman," she admits. "I've had a good relationship with our teacher and with the parents, just as I hoped I would when I joined the group. I've made many real friends."

However much their individual programs may differ in general, owners and boards of directors have the following functions in common:

   Legal responsibility
   Financial control
   Accountability of director
   Site selection and maintenance

Either individually or as a group, they secure the license for the school if one is required, prepare whatever financial reports are necessary, raise and disburse funds, and generally conduct the business affairs of their programs. They select the person who runs the school, and he or she is directly accountable to them. In choosing a site they see that the property meets the various health, safety, and building code standards set by the licensing agency or other regulatory body. If qualified professionally, owners frequently serve as directors and/or teachers of their schools. When this is the case, they naturally assume the duties, responsibilities, and privileges that accompany these roles, too.

Perhaps these comments by the kinds of people you will be working with extend your understanding of a preschool program and your place in it. It takes time to learn techniques for working with staff members and children and to be sensitive to their needs. Knowing something of the roles they play, however, may help you become the kind of teacher you want to be.

TABLE 2-3 CHILDREN UNDER 5 IN THE UNITED STATES
from M. Haberman and B. Persky (Eds.), *Preliminary Report of the Ad Hoc Joint Committee on the Preparation of Nursery and Kindergarten Teachers.* NEA, Stock No. 521-15720, p. 6.

1970	20 million
By 1975	25 million
By 1980	28 million

PATTERNS OF PROFESSIONAL TRAINING

The Need for Teachers

Population statistics as shown in Table 2-3 indicate the estimated number of children likely to be living in the United States in the next ten years. If present trends continue, public kindergarten may become compulsory, voluntary programs will be provided for three- and four-year-olds at public expense and the number of day care facilities expanded. This will mean an increase in school enrollment of five million children aged three to five by 1980. Day care, even if it can be found, will not be enough. During 1968 American colleges and universities graduated only 1200 teachers trained specifically to work at the preschool level. Helping young children develop their potential during the formative years from three to five requires more than concern for physical safety. Special training is needed to meet the demands of rapid change in a human organism with special patterns of learning.

Trained and experienced specialists are needed not only as directors and head teachers of nursery schools, day centers, and other early education programs, but also for college teaching, agency supervision, and community consultants. In addition, highly qualified men and women are needed as assistant teachers. Others with varying degrees of training and experience must be found to serve as aides and volunteers.

Programs of Training

In talks with prospective teachers, certain concerns come sharply into focus over and over again. Students want to know whether the training they are getting will really prepare them for the work ahead. Will they be able to do their part to the satisfaction not only of themselves, but of professionals already in the field? Are they learning enough to be able to hold a job in a "good" school? Young teachers want to know about salaries and what can be expected in the way of advancement and opportunity, of course, but the most central question is whether they will have the qualifications to establish themselves as professionals. What kind of training did other teachers have that qualified them for the work they're doing? An overall view of a typical structure of the training qualifying persons for the various professional steps in the field of early education is given in Figure 2-2.

There is a continual assessment of the particular competencies needed by teachers of young children, and curricula are being developed and revised accordingly. Each state and school with programs has its own regulations concerning such matters as degree requirements, unit hours of work, and transfer of credits.

Position	How Recognized	Training Source
Director / Coordinator / Supervisor	Doctorate, Master's, Bachelor's degree	Universities, Colleges
	Teaching Credential	State Board of Education
Teacher	A.A. Degree	Community and Junior Colleges
Assistant Teacher	Certificate of completion for course work	Colleges and Universities, Professional Associations, School Districts, State, County, and Local Associations
Aides / Volunteers	Unit hours of work	On-the-job training and experience under qualified supervision

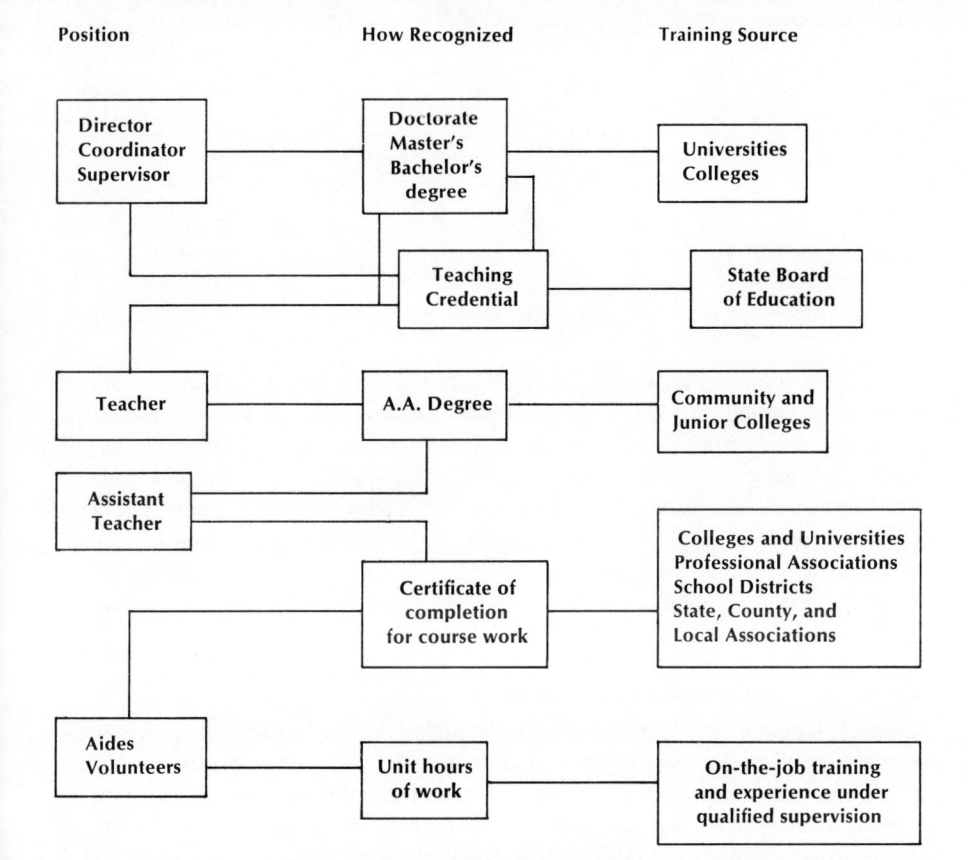

FIGURE 2–2 LEVELS OF TRAINING FOR PERSONNEL IN EARLY CHILDHOOD EDUCATION

At present only a few institutions of higher learning in the United States grant baccalaureate or graduate degrees in Early Childhood Education. Such programs are offered through several different kinds of departments and schools—psychology, education, home economics, arts and sciences—and where formal degree programs are not offered, courses are often available in a number of related areas, such as the following:

Child Development or Psychology
Language Development
Child, Family and Community
Nursery School Theory and Practice
Developmental Psychology
Early Learning
Children's Speech Arts
Children's Literature
Educational Psychology
Observation of Preschool Children
Fundamentals of Testing
Personality Development

Two-year programs for training in nursery school or preschool teaching are offered by many community and junior colleges. Credit is given for courses which apply toward the requirements of an Associate in Arts (A.A.) degree. The course content of these programs overlaps to some extent with programs in four-year colleges and universities.

Colleges and extension divisions of many universities offer night school and home study courses leading to professional upgrading. Workshops and a variety of special weekend and summer programs offered by professional associations and school districts also make continuing education possible. Such training usually carries with it a certificate of completion.

Certification and Licensing Requirements

Degrees or certificates do not automatically qualify one for employment as a teacher. Work in public school kindergartens and in many of the supervisory positions in preschool programs also require credentials. Through separate boards of education, the various states issue teaching credentials based on a variety of requirements. Two of the prerequisites usually required are: 1) a degree from an accredited institution and 2) certain combinations of major and minor course work. California further requires that without a fifth year in education at upper division or graduate level, plus practice teaching, only a provisional credential will be issued and that for a limited period of time.

Private and public nursery schools and other early education programs are often licensed to operate under the supervision of a state or other controlling agency. It is usually not necessary to hold teaching credentials to be hired as a teacher or assistant teacher in these programs. However, persons seeking positions will necessarily have to meet educational and experience standards set by one or any combination of the following groups:

- State licensing agency
- County licensing agency
- City licensing agency
- Business licensing agency
- School district
- Individual owner

Typical educational and experience requirements for teachers in early childhood education programs are given in Table 2–4. Nursery school programs are not usually part of public educational systems. Public schools have their own teacher qualification standards. Kindergartens frequently are an integral part of the schools, and teachers at

DIRECTORS AND/OR HEAD TEACHERS	TEACHERS AND ASSISTANT TEACHERS
At least 21 years of age	At least 18 years of age
University or college degree with emphasis on course work in field of early childhood education	At least 12 semester units of course work in early childhood education
From 1 to 4 years teaching experience in early education programs	At least 3 hours experience per day for 100 days in a calender year under qualified supervision
Either 3 semester units or the equivalent in administration and/or staff relations	

TABLE 2–4 QUALIFICATIONS FOR TEACHERS IN EARLY CHILDHOOD EDUCATION PROGRAMS

this level must meet the same professional requirements as elementary school teachers if they wish to work in public school programs.

In many states, there is more than one way to qualify as a nursery school teacher or assistant teacher. In addition to approved university and college programs, recognition may be awarded for demonstrated on-the-job competence whether or not accompanied by course work or degrees. Such credit is often given with the requirement that in order to maintain a teaching position, the teacher must take course work and special training as they become available.

Training Through Experience

Even after students in early childhood education programs get a background of course work, observation, and laboratory school or student teaching experience, they may wonder whether they are ready to handle a full time job. They are if they recognize that their education does not cease with a degree or certificate; their competence will grow with experience on the job.

The directors and teachers in well-run schools are aware of the value of training through experience for all personnel. They instruct assistant teachers and aides, especially in the details and procedures of their particular organization. Much of this instruction is quite informal, given along with the assignment of a specific task. It ranges from the details of routine rules, which can be picked up readily, to more complex problems of teaching and interpersonal competence. A supervising teacher may say, "I'd like you to be sure that the children use smocks or aprons for water play as well as painting," or "Try to get the children to put away the equipment—they need help in developing a sense of responsibility." This casual way of imparting information, along with the teacher's own example, is one of the most frequent kinds of training. In addition, throughout the day, teachers spend many moments discussing behaviors of the children and techniques for dealing with especially significant examples. The head teacher may take time just before or after school to mention various procedures or methods she wants the staff to follow. Even routine tasks offer opportunities for learning-by-doing. Much training for beginning teachers comes from participating in activities and evaluation of their own performance.

New teachers often express a need and appreciation for curriculum ideas which other more experienced teachers have found useful. Some examples of what to do and how to do it, such as the tasks presented in the companion handbook to this volume (Croft and Hess, 1972), can be a useful resource for teachers, parents and aides.

As part of staff meetings, it is not uncommon for the person in charge of training to present a subject-matter specialist, a film, or a speaker. Regular time may also be set aside for sharing new songs, finger-plays, crafts and supplies with the entire group. Some employers give released time (with pay) for staff members to attend community workshops or local and regional conferences. Often partial or full payment of fees is extended as well. Directors sometimes encourage their teachers to go back to college and work for higher degrees, helping them adjust their work hours to make this possible.

The teacher who wants to keep up with what is going on in her field and develop her own competence can do so in several ways. She can continue to learn through her own experience, from her fellow staff members and from a variety of sources outside the school. These include meetings of local preschool or early education associations, regional conferences and workshops or extension courses offered by universities. Resources are also offered by several major professional associations, such as the National Association for the Education of Young Children, which publishes a journal called *Young Children,* Association for Childhood Education International, which publishes *Childhood Education,* The Child Study Association of America, with its publication, *Child Quarterly,* The Child Welfare League of America, and its monthly journal, *Child Welfare,* and the Society for Research in Child Development, and its publications, *Child Development* and *Monographs.* In addition, the newly established Office of Child Development, under the Secretary of the U.S. Department of Health, Education and Welfare, produces and distributes materials dealing with many aspects of child care, development and education.

Some nursery schools subscribe to journals which provide the staff with information about their work. In addition, many teachers belong to one or more of these organizations, attend conferences, workshops and meetings, and find the publications and resource materials useful in helping them to keep informed about new developments in their field. In a rapidly growing field such as early childhood education, continuous self-education is part of the job.

DIMENSIONS WHICH DIFFERENTIATE SCHOOLS

Few communities are without some program of early education. The wide variety of existing preschools is apparent in the listings in the phone directory of most cities of any significant size. Programs operate under many different names, a sampling of which is given in Table 2–5.

Advertisements accompanying the listings frequently emphasize the "courteous" trained and/or certificated staff; the provision of snacks and hot meals; availability of

Nursery	Day Nursery	Adult Education Preschool
Nursery Home	Cooperative Nursery School	Parish School
Nursery Kindergarten	Real Life Nursery School	Preschool Learning Center
Nursery and Kindergarten	Infant Nursery	Neighborhood Center
Nursery and Preschool	School	Children's Center
Nursery School	Day School	Education Center
Church Nursery School	Community Center School	Child Care Center
Church Co-op Nursery School	Play School	U.S. Govt. Navy Dept. Child Care Center
Temple Nursery	Preschool and Kindergarten	Parent-Child Group
Archdiocesan Opportunity Program	Church Preschool	Head Start Program
Parent's Community Co-op Nursery School	Preschool Training	Infants Day Care Home
Community Association Nursery School	Christian School	Day Home for Infants

TABLE 2–5 TYPES OF EARLY CHILDHOOD EDUCATION PROGRAMS

private transportation; half-day or full-day sessions both summer and winter; academic, social, artistic, physical, and character development as well as expert supervision and guidance; "structured programs" and "non-permissive progressive programs." A few of the schools promise language training (usually French, German or Spanish). Also mentioned are phonics and field trips. When the facilities themselves are described, it is in terms such as "separate buildings," "shaded," and "well-equipped play yard." Groups that have full day programs frequently make a special appeal to "working mothers."

Differences Based on Purpose and Sponsorship

In general, the programs differ on such classifications as organizational structure, the roles teachers are asked to fill, and whether or not parents are directly involved. There are several dimensions which may especially help a teacher understand what to expect and whether her interests will be served by a particular school.

Purpose and Sponsorship Perhaps the most fundamental consideration is the school's *purpose*. From this viewpoint, nursery schools fall roughly into the following categories:

1. Educational and Compensatory

These are schools which have as their goal the improvement of the child's readiness for formal schooling. In compensatory programs they concentrate on helping him catch up in pre-academic skills or in developing his abilities still further.

2. Child Care

These schools serve parents by providing a substitute home for children whose mothers cannot be home because of work schedules, illness, or other circumstance.

3. Commercial or Franchise

The purpose of these schools is generally determined by the owner-investor or corporation which grants the franchise. The program is often organized around a curriculum which promises early attainment of cognitive skills.

4. Social-developmental

Schools of this type give children an opportunity to develop social, emotional and intellectual capabilities in an out-of-home setting. They provide the child another context in which to pursue his natural growth, to learn to deal with other children—perhaps with those from different social and ethnic backgrounds.

SPONSOR (OWNER)	DISTINGUISHING FEATURES
PUBLIC	
Federal or state agency such as Office of Economic Opportunity; Department of Health, Education and Welfare; State Department of Welfare; or State Department of Education	Funds allocated by Congress or state legislatures. Program developers and supervisors may be quite remote from schools themselves. May be experimental programs on a year-to-year basis. Programs exceedingly varied, including those of compensatory education
Local agency such as a neighborhood council, community service organization, or welfare agency	Primarily day care centers in low income areas. May also include schools providing services to special groups such as retarded, handicapped, etc.
PRIVATE	
Individual or group	A small school operated by a single owner or a large enterprise with absentee owners who leave running of the school to a professional director and a staff
Religious group	May use church personnel for staffing and have secular emphasis, or may simply permit use of church facilities
Parents' cooperative	Parents hire professional director and then serve as assistants on a rotating basis with regularly scheduled meetings for families

TABLE 2–6 DIFFERENT FORMS OF SPONSORSHIP

5. Training and Research
Schools established for research and training purposes which also provide teaching experience for students enrolled in colleges and universities.

Schools differ with respect to their *sponsorship*. In many instances, the corporate or individual owner is responsible for the school, but it is possible for an agency to sponsor a program without ownership. Table 2–6 summarizes a number of ways which preschools differ in sponsorship.

The sponsors of schools generally establish the enrollment policy. Most agency programs, including all federally supported compensatory groups, are primarily limited to children of families designated "poor." Many local agencies also use this criterion but perhaps not as rigidly. Church groups may or may not be restricted to children of families who are members of the church; many are available to any child in the community. Private schools and parent coops are selective by virtue of the fees they charge and, in the case of co-ops, the requirement that parents actively participate in the program on a regular basis.

Other Factors of Differentiation

When considering differences among preschools, it is also useful to take into account the following factors: *physical setting, facilities, licensing, staff competence and training,* and *funding.*

Preschools differ as a consequence of *physical setting* which includes location, climate, and the socio-ethnic backgrounds of the available population. The owners of a school in Alaska would have quite different factors to consider from those who run a school in Florida. So, too, would owners of schools in desert country as contrasted with those whose schools are in or near a waterfront community. An inner-city complex

FIGURE 2–3 LOCATION AND CLIMATE ARE FACTORS IN PLANNING A PROGRAM

has an economic and social make-up different from that of a suburban locale. The information in Table 2–7 indicates that teaching in a school located in Aztec, New Mexico, for example, is likely to be quite different from teaching in one in Fargo, North Dakota, or Birmingham, Alabama.

Differences in *facilities* are especially significant since those used by preschool programs conform to no single type. Some exist wherever suitable space can be found; others are an integral part of the planning for a university community center. Young children attend school in many structures from downtown gymnasiums and vacant stores, to church-school rooms. Some preschool groups occupy a series of buildings;

	ALABAMA	NEW HAMPSHIRE	NORTH DAKOTA	NEW MEXICO
TOTAL	3,266,740	606,921	632,446	951,023
Am. Indian	1,276	135	11,726	340,000
Chinese	288	152	100	362
Japanese	500	207	127	930
Mexican-American				95,102
Negro	980,271	1,903	777	17,063
Puerto Rican	663	212	68	433

TABLE 2-7 POPULATION IN SELECTED STATES
adapted from Statistical Abstract of U.S., 89th ed. Bureau of Census, Washington, D.C.: U.S. Government Printing Office, 1968, p. 28f.

others are crowded into a single room of a private residence, a converted garage, or the basement of an office building. A few use rooftops or nearby parks for their outdoor play area; most have fenced-in yards of one kind or another. Anyone touring nursery school facilities soon realizes that for all their variety they are usually geared to the needs of children in a particular program. As long as they meet these needs, uniformity is not only unimportant, it is highly impractical.

Schools sometimes advertise that their facilities are *licensed*. This indicates that they comply with certain health and safety requirements, staff ratios, and other state and/or local agency standards considered minimum for running a preschool program. Not all states require licensing. While it is true that even without licensing some schools may meet appropriate criteria, it is important to inquire whether schools are operating within established state or local standards.

An increasing number of states require a license in order to legally establish and operate a group day care program. In 1940, only three states required licensing; in the mid 1960's nearly thirty states had licensing regulations. In general, licensing is handled through a state department of public welfare. Of concern are requirements covering such factors as staff qualifications, amount of indoor and outdoor space per child, health and safety features, record keeping, financial accountability, and ages of the children. Owners must also meet local regulations such as those covering zoning, building codes, and parking areas. Typical of these regulations covering staff-child ratios are those listed in Table 2-8.

A school reflects the preparation and philosophical orientation of its personnel. The level of *staff competence* and the type of *training* are two of the most important criteria of differentiation.

Staff competence reflects the selection policies of the school both by attention to individual qualifications and personal attributes of teachers, and by the amount of training they have received. The philosophical orientation of the school creates a permissive, child-centered atmosphere or a more structured and predetermined program according to the preferences of the director and staff. Expectations for the teacher are obviously quite different in a school modeled after the relaxed pattern of an English Infant School, than that of a classroom with teaching schedules emphasizing specific pre-academic skills.

Another important dimension of difference in nursery schools regards their *funding*.

AGES	MINIMUM STAFF REQUIRED
3	For each 12 children a trained head teacher and an assistant
4	For each 16 children a trained head teacher and an assistant
5	For each 20 children a trained head teacher and an assistant

TABLE 2–8 SUGGESTED STAFF-CHILD RATIOS IN PRESCHOOL PROGRAMS The Head Start standard for 4's and 5's is 15 children and a trained teacher plus an assistant and community area volunteers.

Operating budgets and per-pupil costs vary widely depending on the type of program and the source of funds. Some private owners and groups raise or borrow money to begin a school and then continue to operate by collecting tuition fees sufficient to make a profit. Many parent co-ops and other group programs depend primarily on tuition, but also raise money through school fairs, raffles, auctions, cake sales, donations, and the like. In such schools teachers may or may not be expected to participate in fund-raising activities. Church programs are usually part of the overall operation of a local group, and their support is budgeted and voted upon at annual meetings.

Government programs are, of course, tax supported and usually funded on a year-to-year basis. Public school programs locally sponsored (for example, by an adult education department) depend largely on state and county tax money allocated by the legislature on the basis of average daily attendance (ADA). Under this arrangement they are provided a certain amount of money per pupil depending on the number of students in school on a given day.

Knowledge of the variety of nursery schools, and some of the ways they are differentiated gives the teacher a basis for judging in what sort of school he is likely to do his best work.

THE IMPACT OF THE PHYSICAL ENVIRONMENT

Interaction with the physical environment is an important part of the learning context for young children. A great deal of what three-to-fives learn in a nursery school program comes from direct interaction with their environment. They explore and discover with their bodies and senses the excitement of high places, the fascination of tunnels, the motion of swings and rope ladders, the texture and shape of a multitude of objects and materials. Their senses continuously bring both general and specific knowledge of all that surrounds them. In creating their own world they use what is in the environment to build and tear down and then to build all over again. From dealing with their surroundings they learn first-hand to choose and judge—they find out which objects and situations they can control and which they cannot. Aware of their influence, knowledgeable teachers plan and use the facilities of a nursery school to provide a constructive as well as pleasant learning environment.

Effect on the Goals of a Program

The space which children occupy in a school can be thought of in terms of how many square feet per child will most nearly assure meeting the goals of the school. Children need room to run and jump, to wheel buggies and ride trikes, to move about freely without jostling and bumping into one another or the teachers. They need quiet corners and out-of-the-way nooks as "escape hatches," and a chance to be alone. They need areas for eating and cleanup and toileting, for activity and rest.

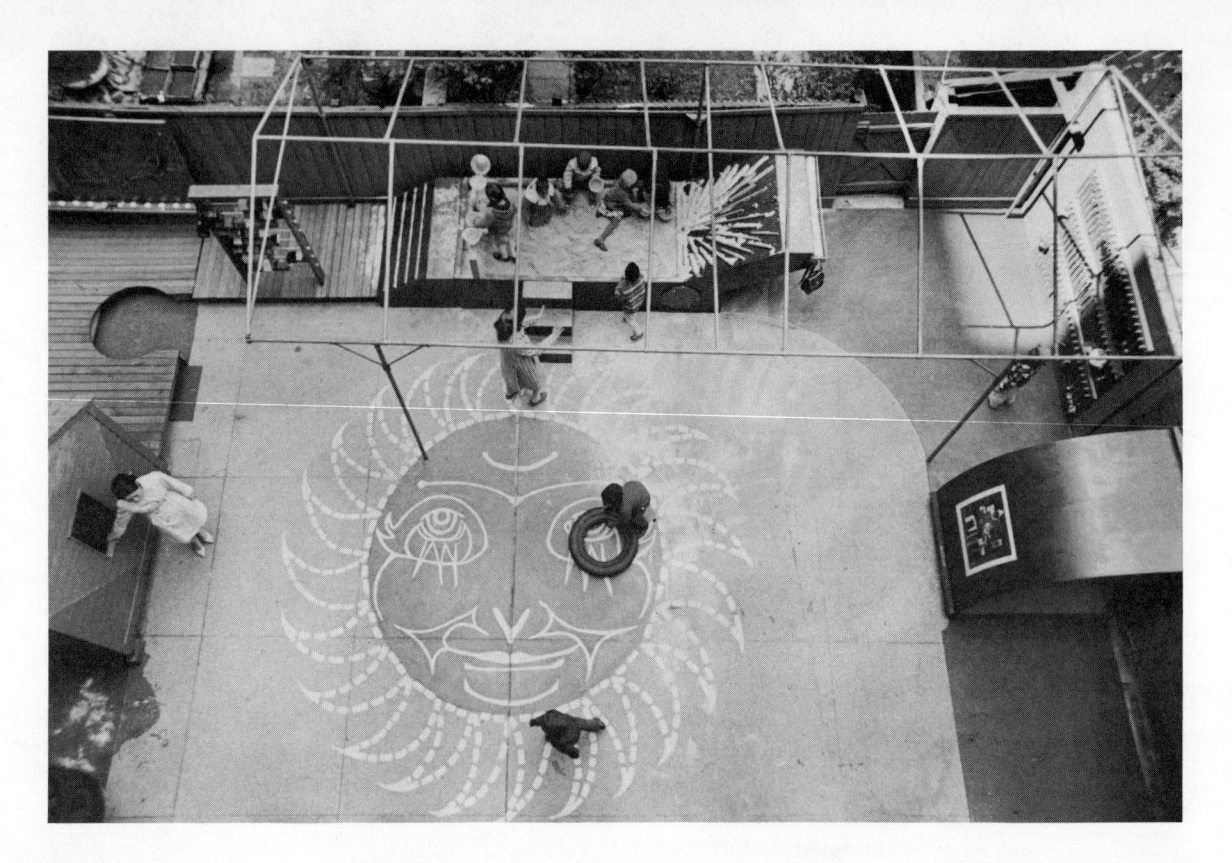

How space is filled has a great deal to do with whether or not a nursery school meets the needs of the children it serves. Well-planned attractive arrangements invite exploration and minimize staff work. When related interest areas are grouped with a thought to traffic patterns and the relationship of noisy and quiet activities, they virtually draw children to them. Arranging and rearranging movable furnishings such as shelves and bins and tables so as to create centers for "house" play, dressups, block building, puzzles, craft projects, science, reading, and art, contribute to a natural flow of activity. Flexible organization of this kind stimulates free choice and varied interests.

Needs differ widely in different kinds of programs—for example, all-day care involves space for meals and naps not needed by half-day session schools. City schools are often more limited in outdoor area than suburban schools. In general, however, desirable ranges are as follows:

    Indoor   50 to 100 sq.ft. per child

    Outdoor   75 to 200 sq.ft. per child

This figure refers to space to be used by the children, not that occupied by storage units, trees, or other relatively permanent items.

Child-height tables and chairs and shelves, together with child-size tools and equipment, invite children to imitate adult activities and to try out ideas of their own. Ample

FIGURE 2-4 SOME PRESCHOOL FACILITIES ARE AN INTEGRAL PLANNED PART OF THE COMMUNITY; OTHERS ARE LOCATED WHEREVER SPACE CAN BE FOUND

bulletin boards and display areas at children's eye level encourage them to mount their own work and to notice what others have made.

The way a room is arranged determines in part the kind and amount of supervision required. If all or most children can be seen from one or two vantage points, less patrolling and check-up is needed. This in turn means that teachers have more time for constructive, individual attention. For planning structured group projects—story hours, films, snacks, music, etc.—space should be provided that requires a minimum of arranging either before or after each activity. Less supervision is needed when toilet areas are located so they can be directly entered from indoor and outdoor play areas. Also when boys and girls share toilet facilities an opportunity is provided for learning about the opposite sex.

School affairs are likely to run more smoothly for everyone concerned if the staff has some space of its own. An adjacent tastefully appointed combination office and teacher room which can also be used for parent conferences, staff training or an isolation room is an asset to a nursery school program.

Well-planned and well-equipped outdoor areas have as great an impact on the goals of a program as their indoor counterparts. Ideally, the one is simply a modified extension of the other. Smooth transition between the two can be achieved by using wide, easily opened doors and windows low enough to extend a child's vision to resources both inside and out. A wide overhang, shaded as well as sunlit spaces, and areas sheltered from the wind, make it more pleasant for children to be outdoors in all but the coldest or most stormy weather.

In such surroundings there is no reason why many activities traditionally thought of as taking place indoors cannot be enjoyed outdoors. Butcher paper tacked along a fence soon becomes a gay mural or garden decoration at the hands of eager artists; juice and crackers under a shade tree turns snack time into a picnic; in mild weather records and musical instruments can be heard as well outdoors as in. Activities in a new setting often tempt children who originally bypassed them.

Traffic patterns are as important in the play yard as they are indoors. Children's tendency to speed on wheel toys, and to run without constraint can be minimized by providing relatively short expanses of unrestricted space. A cement walk that rings a grassy mound allows for distance riding with no sharp corners and therefore fewer spills.

Children develop judgment along with physical skills if the outdoor areas contain a variety of facilities for climbing, crawling, sliding, jumping, balancing and hanging. Low-limbed trees often make better climbing devices than many jungle gyms because they force children into choices not needed when hand-holds all have identical size, and mounting rungs are evenly spaced.

Children should be allowed to discover for themselves the properties and delight of a variety of surfaces and textures. Paper, wood, wire, canvas, cement, grass, sand, tanbark, gravel, hardtop, metal—all have something to impart to the child acquiring knowledge about himself and his relationship to the physical world.

Children are stimulated by their physical surroundings, and nursery school facilities planned with their needs in mind provide a safe environment in which they can explore, create and learn in ways that prepare them for adult life.

Influence on Emotional Climate

Spacious rooms filled with light, color, warmth and order appeal to children as well as adults. They make them feel comfortable and welcome. Play yards enriched by a variety of sturdy, multi-use equipment and different levels and surfaces are not places where children wander aimlessly with nothing to do.

Two factors which influence the emotional climate of a nursery school are light and noise. Natural light coming through doors and windows without glare, yet adequate to brighten the farthest corner of a room, makes for a cheerful atmosphere. When artificial light provides soft, even, overhead illumination, eye strain and fatigue are lessened. The scraping, pounding and clicking, the humming and laughter—all the noises that accompany active children can often be muted to keep from setting nerves on edge or fraying tempers. For example, a nearly square room is a better noise absorber than a long, narrow one, especially when its walls and ceiling are made of sound-absorbing material. Floors should have a surface that can be readily scrubbed yet will not set up reverberations from every running step or pushed-back chair. Occasional rugs and mats help minimize noise. So does a quiet-voiced teacher.

Independence is encouraged when storage areas are within reach of children and they are free to use them. Cubbyholes for boots and hooks for coats and sweaters; individual compartments for personal belongings; special shelves for books and puzzles and paper; food adjacent to animal cages; water easily accessible—all these help cut down work time and encourage freer use of equipment.

Having enough—but not too much—equipment and materials for children to use fosters sharing and taking turns; having too little of popular kinds of equipment may lead to competition, frustration, and feelings of jealousy.

No listing of physical facilities and equipment can be made that insures a "perfect" setting for carrying out a nursery school program that meets individual needs. Not only do choices depend on particular circumstances, but even the most favorable selection and arrangement will only be as effective as the imagination and flexibility of good teaching make them. Keeping the purposes of a program in mind will make choices a great deal easier, however, and more nearly bring about the results you want.

The illustrations that follow represent pictorially many of the specifics that go into planning the environment of a nursery school in order to achieve maximum benefit from the physical facilities.

REFERENCES

Aaron, D. and Winawer, B. P. *Child's play, a creative approach to playspaces for today's children*. New York: Harper & Row, Publishers, 1965.

Bengtsson, A. *Environmental planning for children's play*. New York: Frederick A. Praeger, Inc., 1970.

Bureau of the Census. *Statistical abstract of the United States*, (89th ed.) Washington, D.C.: U. S. Government Printing Office, 1968, 28f.

Croft, D. J. and Hess, R. D. *An activities handbook for teachers of young children*. Boston, Mass.: Houghton Mifflin Company, 1972.

Haberman, M. and Persky, B. (Eds.) *Preliminary report of the ad hoc joint committee on the preparation of nursery and kindergarten teachers.* Washington, D.C.: National Commission on Teacher Education and Professional Standards, National Education Association, Stock No. 521-15720.

Hurtwood, Lady Allen of. *Planning for play*. Cambridge, Mass.: MIT Press, 1968.

Ledermann, A. and Trachsel, A. *Creative playgrounds and recreation centers*. New York: Praeger Publishers, Inc., 1968.

Stone, J. G. and Rudolph, N. *Play and playgrounds*. Washington, D.C.: NAEYC Publications Department, 1970.

U.S. Office of Economic Opportunity, Project Head Start. *Designing the child development center*, by R. W. Haase in consultation with D. Gardner, Washington, D.C.: U.S. Government Printing Office, 1968.

Ideal use of space includes emphasis on separation of active and quiet areas . . . indoors and outdoors as extensions of each other . . . areas of sunlight and areas of shade . . . equipment that is safe and provides a variety of uses.

*The outdoors need not be separate from the indoors but should be an extension of it
... children should be able to move freely from inside to outside.*

Trees and bushes and plenty of grass invite learning about heights, distances, depth perception, and how it feels to be tall.

Equipment should be safe, long-wearing, easily maintained and most importantly, adaptable to a variety of uses . . .

57   SCHOOLS AND SYSTEMS OF EDUCATION

tunnels and complex climbing devices for turning oneself into a pirate, captured princess, sky diver, wild animal, gymnast . . . and in the background a sturdy fence for safety. . .

swings with no boards or handles . . . soft underfooting . . . firm anchorage. . .

equipment that moves or rolls or wriggles and has to be pushed or pulled or thrown or caught or rolled or bounced or chased....

SCHOOLS AND SYSTEMS OF EDUCATION

Children should be able to get at and put away equipment without dependence on teachers . . . equipment should be easy to move from place to place.

Sandboxes help you to be alone together . . . to feel and think . . . to build and destroy . . . to find out how sand feels in hair, eyes, nose, hands.

64 TEACHERS OF YOUNG CHILDREN

Dirt is for discovering that things grow . . . that adding water makes mud pies possible . . . that dirt is more than being dirty.

Even the most experienced and inspired person has limited energy and time. The physical shape of things, carefully selected and arranged, can significantly ease the task. In an environment properly designed for child development, even the doors, walls, floor surfaces, furnishings and fixtures can motivate the child's curiosity, create a potential for learning, and serve as effective assistants to staff. By the imaginative use of the total physical setting, the staff can be freed to concentrate on the activities which are most challenging and beneficial to children.

Ronald Haase, in consultation with Dwayne Gardner, *Designing the Child Development Center,* Project Head Start, OEO, (Washington, D.C.: U.S. Government Printing Office, 1968), p.6.

Materials should encourage imagination . . .

be sturdy, safe, and durable . . .

be easily maintained . . .

have multiple uses . . .

69   SCHOOLS AND SYSTEMS OF EDUCATION

*aid in exploring,
discovering, learning..*

70   TEACHERS OF YOUNG CHILDREN

encourage creativity . . .

and open new worlds.

71   SCHOOLS AND SYSTEMS OF EDUCATION

CHAPTER 3

SCHOOL AND FAMILY: PARTNERS OR COMPETITORS?

THE RATIONALE FOR PARENT INVOLVEMENT

The Separation Between Family and School

In a sense, the child in a program of early education is "on loan" to the teacher, and the school becomes a substitute family. Historically, the family has had the responsibility for socializing and educating the young. Children learned the essential skills, attitudes and information either in the family or under its supervision. A girl learned what to do and what was expected of her by observing and imitating her mother; a boy took on the skills and values of his father in an apprentice-like relationship. This type of family responsibility for rearing young children still exists in many parts of the world, especially where the economy of a country is primarily agricultural. But in highly industrialized societies the pattern of education has changed in fundamental ways.

The kind of education required by a complex social and economic society (reading, mathematics, etc.) is transmitted more efficiently by symbols using verbal instruction than by modeling and demonstration. This type of teaching can be done efficiently in groups and by a person other than the parent. Thus teachers began to substitute or supplement parents in carrying out the educational functions previously performed in the home. The educational process became removed from the family, and control over the curriculum and the decisions about teaching techniques began to shift to the hands of professionals. Instruction began to come from a non-family source and occur away from the home.

More recent educational technology such as instruction by computer or by television —of which Sesame Street is an outstanding example—have separated the source of instruction from both the home and the classroom. In a sense, the distance between the family and the "teacher" and those who control educational input is greater than before, even though the child views the program or console in his own home or school.

This separation between family and school contains an inherent stress that comes from potential disagreement over the way the school carries out its task. If the school or other educational source gets too far removed from the values and needs of the community, there will be some kind of corrective response, protest or objection. Whatever the source or form of schooling, in our society the responsibility for educational decisions ultimately rests with the community.

The case for parental involvement, therefore, is not to be found primarily in the academic benefits for the child or the value it may provide for the teacher. Involvement is not an optional educational luxury; it is an obligation of the adult community.

Community involvement and control is, of course, not a new concept. Schools were traditionally under political and social control in rural areas and small towns in this country. Over the past fifty years, however, the size and complexity of school systems

> *What we're saying is those people who have children in the schools are closest to the situation and ought to have something to say about it. They ought to be able to determine who teaches and what is taught. If they do not have the expertise they need on their lay board to develop the curriculum, for example, they're wise enough and concerned enough to get the people they need.*
>
> Albert Vann, in Poinsett, A., "Battle to Control Black Schools," *Ebony*, 24, No. 7, May 1969, p. 44.

---

increased. A wide tax base was needed to help support schools in low-income areas, and education itself needed to become more professional.

In the growth of professional and specialized training in education, there is occasionally a tendency for teachers and administrators to regard themselves as the educational experts and decision-makers and the parents as clients or customers. This view of education as the business of educators may create a gap of communication between community and school and lead to a school system which is divorced from the needs and values of the community it presumably serves. This happens even more easily in large systems which have centralized administrative functions and control. In recent years such separation has led to demands on the part of parents for community control of the school in which parent groups are asking for much more responsibility for the operation of the school itself. At the preschool level such concern applies especially to publicly-funded programs but may also include private nursery schools.

The school board may be composed of parents from the community who exercise direct control over such matters as the type of program to be adopted and the hiring of teachers. The involvement of parents as advisory groups that participate in decisions made by the school, and in some cases have direct responsibility for such decisions, is a phenomenon that will very likely continue and perhaps increase in the public schools.

Some school professionals have been distressed at this development. They argue that parent groups are difficult to work with and that groups of protesting parents tend to want fundamental changes in the school system itself. It is worth noting, however, that in recent years the most urgent demands for control have come from large cities and minority communities where the schools have separated themselves too much from the community life and the needs of the people which they serve.

This is in effect involvement by neglect. It has led to a kind of revolt in which parents are demanding a voice in the decisions concerning the educating of their children (Hess et al, 1971). This reassertion of parental rights to not only have control of the schools, but to help decide what children should learn, is of great significance to the educational enterprise. The teacher who understands this will be able to engage parents in policy and decision making that will help use the resources of the community effectively and avoid open conflict.

Both the responsibilities and the benefits of parental participation have been recognized by public programs, especially those funded at the federal level. Some schools, such as parent cooperatives and public assistance programs, have guidelines and regulations which specifically stipulate direct involvement in the program on the part of the parents.

For example, a cooperative may specify that each mother assist without remuneration one morning or one afternoon a week for each child enrolled. If unable to work on her regular day, she would be required to furnish a substitute. In addition, each member may be required to serve on the Board or a committee. Often 20 hours of co-op work per family (fathers' skills are often essential for the successful functioning of the school) is a requirement—this may include general maintenance and housekeeping, yard work and repair of equipment.

One of the requirements of a typical funded program is that at least four major kinds of parent participation are necessary for an effective project:

1. Participation in the process of making decisions about the nature and operation of the project through frequent meetings of a Policy Advisory Committee or other parent groups
2. Participation in the classroom and school as paid employees, volunteers, or observers
3. Provision for regular home contact by staff
4. Parent-developed educational and community activities

A number of formal roles and situations in which parents interact with the school were described in Chapter 2, including serving as board and committee members, participating as aides, taking part in a cooperative group and working as volunteers. Parents who assume some of the many responsibilities and chores that go into running a school free the teacher to plan and carry out a broader range of activities than might otherwise be possible.

Stresses in Family-School Interaction

Because the school and family have joint responsibility and both are oriented to the same children in different ways, there are a number of areas of stress which seem to be natural—that is, unavoidable—features of family-school interaction. At the community level, these appear as issues of community control vs. the right of educational experts and professionals to direct the program. There are points of tension, however, in the direct exchange between a specific family and the teacher and other school staff with whom they interact.

One potential source of tension is a subtle competition between mother and teacher for the child. For some mothers, nursery school is the first occasion for separation from their young children, and while the problem of separation is usually seen as a problem for the child, there is a complementary stress for the mother. The child, who as a baby and infant has been almost completely dependent on her, now is dependent upon someone else. Both teacher and mother share responsibility for his care and both expect loyalty and dependence.

In this situation the parent may view the teacher as a competitor for the child's attention. What, for example, will the mother's feelings and attitudes be if the child becomes more attached to the teacher than to her? Or if the school becomes a more pleasant and desirable place than the home in the judgment of the young child? While the question is almost never stated in such bold terms, it appears to be involved in some parent-teacher relationships and can complicate interaction between parent and school.

Parents also occasionally see teachers as potential evaluators and critics. For some mothers, participating in a school program will be their first opportunity to observe their children's behavior in comparison to groups of other children of approximately the same age. ("Behavior" here is used in the full developmental sense, not simply in reference to discipline.) Whether or not they express their doubt, many mothers may fear in the back of their minds that the teacher may find something about their children that indicates parental failure to do an adequate job. No matter how tactful a teacher may be, her expertise carries a potential threat.

Some mothers may worry about how "normal" the developmental skills of their children are compared with those of their peers. The mother's belief about whether her offspring is less bright, as bright as, or brighter than others may have great impact on the future of her child. What she decides from her observation, and through interaction with the teacher, often determines how much she encourages her children to achieve, what she hopes for them and what she will push them to do.

There is also the possibility of difficulty between teacher and mother if the teacher feels that the mother has been neglecting or mistreating the child in some way or is uninterested in his progress. The evaluation may be accurate or it may simply be a reflection of the teacher's tendency to feel possessive about her class. For example, a teacher sees the effort a child puts into creating a picture. Hearing the mother comment that she wishes her child would ". . . paint something I can show his father instead of always making such a mess" can upset a teacher and lead her to feel that the mother is unappreciative. In such circumstances, it is understandable why she might characterize the mother as one who does not give proper support to the child and to the efforts of the teacher.

The question of the extent to which the family and the school share similar goals, expectations, and patterns of achievement is particularly relevant for schools that work with children from low-income families. Because there is often a disparity of cultural background, education, and socioeconomic level between the mother and the teacher, there is potential for problems of communication in their relationship. Some of the elements for misunderstanding and conflict which exist in parent-teacher situations have already been described—i.e., the challenge the teacher represents to the mother's competence, the worry that separation can bring, the competititon for the affection of the child, the feeling that the teacher disapproves. These are heightened when the mother comes from a background which the teacher does not understand or where opportunities were meager in comparison with those of the school staff.

In some instances, teachers have the attitude that mothers from economic and social levels less advantageous than their own lack interest in their children's education. This is a myth (Hess & Shipman, 1968). On the contrary, women with few resources often see the school as the beginning of advantage for their children even when they have little understanding of their own importance as educators, or little time and energy to fulfill this role. If the teacher's attitudes about the parents of her students are stereotyped and biased, they obviously interfere with the communication between school and home.

The Benefits of Parental Participation

Not all relationships between parents and teachers present difficulties for the parent. For some mothers, a warm, understanding teacher may come to be a maternal figure for them as well as for their child. In such a circumstance, the teacher is often the one to whom the mother turns for advice and encouragement with any number of personal problems. Teachers spend many hours in the role of sympathetic friend and counselor. Not only do they want to help, but they may understandably feel flattered to be trusted with confidences of a personal nature.

However, this relationship of confidante presents a number of hazards for both teacher and mother. The teacher's assuming the role of adviser or amateur therapist may change or even destroy the professional teacher-parent relationship. Too often it encourages dependence on the part of the mother, forming an alliance which is essentially outside the function of the school. In addition, the teacher loses the objectivity needed for effective interaction with the total family to the best interest of the child. In being a sympathetic listener to the mother, the teacher typically only hears one side of a situation and thus is not in a position to make valid judgments. Where the confidences are about the husband's behavior as father or mate, the father is often reluctant to come for a conference, not because he lacks concern for the child, but because he may feel the mother-teacher relationship has already excluded him. Perhaps when advice is sought on matters outside the needs of the child, a teacher's most professional and sensible response would be to suggest other resources that are available.

The nursery school gives parents a chance to examine, and in a sense to validate, their own behavior as well as to observe their children. By watching their children in a school environment, they can see whether their own techniques and attitudes are as influential as are those of others. Thus they gain a sense of whether their problems and ways of dealing with them are different or the same as others, and what methods are the most effective. The nursery school affords an important source of information for parents who want to become as adequate and competent as possible in dealing with their young children.

In some instances a mother may need help in handling her preschooler and yet be unaware that she has a problem. She feels, perhaps, that Teddy is going through a "stage" and he will eventually grow out of whatever she finds objectionable. Meanwhile she'll just keep extra close watch on him. Having a chance to compare Teddy's behavior with that of other children his age, and talking over her observations and experiences with the teacher and with other parents, may be all this mother needs to bring about better results with her son. Or a mother may know she has a problem and yet be too proud, or for some other reason unwilling, to ask for help. Close parent-teacher relationships make it possible to share problems of this kind and to work them out together for the benefit of the child.

Where there is effective community participation, schools may also serve as centers where parents can obtain information not only about their children but about themselves and ways to improve their individual lives. This expresses a more general plan to use the schools as educational institutions for communities and families.

Programs have been set up which provide, in effect, training centers for the family as well as nursery school experiences for young children. Such centers make it possible for mothers to watch a skilled staff interact with their children and to work as assistant teachers. This kind of model introduces mothers to alternative ways of dealing with their children and may help them develop more effective techniques of their own. Other specific kinds of information which can be made available to families at these training centers are:

    How to shop
    How to save money
    How to prepare balanced meals
    Birth control advice

Legal advice
Medical advice
How to deal with unscrupulous salesmen and merchants

The benefits which accrue to the family from interaction with the school are part of the rationale for parent involvement. These benefits may come directly through conferences with the teacher, attendance at parents' meetings, and informal discussions with other mothers. Or they may arise indirectly as a mother develops greater understanding of her relationship with her child through classroom observation. Seeing how other children and parents interact gives her a better perspective on her own behavior. In addition, the mutual respect and friendship which grow between women whose children attend the same nursery school program not only help to satisfy women as individuals, but frequently lead to a realization that as a group they can achieve ends not otherwise possible.

Parent involvement often makes possible the expansion and enrichment of a preschool program. Special talents and resources are found among people of all social and economic levels. As mentioned in Chapter 2, the teacher may need to seek out the mother or father who can play a musical instrument, speak a foreign language, take school pictures, or in other ways add to the school program. But the effort is rewarding. Fathers who appear in their roles as firemen, milkmen, auto mechanics, doctors, sports figures, or whatever the composition of the class offers, add interest and substance to any day's schedule. Mothers frequently provide the extra help needed for field trips, library visits, and special projects of all kinds. Parents can also be a valuable resource to teachers in providing and maintaining equipment. Slides, sandboxes, stoves and workbenches are often built by parents; tables, chairs, dolls and swings have been kept usable through parents' skills.

When interaction built on mutual interest and common goals takes place between family and school, the resulting sense of support and harmony can give the child a feeling of security and continuity. His life is less fractionated; he is more free to talk about his experiences at home and at school. There is, in short, less need for him to separate in his mind the things that are separated by distance. On the other hand, home and school may be teaching quite different attitudes and patterns of behavior and this may create problems if the differences are not understood or accepted. But the differences need not always create problems. If close contact is maintained between home and school, teachers are less likely to violate the cultural and personal standards of the family by what they teach children to do and say at school. They can also reduce the

> *At school children sometimes seek to defend their actions by remarks such as, "My mother always lets me," "I don't have to put things away in my house," or "My father says that." A teacher may respond by explaining, "That's probably so, but you're at school now. Some things are different here."*

---

possibility of conflict by helping parents understand the school's goals for the growth and development of the child.

Family Influences on Educability

Perhaps the most important rationale for the involvement of parents lies in the fact that they are critical influences in the early education of the young child even when they themselves are not highly educated. A child's early educational development gains from parental support and participation in the educational process.

As a child begins to walk he explores more of his physical environment. If his natural interest in learning is met, if his mother and members of his family respond by talking with him, by providing him with a rich variety of experiences, and by attempting to satisfy his growing curiosity about the world, he develops an ever-widening scheme for learning.

Families in areas of poverty, however, may not be able to offer the variety of experience the child needs. The mother who is head of a household and who finds it difficult to support the family and who feels frustrated and defeated by the circumstances of her own situation may not have the energy and time to respond to a child's questions and encourage his explorations. If she is part of a migrant farm-labor work force, her work day may begin at five in the morning and after a day of work in the field, she is not likely to want to participate in school activities. Also, her own educational experience has probably not prepared her to do the sort of teaching that will orient the child toward the school and toward academic accomplishment.

The preschool years are normally a time when the child develops *educability, i.e.,* a readiness and capability to learn from a formal institution such as the school. Educability has three basic components:

1. Cognitive skills

Ability to recognize and label objects, to count, to name letters of the alphabet, to pick out colors, to talk and ask questions, to see relationships, to generalize

2. Motivation to succeed in school

Acceptance of school as a reasonable place to commit one's energy and effort—development of a desire to learn and to succeed in the sort of things the school experience represents

3. Acceptance of the role of pupil

Recognition of one's relationship to the school and its rules, to the teacher, and to learning; tendency to adopt an initiating, assertive approach to the world of information, to attend to tasks and persist in them

FIGURE 3-1 COGNITIVE GROWTH AND SCHOOL ACHIEVEMENT ARE INFLUENCED BY MOTHER-CHILD INTERACTION

A child can be taught skills and attitudes which will prepare him to perform more successfully in school. Children tend to develop these in homes where the family has a high regard for education, where parents themselves read and also read to their children; where youngsters have their own books and are encouraged to ask questions; where their questions are respected and answered.

Parents provide children with an orientation toward the school. Those who feel rejected by the school are likely to give their children attitudes that will negatively affect their acceptance of the school and ability to benefit from its teachings. The mother who believes she is respected and wanted by the school and who is made to realize she is assisting in education that will benefit her child is more likely to give the child positive and useful attitudes toward both the school and the teacher, with all that this implies for future success in school (Hess & Shipman, 1968).

GETTING PARENTS INVOLVED

Some Strategies and Techniques

Assuming that a teacher wants parents to be actively involved in the school program, what can she do? How does she let them know that their participation in the life of the school is both desired and expected? It is the responsibility of the teacher to take the initiative, especially in working with families from low-income areas. She should not expect the parent to make the overture but should herself be the one to reach out to let parents know what kind of person she is and what she expects. The program in which she works may have procedures to follow which will help her establish a cooperative, professional relationship with parents, but the responsibility is ultimately hers.

Many opportunities exist for working with parents who expect to be in touch with

Useful Techniques and Strategies for Involving Parents

Greet parents by name and engage in casual, friendly conversation when child is brought to school and picked up

Send notes and samples of child's work home

Make phone calls inviting parents to school programs and suggesting home visits

Provide a place for parents to have coffee

Plan, or have parents plan, more formal meetings

Seek help with special projects

Schedule conferences on a regular basis, not just when child has a "problem."

---

the school and who regularly visit, as well as deliver and pick up their children. Creating an atmosphere that shows that the school is a place where there is someone to talk to and where parents are welcome requires a minimum of effort on the part of the teacher. Any "How To" listing would probably include such familiar techniques and strategies as those shown above. Suggestions such as "Greet parents by name and engage in friendly conversation" may seem obvious and unnecessary. But, not all teachers make it a point to engage in day-to-day contacts of this kind, and some fail to realize that techniques like these build positive learning situations. Simple procedures can go a long way to make parents feel they are welcome and that the teacher is interested in them and in their child. Commenting favorably on the work of the child also tells the mother that she and the child are important in the program.

An occasional spontaneous note pinned to a child's jacket when he's ready to go home encourages interaction between teacher and parent. Criticism of the child, or a report on his lack of achievement should never be handled in this way, however. This kind of discussion, if needed at all, should be reserved for personal conferences.

Parent conferences of a formal nature need to be scheduled with the convenience of the parents in mind. This may require after-school or evening hours, perhaps even a visit to the child's home. Whatever the setting, a formal meeting should be unhurried and directed toward the particular reason for its being held.

Often the most meaningful and helpful conversations will take place informally and spontaneously at the school entrance or over a cup of coffee during a parent's visit. When the teacher or director is available and receptive, parents will often share an immediate concern in an impromptu fashion. Sometimes minor problems which seem too unimportant for a conference, build into crisis proportions if no opportunity exists to air them.

Meetings with groups of parents take many forms. Three of the most common are:

Informational meetings
Open House
Workshop-type meetings

Some parents find it interesting and helpful to see a film or hear what the teacher or outside person has to say about topics such as "When Brothers and Sisters Fight" or "Discipline and Self-Control."

A meeting on "How Children Learn" might present some of Piaget's ideas in an interesting and easily understood format by showing parents some slide pictures and playing a tape recording of some of the children in the school.

Tape Recording	Description of Slide Picture
1. **Child** *I want to play with these buttons.* **Teacher** *Okay. Put them into piles for me.*	1. Teacher and child examining a cigar box filled with buttons
2. **Child** *Can I make any piles I want?* **Teacher** *Yes.* (other chatter and conversation)	2. Child selecting buttons
3. **Teacher** *Good! You sorted these buttons into how many piles?* **Child** *One, two, three.*	3. Child with three piles of buttons
4. **Teacher** *Why did you put these buttons in this pile, Lonnie?* **Child** *'Cause they're red.* **Teacher** *Yes, now why did you sort these buttons into this pile?* **Child** *'Cause they're big.* **Teacher** *And these?* **Child** *Um-m, let's see, I don't know. Oh, wait, I know. Because, see . . . this has two holes and this one has two holes and this, and all of them have two holes.*	4. Teacher and child pointing to a pile of buttons
5. **Teacher** *That's good, Lonnie. You sorted the buttons three different ways. I like what you did.* **Child** *Let's do some more.* **Teacher** *Okay. Let's think of some other ways we might sort them.*	5. Picture of teacher hugging child. Both smiling

After the visual demonstration, a guest speaker tells how children tend to learn and retain more if they are given an opportunity to interact physically with the materials; in other words, "show them and let them do it, rather than lecture to them or tell them."

The parents also heard some theories and ideas about reinforcing the positive things that a child does and rewarding him for behavior that is "right" rather than punishing him for incorrect behavior.

After the speaker's presentation, the teacher leads a discussion with the parents asking how they might have sorted the buttons. She points out the importance of letting the child sort the buttons his own way, rather than suggesting how he should do it. Many of the parents will become intrigued with the different possibilities, remarking that it had never occurred to them that children's minds could be so unique. They are excited about the meeting and eager to try out some of the ideas on their children. They acquire some useful information which they can immediately adapt to their own needs.

If the presentations give parents a better understanding of their child's growth and development, their involvement is more readily achieved.

Open House meetings, especially those that are informal and include the entire family, are an effective means for involving parents. The following description by the director of a cooperative nursery describes an especially successful Open House at her school:

> ...We took examples of the children's art work such as paintings, collages, crayon and felt pen drawings and had each child "dictate a story" about his creation which we then typed out. We mounted these stories and pictures next to a snapshot of each child and displayed them at the children's eye level. Then we invited the entire family to an early potluck supper at school where the proud youngsters were able to show their work to the visitors.

The teachers and children also demonstrated how they used some of the materials and equipment at school, such as listening individually through earphones to a recorded lesson about "right and left hands" while following along with corresponding pictures in a book. One teacher had prepared a tape recording of the children's responses to questions about a story and placed the recording alongside the appropriate books so the children could turn the tape recorder on and play it for their parents.

Some parents welcome an opportunity to attend workshop meetings where they find out what the children are learning and can thus reinforce the same behaviors at home. This might include math concepts such as teaching the child to count, to give someone

Activities in which Parents Can Become Involved Directly or Indirectly

Supervise kitchen activities on "cooking" days

Repair books

Transcribe tape recordings

Supervise pasting of pictures for scrapbooks and displays

Cut out art materials

Help prepare and plant school garden

Address and stuff envelopes for mailings

Print children's names on "book" covers

2 or 4 or whatever number of something he is asked for, to choose the third or fifth (or any other such as the middle, last, or fourth), and to know how many of something he will have if he adds one more.

Some parents comment that their children expect them to know the words to songs and finger plays learned at school. The teachers can demonstrate some popular activities and have the parents participate. Parents often repeat the songs and finger plays with apparent delight, asking for copies of the words to take home.

Many adults have never had experiences with easel or finger paints, mobiles, collages, tie-dyeing or many of the other activities through which nursery schools encourage creative expression. The chance to learn about these often leads to a willingness to be involved in other aspects of the school program.[1]

Not all contacts with parents require their physical presence. Some teachers find that telephone calls keep them in close touch with parents—especially mothers who live some distance from the school or who work during school hours. Rather than waiting for a "problem" to develop before getting in touch with a parent, the teacher phones to introduce herself and subsequently to report progress or seek information. This makes it possible for her to involve the parents in the child's education even though she may or may not meet them during the entire school year.

Another technique for involving parents is one used widely in grade schools through the system of "room mothers." This entails more than asking parents to furnish empty juice cans, old magazines, egg cartons, or supplies needed for various projects; it may involve a request for the parents to come to school and help with activities such as those listed at the top of this page.

With little extra effort teachers find it possible and rewarding to involve most parents both directly and indirectly in the nursery school program.

Involving Low-Income Families

The problems of actively involving parents of middle-class communities and parents of low-income communities are quite different. The differences stem not from lack of

---

[1] See Croft, D. and Hess, R. *An Activities Handbook for Teachers of Young Children* (Houghton Mifflin Co., 1972).

interest in education on the part of either group, but from the different orientations of the two groups about school.

To fathers and mothers from low-income areas the teacher is often a formidable figure. Before her they are uncertain about their language and their dress; they are unsure whether they will be acceptable. In short, these parents tend to be shy in the presence of the teacher and reluctant to participate unless it is clear that they are welcome. They often have had unfortunate experiences in schools. Many of them have limited educational achievement; teachers do not remind them of success or pleasant memories.

Also, the realities of their lives may make participation quite difficult. The mother who travels two hours on public transportation to an eight-hour job and back within a day has little opportunity to drop in on a nursery school or day care center, even if she feels confident of herself. Other opportunities must be provided for contacts with her. Mothers who live under such conditions often want to do what they can, if the teacher makes it possible for them to participate.

This greater difficulty in involving mothers from low-income areas means that the techniques the teacher uses will have to be quite different. Sometimes circumstances at home may make the mothers and fathers sensitive and reluctant to have the teacher visit. Often the best way to get in touch in this case is to make some kind of personal contact with the mother at home, since she is unlikely to be able or willing to attend parents' meetings.

An initial visit may be easier for both the teacher and the parent if the teacher can establish an atmosphere of friendliness and informality. The mother should know that the teacher is coming—a phone call or a note sent home may help. This preliminary step and the dress and manner of the teacher should help make clear that the teacher is not coming on a survey or simply to have the mother fill out school forms. Most low-income mothers have had many contacts with government agencies and these contacts have often been negative and frustrating. Sometimes mothers fear representatives from agencies because they know of instances when an inquiry eventually led to a reduction or cutoff of welfare funds. Low-income mothers know, too, that representatives of the middle-class establishment often come for purposes of policing or of enforcing the rules of bureaucratic organizations. Therefore teachers need to take particular care to see that their interaction with mothers does not in any way create this kind of atmosphere. It is important that the mother understand that the teacher is interested in the child and in working with the family to help the child do well in school. It may take a while to convince the mother of this intention, but teachers who have taken the initiative and planned visits to the homes of low-income families have been gratified by the results.

Showing samples of the child's work to the mother and praising his efforts can help overcome much doubt and suspicion. It is not recommended that the teacher bring gifts or food since this might imply that she felt the family was unable to provide for the child. A student teacher involved in a visit of this kind said:

> *When they offered me coffee and cookies I didn't know whether to accept or not, but I did and then I found it made for good feeling between us and we were able to talk together much more easily. From my visit I began to feel I knew Lou Ellen better because I had met her family and knew what her home was like. At school Lou Ellen had been shy but afterwards she was eager to have me talk to her about my visit. She reminded me on several occasions that she remembered my coming and used this to start a conversation with me.*

Visiting a child's home often helps the teacher understand something of the reasons behind the child's behavior and his patterns of activity in the class. She is likely to understand better the kind of person he is and the problems he and his parents have to face. Because of her increased understanding she can often give more individualized attention to particular children.

This building of rapport between the teacher and individual mothers often makes it possible for the teacher to get a group of mothers to meet with her. One of the least successful strategies in getting parents together from low-income areas, however, is to plan discussions of child development. In their personal lives low-income families tend to deal with fairly specific and concrete things. To move from direct, practical matters to abstract principles of child rearing may make the session seem irrelevant. The kind of "Let's-talk-about-our-program-and-our-problems" approach so common in middle-class communities does not work well in all environments. Parents might be persuaded to talk about the school and its needs, or about community needs, but these subjects should be handled cautiously and with a great deal of care to keep the discussion on the kinds of problems that directly concern the people in the group.

One teacher tells of meeting with a dozen black mothers and using all the techniques she'd been taught during training—chairs in a circle, paper and pencil available for note taking, name cards that all could see and read, formal recognition from the chair for each speaker, and everything kept business-like. She remembers that her subject was "Individual Children and Child Development."

She admits the meeting was anything but a success. Afterward one of the mothers told her if she wanted to have a good meeting, one that would *really* do some good, she ought to bring food and let the children come with their parents, as many as want to, no matter what their age. And she should have soul music. The teacher followed this mother's advice. According to her standards the session was unusual, but the parents came and participated. They talked about what mattered to them even though their concern was not by any means primarily about child development. But they talked and they wanted to meet again.

Another teacher faced the reluctance of a group of Chinese mothers to let their preschoolers go on a field trip to a city park. They worried about the bus being in an accident, about the children going so far from home, and about what the children would eat and wear. The teacher invited them to go along. She also asked that they bring fruit for a salad. At the park, while the children explored nearby under a teacher's supervision, the mothers made a salad and prepared other food which had been provided by the school. With something to do, and their children within sight and hearing, the mothers felt at ease. During lunch they talked freely with one another and with the teacher. In the following weeks the teacher was able to carry out several somewhat more formal meetings at the school based on what she had learned at the park of the ways and concerns of the mothers in regard to their children.

Involving Fathers

There is a good deal of confusion as to how much fathers have participated and should participate in preschool programs. Perhaps some of the reason for the controversy over this issue is that the father's presence or nonpresence at school has often been equated in the teacher's mind with his degree of interest in his child. Obviously, a father is involved with his child in many ways other than putting in an appearance at school and does not necessarily see his physical presence there as a measure of his concern. Discussion about father involvement also tends to pair his role with that of the mother when it might be quite helpful to see their relationships to the school as separate and different.

Fathers may contribute to the education of their young children in many ways. In the home, support of their children's interest in learning, and their reinforcement of school achievement, shows the child that his father cares. By going to school and participating in a program a father would acknowledge his support of the mother's interest and involvement, but this might or might not influence his child's performance. Also, his attendance at various ritualistic events such as Parents' Night and Clean-Up Day would encourage the teacher to feel that he cares about what she is doing in the school program. Yet it is an obvious truth that many fathers do not come to school meetings, do not visit the classroom, and are not especially eager to know what the school is doing. This does not mean that they are not concerned with their children.

Perhaps it is useful for teachers to consider their own motives for wanting fathers involved, and what kinds of activities would meet the interests of the fathers. Before setting up any kind of program, however, it might be well to consider why fathers haven't participated in school affairs more often.

Traditionally the father has been asked to play a role which is often awkward and even embarrassing to him. In his visits to school his abilities or preferences are not really differentiated from those of the mother and the teacher. That is, many fathers walk around the classroom looking at drawings in which they have little interest except to find a name so they can later say to their child, "I saw the picture you drew." While there is some point to be served in their attempt to be cooperative, their effort is frequently motivated by a sense of obligation and they are made to feel guilty if they don't participate. Their expression of interest is often the result of external pressures rather than an indication of their own concern about the school and the child's activities in it.

This is not to suggest that fathers are not interested in schools. They are. But they should be offered appropriate ways in which to express their true interest. Many seem not to be interested because they are asked to do things which from their point of view may be "silly" or "childish."

Of course, many men do not become involved simply because they have no free time that coincides with the hours of a nursery school program. The employed father quite naturally puts the demands of his job ahead of those of a school program. The unemployed father is either too busy looking for work or too involved in dealing with his failure to participate in school affairs.

A factor which keeps many men with limited education away from school (and which in some instances applies to mothers as well) is that they fear the teacher will ask them for information or help they are unable or unwilling to give. Understandably they are reluctant to expose themselves to the sophistication and expertise of a trained teacher or of other parents. But fathers can and should be involved in school affairs in ways that reflect their real interest and abilities.

Perhaps one of the most effective beginning strategies is to call upon them for specific "helping" types of jobs—tasks such as construction, moving of equipment, and main-

FIGURE 3-2 FATHERS CAN MAKE VALUABLE CONTRIBUTIONS OF TIME AND TALENT TO THE PRE-SCHOOL PROGRAM

tenance—tasks commonly considered to be "men's work." However, it must be remembered that not all men are competent in these areas and may be quite unwilling to display their ineptness. Once fathers come to school they often see for themselves what needs to be done to help the children. One teacher recalls such an instance:

> This father was a somewhat older man and you could sense that he didn't particularly feel part of the group of men who had come to help one Saturday morning. But he noticed that the children had no way of hanging up their coats or sweaters, that these garments were folded and placed at the bottom of small lockers. He offered to install hooks and from then on took an active interest in the program of the school.

It sometimes helps to make fathers aware that other men are making a contribution of time and talent to the school. Men who know that others participate in and contribute to a preschool program, especially that of their own child, feel better about making an effort themselves. Seeing clippings and news items concerning the importance of preschool education, and hearing about fathers who have come to school and demonstrated their special skills as hair cutters, fishermen, and kitemakers, or simply served the ice cream cones at an all-school party, helps other men understand how they might be involved in a way they consider "worthwhile."

Initial contacts with fathers can sometimes be made by scheduling a home visit at a time when both parents are likely to be there and by including the father in whatever conversation takes place. A teacher tells of the following experience:

> The father was at home; in fact he was the one who opened the door and invited me in. He did most of the talking because the mother spoke very little English. The visit wasn't going very well until I happened to notice some flowers he had planted. I admired them and with that he went into a long explanation about varieties and told me a great many details about their care. He cut some for me and insisted that I take them back with me. When I finally left we still hadn't talked about his son and the boy never came into the room. But several days later Mr. Y. brought some flowers to school for a holiday celebration. We talked to him and he returned the following week to show the children how to plant a garden. I was able to tell him how much we appreciated what he was doing for the children and he promised he would come again.

As in all human relationships, appreciation goes a long way with fathers, too. Those who are made to feel that their efforts count, that their interests and opinions are important, obviously will tend toward involvement far more than those who feel unwelcome, unwanted, or merely supportive of the mother and teacher. One of the most rewarding aspects of fathers' involvement is the chance it gives children who are without fathers in their homes to identify with a male figure—especially one who is interested in children and wants to help with their education.

Perhaps the most effective way for a teacher to involve fathers is to take time to let them know the educational goals of the program and the role she wants them to play. If she wants them in the role of lending moral support to the school—that is, nodding and smiling as they walk around the classroom—then she invites them to a Parents' Night. If she wants them to help teach their children skills that will prepare the children for formal schooling, then she makes sure they know what the curriculum is and how they can reinforce her teaching and help their children learn.

The problem of getting fathers to participate in school activities is often severe. Their time is limited and their preoccupation is generally with their own work; they feel that the care of the young child is primarily the responsibility of the mother. But these are circumstances that can be overcome. Certainly it is in the interest of the child to do so.

PARENTS AS TEACHERS

The Influence of Parental Behavior upon Academic Achievement

Traditionally, the schools have had responsibility for scholastic and cognitive development of children and the family has had primary responsibility for social-emotional and moral development. In its early stages, however, the nursery school often was organized to deal primarily with social development with little direct attention to cognitive aspects of growth. There were, of course, some notable exceptions, especially the Montessori schools. Educational and social changes in this country, however, have blurred the lines of responsibility and participation, and a great deal of attention has been given to the family's contribution to the child's intellectual development.

This is a question which has been examined in various ways during the past twenty-five years and there are many studies of the relationships between the child's achievements in school and other forms of mental activity and parental behavior and attitudes. In considering how a program of early education can contribute to parent-child interaction in ways that will benefit the child's school achievement, a summary of the findings of these researchers may be useful (Hess, 1969).

The parental behavior examined by these studies falls into three broad categories: 1) behavior that deals with intellectual interaction of some kind; 2) behavior that touches on affective exchange between parents and child; and 3) behavior which is related to patterns of regulation, control and other similar forms of interaction.

Interaction Around Intellectual and Scholastic Activities   One of the most significant areas of parental influence involves the intellectual interaction between parent and child. Studies concerned with the extent to which parents affect the cognitive growth of their child identify five types of parental behavior related to child performance:

1. Parental demands or expectations for high achievement
2. Extent and variety of verbal interaction between parent and child
3. Mother's participation in mental and cognitive activities with the child
4. Mother's strategies as a teacher in the home
5. Amount of diffuse intellectual stimulation provided in the home by parents

Parental demands for high achievement may take the form of interest in grades and test scores, class assignments, essays and other school work, keeping track of how well the child does in relation to his peers, and clearly stating their expectation that the child should do his best to succeed in school. Good performance is praised; poor work is criticized and rejected.

FIGURE 3-3 SCHOOL ACHIEVEMENT CAN BE AFFECTED BY OPPORTUNITIES FOR CONVERSATION WITH ADULTS

Several studies have pointed out that the child who is given opportunities and praise for engaging in conversation with adults, and who participates in experiences that tend to enlarge his vocabulary, is likely to show more advanced achievement in school. Apparently, even for a young child these opportunities can be tied to school performance. They include the mother's correcting the child's use of a word, persuading him to talk in sentences and asking him questions which stimulate verbal response.

Perhaps the most important type of behavior, from the standpoint of future school success, is the mother's tendency to become engaged with the young child's mental and cognitive activity—to mesh with his ideas and responses and to monitor his performance. This kind of behavior is indicated by the mother's knowledge of what he's doing in school, her concern and interest in the child's activities at school and at home and her desire to contribute to his efforts. This kind of behavior is applicable not only to definite tasks at school, but also to the interests and games that small children get involved in at home. The mother's interaction with the child and her sensitivity to him are effective.

The mother's ability to teach her child in ways that help him define and master tasks also influences cognitive growth and achievement in school. This may include giving the child specific instructions and providing him with feedback on how well he has done. It presents another person's point of view and encourages the child to talk and ask questions about the task in which he's engaged. In these activities the mother acts both as model and as a specific source of information.

Children who score well in school and who seem to do academic work most easily tend to come from homes where the parents are involved in a variety of activities which may indirectly stimulate their children intellectually. Books, magazines and other printed materials are available to explore. The parents read a great deal, listen to music and discuss contemporary issues and their intellectual interests with their children and one another. There is a tendency to encourage the child to view educational television programs. Activities are planned to arouse curiosity, and the child is taken on trips often for the express purpose of finding out something about the world.

Affective Relationships A second important group of parental behaviors related to academic achievement derive from the affective relationship between parents and the child. Parental behavior of this type can be divided into two general categories:

1. Establishment of a warm, emotional relationship with the child
2. Expressions of positive self-esteem

There is some evidence that a mother's support and affection for her child as shown in her physical and verbal response to him, and her positive regard for herself and her child, seem to have a good influence on his level of achievement. These supportive attitudes tend to release the child's ability to concentrate on mastery of the task in hand and to increase in a diffuse way his sense of competence and willingness to explore and test his ability. Children who are worried about their relationship to their parents or family may be distracted and fail to complete whatever they are doing. It is not entirely clear just how maternal affection influences school achievement, but it seems likely one of the significant effects is that it may free the child to turn psychic energy to the tasks of the school. It may also give him a sense of a supporting and rewarding audience at home which cares about his school experience.

Patterns of Regulation and Control A third area of parental behavior affecting school achievement includes patterns of interaction between the mother and the child. These fall roughly into three categories:

1. Encouragement of self-reliance and independence
2. Consistency in enforcing discipline
3. Utilization of control strategies

Parents encourage self-reliance by teaching children to dress and feed themselves, by making them responsible for their own belongings, and by seeing that they have a chance to solve many of their own problems. Three-year-old Mark's mother used the latter technique the day he rode his tricycle into a corner and fussed because he

FIGURE 3-4
RESOURCES FOR
INTERACTIONS ARE FOUND
WITHIN THE HOME

couldn't get it out. She made no attempt to come to his aid but suggested that he could work it out himself. When he accepted the fact that he was on his own, he stopped fussing and considered his alternatives. After a moment he climbed down, shoved the trike through a 180° turn, remounted and rode off.

Children who achieve well in school tend to come from homes where discipline is made clear. Parents set specific limits and enforce them consistently. Quite apart from the kind of discipline imposed is the *way* it is presented by the parents. The strategies utilized may be expressed in several ways. In one type, the appeal is to social *imperatives* and *norms of conduct*. For example, the mother may demand compliance by giving some reason in justification, such as "Girls don't behave that way," or by merely stating, "You'll do as I tell you!" In the latter case she is using norms and rules which she expects to be followed without need for explanation. The child is offered no alternatives to consider, to compare, to evaluate, to select.

Another way she might interact with her child would be to use personal-subjective control strategy and call upon the child to understand the feelings of others. Where the imperative-normative system imposes the rules of the group, the personal-subjective attends to the motivations, the intent, the inner states of the individual. Control statements such as "You shouldn't say things like that—they hurt your sister's feelings" or "You know it makes Mommy sad when you cry" are examples. Appeals of this kind require that the child think about his behavior by trying to put himself in another's place.

In still another use of control strategies, the appeal is to the results of a sequence of events or the rationale behind a demand. The child is asked to think about long-term consequences of his action, or at least what might seem to be long-term to him. Typically, he might be denied food in the late afternoon not because it's a rule, but because if he ate then he would not enjoy his supper so much. Or he is made to wear his sweater when he goes out "so you won't catch cold and have to stay in bed."

The use of different types of control has various consequences for the child and his

... AND OUTSIDE THE HOME

relationship to his parents and teacher. All of the techniques can be misused. For example, continually asking a child to think about how unhappy he makes his parents may easily induce a sense of guilt and anxiety, and asking a child always to think about the long-term effects of his behavior may put a constraint on his spontaneity.

Different control techniques may also influence mental growth and activity. Children whose parents use imperative statements almost exclusively tend to think of restrictions on behavior in terms of rules and prohibitions. Children whose parents use personal-subjective techniques may come to be more sensitive to what people think and feel. Strategies which call upon the child to reason and anticipate the consequences of ignoring rules or restraints encourage him to see his behavior in relation to its eventual outcome and effects. Reacting to imperatives requires little thought, but the other strategies elicit more elaborate mental responses on the part of the child.

Other Considerations The circumstances of the home and community, as well as direct interaction with the mother, are related to the child's school achievement. Studies show that the amount of crowding in the home affects performance at school. Where space is scarce and the number of children per adult is high, children are less likely to do well. There is also some reason to think that if the mother is interested and active in community affairs—club work, church circles, civic committees, study groups, and the like—she will have a wider perspective on what it is possible for her to do with and for her child and gain a greater feeling of control over her environment. On p. 96 is a partial listing of the kinds of resources she can call upon both within and outside the home for interaction with her child.

Research shows large differences in the uses mothers make of the resources available to them. These differences occur in middle-class as well as low-income families. The question this kind of evidence raises for the nursery school teacher is the extent to which a preschool staff can help the mother and family become more active and effective in promoting educability in their children.

Resources Available for Mother-Child Interaction

Utensils and furnishings in the home
Play areas afforded by porches and yards
Neighborhood parks and playgrounds
Community Centers and amusement areas
Libraries, museums, children's theatres
Church schools and family programs

Training Programs for Families

The last few years have seen a number of programs developed to convey to low-income families attitudes, strategies, and techniques that will help raise their children's performance in school. Such programs generally concentrate on one or more of three broad areas.

1. Parents' sense of competence
2. Specific teaching strategies in the home
3. Parents' participation in school programs

In low-income areas, parents are often convinced they have little influence over the education of their children. However, their concepts of themselves and their feelings of ineffectiveness seem to have considerable bearing upon how well their children do in school. If they believe that no teacher, principal or official will pay attention to them, even if they have a justifiable complaint or suggestion for improvement, they may come to accept things the way they are. They seem to be saying, "No sense getting put out when you have no choice and know you can't change anything."

Feelings of powerlessness and pessimism about oneself and the future have a way of rubbing off, of spreading to the child. Parents who have few alternatives and low self-esteem are not likely to see the world as a place of opportunity (Hess, 1970). Transmitted to the child, the parents' acceptance of the status quo may come out as a lack of enthusiasm or as an unwillingness to consider as possible the things which teachers and other adults tell him he should be able to do. Self-esteem and feelings of efficacy tend to rise, however, when parents feel competent as parents and have a chance to be effective in school affairs.

Schools and teachers use various means to try to elicit a sense of competence and a willingness to participate on the part of mothers and fathers from low-income areas. To help them develop strategies and techniques that will improve their children's school performance, some programs engage parents as assistants in the teaching process. However, in dealing with mothers who face extreme poverty, other considerations often come first. Until the mother gets assistance and relief in problems of her daily life it is difficult for her to spend much time doing anything about the educational and developmental aspect of her child's life.

Given reasonable circumstances, mothers can learn how to deal with their children in more effective ways by observing and assisting the teacher in the classroom. In a classroom setting, they have an opportunity to see the behavior of other children and compare it with that of their own children. In addition, they can be given information

Some Useful Learnings Preparing the Child for Formal Schooling

Attending to assigned tasks until completed
Following simple directions
Listening to instructions
Verbalizing ideas
Planning ahead
Being able to take turns
Knowing names of letters, colors, numerals

---

about nutrition and child care. In short, they can learn something about early childhood education through observing activities in a nursery school setting.

Mothers involved either as observers or teaching assistants often learn incidentally and indirectly many techniques for educating their children—techniques which can be carried over into their interactions at home. But they can also be given systematic and specific instructions which will help them as teachers in the home. Presenting a mother with a formal program of instruction gives her, in effect, a script to follow. It may not necessarily be any more effective than an informal approach, but it is a useful method for helping parents become involved in the education of their children.

It may very well be that mothers who are not accustomed to teaching in any usual sense can more easily acquire some understanding of what it means to be a teacher if they first participate in a specific curriculum. From this they can develop a way of teaching concepts, colors, directions, numbers, relationships and other cognitive skills as a matter of course, rather than just at specified times. In this perspective, the formal program becomes a learning experience for the mother who may then generalize and transfer what she knows to more informal types of interaction with her child.

Perhaps a useful background for any program that helps mothers teach their children is some notion of what the child should know as he enters the first years of formal schooling. A teacher needs to work out for herself (or in cooperation with her director and other members of the staff) detailed goals of the preschool program in which she is involved and should also let the parents know what she is attempting to teach. At the top of this page there is a list of some learnings that would be useful preparation for the child entering the primary years.

Equally important, perhaps, are several less tangible types of learning. By the end of a preschool experience, a child should be aware that there are many things he can learn. Hopefully he will know there are things he can learn on his own. In addition, a child should have developed confidence in his ability to master the tasks that are set for him by the teacher. This may be more important than the actual number of tasks he has mastered. Confidence in his ability to learn may be one of the most important components of self-concept for the child who moves into a formal educational situation such as first grade.

Before entering school, it is helpful if a child has developed some ability to orient himself toward a future goal, to control his impulses and to engage with others in tasks set by the teacher. Ideally, he will also have developed some sense of assertiveness and initiative in dealing with the teacher and with the tasks that he has been assigned. The child who is able to use his energy to find ways of doing what he is asked to do is better prepared for formal schooling than the child who waits passively to be told how.

Teaching Parents to Teach Although methods may vary greatly between families, many parents are able teachers of young children whether specially trained in teaching techniques or not. Through interest, observation, and experience they develop effectiveness. Yet numerous parents who want to help really don't know what to do, and many others are virtually unaware of how significant a part they can play in the education of their children.

Home and school are probably the two most important influences on young children's learning, although television is increasingly becoming a factor. In the United States the school has become large and powerful, and as it has grown has tended to become more and more separate from the family. This is especially true in low income areas of cities. However, the development of programs to raise the educational attainment of children from these areas has made it clear that the home and school must work together if children are to experience success in school. Therefore, many students trained to teach in programs of early education will increasingly be involved in teaching parents how to help their young children. They will more and more often be called upon to work with parents who themselves may have had poor school experiences. Such parents are frequently suspicious of the system in general and mistrustful of teachers in particular. More than likely they themselves or their older children experienced disciplinary or academic problems. Such a background does not often lead them to feel capable of helping with a child's education.

Contacting Parents General methods of contacting parents were discussed in the section on strategies and techniques for parent involvement. Because involving mothers from low-income families so often requires special effort on the part of teachers, some details which may prove helpful in making initial contacts when you expect to set up a home-teaching program are offered here.

Mothers from low socio-economic minority backgrounds are not likely to respond to invitations (especially dittoed ones) to come to parent meetings. The first task of the teacher, therefore, is to establish contact and rapport with the mother. In any note, or phone call, or personal conversation, the teacher needs to explain why she wants to see the mother and help her understand how she herself can assist in the child's work at school.

To some extent, the individual style and preference of a teacher must be taken into account as far as the initial contact with the family is concerned. If at all possible the father should know that he also is welcome to come to school or to be present during any home visit. Following are some of the means teachers may use to make the first contact:

    Handwritten, personal note sent home with the child
    Telephone call
    Class announcement asking children to talk at home about teacher coming to visit

It would appear that the genuineness of the teacher's expression of interest and of her desire to talk with the parents, rather than the way she goes about it, may be the most decisive factor. But whatever approach is used, the teacher should confine her first visit simply to getting acquainted with the child's mother and other family members. The visit may last an hour or only a few minutes. In any event, its length need not be taken as an indication of success or failure. As one participating teacher explained:

> More than anything else, on a first visit I try to make sure the mother understands I haven't come to complain or because of any difficulty her child has been having at school. I let her know that I feel I can do a better job if I'm acquainted with the family. Naturally I wear informal clothes, I don't carry a notebook or any papers with me (except perhaps something the child has made), and we talk about ourselves and TV and the weather as much as we do about school.

Teaching by Modeling   Once in touch with the parents, the techniques used to engage them in teaching their children are perhaps the most critical aspect in the success of the school program. The teacher needs to keep in mind that she will be dealing occasionally with mothers who do not easily learn from verbal instructions.

How then will the teacher go about getting the mother to understand what she wants her to teach and showing the mother how to teach?

Many experimental parent-involvement programs include the four strategies summarized on p. 100. Even where relationships with the mothers were already friendly and cooperative, when teachers came to the home to work with a mother on a teaching task they took time to re-establish these feelings at the beginning of each visit. Some general principles of working with the mothers were:

1. Take enough time so that you do not appear rushed.

Ways to Help Mothers Teach Their Children

Establish rapport

Be honest and explicit

Demonstrate with the child in the mother's presence

Teach only a few simple techniques

---

2. Show the mother your own enthusiasm in what you and she are doing together.

3. Engage in person-to-person conversation (not teacher to parent) about cooking, gardening, housekeeping, etc. It should be spontaneous, not contrived. One father just wanted to reminisce about the wonderful first-grade teacher who had befriended him.

4. Be certain that the mother knows what you are going to do—that you will teach the child.

5. Sometimes mothers will want to talk about other things—let them. They may hesitate to introduce a topic that may be bothering them if the atmosphere isn't leisurely or friendly. These tangent subjects often turn out to be more constructive than the subject you came to discuss (because they reflect a mother's concern for her child and are more meaningful to her).

It is important for the teacher to make statements that are clear to the mother who probably does not understand jargon or educationese. At the same time, the parent needs to be told about the child's progress. The teacher should be honest in such matters. For example, some mothers believe their children "know the numbers from one to ten" when they can count by rote. When some of these children could not give the visiting teacher six crayons, the mothers understood that the job was only begun and eagerly went on to teach object counting (and eventually numeral recognition and making numerals).

When the teacher is going to teach a new technique she should be certain that the child will be present when she visits the home. In modeling with the child, the following procedures are effective:

1. Have specific things prepared for the mother to do.

2. Be prepared to show the mother how you work with her child on the task you have selected.

3. Do not begin until you feel that the mother is sufficiently at ease to understand and remember what you are doing.

4. In the teaching demonstration, use all the techniques you want the mother to imitate—praise, reinforcement, attention, small steps, moving to easier task if child can't do what you ask, etc.

5. When you teach the child in the mother's presence, talk only to the child; give him your full attention.

6. Talk with the mother later. Allow her to raise questions or bring up concerns of her own.

7. On subsequent visits, the mother may volunteer to show things the child has done—lessons he has completed. Encourage this; show interest and praise, not criticism.

FIGURE 3–5 PARENTS OFTEN WELCOME DIRECT INVOLVEMENT WITH THE PRESCHOOL PROGRAM

You may make suggestions about how the mother may go on to a more difficult stage or go back and review a lesson.

One teacher summarized her experience in modeling by commenting:

> I find modeling more successful than explanations and samples. I sit down with the child and run through the whole activity while the parent watches. On subsequent visits I try to watch the mother run through the activity with the child. "Andy, will you and your mom please show me how you play your color game?" Some of the mothers have altered and improved a game. A few moved on to a more advanced stage but seem to accept my suggestion that the child work on the first stage until he can perform the task with ease.

Teaching is a very complex and subtle form of behavior. The style of the teacher, her tone of voice, her manner, the pace of her instruction are difficult to explain. Therefore, perhaps the best technique is to demonstrate to the mother or to model for her the way to get across to the child the ideas you want taught. In this way the teacher can provide an example in the most unobtrusive way possible. That is, rather than saying, "Now watch me; I'm going to show you how to do it," her interaction with the child in the home provides an opportunity for the mother to observe and imitate.

Whatever method the teacher uses to communicate to the mother what she wants her to do, there are a number of teaching principles the mother should be encouraged to follow in some way. The experiences of the teacher can often suggest sources and strategies that mothers might try for themselves:

1. Teach the child even when he doesn't realize he is being taught; use the many opportunities that come up in talking with him. There are things you can do when you are talking with him during the day:

> Get me your *red* shirt.
> Put the fork on the *left* side of the *round* plate.
> Bring me *two* spoons.

2. Do not be surprised if the child forgets; review the things he has already learned.
3. Teach only one color or idea at a time, use small steps in teaching.
4. Do not start on a new task until he has learned the first one well.
5. Work regularly, some each day, for short periods of time—perhaps ten or fifteen minutes.
6. When working with the child, pay attention only to him if you can. Make him feel important.
7. Work when you and the child feel like it. If you are cross or angry with him, do not try to teach him; wait until you both feel better.
8. Work at a time when the house is quiet and stop when the child loses interest. Do not make him work if he doesn't want to.
9. Work when you can get his interest—not in the middle of his favorite television program.

Teachers may stress the importance of teaching the mother to show her interest in the child and to encourage him for his efforts. The mother should be taught to reward or reinforce the success of the child and come to realize that praise is much more important than blame in shaping behavior. The following are suggestions in regard to this aspect of helping mothers know how to teach their children:

1. Praise the child often. Praise him and talk about his work in front of others.
2. Praise him just as soon as he gets the task right.
3. Encourage the child but do not force him to work when he has lost interest or is worried about something.

4. Do not criticize or scold him when he is wrong; say nothing about it if he makes a mistake but go back to a task you know he knows so he can feel success, then go on to a task a little more difficult.

5. Start each lesson with something he has already had and knows; have him do something he knows before starting a new color, numeral or other task.

6. End each lesson with a success—with something he knows.

Of the various techniques and practices suggested for teaching mothers, these four may be the most important of all:

1. Concentrate on the successes of the child.
2. Proceed slowly and be certain the child understands what he is to do.
3. Present material in small units.
4. Provide an example for the child to show him what you expect him to do.

Helping parents teach their children can be of great benefit to both the child and to his family. It can also be the beginning of a long-term, effective and close relationship between family and school.

REFERENCES

Badger, E. *Mothers' training program: the group process,* Urbana, Ill.: ERIC Clearinghouse, 1970.

Croft, D. J. and Hess, R. D., *An activities handbook for teachers of young children.* Boston, Mass.: Houghton Mifflin Company, 1972.

Gordon, I. J. *Early child stimulation through parent education.* A progress report to the Children's Bureau, Department of Health, Education, and Welfare, Grant No. PHS-R-306, Gainesville, Florida, 1968.

Hess, R. D. and Shipman, V. C. Maternal attitudes toward the school and the role of pupil: some social class comparisons. In A. H. Passow (Ed.), *Developing programs for the educationally disadvantaged,* New York: Teachers College Press, 1968, pp. 109–129.

Hess, R. D. Intervention in family life. Seminar No. 5 in E. H. Grotberg (Ed.), *Critical issues in research related to disadvantaged children,* Princeton, N.J.: Educational Testing Service, 1969.

Hess, R. D. Social class and ethnic influences upon socialization. In P. H. Mussen (Ed.), *Carmichael's manual of child psychology,* (3rd ed.), New York: John Wiley and Sons Inc., 1970, Volume 2, pp. 457–557.

Hess, R. D. et al. Parent involvement in early education. In E. H. Grotberg (Ed.), *Day care: resources for decision.* Office of Economic Opportunity, Washington, D.C.: U.S. Government Printing Office, 1971, Chapter 9.

Hess, R. D. et al. Parent training programs and community involvement in day care. In E. H. Grotberg (Ed.), *Day care: resources for decision.* Office of Economic Opportunity, Washington, D.C.: U.S. Government Printing Office, 1971, Chapter 10.

Poinsett, A. Battle to control black schools. *Ebony,* May 1969, *24,* No. 7.

CHAPTER 4

SOCIAL OPPORTUNITY AND EDUCATIONAL ACHIEVEMENT

THE NATURE OF THE PROBLEM

Influence of Socio-Cultural Factors on Behavior

In any group, children differ from one another because of individual circumstances such as genetic endowment, age, sex, and the unique aspects of their personal experiences. There are other influences upon individual behavior, however, which operate in less apparent, though equally powerful, ways. These affect the child through the social, cultural and racial backgrounds from which he comes.

These are influences which create differences not only between individual children but between *groups* of children. In great part they arise as a consequence of the way our society treats individuals from cultural, social and racial backgrounds which differ from those of the majority. Because they often come from outside the child and his family group, they may be beyond his power to change. For children from such backgrounds, educational experience has a particular significance because of its potential for helping the individual deal with his own circumstances and for helping change the attitudes and opportunity structure of society.

The problems of children from low-income and "minority" groups are obviously important to the teacher of young children. She needs to know how they follow from the child's social and cultural experiences so she may better understand the individual child and his behavior and help him get as much from school as possible. She also needs an understanding of these social processes in order to evaluate the usefulness of programs of intervention that may be urged upon her from various sources.

In working with a child whose socio-cultural background has placed him at a disadvantage, the teacher has a major problem. She must deal with the question of how to support him as an individual, respecting his background and social heritage, and at the same time give him skills that will make him more likely to succeed in the larger society. To help make the decisions involved in offering an educational experience she needs to understand how the social system works and the ways it has affected the child and his family. This chapter deals with the social structure of society and its consequences for the child in an educational setting. To describe how group differences arise and how they are perpetuated by the social structure is not to suggest that they are desirable or inevitable. Rather it is to provide information that will permit a teacher to take effective action.

Poverty in the United States

For all its wealth, the United States has thirty million people who are living in poverty, a population of poor that equals or exceeds the total population of 85 percent of the countries in the world. Within the United States a household is officially labelled "poor" by the Social Security Administration if it meets the definition shown in Table

Poverty in the United States is officially measured by a fixed standard of real income based upon the cost of a minimal human diet. Any household is officially defined as "poor" by the Social Security Administration if its annual money income is less than three times the cost (in current prices) of a minimal diet for the persons in that household.

Poverty-level income for a four-person household in 1968	$3,553
Total population designated as "poor" in 1968	25,400,000
Racial breakdown: White—approximately 66%	
Nonwhite—approximately 33%	
(From 1959 to 1968 the total number of poor persons *dropped* by 14.1 million, or 36%.)	
Percentage of all U.S. citizens in poverty in 1968	12.8
Number of those designated "poor" and living in urban areas in 1968	12,900,000
Percentage of metropolitan area population in poverty 1968	10.0
Percentage of metropolitan whites who were "poor" in 1968	7.6
Percentage of metropolitan nonwhites who were "poor" in 1968	25.7

TABLE 4-1 THE OFFICIAL VIEW OF POVERTY
figures from Anthony Downs, *Who Are the Urban Poor?* Supplementary Paper No. 26, Revised Edition. Committee for Economic Development, September, 1970, pp. 7-15.

4-1. Figures change somewhat from survey to survey but the relationships and magnitudes represented by this example have remained relatively constant over the last two decades. When the official definition of poverty is based on an absolutely fixed level of income, continued national prosperity that raises all incomes in society causes the number of poor to decline steadily. But if poverty is considered a relative matter, it is clear that its disadvantages will continue to affect all people in the lowest income groups until there is a significant change in the distribution of income.

A Bureau of Labor Statistics study in 1967 estimates that an income of approximately $9,300 would be needed for a family of four to achieve a moderate standard of living . . . or almost three times as much as the poverty income threshold at that time. Using this standard would greatly increase the official number of "poor" people in the United States.

In a broader sense, poverty is not only having too little money; it is a matter of how much opportunity one has to get more. Many institutional arrangements in our society, presumably designed to furnish assistance, in actuality may reinforce dependency and a sense of failure and defeat. Welfare regulations may penalize initiative (such as part-time jobs). Our economic institutions exploit the ignorance of the poor by charging higher prices for housing, food, goods and services than in middle-income areas; and perpetuate poverty by omitting low income people from social insurance plans, measuring welfare services in quantity rather than quality, by providing poor quality schools and often the least qualified teachers.

The pictures and descriptions on the following pages show some of the conditions of poverty under which millions of young children live in the United States.

Speaking at the First Texas Conference for Mexican-Americans, Congressman Henry B. Gonzales (1967, pp. 112, 113) expressed the meaning of poverty in these words:

> If one is hungry, hope itself is a distant thing, if one is defeated, promises of things to come ring empty. If one's world is limited by dirt floors and tin roofs, tomorrow holds no promises, as the greatest ambition is to live through today.
>
> Society as a whole has never cared much about the poor because they have always been there, and because there has never been much reason to believe that poverty would, or even should, be eradicated. We decided somehow that

TABLE 4-2 FAMILY SIZE AND POVERTY
from Mollie Orshansky, "Counting the Poor: Another Look at the Poverty Profile," *Social Security Bulletin,* Vol. 28, No. 1, Jan. 1965, p. 9.

NUMBER OF CHILDREN IN FAMILY 18 YEARS AND UNDER	PERCENT OF FAMILIES WHO WERE POOR
2 or less	12
3	17
4	23
5	36
6 or more	49

a poor man is poor only because of his own failure, and we have too often said that a poor man deserves to be poor and should get no help. In recent years, however, there has been a change in attitude among us. We have realized that the great American dream is not open to everyone; and we are now able to understand that poverty is a symbol of waste and that it can be ended. We have come to understand that some men are poor because society has denied them a chance to be anything else; and the poor should not and need not be despised or forgotten. . . . One thing we have been doing is to make an effort, for the first time, to understand why people are poor and what can be done about it.

Traditionally one of the principal routes out of poverty and discrimination in the United States has been through education. Oscar Ornati (1966, p. 67), in a report to the directors of the Twentieth Century Fund, summarizes the importance of this avenue for upward mobility.

There was a time when it could generally be assumed that individual effort matters, that human beings could control their future. It is no longer clear that this can happen if individual efforts are not crowned by a diploma. It is also clear that many of the poor, possibly believing that this means growing up absurd, are not getting and will not get their diplomas. That if they do not get their diplomas they will stay poor is certain.

Many young people who do not finish high school still maintain faith in education as a means of equalizing opportunity. They assume that education prepares the young for higher paying, more prestigious jobs in the economy. National and local government planning reflects this assumption; the introduction of multicultural programs in public schools and colleges illustrates one effort to offer more effective education. The society is also turning to programs of early education as a way to give children from all socio-economic and cultural backgrounds a more nearly equal opportunity to receive quality education. However, intervening through education in the problem of socio-economic and cultural disadvantages is a complex and difficult task and consequences are not always predictable.

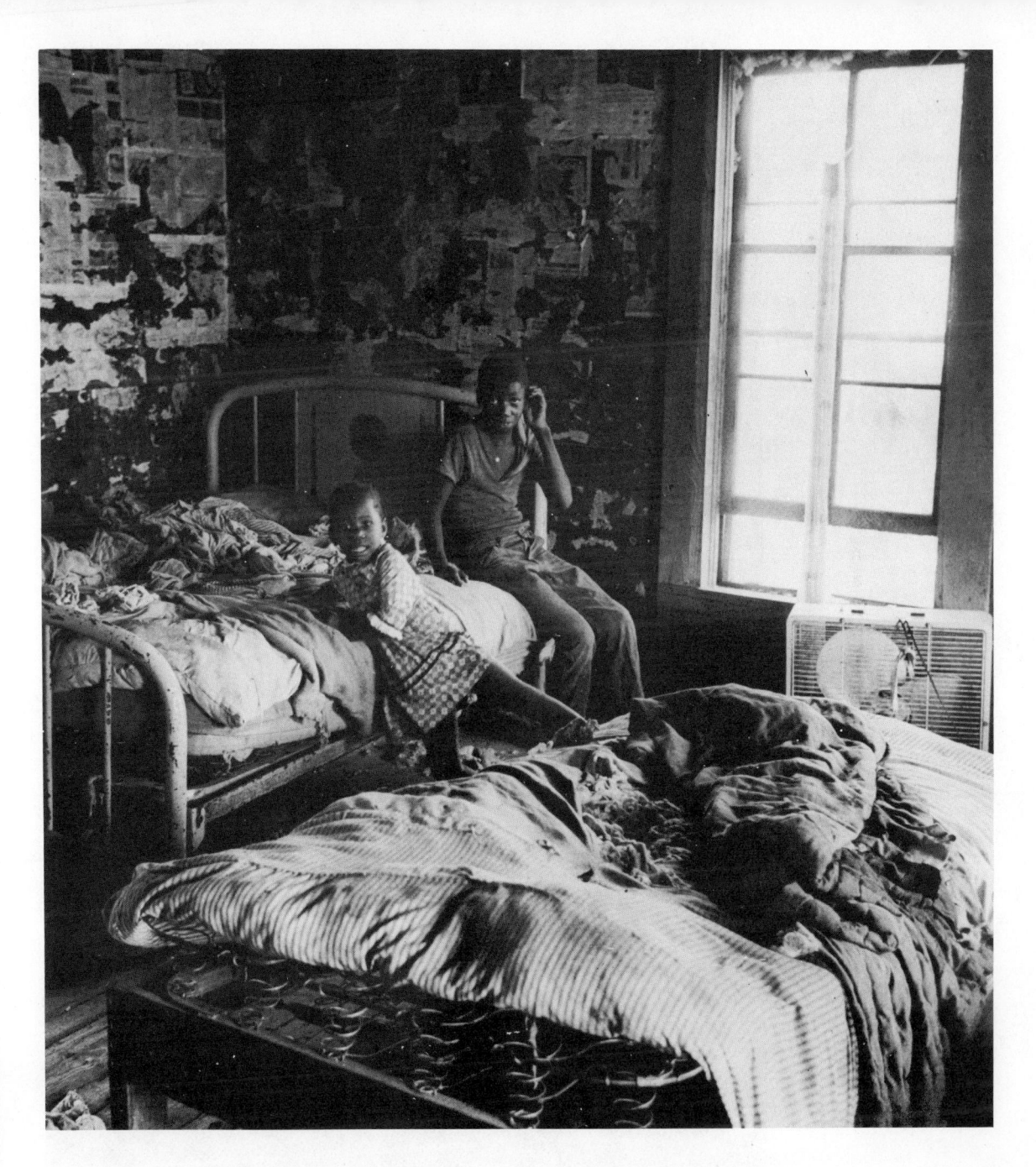

Poor children are inadequately housed . . .

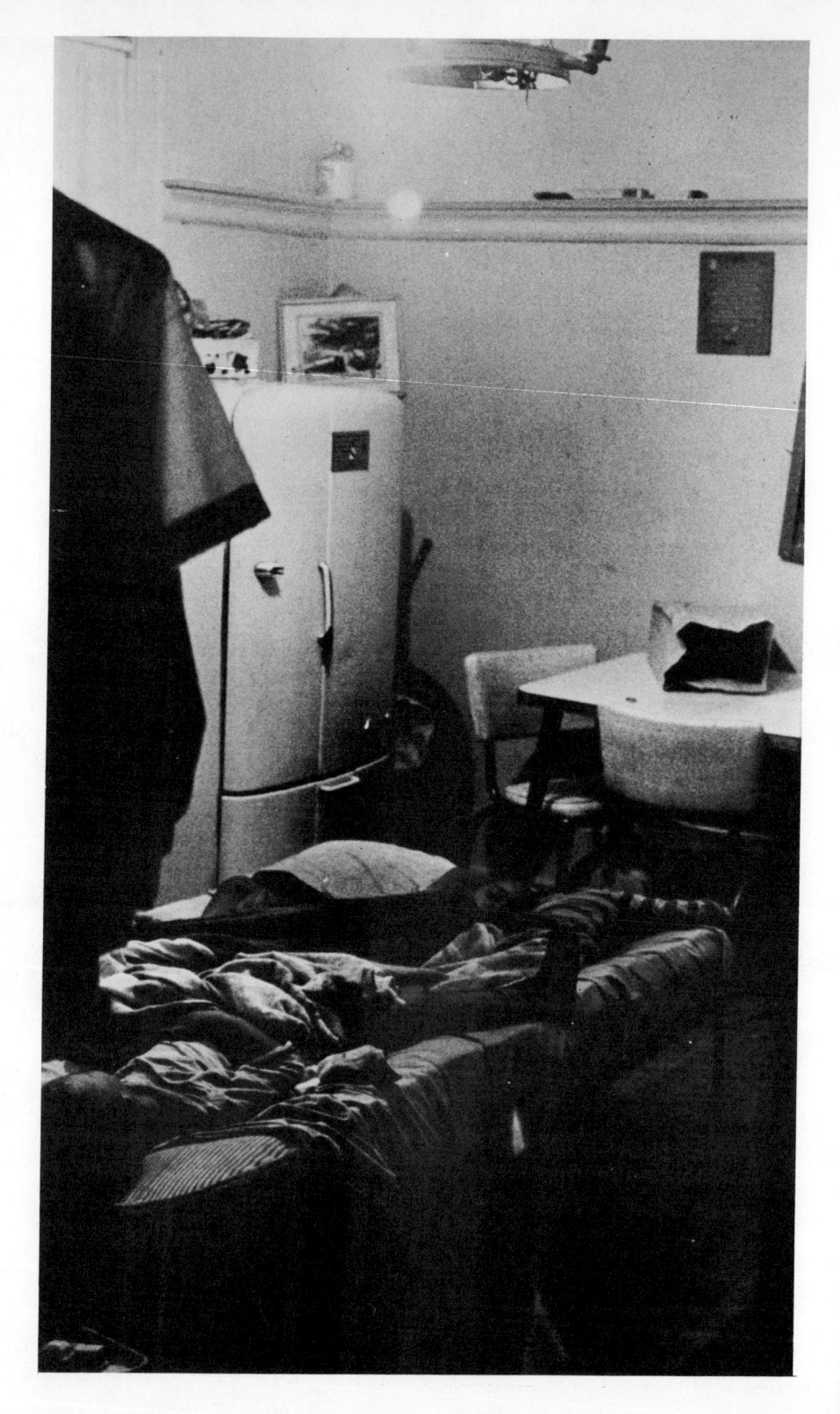

they are crowded...

they are often hungry . . .

109 SOCIAL OPPORTUNITY AND EDUCATIONAL ACHIEVEMENT

and often ill.

110 TEACHERS OF YOUNG CHILDREN

Their clothing is inadequate....

They have few suitable places to play . . .

and not much to play with.

113 SOCIAL OPPORTUNITY AND EDUCATIONAL ACHIEVEMENT

They are often lonely.

THE SOURCES OF INEQUALITY

Poverty is one extreme indication of inequalities in a social and economic system. In this country, it is often the consequence of two conditions: first, *socio-economic inequalities* related to industrialization and competition, and second, *discrimination* against groups on the basis of racial or cultural characteristics. Poverty and other social disadvantages are rooted to a great degree in these sources. Both socio-economic influences and racial-cultural prejudice limit opportunity and resources for large numbers of people, creating conditions which affect the educational and occupational achievement of both young and adult.

Socio-economic and ethnic discrimination creates inequalities in the availability and kind of education, housing, job opportunities, income, political power, tax assessment, economic resources, and civil rights within the system. These inequalities in turn often determine how children are treated and how well they are respected as people—factors which in turn greatly influence behavior.

Evidence of differences based on socio-economic factors and ethnic discrimination appears in many forms. That there is inequality implies, of course, that someone has more of something than someone else. If the differences are great, some members of a society will be quite rich, others very poor. Affluence and poverty are not absolute, of course, only relative, and a man's subjective sense of poverty depends somewhat on his frame of reference and on his own particular biases. Conditions which seem inadequate in one society may be considered quite satisfactory in another.

The people in a society who occupy a socio-economically dependent or a culturally subordinate status, and who do not share opportunities to obtain the rewards of that society, are disadvantaged. Poverty and lack of opportunity separate them from the mainstream.

Socio-Economic Basis of Inequality

Societies, especially modern, complex, industrialized societies (of which the United States is but a single example), are highly stratified. They have an hierarchy along which privileges, wealth, and power are distributed. In some societies, even today, these different strata take the form of castes—that is, hereditary social categories sanctioned and rigidly enforced by custom, law or religion. In a caste system, members find it virtually impossible to escape the social position they enter at birth.

Distinctions of this kind are not so rigid in the United States. We speak of "lower class" and "middle class," but our use of such terms is diffuse and vague. In the face of social and economic hierarchies we cling to an ideology of equality; we claim that anyone has a chance to be President if he meets the basic qualifications specified by the

> *No person except a natural born citizen or a citizen of the United States at the time of the adoption of this Constitution, shall be eligible to the office of president; neither shall any person be eligible to that office who shall not have attained to the age of thirty-five years and been fourteen years a resident within the United States.*
>
> from the Constitution of the United States. Article II, Section I, Clause 4,

Constitution. The Horatio Alger myth that a youngster starting at the bottom and working hard can rise to financial success and all attendant rewards has not disappeared from our national values or social reality—approximately one-fifth of our population still tends to rise substantially along the socio-economic scale.

The unequal distribution of privileges and resources in the United States today results in part from the differentiation of roles, functions and tasks upon which an industrial complex depends. Within a factory, for example, or in a school or a business corporation, there are different types of tasks to be done. Such specialization means that some people will be policy makers and some will be delegated to carry out policies. Except in very small companies or organizations, the people who work with ideas are not usually those who deal with personnel, and the personnel staff isn't likely to be involved in procurement or manufacture, record keeping or maintenance.

Different parts of the system create different demands. The skills needed to assemble a watch are not at all the same as those needed to sell the finished product. A TV repairman would scarcely be trained to tune pianos; waitresses are not expected to prepare the food they serve.

Because all but the least skilled jobs in a socio-economic hierarchy require some degree of training, the rewards and privileges accruing to the job are generally related to how long the needed training takes, how specialized it is, and how many people are qualified to perform the same task. Most work requires cooperation among persons who perform a wide variety of tasks. Each role has rewards in terms of prestige, income, security, working conditions, or personal satisfaction. Those who fill roles at the top levels—roles requiring the most skill and training and involving the greatest responsibility—expect and usually receive the highest return for their efforts. People at each level compete for prestige, power, and opportunity for themselves and their children to acquire material wealth, education and a high standard of living.

Although it appears to be inevitable that complex organizations require specialization of tasks and thus create differentiation and a hierarchy, this does not indicate the extent to which these differences will result in unqual rewards, such as salary, privileges and prestige. These are distributed in part on the basis of the values of the group and the power which sub-groups can exert to improve their share of the benefits. The change in prestige and income of workers in certain industries in this country over the past 30 years is an example of how the relative advantage of levels within the system can be altered.

Racial and Ethnic Discrimination

A second major source of poverty and disadvantage in the United States is racial and ethnic prejudice. It is ironic that this should be so, since the history of this country is the

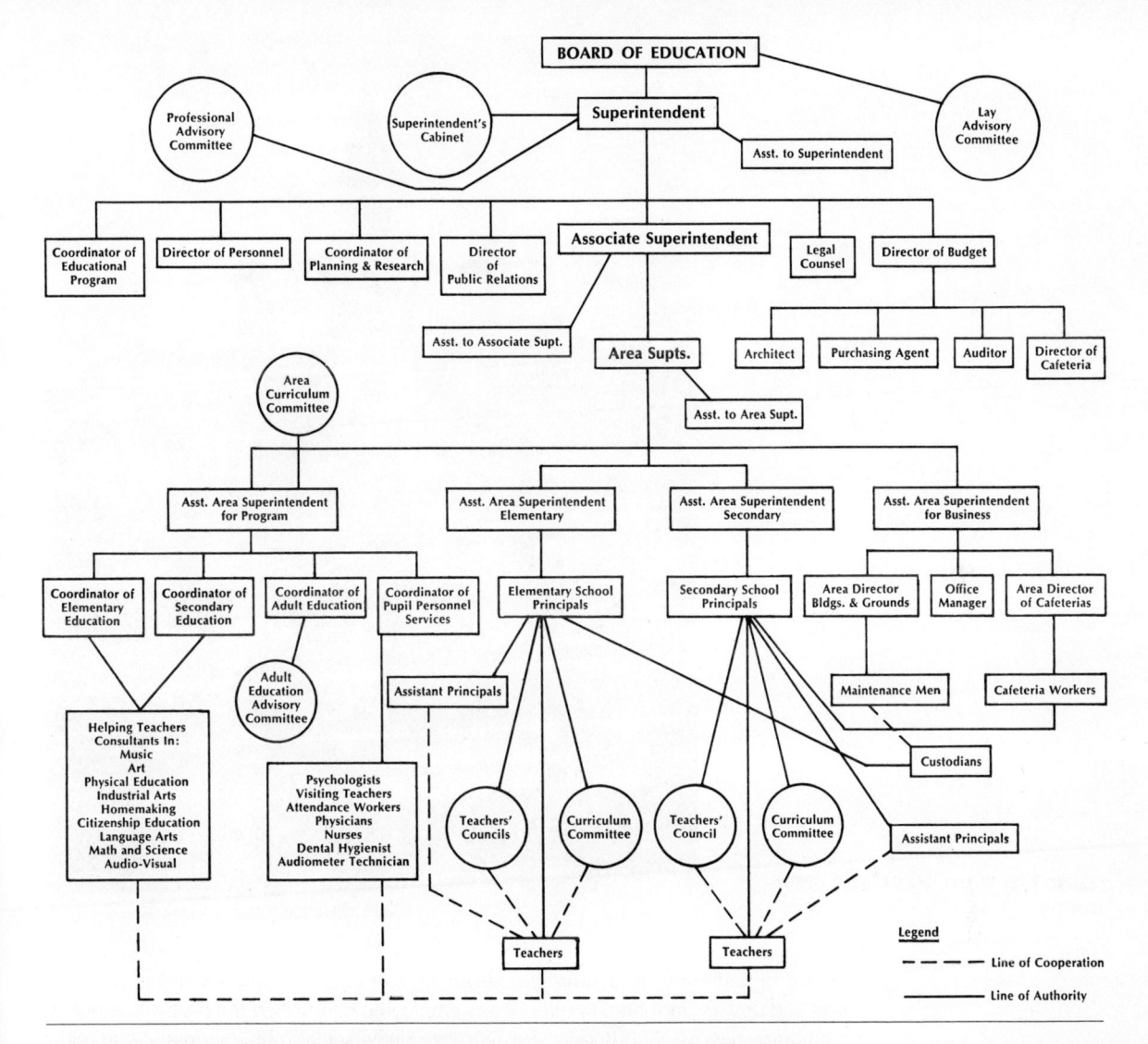

FIGURE 4-1 TYPICAL ADMINISTRATIVE ORGANIZATION OF A LARGE CITY SCHOOL SYSTEM
from Griffiths, Clark, and Wynn, *Organizing Schools for Effective Education,* Danville, Illinois: Interstate Printers and Publishers, 1962, p. 14.

history of various ethnic groups that despite their differences eventually achieved a national identity. The need to establish a sense of national belonging and loyalty and to minimize ethnic distinctions gave rise to the insistence that new arrivals learn to speak the same language and to identify with traditions and heroes of this country rather than (or at least in addition to) those of their native origins.

Thus the notion of the United States as a vast melting pot of different peoples was created. In this tradition change was possible for many and schools were the principal instrument for change. Although often facing discrimination, members of most ethnic minorities were relatively free to move from one socio-economic stratum to another and thus become integrated into the dominant element. Public schools and social centers

SOCIAL OPPORTUNITY AND EDUCATIONAL ACHIEVEMENT

FIGURE 4–2 ROUTE TO GREATER OPPORTUNITY?

offered opportunities to acquire the language, training, and culture needed for better jobs and upward mobility. In turn, steady employment furnished the means to move to more attractive neighborhoods; and marriage made social mobility possible. In addition, some ethnic origins could be disguised by a change of name and adoption of different ways and values. Thus, acceptance into the mainstream of society was within the reach of many who availed themselves of the opportunity.

But the American melting pot has not been effective for everyone, including citizens who have been here for generations. Many of those who are ethnically identifiable, such as the Negro, the Mexican-American, the Puerto-Rican, the Chinese-/or-Japanese-American, or the American Indian, have encountered prejudice and discrimination so pervasive that regardless of education, skill, talent or background, they have been kept in an inferior status.

Concepts of the "inferiority" of certain ethnic groups, which have sometimes been used to justify the reprehensible social, economic and psychological treatment afforded some minority groups, have been overwhelmingly discredited. In general, social scientists hold the view that the cornerstone of ethnic prejudice is in fact ignorance and

> *Few middle-class individuals seem to understand the true meaning of the word prejudice—to judge without reference to the facts or before the facts are in—believing instead that it simply means "to dislike someone."*
> Mario D. Fantini and Gerald Weinstein, *The Disadvantaged: Challenge to Education.* Harper & Row, 1968, p. 37.

> *Prejudice brings in its train fear, suspicion, revulsion, hatred all unfounded and all leading inevitably and irrationally to discrimination, social upheaval, and the denial of human dignity.*
> Rev. Theodore M. Hesburgh, C.S.C., in the Foreword to *Prejudice, U.S.A.,* Charles Y. Glock and Ellen Siegelman (eds.). Frederick A. Praeger, 1969, p. vi.

---

endorse the statements issued by psychological and sociological societies. David Tyack (1969, p. 8) further reminds us that:

> Even if it could be scientifically demonstrated that certain groups had different innate capacities, [as] one anthropologist has recently asked, would that alter their constitutional rights or their need for equality of opportunity? If, for example, Chinese-Americans on the average had larger brains than Caucasians, would that mean that they should be a dominant caste?

Although many of the laws restricting identifiable minorities have been declared unconstitutional (for example, the laws calling for segregated public facilities such as schools, transportation, rest rooms and theaters), the conditions that created them have been only partially eradicated and some such laws remain.

In recent years job opportunities have increasingly opened up to minority group members. Selection procedures sometimes still have a subtle or hidden bias, however. The use of forms or tests alien to a nonwhite frame of reference may jeopardize the chances of some applicant for equal consideration. Differences in the quality of education received by applicants may eliminate some who would otherwise be qualified. To discover whether discrimination based on ethnic prejudice exists in your community and in this country consider the following questions:

1. Can an educated, regularly employed, ethnically identifiable resident of your community
    a. Buy or rent any available house or apartment?
    b. Register for a room in any motel or hotel?
    c. Become a member of the same churches, social organizations, country clubs, and civic groups as whites?
    d. Enroll his children in all schools including dancing classes, horseback riding academies and swim groups?
    e. Get appointments with doctors, dentists, attorneys, bankers, or in barber and beauty shops on the same basis as whites?
    f. Enter the nearest hospital as a patient?
    g. Be buried in the nearest cemetery?
    h. Buy property, secure building permits and business licenses, or get loans on an equal basis with whites?
    i. Join a trade union?
    j. Realistically hope to become president of the company or director of the organization for which he works?

> *The basic principles of equality of opportunity and equality before the law are compatible with all that is known about human biology. All races possess the abilities needed to participate fully in the democratic way of life in modern technological civilization.*
> David Tyack, *Nobody Knows: Black Americans in the Twentieth Century.* Macmillan Co., 1969, p. 8.

2. What is the ethnic or racial origin and sex of the following people?
   President of the United States
   Chairman of the Board of General Motors Corporation
   National Director of the American Red Cross
   Archbishop of New York
   National Commissioner of Baseball
   President of the American Medical Association
   Chairman of the Joint Chiefs of Staff
   National President of the P.T.A.

Being ethnically identifiable obviously subjects people to stereotyped labelling without reference to individual merit. Additionally, since many of the members of some ethnically identifiable groups have low incomes, relatively little education and live in slums and ghettos, all are presumed to share these circumstances. However, just as a society has various strata along which rewards are distributed, so does each ethnic group within that society. The black community in America, for example, has doctors, lawyers, politicians, scientists, businessmen, factory managers, teachers, shopkeepers and artisans along with unskilled laborers and unemployed. This does not prevent prejudice, however, even where some of the economic inequalities have been ameliorated. Numerous Mexican-Americans have made names for themselves as legislators, writers, attorneys, teachers, priests, athletes and musicians. Many Americans of Chinese and Japanese ancestry in this country own their own businesses and are involved in professional services and careers. They, too, are vulnerable to prejudice. Although some individuals from groups that have been discriminated against have found recognition and acceptance in the mainstream of society, prejudice is still persistent. It can be found in discriminatory employment, education, housing and social practices. Educated, skilled and well qualified persons repeatedly come up against the barrier of discrimination that exists in this country. Prejudice applies to members of all ethnically visible minorities, but perhaps the plight of the Negro has received widest publicity.

While there are many individual examples of the insults of racial discrimination, the total impact is perhaps best documented by the effects upon the crucial area of income. The estimated life earnings of nonwhites are dramatically lower than those of whites, *at every level of education* and for both men and women. Thus discrimination applies to middle- as well as working-class levels of our society (Table 4–3).

Although recent social, economic and political developments have improved the status of nonwhite women workers, there still are substantial differences in the employment patterns of nonwhite and white women. Department of Labor statistics on women

LEVEL OF EDUCATION	NONWHITE	WHITE	NONWHITE AS PERCENT OF WHITE
Elementary school			
Less than 8 years	$ 95,000	$157,000	61%
8 years	123,000	191,000	64
High school			
1 to 3 years	132,000	221,000	60
4 years	151,000	253,000	60
Higher Education			
1 to 3 years	162,000	301,000	54
4 years	185,000	395,000	47
5 years or more	246,000	466,000	53

TABLE 4–3 EDUCATION AND DIFFERENTIAL LIFETIME EARNINGS BY COLOR (FOR MEN AGED 18 TO 64)
derived from 1960 Census data. See U.S. Senate, 88th Congress, 1st Session, Hearings before the Committee on Labor and Public Welfare on Bills Relating to Equal Employment Opportunities, July and August 1963.

workers reveal that a higher percentage of nonwhite than white women are in the labor force, are working wives, and are working mothers. In general, nonwhite women have higher unemployment rates, lower income and less schooling than white women. Also, more of them are concentrated in low-skill, low-wage occupations.

For example, in the major occupational group of women workers, 13.7 percent of the professional and technical workers were white, 8.4 nonwhite; 34.1 percent of the clerical workers were white, 11.8 percent nonwhite; 8.2 percent of the sales workers were white, 2.0 nonwhite; 5.6 of the private-household workers were white, 30.3 nonwhite; and 14.0 percent of the service workers (except private household) were white, 24.5 nonwhite.

Almost 67 percent of nonwhite women (59 percent of white) reported some income in 1964. Their median income, however, was $1,066 compared with $1,513 for white women. Income of less than $1,000 was reported by almost 48 percent of nonwhite women, 39 percent for white. The median wage or salary income of nonwhite full-time year-round women workers ($2,674) was 69 percent of that of white women ($3,859) (Table 4–4).

THE DISADVANTAGED EXPERIENCE

In a society that increasingly depends on technology and science for its well-being, unequal distribution of resources means poverty for many who lack the opportunity to acquire the skills needed to compete. In a country where prejudice may be directed against appearance regardless of accomplishment, ethnic group members who are visibly different face unequal opportunity based on discrimination. Separately, poverty or discrimination signify disadvantage; in combination they ensure despair.

Features Common to Disadvantaged Groups

However dissimilar disadvantaged individuals may be from each other or however different one ethnic minority may be from another, they share various experiences. Unlike members in the mainstream of society they fill places in two worlds—their own

INCOME	WHITE	NONWHITE
Some	59%	67%
Median	$1,513	$1,066
Less than $1000	39%	48%
Median full-time year-round	$3,859	$2,674

TABLE 4–4 INCOME REPORTED BY WHITE AND NONWHITE WOMEN, 1964
from Department of Labor Statistics, U.S. Department of Labor. Women's Bureau. *Fact Sheet on Nonwhite Women Workers, Washington,* D.C., October, 1966, p. 2.

and that of the dominant majority. In their environment they may hold roles of leadership and trust, yet they are often subjected to stereotyped attitudes and treatment; they may be considered unambitious, disinterested in planning for the future, lazy or shiftless. There is little overlap between the majority population and the disadvantaged. Young children of the poor are more frequently seen by the comfortable majority in documentary films or as part of advertisements for camp and club donations than on the streets where they play. However, by means of television, radio, billboards, newspapers, and magazines, the poor are in contact with a culture and standard of living unlike their own. They see what resources and material comforts are available. In addition, they work in the same factories, buy many of the same kinds of food and clothing as those better off than they, but in direct contact with the middle class the poor are usually in subordinate roles and unseen by the people they serve. However, whether or not these circumstances can appropriately be called a culture of poverty (Lewis, 1959), lower-class life differs dramatically from that of the middle class, especially where it is also influenced by ethnic culture. Gordon Parks, (1966, p. 48) writer and film-maker, recalls this one-sided view.

> The world inside the M. Club was one of spacious rooms . . . of thick carpeting, of master and servant, of expensive wines and liquors, of elegant table settings and epicurean tastes. Influential men . . . sat about smoking long cigars and ornate pipes . . . and I, in a suit of blue tails, white tie, and striped red vest, would stand near them discreetly listening to their confidential talk of financial deals, court decisions . . . families . . . and weather. To most of them I was invisible and unhearing, a sort of dark ectoplasm that only materialized when their fingers snapped for service.

As a whole, the disadvantaged poor have little to say about what will or will not be done on their behalf. No one stops to ask, "What do you think should be done?" Decisions of this kind are made for them. They are subject to economic control by a variety of government agencies: medical services from public health and welfare groups, and education based on decisions made by remote boards of education. In many instances their lack of education handicaps them in knowing where or how to get information and even how to take advantage of the information that may be available to them.

Knowledge about what they might do to improve their situation is often not available and may be deliberately withheld from them. This results in ignorance which makes them susceptible to exploitation by members of their own social community and by con men, unscrupulous repair men, loan agencies and other individuals, agencies and groups. Thus lotteries and other long-shot ventures hold great attraction.

> *One of the sorest points of "justice" until recently was the difference in treatment for the rich and the poor. A rich person could pay his fine in a criminal case and go free. A person unable to pay his fine often was kept in prison to "work off his fine."*
>
> *Early in July 1970, the United States Supreme Court, in an 8–0 decision, ruled this procedure as unconstitutional. The case involved a convicted thief who remained in jail a year, then was ordered to remain another 101 days to work off a $500 fine.*
>
> *A new federal law gave a break to the poor at about the same time when a new law, Title III of Truth-in-Lending, came into force. It prevents a creditor from garnishment of all of a worker's wages. Anyone making $48 a week or less could not have any of his wages seized by a creditor.*

The life circumstances of the poor restrict their range of alternatives of action. Lack of economic resources, power, education and prestige drastically reduce physical mobility and the availability of different options for residence, housing, employment and other areas of their lives.

As a group, they are dependent upon the policies and resources of the federal, state, and local public health and welfare agencies who supply them with services. The range of medical services open to them is severely restricted and their bodies are likely to be exploited for medical education and research as a contingency of medical services at low cost. A low level of literacy and education and lack of experience about how to obtain information make it difficult to discover and take advantage of those alternatives that may be technically available.

The disadvantaged are frequently more subject to arrest and detention with little regard for their rights. Coretta Scott King, wife of the Nobel Peace Prize winner, Martin Luther King, Jr., recalls an incident of this kind that occurred several years after the Montgomery bus strike had been won (King, 1969, p. 163). She and her husband were standing quietly outside a courtroom with a friend who was to testify in a private case. A policeman ordered them to move on. When Dr. King stood his ground, courteously explaining that he was waiting to see his attorney, the policeman threatened him and together with another officer grabbed him, twisted his arms behind him, and pushed Dr. King down the stairs.

> ... I ran to get our friends, and when I came back into City Hall Martin had disappeared. He was kicked and roughed up, and then, when they discovered who he was, he was charged with disobeying an officer and released on his own recognizance.

Not only are the civil rights of the disadvantaged often ignored, but the services they are provided, from emergency care in hospitals to visits by welfare agency workers, are often inferior and made with little consideration for human dignity or concern about the invasion of privacy.

Poverty and its consequent powerlessness leaves people overly vulnerable to disaster. Many disadvantaged people are in the ranks of unskilled and semi-skilled labor and therefore are usually the first to be laid off when work is slack and last to be hired when work picks up. The poor typically are not only without financial reserves of their own, but are most likely to be given little advance notice when laid off from work.

Because of their record of intermittent employment and lack of property or financial reserves, the disadvantaged possess little credit or borrowing power and are unlikely to have friends who can help them (Cloward & Elman, 1966a; 1966b). If a crisis develops in their lives, recovery is more difficult and requires more time for them than for people with some resources (Koos, 1950). The poor live on the edge of incipient tragedy which they are powerless to avert.

Consequences of Disadvantage

These conditions of poverty—*powerlessness, low status, lack of alternatives* and *little access to experience or information* inevitably bring their own consequences. Individual differences in ability to cope with adverse circumstances cannot be overlooked, of course, for some men and women manage somehow to rise above severe socio-economic and cultural handicaps. Nevertheless, certain consequences result for the majority of people who lack opportunity and face discrimination.

Because powerlessness is at the core of their condition, their own relationships are often oriented to power, coercion and force. Physical punishment is a common form of discipline in families. In verbal interaction, mothers govern children largely by phrasing their comments and instructions as imperatives; fathers may see their children's respect for them as expressed in their obedience to commands. Because adults have little power outside the family, they frequently blame those who are in control for the problems and misfortunes that daily beset them.

Self-esteem is low among the disadvantaged largely because of an accumulated sense of ineffectiveness. Their response to this frustration is often apathy and resignation. It is not that parents *teach* their children to be passive; rather the unpredictability of their lives and the lack of order and stability in their experience with their environment bring a realistic sense of caution and apathy.

On the whole, disadvantaged people tend to embrace familiar experiences and routines rather than attempt novel or unfamiliar circumstances. In general, a disadvantaged person has little opportunity to make the kind or number of decisions he would if he were in a middle-class environment. For example, he cannot be concerned whether an apartment is of a certain size or on a certain floor, when there is a question whether he will have an apartment at all or be able to meet the rent payments. People who know they are going to have to live in a hovel are not as likely to worry about how far it is from the bus stop.

Also, the life circumstances of the poor orient them to practical action. Their participation in their jobs has not typically been that of policy making. The world of abstract ideas has less place in the practical realities that must be dealt with day after day.

GROUP A	GROUP B	GROUP C	GROUP D
College education, professional, executive and managerial occupations	Skilled blue-collar occupations, not more than high school education	Unskilled or semi-skilled occupations, predominantly elementary school education level	Same occupational and educational level as Group C, but fathers absent from home and families supported by public assistance

TABLE 4–5 SES GROUPINGS FOR HESS AND SHIPMAN STUDY

Since the disadvantaged do not participate in policy making or any long-range planning either for themselves or others, it is essential to deal with the immediate present.

The impact of conditions of poverty upon families are expressed in many ways. One particularly significant manifestation of the process by which social circumstances are translated into behavior is in the way mothers prepare their children for entry into school experience. The orientation a child receives and the attitudes he develops toward teachers, toward learning, and toward his own role as a student in the classroom may affect his subsequent school achievement as well as his self-esteem in areas of scholastic performance.

In a study conducted by Hess and Shipman in Chicago (1965), it was found that mothers from different socio-economic backgrounds in the black community prepare their children in different ways for their first school experience. To obtain the mothers' definitions and perceptions of school, 163 Negro mothers from four SES (Socio-Economic Status) groupings (Table 4–5) were asked to imagine that it was the first day of school and then to respond to the question:

> Your child is going to school for the first time—what will you do, what will you tell him?

The responses showed that mothers in low income levels tend to conceive the problems that the child will have at school essentially as getting along with the teacher and dealing with the school as an institution. Accordingly, they tend to teach their children to comply, to "be good," to "mind what the teacher says," and to stay out of trouble. Mothers from professional homes are more likely to talk to their children about the teacher and to present her in a more favorable light. They describe the school situation as one in which the child will learn and, in general, enjoy learning. Her attitudes are related also to her place in the society and the way she and her family have been treated by its institutions.

As discussed earlier in this chapter, each mother sees the social world from her own point of advantage or disadvantage, and her attitudes and responses reflect the nature of the society in which she lives. The child who comes from a low-income home is oriented more towards questions of discipline and authority and whether or not he will conform to the rules, than he is toward the school as a place in which he can and will be expected to learn. This conception of school and of the school situation reflects, in part, the differences in the control strategies and techniques that the mothers use. Mothers from low-income homes are more likely to be concerned with external appearances and behavior and less oriented towards subjective experiences with which the child will be involved.

The images that mothers transmit to the young child in some form are particularly relevant for early education and the child's success in school. The mothers' attitudes in the Hess and Shipman study indicate that the problem is not due to a lack of respect for the school, lack of interest, or to the belief that it is ineffective. The low-income mothers regard the school as a distant, formidable institution with which they have very little interaction and over which they exercise little control. Thus the initial relationship between many children and the teacher is posed in terms of authority rather than interaction; as a matter of rules and obedience rather than inquiry and exploration. These patterns arise in response to the circumstances of their own lives.

Many of the programs developed in the past ten years, especially for children from poor families, adopted the concept of *deficit* as their central theme for program design. That is, they were based on the assumption that the child has come to school lacking in experience, concepts, language development, social abilities and the like. From this simplistic (and incorrect) diagnosis of the educational problem, programs of "cultural enrichment" were created. The school became responsible for seeing that children had experiences which would overcome the "deficit" they faced. Gradually it has been recognized that children come to school with a wide range of skills, adaptations and coping strategies. The problem is that many from low-income areas come with behaviors which are not readily applicable to the tasks expected by the school or oriented to middle-class values and expectations. Some mutual accommodation is needed; the child must be helped to develop attitudes and behavior necessary for success in a school setting and the school must revise its program and expectations to respond to the particular needs, talents and experiences of the child from a low-income community.

DIFFERENCES IN EDUCATIONAL ACHIEVEMENT

Performance Related to Socio-Economic Level

Children share the consequences of disadvantage and the effects are evident in many areas of behavior. Of particular concern to teachers of young children are the effects of disadvantage upon capabilities and attitudes which are instrumental in performance in school, and which ultimately determine the skills and abilities needed to work and live effectively in a complex social community.

Children from families with unskilled and semi-skilled occupational backgrounds tend to be less successful in school than children from families of professional, managerial and executive occupations. These differences have been evident for many years and appear in most types of school achievement and test scores.

These discrepancies in performance between children from low-income level and high-income level families appear early in the child's educational career; the traditional school has not been very successful in improving the relative achievement of many children from low-income homes.

To recognize the scope of the problems involved in dealing with inequalities of educational opportunity, it may be useful to review the differences among socio-economic and ethnic groups on tests. In the early years of this century the French psychologist Alfred Binet devised a test to detect children who were likely to have serious academic problems. The individual intelligence test which he worked out, and which was later revised, is still one of the classic and most-used measuring instruments in the field. In early uses of this test it was discovered that children from so-called working-class backgrounds scored at a lower level than those from middle-class homes. This finding has been repeated many times, not only on the Binet test and its revisions, but with other measuring instruments as well.

The size of the difference varies with the test used and to some extent with the population to which it was administered. Children from middle-class homes show a clear advantage; generally the discrepancy is on the order of 10–15 IQ points.

There are a number of theories as to why these differences exist. Most of them present explanations about the effect of environment upon the development of mental capabilities, although some claim that achievement differences between socio-economic groups are based on genetic factors. As was indicated in Chapter 1, this is a very complex problem. To think of it in terms of genetic factors seems unproductive and somewhat futile; such an approach discourages attempts to improve the child's educational experience. Rather, we need to consider the kinds of learning contexts that can be provided in the child's environment so that no matter what his native or biological talent he may develop his abilities to their fullest extent.

One of the common criticisms of intelligence tests is that the items were constructed by middle-class, academic persons with knowledge obtained from their middle-class, philosophy-oriented language, objects, and experiences. Many of the test items contain a bias, however unintentional, which favors children from middle-class homes (Davis, 1948). This criticism of the application of intelligence tests to children from quite different backgrounds holds that many of the activities, skills and adaptations needed for successful performance are acquired only within the context of middle-class community and school situations. Children from city slums and rural communities develop aptitudes that are not always readily assessed by middle-class, academically oriented testing devices. Children from dissimilar socio-economic and ethnic communities even within the United States have vastly divergent experiences and the initial and most urgent efforts of education should be to assess the effects of environments and examine differences in achievement in these terms before surrendering to the genetic arguments with their easy answers of inevitability and despair. The first place to look for explanations, though not the only one, is in differences of opportunity and experience.

Discrepancies that appear on IQ scores have a parallel in other devices intended to test levels of educational attainment, in dropout rates, in college attendance and in aspirations and expectations for achievement. This is not surprising since the so-called general intelligence tests are strongly weighted in the direction of reading ability and school-related information. The differences in level of achievement in reading, arithmetic and other academic subjects have shown up in the early grades and were maintained as the child progressed through elementary and high school.

Although achievement of middle-class children compared with that of children from unskilled and semi-skilled occupational levels might seem to be higher on items that have to do with verbal performance, this may not generally be the case. Rather, the art of test-taking itself appears to influence a fairly wide range of item types.

A survey conducted in a large metropolitan center in the midwestern United States illustrates the extent of difference in educational attainment between such groups. In this survey twenty-one school districts were ranked by criteria consisting of a composite of median level of income and median level of education of the adults in the school districts. These were compared with a crude index comprised of the combined scores of two reading tests and two tests in arithmetic at the fifth grade level. In those districts which were in the top third of the socio-economic scale, student performance ranged from achivement at grade level to achievement roughly one grade or one full year above the norms for the city. Students from all districts that were on the bottom level of the income scale performed about one year below expected grade level. Similar patterns were apparent in reading readiness scores for first grade children where only 40 percent of the districts which fell in the bottom third of the socio-economic ladder were up to national average in this crucial set of skills.

In another survey, a comparison of the performance of children in twenty-six schools in California showed that differences among the schools varied considerably according to subject matter. The greatest disparities appeared in science where the percentiles ranged from approximately 83 for the highest socio-economic level schools to a percentile of 14 for the lowest—where the schools had been categorized into four socio-economic levels. The smallest differences were in writing where the highest socio-economic group was at the 76 percentile and the lowest at 37.

Another index of difference in educational attainment between middle-class and low-

TABLE 4–6 COLLEGE ENROLLMENT FROM DIFFERENT SOCIO-ECONOMIC LEVELS, 1967
from U.S. Department of Commerce, *Current Population Reports,* Series P-20, No. 185, July 11, 1969, Washington, D.C.: U.S. Government Printing Office, 1969, p. 6.

FAMILY INCOME	PERCENT OF HIGH SCHOOL GRADUATES ENTERING COLLEGE
Under $3000	19.8%
$3000 to 3,999	32.3
$4000 to 5,999	36.9
$6000 to 7,999	41.1
$8000 to 9,999	51.0
$10,000 to 14,999	61.3
$15,000 and over	86.7

income children has to do with the tendency of young people to drop out of school rather than to continue and go on to college. The number and proportion from low-income areas who leave before high school graduation is disproportionately high especially when combined with ethnic considerations. It is also significant that young people who have the ability to go on to college tend less often to do so if they come from poor backgrounds or backgrounds where the education of the parents seems to be low (Table 4–6).

Cultural and Ethnic Differences

The varieties of behavior shown by individuals from dissimilar cultural and ethnic groups is one of the most fascinating topics of study in human activities. In the United States variations in cultural and ethnic (including racial) patterns of living and working are part of our national life. These ethnic differences appear in regard to academic performance as well as in other areas of daily life. They are not fully understood but they reflect to some degree an inequality of educational opportunity. Not all ethnic groups have been allowed to realize their intellectual and scholarly potential, even in a society which is concerned with developing the ability of all children.

One of the most comprehensive surveys showing ethnic differences in school achievement was made by Coleman (1966). This was a national study of the academic performance of children from low-income communities and racial minority backgrounds. The study revealed a discrepancy in the performance of children from the different ethnic groups tested. These discrepancies were apparent in grades one and persisted through grade twelve.

Lesser and his associates (1965) designed a project to explore the relative effects of social class differences and ethnic-racial variations on intellectual performance of young children in New York City. They selected or constructed tests and developed conditions that were intended to minimize cultural and social bias. The tests, covering four mental abilities—verbal ability, reasoning, number facility and space conceptualization—were administered to 320 children in first grade (ages 6 years 2 months through 7 years 5 months) from four different ethnic groups. These groups—Chinese, Jewish, Negro and Puerto Rican—were themselves subdivided into middle and working-class. These SES categories were not comparable from one ethnic group to another, however. The "low" SES Jewish group was probably closer to the "middle" than to the "low" SES Negro group.

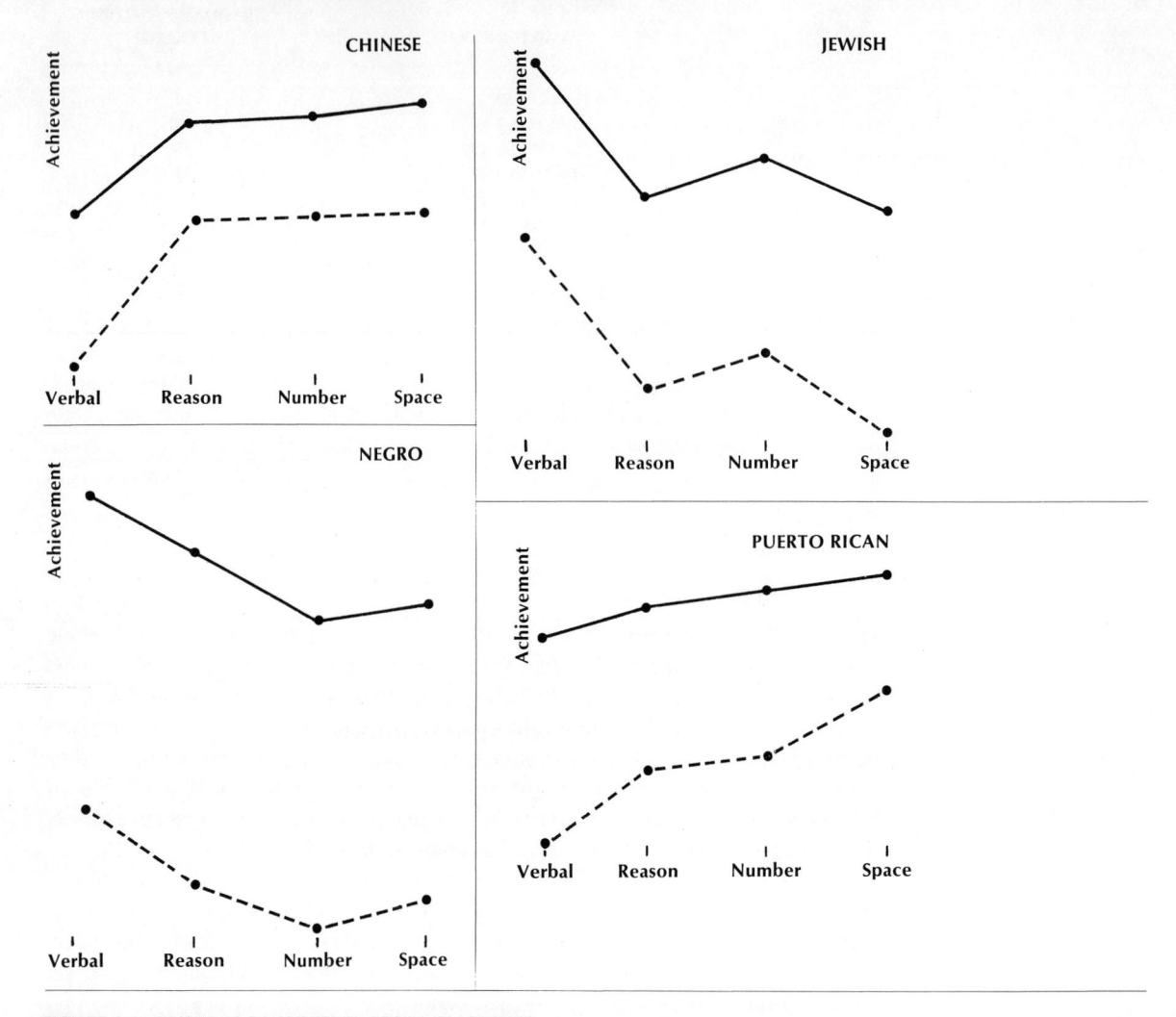

FIGURE 4–3 PATTERNS OF ABILITY BY SOCIAL-CLASS LEVEL
adapted from Lesser, Fifer, and Clark, "Mental Abilities of Children from Different Social-Class and Cultural Groups," in *Monographs of the Society for Research in Child Development*, Vol. 30, No. 4, Serial No. 102, pp. 65–68.

The study, which was replicated later in Boston, confirmed that both socio-economic status and cultural background exert strong influences upon mental ability. These influences, however, act in quite different ways. Cultural background affects the *pattern* of mental ability such as in the test performance regardless of social class background; social class background affects the *level of achievement* in the different abilities tested. This is apparent in the data presented in Table 4–7 and Figure 4–3.

The essential points of the Lesser findings are first, there are different *patterns* of ability among children from different cultural backgrounds. Second, within each group there are different *levels* of performance based perhaps on unequal opportunity, presumably of broad educational experience.

TABLE 4-7 RANK OF MENTAL ABILITIES WITHIN CULTURAL GROUPS
adapted from Gerald S. Lesser, Gordon Fifer and Donald H. Clark, "Mental Abilities of Children from Different Social Class and Cultural Groups," *Monographs of the Society for Research in Child Development*, Vol. 30, No. 4, Serial No. 102, 1965, p. 82.

ABILITY	CHINESE	JEWISH	NEGRO	PUERTO RICAN
Verbal	4	1	1	4
Reasoning	3	3	2	3
Numerical	2	2	4	2
Spatial	1	4	3	1

Implications for the Classroom

A careful examination of the nature of socio-economic and cultural differences in the United States and of the extent and impact of racial discrimination brings some understanding of the seriousness of these problems and of the complexity of any effective solution. It becomes clear that the problems of poverty and discrimination are related to a total life pattern and that any simple or single solution is not likely to be sufficient. This means, of course, that educational gains and advantages will be even more effective if they are accompanied by changes in other areas of life—employment, housing, health, physical safety and security. These interrelationships are recognized at high governmental levels and programs such as the 4 C's (Community Coordinated Child Care) are established to coordinate child care services.

The desire or the decision to intervene in the life of a young child or his family and the attempt to change his style of life, cultural pattern or socioeconomic level is a critical decision. The teacher will often find herself torn by the inconsistencies which arise between her own values and those of the child's home.

How much should she try to alter the cultural and social patterns that the child brings to school? Why? Assuming that she could be effective in her efforts, the teacher needs to be aware of the impact of attempts to change the values of a child or family. However, part of the opportunity which a school can offer is the chance for educational routes out of poverty and disadvantage. To develop a child's potential to read and to succeed in school is to increase his alternatives. The teacher can help give the child more alternatives than he would otherwise have and help his family see that there are more options and possibilities which they may not have realized were available. This will not happen in dramatic ways with every child, of course, but will happen often enough to justify her efforts.

It is important, also, that we not promise more than our programs can achieve. In the early days of compensatory education, the impression was conveyed (through titles like Upward Bound, Higher Horizons, Head Start, etc.) that these new efforts held a special sort of immediate promise for many children. They were often less effective than the publicity might lead parents and community leaders to believe and the resulting disappointment added to the mistrust of the system.

Perhaps the most significant implication of the facts of socio-economic and ethnic circumstances is that the educational needs and goals of individual families and of poor communities and minority groups should be taken into consideration.

In a real sense, these are philosophical and political problems as well as educational ones. The ethnic communities in this country are increasingly insistent upon participating in the decisions that affect their children, and schools are becoming responsive and sensitive to these community pressures. This is a familiar pattern in American education. Schools are instruments of the community and are supported to carry out the community's educational plans. In the past, those who set the curriculum for low-income and ethnic groups were not from the communities themselves but a part of society far removed from the realities of the low-income groups and ethnic families. This trend to community participation in setting goals for children who have been disadvantaged is in line with an historic educational tradition in this country.

The teacher thus needs an understanding of the kind of behavior she may expect from the children with whom she works, whether from middle-class or low-income backgrounds, and a sense of how she may best assist each child to achieve the goals his family and community set for him. Perhaps the most difficult and important task she has is to give the child a versatility and competence to be successful in both his own world and in others he may encounter and wish to enter.

REFERENCES

Bureau of the Census. *Current population reports.* Series P-20, No. 185, Washington, D.C.: Government Printing Office, U.S. Department of Commerce. July 11, 1969, p. 6.

California Elementary School Administrators Association. *The neighborhood and the school: a study of socio-economic status and school achievement.* Burlingame, Calif. 1962.

Cloward, R. A. and Elman, R. M. Poverty, injustice and the welfare state. An ombudsman for the poor? *The Nation,* February 28, 1966, Part 1, *202,* No. 9, 230–235.

Cloward, R. A. and Elman, R. M. Poverty, injustice and the welfare state. How rights can be secured. *The Nation,* March 7, 1966, Part 2, *202,* No. 10, 264–268.

Coleman, J. S. et al. *Equality of educational opportunity.* Washington, D.C.: U.S. Government Printing Office, 1966.

Davis, A. *Social class influences upon learning.* (The Inglis Lecture), Cambridge, Mass.: Harvard University Press, 1948.

Downs, A. *Who are the urban poor?* Supplementary Paper No. 26, (revised edition), New York: Committee for Economic Development, September 1970.

Fantini, M. D. and Weinstein, G. *The disadvantaged: challenge to education.* New York: Harper and Row, 1968.

Gonzales, H. B. The hope and the promise. In D. Estes and D. Darling (Eds.), *Improving educational opportunities of the Mexican American, Proceedings of the first Texas conference for Mexican Americans.* Austin, Texas: Southwest Educational Development Laboratory, 1967.

Griffiths, D. E. et al. *Organizing schools for effective education.* Danville, Ill.: The Interstate Printers and Publishers, 1962.

Hesburgh, T. M. Foreword. In C. Y. Glock and E. Siegelman (Eds.), *Prejudice, U.S.A.* New York: Frederick A. Praeger, 1969, pp. v–viii.

Hess, R. D. and Shipman, V. C. Early experience and the socialization of cognitive modes in children. *Child Development,* 1965, 36, No. 4, 869–886.

King, C. S. *My life with Martin Luther King, Jr.* New York: Holt, Rinehart and Winston, 1969.

Koos, E. L. Class differences in family reactions to crisis. *Marriage and Family Living,* 1950, *12,* 77–78.

Lesser, G. S., Fifer, G., and Clark, D. H. Mental abilities of children from different social class and cultural groups. *Monographs of the Society for Research in Child Development,* 1965, *30,* No. 4, Serial No. 102.

Lewis, O. *Five families.* New York: Basic Books, Inc. 1959.

Ornati, O. *Poverty amid affluence.* New York: The Twentieth Century Fund, 1966.

Orshansky, M. Counting the poor: another look at the poverty profile. *Social Security Bulletin,* January 1965, *28,* No. 1, 3–29.

Parks, G. *A choice of weapons.* New York: Harper and Row, 1966.

Tyack, D. *Nobody knows: black Americans in the twentieth century.* New York: The Macmillan Company, 1969.

U.S. Bureau of Labor Statistics. *Three standards of living for an urban family of four persons, Spring 1967.* Bulletin No. 1570–5, Washington, D.C.: U.S. Government Printing Office, 1969.

CHAPTER 5

PROGRAMS ARE TOOLS, NOT RELIGIONS

HEAD START BRINGS A NEW ERA

National Concern About Equality in Education

Shortly after 9 p.m., January 4, 1965, reading slowly and pausing often to emphasize his points, President of the United States Lyndon Johnson called for legislation that was to lead to far reaching changes for early education in this country. He spoke from the rostrum of the House of Representatives, not only to a packed chamber and gallery of those attending the opening sessions of the 89th Congress, but also to a vast radio and television audience. It was only the second time in the history of the United States that a State of the Union message had been delivered at night. During his speech, the President said:

> I propose we begin a program in education to ensure every American child the fullest development of his mind and skills. . . . Every child must have the best education our nation can provide. . . . In addition to our existing programs, I will recommend a new program for schools and students . . . .
>
> . . . For the preschool years we will help needy children become aware of the excitement of learning.

Never before had education at the preschool level been singled out for this kind of attention. Eight days later the President sent a message to Congress devoted entirely to his plans for all levels of education. His recommendations regarding preschool education, although brief, showed an awareness of the lack of school achievement on the part of children from backgrounds of poverty, and a belief in the importance of early education in the lives of all children. He called for an initial expenditure of 150 million for preschool programs:

> Education must begin with the very young. The child from the urban or rural slum frequently misses his chance even before he begins school. . . . Action on a wide front will begin this summer through a special "head start" program for children who are scheduled to begin school next fall.

And so was launched Operation Head Start and the variety of programs it stimulated. A number of trends and events brought about this response at the national level to the educational needs of poor children. Perhaps the most significant was the growing concern over the inequality of educational opportunity for black children in the United States and the more general concern for economic, legal, social and civil rights of minorities.

The work of a few social scientists in scattered parts of the country was another important influence. These men and women had been conducting research on the educational development of poor children and constructing experimental programs intended to raise school achievement. Most of these programs were sponsored by universities and funded by private foundations. There were a few formal programs of instruction, particularly of the sort represented by Montessori (1870–1952), who began her work with poor children in Rome. But, on the whole, prior to the mid-1960's, little systematic effort had gone into devising effective preschool programs based on learning theory and research. The concern expressed by the President led to increased interest in early education and a wide variety of programs for intervention. Each of the publicly financed programs was different from the others, but all sought to help children avoid educational failure.

The interest in the concept of "Head Start" and the availability of funds from private as well as government sources evoked a great deal of professional response. Intense efforts were begun to construct programs and develop theories of early education. The activities of these professionals were concentrated on experimental programs and on research that would increase the effectiveness of methods of instruction in the classroom and other settings.

As ideas were put into practice, their proponents argued the merits of alternative programs. Competition among programs stimulated a process of evaluation which still continues and very likely will for some time to come. The relative value of different programs is a major controversy; the advantages of investing in curriculum as opposed to investing in teacher training or other aspects of early education (use of aides from low-income communities, for example) are issues still under consideration. The impact of Head Start and its attendant experimental and research efforts has been enormous, however; early education has gone through an irreversible transformation.

Support for these programs of educational intervention came largely from concern over the effects of poverty and discrimination on the cognitive growth of children. It was inevitable, therefore, that the programs which emerged would be based on assumptions or theories about the nature of the problems of children from slum areas. However, considerable attention was also given to learning process, and this has had an effect on preschool education for all children—advantaged as well as disadvantaged.

Different experimental programs and points of view have evolved a number of distinct philosophies and teaching techniques for early education. Although ideally a teacher selects and adapts programs to fit her own teaching style or the child's needs, there is a tendency for her to align herself with a particular philosophy, sometimes rejecting programs as "too unstructured," "mechanical," "academic," or "traditional," or because she intuitively doesn't like them.

Programs do indeed reflect different theories and techniques, but these can be seen as providing the teacher with a variety of tools and resources. Although she will probably prefer one type of approach, she need not reject other techniques and ideas,

FIGURE 5-1   WHERE DOES THE PROBLEM LIE?

if they can contribute to her program. It might be useful for a teacher occasionally to vary her methods if only to see more clearly how her own ideas and practices contrast with those of others. Obviously, a teacher can more effectively select the methods and techniques she needs if she is familiar with various contemporary and historical points of view about the educational process.

Assumptions About the Impact of Poverty and Discrimination

Many of the recently developed programs were designed for use with children from low-income backgrounds and are thus oriented toward the needs of children from underprivileged areas. These new programs and related reports have offered various explanations as to why children from poor families (and especially those who also face ethnic discrimination) don't do well in school.

The center of the problem is seen by some to be within the child. Others direct attention to family relationships and community influences. Sometimes the school system, with emphasis on the interaction between teacher and child, is considered a principal cause of children's failure to achieve the cognitive development needed for school success. A fourth explanation focuses on the structure of society itself, and how this structure creates disadvantages which affect children's learning and educational performance (Figure 5-1). Each viewpoint has its proponents. Learning something of the assumptions helps make clear the nature of the programs which evolved from them.

The Child as the Locus of the Problem: The Deficit Model   One of the first and most popular explanations of why certain groups of children fail to achieve in school is that they suffer a deficiency of school-related experiences. Such children, in this view, have not been adequately exposed to the beneficial stimulation and care that build the basis for academic achievement in our school system. Indeed, one of the most widely read books on education of low-income children in the early 1960's expressed this view in its title, *The Culturally Deprived Child,* and this sort of terminology persisted for many years and is still found in some writings about low-income children. The analogy that comes to mind is to compare a physically undernourished child who has never been given enough vitamins, proteins, or other body-building nutrients to establish and maintain good health, with a picture of the socio-economically and culturally "malnourished" child who lacks the skills and experiences most needed for success in school.

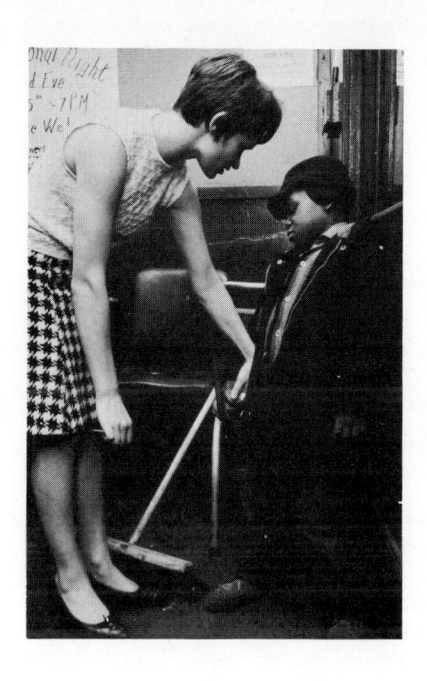

This view of the role of early experience is an echo of the writing of John Amos Comenius (1592–1670), who wrote of the School of the Mother's Knee where, during the first six years of life, the child was taught by the mother so that when he reached school age he possessed simple facts and skills that prepare him for school. It also borrows from the ideas of John Locke (1632–1704) that described the mind of the young child as a *tabula rasa,* a blank tablet, on which experiences were to be impressed and transcribed. In this view, the disadvantaged child was an empty vessel, lacking and insufficient.

From this viewpoint, in terms of program planning, the locus of the problem is in the child himself who comes to school with an educational and cognitive deficit. Writers holding this view elaborate this notion in the following ways:

Lack of Stimulation. This perspective suggests that the poor have not been sufficiently exposed to "beneficial" stimuli at home or in their neighborhoods to provide adequate background for school experiences. In this sense "beneficial" means exposure to middle-class language patterns, social experience and achievement training. Stimulus deprivation, in this view, also includes lack of exposure to the geographically wider community, books and libraries, magazines, concerts, art galleries, and

137 PROGRAMS ARE TOOLS, NOT RELIGIONS

other of the "educational and cultural" experiences which presumably prepare children for school. A writer in the mid 60's (Lyford, 1970, pp. 49, 51) expressed it in this description of a child's life in Harlem:

> It is the crowds of children most of all who contribute to the neighborhood atmosphere. According to my census there are about three dozen of them, mostly Negroes. Some belong to the Methodist Church Sunday School and sell Girl Scout Cookies. All of them spend the summer racing up and down the block looking for something to do. Since they do not have any equipment for the usual games, they invent their own, which is a misfortune for the city because the major emphasis—in spite of Sunday School—is on breaking bottles, setting fire to trash, opening hydrants, and sending in false alarms. But with all their rushing about and daredeviling, the children regard the four corners of the block as the outermost limits of the universe. Whatever travels they take are imaginary ones in the hulk of an abandoned car that periodically turns up along the curb. Very few of the children leave the block even to climb the big rocks that loom up on the edge of Central Park a few hundred feet to the east.[1]

This view of the lives of poor children who lack the parties, vacations, experiences with pets, trips to beaches and jaunts at amusement parks which are often a part of the lives of middle-class children, is a familiar one, especially in the early literature of Head Start.

Another related but distinct view is that there is a *lack of pattern in experience* in poor neighborhoods. One may distinguish between random experience and stimulation and the ordering of experience into patterns of meaning. As the young child explores the world around him he learns that his actions elicit response. Adults approve of or respond to certain behaviors and disapprove of or ignore others. Some people pay attention to him, others appear not to notice his presence. The consequences of his action may vary according to the occasion. Through his experiences the child builds an array of patterns and associations linking what he does to its consequences, and these make it possible for him to understand his world. If the responses he receives are random and therefore not predictable, he has no way of knowing where he stands. Unless the stimuli to which a child is exposed are presented in a pattern that permits him to generalize from them in coping with future situations, he won't be able to make sense of his world. A deficit of this sort results not from an absence of stimuli, but from the absence of a

---

[1] From "In My Neighborhood An Adult Is a Dead Child." Reprinted, by permission, from the November 1970 issue of *The Center Magazine,* Vol. III, #6, a publication of the Center for the Study of Democratic Institutions in Santa Barbara, California.

> A study of 195 Apache children between one and six years old disclosed that one-third of them had anemia and deficiencies in vitamins A and C. Virtually all 165 children examined in one clinic had dental disease; half the cases were described as severe. In another group of 126 families, marked growth retardation was seen in children through age five years.
>
> M. S. Read, *Malnutrition and Learning.* National Institutes of Health, 1969, p. 4.

pattern to the stimuli presented. According to this interpretation of the effects of poverty upon early cognitive development, a child who is not accustomed to seeing patterns of cause and effect and who has lived with inconsistency, is likely to reach school less able to cope academically with what is expected of him.

Another facet of the malnutrition or deficit approach emphasizes *the substandard conditions of the poor* and the consequences of this economic fact upon their lives. Unable to purchase necessities in the form of goods and services of various kinds, they lack a balanced diet and nutritional problems become severe. The National Nutrition Survey begun in 1968 suggests that multiple deficiencies of specific nutrients occur in higher than expected proportions among poor people (Read, 1969, p. 11).

> Those who have worked with undernourished or hungry children know that they exhibit behavioral alterations. These include apathy, lethargy, inability to pay attention, and perhaps overconcern about food to such a degree that responses to classroom stimuli do not occur.

The notion that the disadvantaged child is deficient in the learning he brings to the classroom was the basis of the first major wave of programs for intervention. Often called "cultural enrichment," the programs included trips to museums, zoos, parks, stores, gardens, factories or wherever children might gain needed experience. Some youngsters visited overnight in suburban homes. Others received special attention in language training. Underlying this approach was the general philosophy that children who lacked advantages should be exposed to the world of those who had them, thus making up the deficit.

The Misfit Between Cultures: The Cultural Disparity Model Sociologists, linguists and anthropologists interpret the difference in school performance between poor children and middle-class children from the *viewpoint of cultural differences*. According to this theory, the ghetto child, rather than suffering from a deficit in learning, faces a conflict in values and goals because of the difference between what he has learned at home and what he needs to know in order to succeed in school. This approach, which places the locus of the problem within the family and community, takes several forms.

Cultural Pluralism. Family ways and values differ from culture to culture and along a socio-economic hierarchy. Differences in food preparation, religious beliefs and holiday customs do not usually affect school performance, but some cultural patterns and customs do cause difficulties in the classroom. For example, many Puerto Rican and Mexican-American children are taught to show respect for their elders by turning their eyes downward when they are spoken to. If the teacher's reaction is that shown in

FIGURE 5–2
"José! Look at me when I am speaking to you!"

Figure 5–2, this is obviously a problem in communication. For some tribes, American Indian life traditionally centered around sunrise and sunset; time was relative and unimportant. Even today it is frequently difficult for Indian children and their parents to adapt to the ways of a school program which is regulated by clock time, yet they are judged by school norms of punctuality.

Perhaps one of the most significant aspects of cultural pluralism concerns language usage in the home and in school. Many poor children speak either a dialect of English or an entirely different language. In either case, however well they communicate at home, their speech is often not that approved for classroom use. Although these children may daily hear standard English on television, they often have little occasion to use the forms themselves and so come to school linguistically different, only to find that they are expected to speak, read and comprehend standard English.

The educational and occupational opportunities of disadvantaged minority children and their families are limited not only by discrimination, but also by lack of accurate information. They often have few contacts with levels of society other than their own, and their knowledge of the economic and occupational aspects of the larger world is based mainly on hearsay rather than personal experience.

The cultural patterns of poor children, especially those who also face racial or ethnic discrimination, may conflict with those the child is expected to follow at school. If they do, he has to make choices. This may be difficult, for he does not come to school ready to change what he already knows and embrace a new set of values. If he does not succeed in school, he becomes more isolated. From five to 15 he learns to know his own culture even more perfectly, the school culture less and less. Therefore many children explicitly reject the school and its values long before high school graduation; others choose to hide the conflict from view.

Acquisition of Behavior Not Rewarded at School. The child who lives in a ghetto or impoverished rural community learns to deal with and adapt to the environment in which he lives, not matter how poor, dangerous or unrewarding it may be. He learns to cope with the threats of exploitation and of physical danger from fire, rats, traffic, etc., to deal with harassment from police, and to hold his own physically with peers and older children. He learns not only to protect himself in an often hostile environment, but to extract from it some of the things he wants or needs. The inner-city ghetto is not always a friendly or happy place. Its inhabitants are painfully aware of the contrasts between the wealthier, more powerful, established dominant culture and their own problems of dealing with the life of the street. It is a way of life that demands special resources and coping abilities but these are not of a type likely to bring success in the classroom. This analysis does not hold that the "inner-city" child has failed to learn during his preschool years, but that he has learned the wrong things, from the teacher's point of view.

Schools as the Locus of the Problem: The Miseducation Model The following statement from a report made to the United States Commissioner of Education (Panel on Educational Research and Development, 1964, p. 30) is typical of some assessments of the quality of education in the slums:

> By all known criteria, the majority of urban and rural slum schools are failures. In neighborhood after neighborhood across the country, more than half of each age group fails to complete high school and 5 percent or fewer go on to some form of higher education.

In the face of this kind of evidence, the schools themselves have come under attack. In effect, those who blame the schools for low achievement of poor children are saying, "We spend money on schools, buy books, provide equipment, pay good salaries—why aren't the schools doing their job?" They see children's failure to be one of teaching, not learning. Therefore they also ask, "Why haven't teachers been better trained? Why are so many unable to understand children from backgrounds other than their own?"

To these critics, the teacher's inability to comprehend the circumstances of the poor and minority groups represents a lack of sympathy for the child and his problems. They see it as the teacher's ineptness in communicating with children and general failure to help them learn about and relate to the larger society. They grant the possibility that some children from low-income families have learning problems, are poorly disciplined, and have had little practice with abstraction. But to them this does not explain why many teachers are ignorant of the needs of these children, perceive poorly the abilities the children do bring to school and have not acquired the skills needed to teach them.

FIGURE 5–3   PICTURE BOOKS, SONGS, AND STORIES USED IN SCHOOL CAN REFLECT AN UNREALISTIC LIFE

The picture books, texts, stories and songs used in the early grades show a life and a people far removed from the world experienced by children who live in slums, on sharecropper farms, or in migrant work camps. Poor children's imaginations encompass giants and fairies, talking animals and tug boats, but fail to respond to a life for boys and girls that is shown to consist of:

. . . happy, neat, wealthy white people whose intact and loving families live only in clean, grassy suburbs. . . . and the most serious crises they have to face are the loss of the family pet or who in the household will have the use of the car (Fantini and Weinstein, 1968, p. 133).

Discontent with teaching has led to demands for schools oriented to ethnic and ghetto cultures, new ways of teaching and better teacher training. Those who blame the schools sometimes give the impression that the best solution is to do away with the entire system and start anew. Their reform movement is less formal and less coordinated, perhaps, than some of the others, but the voices of their representatives are clearly heard.

Society as the Locus of the Problem: The Destructive System Model   Disadvantage is inherent in a highly differentiated social system such as that in the United States. In turn, the disadvantages incurred affect individual cognitive activity and achievement. Those who view the social structure as being responsible for the many school failures among poor children see socio-economic disadvantage, combined with discrimination, as placing individuals in situations which permit little latitude for choice or comparison. For example, children are expected to comply with rules without explanation, just as parents themselves must comply with seemingly arbitrary decisions made for them by institutions on which they are dependent—the housing authority, medical service, or school board. Alternatives and reasons are not given or thought necessary, and decisions are often based simply on expediency or availability.

Since the mother has few chances to evaluate or choose among alternatives in her own life, she is not likely to provide situations in which the child is encouraged to compare, to select or to think for himself. As a consequence, the cognitive operations (ability to plan, categorize, select, order, etc.) needed for success in public school are less often stimulated in children of the poor.

A graphic expression of this viewpoint appears in Lyford's article (*op. cit.*, p. 53):

> One of the tidal facts that has impressed me most is the continual waste and loss of human life that is taking place in our city. I am not talking about the murders or assaults that have terrified most of the people I know—poor people, middle-class people, well-to-do people. I am talking about the destruction of children. Of the enormous number of crimes that take place in the city, the largest amount and the most terrible are committed against children. Only a small portion of these crimes have to do with outright physical abuse. From the time tens of thousands of newborn infants are removed from the hospital, they become subjected to what I call "the process." That is, they are introduced to a style of existence that eventually cripples or destroys huge numbers of them, and occasionally other people with whom they have come in contact. . . . . The children who do survive this tempering process become adults, but in my neighborhood an adult is a dead child.

And again (*op. cit.*, p. 55):

> What has happened is that we are in the middle of a system that makes the "process" inevitable; that requires more and more human beings in various parts of our country—Appalachia, Selma, Watts—to grow up to be dead children, or, as some people put it, welfare babies. The system I am talking about is turning more and more of our resources away from the nurture of human life and into the destruction of it.

If the structure of modern American society contributes to school failure, so also does discrimination against minorities. Discrimination affects learning and cognition by creating a sense of incompetence and low efficacy, and consequently an unwillingness to be assertive in the environment.

President Johnson's public acknowledgment of the already known discrepancy in school achievement between middle-class children and those from low-income families stimulated broader interest and public funding to deal with this problem. Although all of the above assumptions have some validity, planners who began to develop programs often preferred one to the exclusion of others. Obviously, decisions as to whether the root of the problem lies in the child, the family, the school, society, or in some combination, determined the types of programs of intervention chosen.

APPROACHES TO EDUCATIONAL INTERVENTION

One of the features of programs developed in response to the educational needs of low-income and minority children is that they were more focused to the needs of a particular part of the population than had generally been true in the past. Different conceptions of the problem, however, gave rise to a variety of approaches. Some of these are instructional programs in the usual sense; others are more general strategies for changing the environment in various ways or attacking the educational problem in a supposedly more effective way.

Strategies of educational intervention tend to fall into the following broad categories:

1. Enriching the cultural and educational environment
2. Engineering an instructional program
3. Involving parents in the educational process
4. Giving communities greater control over the school
5. Beginning instruction at earlier ages

Enriching the Cultural and Educational Environment

Perhaps the most popular and extensive educational effort has been in response to the concept of cumulative deficit. The idea that children's cognitive experiences can be incomplete—that children need exposure to the elements of a wider (middle-class) society to help raise their performance in school—excited the imagination of many educators. In an enrichment program, therefore, children engage in numerous cultural and social activities and the classroom environment provides an opportunity for the development of language and cognitive skills.

Engineering an Instructional Program

Another early response was that which led to a highly engineered environment. Research had shown that disadvantaged children, even before they reach school age, are behind in a number of the verbal and cognitive skills needed for school success. Selecting specific and significant educational objectives and gearing the teaching effort explicitly to their attainment seemed to some to offer the hope that inequality might be overcome. Accordingly, instead of permitting children in nursery school to engage in

Introducing "I Don't Know" Statements

These are valuable because they help the children articulate what they know and what they do not know about an object. The "I don't know" statement sets the stage for deductive processes that require more than a single step.

Show the children two juice cans, both at room temperature. Hold one up and ask, "Is this can cold?" If a child offers an answer, explain; "You are guessing. You don't know that this can is cold. How can you tell? You have to touch it."

Let the children feel the can and determine that it is not cold. The second can is introduced unopened, and the procedure is repeated.

The children are likely to assume that this one must be cold. "You are guessing. Do you know? Did you touch it? . . . No. You don't know. Say, 'I don't know.' Say it."

from C. Bereiter and S. Engelmann, *Teaching Disadvantaged Children in the Preschool,* Prentice-Hall, Inc., 1966, p. 149.

---

whatever catches their interest, they are taught systematically, in an engineered program. The exact behavior desired and the sequences for achieving the objectives are defined and structured, whether the task is to identify a color, name a letter, describe a space relationship or respond, "I don't know." Project directors set up an environment to elicit the desired behavior and work out a reinforcement schedule. Teachers are then trained to teach according to techniques specified in the program.

This approach to intervention proceeds from a belief that children who are behind the norm in school-related learning need to be given more than the opportunity to learn. In effect, they need a kind of forced feeding of the skills and concepts which will best serve them in the school experience and enable them to begin formal schooling with an ability equal to that of middle-class children. From this point of view have come a number of engineered programs as well as considerable controversy.

Involving Parents in the Educational Process

Involving parents was discussed in Chapter 3 and no attempt will be made here to develop further the ramifications of this subject. However, one point needs emphasis regarding parent involvement as an approach to intervention.

Research shows maternal behavior to be influential in children's early cognitive and academic development. The ways mothers talk to their children and develop their language skills, the ways they attend to and interact with children's activities, the expectations they have for their children and the control techniques they exercise have a bearing on school achievement. This suggests that success in public school depends on far more than the few hours a day spent in a nursery school regardless of the level of teaching, the ratio of teachers to children, or the kind of program offered. If it is to be lasting, cognitive development seems to require reinforcement beyond that which the school can give. Family support which results in consistency between what goes on at home and in the classroom is essential. Such a relationship not only improves the child's orientation toward school, but also helps the mother see her importance as an educator.

On the whole, parents are interested in the education of their children. When this interest is translated into active support of the school, it reinforces the goals of the school by helping children develop positive attitudes toward themselves and toward learning. In family-oriented programs, decisions as to what is to be done for the child and how to do it remain the responsibility of the school, even though the impact on the child is made primarily in the home by the parents.

Giving Communities Greater Control over the School

Those who conclude that the core of the educational problem is in the failure of the schools and the dominant society, believe that it is not sufficient to concentrate on reforming instructional programs and the curriculum. Their conviction leads to quite different approaches to educational intervention—approaches which are aimed not only at the child and his learning but also at the social and institutional context in which he learns. Accordingly, there have been vigorous attempts recently to involve parents as power groups and to shift responsibility for the school directly to the local community.

This feeling is especially intense in ethnic communities. Many members of ethnic groups feel, with considerable justification, that they have been ignored in the formulation of educational policy. Many of today's minority groups not only see their cultural ways as "right" for their children, but they resent the omission in the curriculum of the contributions made by ethnic leaders to the development and well-being of the country. When the schools fail to take into account the important values of children from different backgrounds and fail to offer programs relevant to their cultures, the families and community leaders quite naturally blame the schools for their children's failure to succeed.[2]

In recent years, therefore, a general strategy of shifting responsibility and power for decision-making from the schools to organizations within the community has been gaining strength. A community-oriented program sees the community as exercising specific influence and control in decisions concerning the hiring and firing of school personnel, the choice of curriculum, and the setting of policy as to how the school shall be run.

This approach to education can bring about many changes:

1. People called upon to make decisions about hiring and firing soon develop a sense of power.

---

[2] See specific example regarding test bias, Chapter 10, p. 304.

2. People responsible for deciding what children are to learn and the means to be used develop a sense of control.
3. People in charge of anything as complex and important as a school acquire status in their own eyes and in the eyes of the community.

In addition, children recognize and respond to their parents' positive orientation to the school with a greater commitment to education. Although the goals of various approaches to education may be alike—that is, the socialization and welfare of children—the political and social consequences of community control are unique.

Beginning Instruction at Earlier Ages

Because one of the most obvious measures of school failure in ghetto and poverty areas is the high rate of dropout in secondary school, some of the first efforts at educational intervention involved work with adolescents. This proved relatively ineffective, however, and attention was turned to programs for children in the elementary grades. Success in these measures was not spectacular, and many scholars became convinced that effort was needed at even earlier levels. Head Start, involving four- and five-year-olds, was a recognition of the importance of learning during the preschool years.

More recently, emphasis is being placed on infancy as the prime time to establish a base for later learning in specific skills and concepts. In addition, Parent-Child Centers —federally funded programs established for children as young as two years—carry with them the notion of specific instruction under the supervision of personnel trained in early childhood education. This is in contrast to the more traditional day care center where the emphasis is simply on caretaking during the time the mother is at work.

THE GROWTH OF PROGRAMS OF EARLY EDUCATION

Recent Developments in Curriculum and Programs

The concentration of research and developmental efforts to create programs particularly effective with children from low-income backgrounds had dissimilar results for preschool children of varying backgrounds. Initially, these were experimental programs or modifications of established programs which had achieved a new popularity, as in the new impetus given curricula based on Montessori's theory and procedures. Although they were designed for disadvantaged children, the principles on which they were based and the imagination that went into their construction made them appropriate for children from a variety of ethnic groups and socio-economic backgrounds.

The energy and interest that were generated by Head Start, as well as the experimental work that preceded this national effort, has taken many forms, most of which are variations on major types of programs. Some were created and used in local schools and received little publicity. The time pressure under which Head Start was organized made innovation necessary, and it is possible that a great deal of the imagination utilized in local programs was not publicly disseminated. Programs with a definite form, practice and philosophy do not easily develop, and it was the combined efforts and funds of national educational projects that accelerated the emergence of special curricula and made them more widely accessible.

It seems likely that future historians of early education will regard Operation Head Start and Project Follow Through as the two major forces responsible for the growth of differentiated programs of early education in the sixties and seventies. Project Follow Through came about as an attempt to continue into the early grades the educational advantages of Head Start. It provided an opportunity to develop specific programs for children in the early grades from low-income communities.

At the invitation of the U.S. Office of Education, professionals who were working on experimental curricula and programs for young children were asked to develop these for kindergarten and the primary grades. The resulting programs were implemented under their supervision and "sponsorship" in schools in various parts of the country, located in communities representing several different ethnic groups. The expansion and visibility of early education also stimulated the development of other approaches which later joined Follow Through as sponsored projects. The curricula and instructional methods of Follow Through, which were more specific and elaborate than most available preschool programs, were adapted to age levels included in Head Start. This planned continuity between the two programs reduced the traditional gap between the "preschool" and the school curricula.

A part of the total Follow Through effort was an evaluation of the relative effectiveness of different approaches and curricula components. The results of this evaluation, not yet announced, will be of great interest to professionals in the field and will have a significant impact on the future of the programs involved—an impact which the teacher will have to consider carefully in light of her own and her school's objectives. For example, results of one program may show impressive changes on one kind of behavior (number skills, letter recognition, IQ, etc.); others may be more effective in promoting affective and social development.

Publicity about evaluation programs through the mass media often simplifies and even distorts what a program has accomplished. *Announcements of evaluation results, therefore, should be examined with skepticism and great care* (see Chapter 10).

It is not possible to describe all the new and modified programs of early education which were inspired by the wave of enthusiasm of the sixties, but some of the prominent examples will indicate the variety in point of view and practice that is available. The summaries cover basic issues in philosophy and implementation but do not attempt to describe parent community involvement or in-service teacher training, all of which are specified and employed to different degrees in each program. Most of these programs have some objectives in common but differ in emphasis and manner of implementation. Some are more widely known and may be identified by the sponsor's name.

SOME ILLUSTRATIVE PROGRAMS[3]

THE TUCSON EARLY EDUCATION MODEL

Marie Hughes and Ronald E. Henderson
*Arizona Center for Early Childhood Education,
College of Education, University of Arizona
Tucson, Arizona*

Rationale and Objectives

Originally designed for Mexican-American children. Based on belief that children bring different sets of attitudes and skills to school. Must begin from where they are. Language and cognitive skills, positive attitudes toward school, and societal arts and skills are stressed.

Description and Implementation

Frequent opportunities for one-to-one adult-child interaction, modeling (imitation), reinforcement through praise, attention, etc.; generalization of curriculum skills through frequent field trips and extension of the learning environment.

Teachers learn to use the experiential backgrounds of the pupils.

No demands are made on the child to learn. The physical environment is organized "to facilitate interaction between the child and his environment, between the child and his peers, and between the child and adults in the classroom." The child is given opportunity to engage in a variety of behaviors and the teacher encourages those which are "congruent with her educational aims."

---

[3] Up-to-date information about Head Start and Follow Through programs as well as for more recent materials may be obtained from Follow Through Program, U.S. Office of Education, 400 Maryland Avenue, S.W., Washington, D.C., 20202 or The Office of Child Development, Department of Health, Education and Welfare, Washington, D.C. Other sources include Maccoby, E. E. & Zellner, M. *Experiments in Primary Education: Aspects of Project Follow Through.* New York: Harcourt Brace Jovanovich, Inc., 1970; and the ERIC Clearing House for Early Education, College of Education, University of Illinois, Urbana, Illinois. In the descriptions of programs in this section, quotes are taken from *Follow Through Program Approaches,* 1969.

BEHAVIOR ANALYSIS MODEL

Don Bushell, Jr.
Department of Human Development
University of Kansas
Lawrence, Kansas

Rationale and Objectives

For children of poverty, success or failure in school is often judged by middle-class standards. These children do not have the same skills as suburban children, nor are they motivated by the same kinds of reinforcers. There are basic skills essential for success in the classroom. This program seeks to identify and define precisely the necessary academic and social skills and use effective reinforcement procedures to teach these skills.

Description and Implementation

Uses systematic reinforcement through a token system. Activities which the children prefer, such as movies, records, recess, favorite materials, are identified for each classroom. Children earn tokens to buy these special events as a direct result of their own achievement. "For example, a recess might cost 20, and the correct solutions to math problems could then be exchanged for recess;..." "...the child makes the decision concerning when and for what he shall exchange his tokens. It is the teacher's responsibility to make sure that events are available which are important to the child." The tokens also "provide a reminder to the teacher to give her attention to *all* children", and especially to question her teaching techniques with those who are not earning many tokens.

THE RESPONSIVE MODEL

Glen Nimnicht
Far West Laboratory for Research and Development
Berkeley, California

Rationale and Objectives

"The major objective... is to begin an educational process that will produce adults who have both the ability to solve unique problems and the self-confidence to tackle them." "The program is called *responsive* because it stresses responding to children rather than having them respond to you. Three principles support this approach:
1. Children learn at different rates
2. Children learn in different ways
3. Children learn best when they are interested in what they are learning"

"Problem solving is the essence of learning" and the child "better remembers what he discovers for himself." The program emphasizes "learning how to learn rather than learning specific content." This program is based on intrinsic motivation and the development of positive self-concept.

Description and Implementation

The classroom is designed and equipped so that the child has many opportunities to explore and experiment with materials which provide him with immediate feed-back and which help him make a series of "interconnected discoveries about his physical and social world."

"The essential satisfaction should come from the activity and not from something not built into the experience itself." Examples of self-correcting toys are nesting cups, puzzles and depth cylinders.

The class is equipped with (among other things) a "learning (typing) booth" in which the child is invited by the adult booth attendant to play each day. He is allowed to explore the electric typewriter freely while the attendant names the symbols and letters he strikes. This free exploration leads to transcription and dictation of stories and finally to the child transcribing his own stories.

THE FLORIDA PARENT EDUCATION MODEL

Ira Gordon
Institute for Development of Human Resources
College of Education
University of Florida
Gainesville, Florida

Rationale and Objectives

The reason disadvantaged children fail in school is because their mothers are too involved with failure themselves to provide adequate models. Therefore, if a program of intervention is to succeed, education must start early and it must start in the home. Both home and school must engage in curriculum development.

Description and Implementation

One or two mothers are trained to work as aides with each classroom. These parent aides also pay periodic visits (preferably once a week) to the homes of the children to teach the mothers tasks which have been devised in school. Much language is used to accompany the child's activities in order to help him learn to classify and label. Much of the curriculum is based on Piagetian type tasks.

Effective development of the curriculum requires very careful observation of home and school behaviors on the part of aides and parent educators.

COGNITIVELY ORIENTED MODEL

David P. Weikart
High/Scope Educational Research Foundation
Ypsilanti, Michigan

Rationale and Objectives

This is a cognitively oriented program based on the belief that "the *process* of education is the most important element in achieving success in educational programming, not the specific curriculum employed." This process of educational reform is dependent on the teacher for planning and implementation, and on a carefully structured program for teaching "cognitive habits and educational attitudes."

Description and Implementation

"While the project provides general guides toward major curriculum goals, it is the teacher's responsibility to make detailed lesson plans so that the general goals will be appropriate to her class . . ." ". . . learning objectives are stated in terms of behavioral goals which describe the behavior expected from the child as a result of the learning activity . . . The sequence is always from the simple to the complex, from the concrete to the abstract."

INSTRUCTIONAL GAMES—INDEPENDENT LEARNER APPROACH (NYU MODEL)

Lassar G. Gotkin[4]
School of Education, Institute for Developmental Studies
New York University, New York, New York

Rationale and Objectives

Children from lower class backgrounds display a unique style or "rhythm" in their culture. This program uses games based on the principles of programed instruction. The games are sequenced in complexity so each child can proceed at his own rate. These provide opportunities for independent learning and leadership roles.

Description and Implementation

A "Quiet Work Time" is set aside at the beginning of the school day for instructional games. The mastery of materials stressing perceptual, verbal and conceptual skills "requires some privacy, orderliness in the room and a moderate noise level." Materials and activities which lead to noise-making are eliminated at this time of the day, not because of any opposition to those activities (e.g. block play), but only to avoid noise and distractions. "In order to establish a Quiet Work Time, the teacher must help the children develop and internalize the habits of working either independently or in small groups for extended periods of time, and of working relatively quietly. At the outset we have relied heavily on puzzles and building materials which can be used with a minimum of direction or instruction." (Small table toys, plastic linking blocks, etc.). As children become accustomed to the established period, games of a more conceptual nature are introduced, such as "What's Missing," which requires the children to figure out which picture from a matrix has been removed while their eyes are closed.

---

[4] Deceased, 1971. Program now directed by Don Wolff.

ENGELMANN-BECKER PROGRAM
THE SYSTEMATIC USE OF BEHAVIORAL PRINCIPLES

Wesley C. Becker & Siegfried Engelmann
University of Oregon
Eugene, Oregon

Rationale and Objectives

"Culturally and economically deprived children have lived under conditions which have failed to build skills which would allow them to progress at a 'normal' rate with typical group teaching methods and approaches to curricula." First priority in the classroom is given to accelerated acquisition of the necessary skills in language, reading, writing and arithmetic. Teaching strategies are based on the Bereiter-Engelmann Programs "premised on the belief that every child can achieve well in the academic arena if he receives adequate instruction. The instruction has to be designed so that the child learns at a faster rate than he would learn in a more traditional setting."

Description and Implementation

Children are placed in small groups (5 to 10) according to ability. The format "(1) requires a far greater number of responses from the child. (2) uses systematic reinforcement. (3) programs the material so that the child works on the essentials that are needed for future tasks."

Teachers reinforce correct responses by giving extrinsic rewards such as a cookie until the child learns to become motivated through praise. Tasks are taught with much repetition, rapid fire drill and clapping to accentuate the rhythm of language patterns.

BANK STREET APPROACH

Elizabeth C. Gilkeson & Herbert Zimiles
*Bank Street College of Education
New York, New York*

Rationale and Objectives

This program focuses on the development of the "whole child" . . . "to organize education for 'disadvantaged' children as remediation of 'deficits' or to focus solely upon the development of narrowly defined intellectual skills is self-defeating. Such definitions may even perpetuate more permanent damage by depriving these children of precisely those opportunities they need to develop active, thinking, creative ways of coping with the real problems of our culture." The child's mastery of skills and his total development are interrelated. He integrates his knowledge and feelings through play.

Description and Implementation

The environment is planned to provide maximum opportunity for exploration and discovery. The teacher is a knowledgeable, trustworthy person the children can count on. "She introduces central themes of study or activities which will help the children to become sensitized to the world around them. First, themes are elaborated from the planned environment of the classroom (organizing chores, caring for pets and plants, cooking, building, etc.) then from those aspects of the community in which the children can see relationships, solve problems and use their skills (food marketing, traffic control, sources of water, etc.). She encourages direct observations of the important aspects of the environment through a wide range of relevant field trips. The teacher provides systematic instruction for the development of mastery, but the vitality of classroom life for children and their own investment in that life exert direct influence upon their motivation to learn."

THE COMMUNITY CONTROLLED SCHOOL[5]

Rationale and Objectives

Public schools represent middle-class standards and therefore do not succeed in educating children from poor families. The solution is not to blame the child, but to change the relationship between school and community in order to make the school more responsive to the real needs of the families they serve.

Parents should have more to say about what they think is good for their children. In this way, a community controlled school will break down "the disjunction between home and school—a child's sense that what he does at home is not approved in school, and vice-versa." Community control can help prevent expressions of negative feelings by teachers as well as create a positive attitude toward different cultures. Perhaps the most important aspect of community control is that the children "see their parents and neighbors, people of their own race and language playing an important role in the daily life of their school."

Description and Implementation

The community should be involved in planning and decision making at the earliest possible moment. People are invited through existing organizations and publicity to attend initial information meetings where ad hoc committees are established. Selection of the kind of curriculum is then left up to community groups that emerge. A continuing community organization coordinates community resources to participate in the educational process to make education more relevant. The community is kept informed about the educational program and innovations and families participate in policy decisions. Community people are engaged as paid staff members and the school buildings are utilized as resources for the total community.

---

[5] No single program is referred to as an example because there are many schools throughout the country operating under this philosophy.

PRIMARY EDUCATION PROJECT

Lauren B. Resnick
Learning Research and Development Center
University of Pittsburgh, Pittsburgh, Pennsylvania

Rationale and Objectives

Children learn through active involvement, self-direction and at their own rate. Instruction should be adapted to the individual learner; the learner should play a major role in evaluation of his own progress. In order to achieve optimum learning, the curriculum must include the following: (1) attending skills (listening, following directions, etc.) (2) perceptual-motor skills (large and small muscle, visual and auditory skills) (3) conceptual-linguistic skills (reasoning, classifying, language, etc.)

In order to teach these skills, each child should be tested carefully to determine which skills he possesses. The objectives must be clearly defined and the tasks carefully sequenced.

Description and Implementation

A hierarchy of skills is specified for each level of learning. Diagnostic tests are administered to determine where each child stands and tasks which have been designed to teach the desired skills at the child's level are then given by the teacher. The child learns from interaction with the materials and the teacher plays a supportive, reinforcing role. The diagnostic test results enable the teacher to provide the correct materials for each child.

UNDERLYING ASSUMPTIONS OF PROGRAMS

A number of assumptions about teaching and learning underlie all contemporary programs of early education intended for low-income children. Some of these common views are described below.

Education must begin at the level of the children's abilities. Because what children learn depends largely upon what they already know, it is important to determine where a child "is" along the continuum of growth and development when setting up a program of early education. This is, of course, not a new idea. Maria Montessori, in her focus on individual learning, established procedures for evaluating the ability level of children in her classes so that instruction could begin with the child's edge of mastery. This basic principle of learning and motivation appears in many forms, especially in individualized pupil instructional programs which plan sequences of learning steps which build on one another. Diagnostic examination to assess levels of mastery can provide the detailed information needed to determine children's capabilities. There are many ways to carry out this sort of assessment, some of which are highly informal and impressionistic, others formal and systematic. The principle, however, is that teaching most effectively proceeds from what a child already knows.

Teaching should be adapted to the needs of the individual child. No matter how similar the experiences or endowment of a group of children, as individuals they differ greatly. Each will have his own store of skills, his own special interests and talents, his own worries about achievement. Therefore, in order to be effective, teaching must be individualized to a larger degree than is presently accomplished in most classrooms.

A child learns best when motivated. Exposing a child to numerous experiences, providing him with a wide variety of materials, or giving him the opportunity to participate in numerous activities, alone or in a group, does not always mean a child will learn what you want him to, or be willing to learn at all. However attractive the environment from the teacher's viewpoint, many children need other stimulation; they require special direction in the form of a teacher's interest and enthusiasm, and they need help in finding out where and how to start, before they are capable of proceeding alone. Some children respond to rewards such as stars on a chart, a cookie or sweet, or special privilege. For others, social approval is sufficient. During the early stages, at least, choosing a technique that engages the child may be more important than utilizing one because it meets with universal or personal approval.

Children must learn the role of pupil in order to succeed in school. Behavior appropriate to the role of pupil includes the ability to pay attention, to follow directions, to understand what the teacher expects of him, to work in groups, and to be able to take the initiative in learning situations rather than waiting passively for things to be done for him and explained to him. His role as pupil also requires that he avoid disruptive behavior, noise, fighting, teasing, shouting, or conversely, withdrawing or refusing to participate. To become a successful learner, the child must be able to master tasks as well as cognitive materials.

Disadvantaged children can acquire school-related skills and concepts. Because of their record of low scores *on the average* compared with those of middle-class children, children from low-income backgrounds have sometimes been thought less capable of doing satisfactory school work. When children do not learn, however, the fault may be in the materials or the techniques of teaching, rather than in the children. Once dimensions of "readiness" have been ascertained, and subject matter has been chosen to correspond with their level, large numbers of disadvantaged children show themselves to be apt learners. It would seem that the learning capacity of these children has been grossly underestimated. The task may be to engage their interest and show them that learning is possible.

ISSUES THAT DIFFERENTIATE PROGRAMS

Early educators dealt in various ways with issues involved in preschool education and today's programs, whether innovative or based on old forms, take a stand on many of the same issues. These issues themselves provide categories by which programs can be classified or defined. The name, size or location of a school tells very little about what its staff intends to do for children. The stand a school takes on various basic issues, however, immediately gives a prospective teacher an idea of its philosophy and the direction her teaching will be expected to take. It helps answer the questions, "What kind of program is it?" and "What can be accomplished by working in this program instead of another?"

Structured vs. Unstructured Curriculum

When trying to understand a program, one way is to determine to what extent and in what ways it is structured.

The term *structure,* as applied to curriculum, is frequently used in discussions of early educational programs, but it means different things to different people. Most frequently, perhaps, it brings images of a rigidly disciplined, prearranged, organized pattern of ac-

FIGURE 5-4 WHAT KIND OF SCHOOL? WHAT DO THEY TEACH?

162 TEACHERS OF YOUNG CHILDREN

tivities in which the teacher directs the components of the daily routine. "Unstructured" may suggest free play and other activities which are initiated by the child and reflect his own preferences and interests. In general, traditional programs are thought of as having less structure (and being less "cognitively" oriented) than some of the newer, innovative programs.

Some early educators had firm views on this subject. Pestalozzi (1746–1827) argued that teaching should proceed not from structured programs but from the unfolding of the child's natural interest and capability. Comenius (1592–1670), on the other hand, emphasized the importance of systematic early training and believed that all knowledge could and should be introduced early and systematically. Rousseau (1712–1778) was relaxed about the problem—he maintained that children would learn to read and write in due time according to their own inclination.

The term "structure" may have a negative connotation to some, because it suggests the image of mechanical, insensitive rigidity. This is only one meaning of the term and perhaps not the most significant one.

Structure—in terms of the arrangement of learning experiences—exists in two forms: 1) a constant *awareness in the teacher's mind* of an underlying design to a total curriculum, or 2) a prearranged *sequencing of materials for presentation* to the child.

In the first form, the teacher keeps in mind overall goals which she uses to help organize and provide learning experiences for the child. The sequence of presentation of this underlying curriculum has not been arranged. (A casual observer might think it unstructured.) The teacher makes constant use of incidental experiences to provide teaching situations. When a child comments about her dress, for example, she may help him label colors, count buttons, and the like.

In the second form, the structure lies in the arrangement and presentation of information. This kind of structure may be highly similar from school to school and can easily be programed and used somewhat like a script. The most highly structured programs of this form utilize definite lesson plans in which one "lesson" is presented and presumably mastered before the next is introduced.

A truly unstructured program in our view, is one in which *neither* is the implicit curriculum in the teacher's mind *nor* is the presentation organized and thought out. There is no statement of objectives in behavioral terms. Consequently, neither the physical nor the human environment has a design and the program lacks specified objectives. In programs of early education for children whose educational opportunities are likely to be limited, this is unacceptable no matter how skillfully a teacher might entertain her class and keep them interested and well behaved.

```
Name of Program_____

Location_____ Date_____

        STRUCTURED  _____  UNSTRUCTURED


Cognitive  [_____]      Instruction [_____]
Affective  [_____]      Discovery   [_____]
           Little  Some  Much                  Little  Some  Much


Content    [_____]      Extrinsic   [_____]
Process    [_____]      Intrinsic   [_____]
           Little  Some  Much                  Little  Some  Much
```

FIGURE 5-5 RATING SCALES FOR PROGRAMS OF EARLY EDUCATION

In some instances, the importance of structure in the presentation of materials has been overemphasized and the importance of structure in the teacher's mind has been neglected. A teacher who is able to use spontaneous experiences in the classroom to help teach concepts, and who knows how to serve as a model for the children, may be very effective even though the learning situation itself has not been preprogramed.

Proponents of programs which are structured both in their underlying design and in the way of presentation to the child argue that learning principles which such programs incorporate, such as properly timed rewards, make for more effective and efficient learning. Perhaps something can be said for giving an inexperienced teacher a script which relieves her of some of the responsibility for planning the children's learning experiences. It is more desirable, however, for teachers to have an underlying curriculum in their interaction with children. The most effective teacher can make use of a structured presentation of materials when this suits her purposes and can also utilize spontaneous opportunities to accomplish her goals.

Perhaps the real issue is whether the teacher is in charge of learning situations in the classroom, or whether decisions are made by some group who provides her and the classroom with predetermined educational experiences. A script strictly adhered to is better than nothing but not as desirable as a creative teacher with a curriculum in mind.

In gaining experience in evaluating the degree and kind of structure in a curriculum, it may be helpful to use a crude rating scale, similar to the one illustrated in Figure 5-5.

Depending upon the degree to which a program is structured, its staff emphasizes certain kinds of teaching more than others and has specific goals and techniques. Evaluating a curriculum on each of the following dimensions adds perspective to the specific type of program.

Cognitive Skills	vs.	Affective Skills
Content	vs.	Process
Learn by Instruction	vs.	Learn by Discovery
Extrinsic Motivation	vs.	Intrinsic Motivation

WHEN CONTENT IS STRESSED	WHEN PROCESS IS STRESSED
Names of letters of the alphabet	Initiative in tackling problems
Identification of geometric shapes	Inquiry skills
Numbers and their ordering	Problem solving skills
Specific labels	Skills in carrying on a discussion and exploring meanings
Discrimination of speech sounds	
Perceptual discrimination	Consideration of alternative solutions
Self-concepts (name, relationship in family . . .)	Obtaining of information

TABLE 5–1 EXAMPLES OF SKILLS TAUGHT IN CONTENT- AND PROCESS-ORIENTED PROGRAMS

(The order is not significant.) The two poles of each of these dimensions are not mutually exclusive. A program can teach both cognitive and affective skills, can emphasize content in one area and process in another. Usually, however, emphasis is placed more toward one side of the dimension than another. Where a program fits in regard to these dimensions can often be assessed by observation (and perhaps a few questions) if one knows what to look for.

Cognitive Skills vs. Affective Skills

Programs which emphasize development of *cognitive skills* are likely to stress teaching of language, shape, color, concepts and prereading skills. They may be prepared to teach reading itself. The staff will see that children work with numbers and number concepts. Children's speech habits will be closely attended and frequently assessed. In short, the teaching will concentrate on a curriculum which makes it possible for children to move more easily into the primary grades.

At the other end of this dimension a school will place primary emphasis on developing the child's *affective skills*. Teachers in this kind of program spend a major portion of their time helping children build positive self-esteem, seeing that they gain confidence in themselves and in their ability to learn and interact with them on a personal level. Their primary concern is with humanistic qualities. Most programs fall somewhere between these two extremes, emphasizing both to some degree.

Content vs. Process

Some preschool teachers believe they should stress content in their programs by teaching specific information and academic skills. Others are less concerned with content, stressing instead the importance of *process*. Those who concentrate on content think in terms of what is learned and try to make sure that preschool children acquire skills and concepts and a store of specific knowledge. Those who focus attention on process think in terms of teaching how to learn. They attempt to start the young child on his way to becoming self-sufficient and autonomous in the school setting, and able to find and use information on his own initiative. In a program that emphasizes process, the teacher assumes it is more important to know how to solve problems than to store specific knowledge in one's memory, however efficient that memory might be.

These objectives are not contradictory and elements of both are found in many preschool programs. The teacher's having her own ideas about the importance of content and process is essential as she plans curriculum and makes decisions on how best to achieve the ends she has in mind.

Planned Instruction vs. Self Discovery

A third dimension along which programs group themselves concerns how learning and teaching can best take place. Do children learn best from specific instruction or by discovery? Is it better to give children information deliberately or to encourage them to find out what they are expected to know?

This is a question on which early educators had a great deal to say. Froebel (1782–1852), the founder of the kindergarten, argued that the child is the source of his own curriculum and that the teacher merely follows. In his view, learning takes place through following one's interests. He did, however, see the need for children to be presented with an orderly series of phenomena which challenged and stimulated mental activity and produced inner organization and integration, an idea developed in greatly elaborated form by Piaget (1952). In contrast to Comenius' position that knowledge should be introduced in systematic fashion was Rousseau's proposition that everything one learns should come from within, and that the child should be allowed to acquire knowledge for himself and acquire a power to learn on his own.

Two modern psychological theories—the learning theory associated with the American psychologist B. F. Skinner and the cognitive developmental theory based on Piaget's work—have widely influenced the more recent answers to this question but have by no means resolved the apparent difference in point of view. Skinnerians emphasize the acquisition of knowledge through instruction, while Piagetians stress the discovery-developmental method.

The Skinnerian holds that the goal of education is to produce specific behavioral changes. School programs based on this theory begin by determining the specific behaviors desired and proceed by building up the child's repertoire of responses one at a time. For example, in learning to write his name, a child would first need to know something about writing materials and their uses as well as the shape and sequence of certain letters. A child's responses are regulated by stimuli which the teacher introduces in a planned sequence. The process by which a child thinks is immaterial according to this view, since it deals only with what can be observed and controlled.

The Piagetian sees early learning as a matter of building cognitive structures in the child's mind. Rather than being governed by external stimuli, it is the child himself who controls stimuli. Through his own experience (discovery) "structures" emerge in his mind which guide further perception and the acquisition of concepts. The child can learn only if he has already built up the store of structures needed to master a new task. According to Piaget, children make their own contributions to the learning process. Therefore, teachers need to provide materials that serve the child's desire to see how new information compares with his present knowledge and concepts and permit him to revise his ideas through examination and questioning. Only by changing internal structures does the child progress from one state to the next and so acquire new learning.

Because of the emphasis placed on the developmental nature of learning and its reliance on maturation, critics of Piaget's theory claim it does not permit teaching, that one waits for the child to reach a particular stage in order for learning to take place as the child explores and discovers the world about him. Those who favor the cognitive-developmental view tend to feel that the Skinnerian emphasis on "acquiring responses" is merely rote learning without understanding. To their way of thinking, it follows that without understanding (*i.e.*, relating new materials to what is already known), a child has not really learned.

Proponents of both theories agree that teaching must begin from where a child is when he comes into an educational program. To a Piagetian this means determining what a child is ready to learn by discovering his present level (stage) of understanding and presenting materials appropriate to that stage. A teacher more nearly oriented to Skinner's ideas would attempt to find the child's present or basal level of skill or performance through diagnostic assessment, by using simple appropriate tests or performance measures, and begin the sequence of instruction at the edge of the child's knowledge and ability, without involving the notion of stages.

The effectiveness of both learning theories greatly depends on proper sequencing of tasks, but the Piagetian is inclined to be concerned with the total organization of thought, and the Skinnerian tends to deal with specific step-by-step increments. This latter approach recognizes that teaching a particular skill often depends on prior learning—for example, it is unlikely that a child could be taught the concept of equivalent sets without knowing how to do one-to-one matching—but the Skinnerian feels that once started, a child can be taken step-by-step through a well designed learning sequence, regardless of "stage of readiness."

Extrinsic vs. Intrinsic Motivation

At some level, all educational programs are based on assumptions about what it is that stimulates learning and makes the acquisition of skill and knowledge a rewarding experience. There are several quite different conceptions about the motivational processes involved in learning and how they can be used to develop effective teaching procedures. There is not disagreement, of course, that children learn best when they are engaged in the task and activities of the curriculum; the disagreement comes in deciding how best to arouse and maintain their interest.

At one end of this second dimension are programs (usually academically oriented) which emphasize the value of *extrinsic motivation*. Those who emphasize its use do not

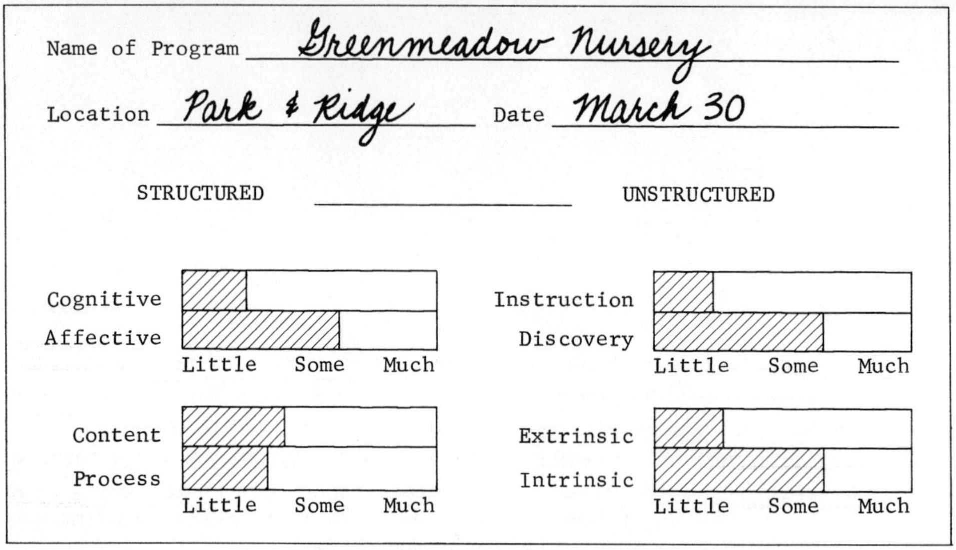

Name of Program __Greenmeadow Nursery__

Location __Park & Ridge__ Date __March 30__

```
        STRUCTURED                          UNSTRUCTURED
```

Cognitive
Affective
  Little Some Much

Instruction
Discovery
  Little Some Much

Content
Process
  Little Some Much

Extrinsic
Intrinsic
  Little Some Much

FIGURE 5-6 RATING SCALE OF EMPHASIS IN A PARENTS' CO-OP PROGRAM

deny that children are normally curious and want to learn. They simply feel that children's interest should be aroused and their effort sustained deliberately rather than waiting for evidence of "readiness" or natural desire. In these schools, the teaching includes some kind of tangible reward for the child other than satisfaction from completing the task. Although social reinforcement, such as words of praise and approval, or physical contact (pat, handshake) of some kind, is usually sufficient to keep a child working, in many instances, a more tangible symbol of approval is given. This is often candy, a cooky, raisins, a chip or token of some kind which can be exchanged for special privileges, or a toy or other object desired by the child. Occasionally some difficulty is encountered in deciding on what tangible reinforcers to use. Rewarding one child with a special mark that all can see may be so nonrewarding to all others as to defeat its total, broader purpose. Tokens have been shown to be effective not only in motivating children but also the teachers. The frequency of a teacher's attending individual children and praising performances increases sharply when she has tokens as well as words to give.

At the other end of the dimension of motivation are programs which emphasize the value of intrinsic motivation. These programs are designed on the philosophy that learning and mastery of a new skill are basically satisfying experiences that are not only sufficient to hold interest, but may often be exciting to the child. In such programs, the teacher attempts to use the child's interest in activities and problems to begin the teaching experience. In this way, the mastery of the problem or completion of the task are goals that are set by the child and are themselves interesting and rewarding. One underlying principle of this approach is that mastering a task just slightly beyond the child's present level of ability or knowledge is sufficiently satisfying to make a child willing to continue learning. Tasks too easy fail to hold attention; those too complex are soon abandoned. The things that interest and motivate a child, in this view, are those which fit his present level of competence yet offer a challenge of mastery in which learning for its own sake can take place.

```
Name of Program   Main Street Nursery School
Location   Main & Front Sts.   Date   May 17
```

STRUCTURED ─────────────── UNSTRUCTURED

Cognitive / Affective — Little Some Much
Content / Process — Little Some Much
Instruction / Discovery — Little Some Much
Extrinsic / Intrinsic — Little Some Much

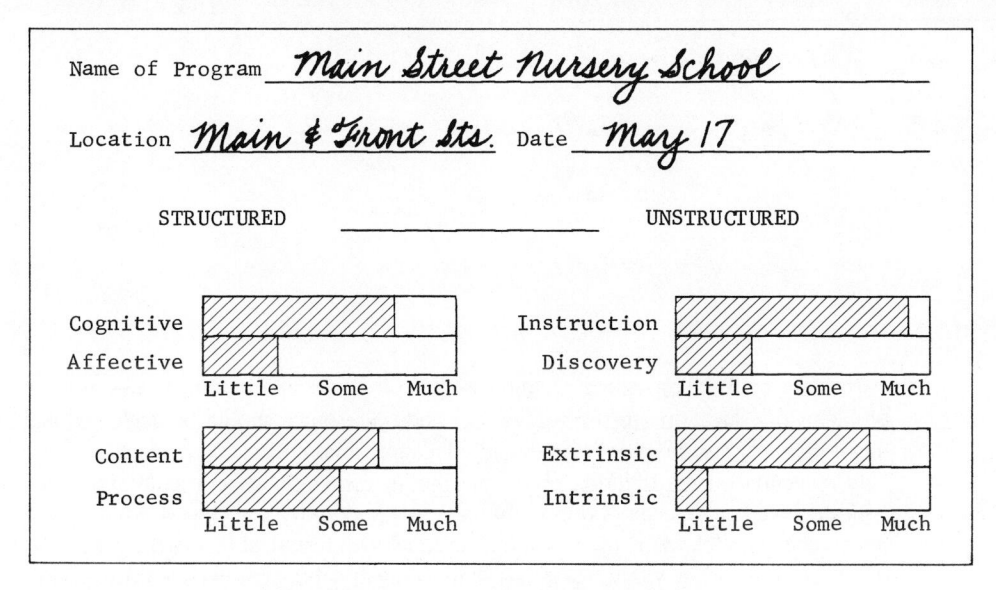

FIGURE 5–7 RATING SCALE OF EMPHASIS IN A COMPENSATORY PROGRAM

How can these dimensions be applied to ongoing programs? Figures 5–6 and 5–7 show two rating cards filled out. One represents the dimensions emphasized in a parent's co-op program, the other a compensatory program for three- and four-year-olds.

Compiling information of this kind from her own observation can give a teacher some idea of what to expect of a particular nursery school and a way of choosing a program in which she feels she can teach most effectively.

There are other dimensions, of course, for viewing a program of early education. Programs vary, for example, in the emphasis placed on diagnostic testing, or parent involvement. But from the standpoint of teaching and learning effectiveness, the major differences are those discussed above. A teacher who is aware of the distinctions underlying various programs can more readily categorize the learning and teaching procedures of a school which she observes or which she hears described.

In every program, no matter how structured, there are occasions when the teacher is on her own or wants to work individually with a child for a specific goal. She must eventually come to her own conclusions as to what technique is most effective for that particular child. Her judgment will be related to the characteristics and needs of the child at that time. By attending to individual differences she can be more effective in her teaching.

Controversy among proponents of the various programs sometimes polarizes feelings and loyalties towards one program or another. Attitudes of this kind may lead to a refusal to look closely enough to see the merits of a competing technique. For example, some teachers see the use of tangible rewards such as tokens or candy as materialistic and mechanical bribery. Perhaps before making judgment, these teachers might seek the opportunity to observe a program where tokens are used effectively. Or they might come to a conclusion about the usefulness of tokens by trying them and determining for themselves the various limitations and advantages. This same suggestion is perhaps worth following by anyone who so favors any single dimension or combination of dimensions over others.

The task of teaching young children is difficult under any circumstances and the problems of education are severe. No tool and no resource should be neglected that might help teachers be more effective in educating children.

In reflecting on the differing points of view in contemporary curricula and in the issues debated by educators during the past two hundred years, one is struck with a remarkable parallel. Many of the same issues on which historical figures disagreed also divide our colleagues today. There is a shared concern about the need to provide conditions for optimal development of the child's resources, especially his mental faculties, but there is a dramatic divergence among them in theory and practice as to how this should be accomplished.

One finds it easy to be skeptical about whether recent findings and program developments have resolved these basic issues in any real sense. Perhaps the persistence of these problems and questions and the sharp disagreement among scholars and researchers means that they all represent different facets of reality and that, if we could gain sufficient perspective we could see that they are not really inconsistent except as we are too simplistic in our own interpretation and application of our knowledge. Perhaps some things are learned best by discovery, some best by direct instruction; it may be that intrinsic motivation may be ideal in one phase or situation and external rewards still are a necessity in another. It is possible that the question is not *whether* these different points of view are true but *when* and in what circumstances they are valid.

We must, perhaps, learn to think and work in a field which is becoming more complex and in which a mastery of our trade requires that we discard the simple solutions and absolute statements and make finer and more subtle discriminations in trying to comprehend the complexities of early learning and teaching. We can then select more freely from a range of techniques and strategies, viewing them as tools to use, not as articles of faith to defend.

REFERENCES

Bereiter, C. and Engelmann, S. *Teaching disadvantaged children in the preschool.* Englewood Cliffs, N.J.: Prentice-Hall, Inc., 1966.

Fantini, M. D. and Weinstein, G. *The disadvantaged: challenge to education.* New York: Harper and Row, 1968.

Follow Through program approaches. Washington, D.C.: Follow Through Program, U.S. Office of Education, March 1969.

Lyford, J. P. In my neighborhood an adult is a dead child. *The Center Magazine,* November 22, 1970, Vol. III, No. 6, 49–56.

Maccoby, E. E. and Zellner, M. *Experiments in primary education*. New York: Harcourt Brace, Jovanovich, Inc., 1970.

Panel on Educational Research and Development. *Innovation and experiment in education*. Washington, D.C.: U.S. Government Printing Office, 1964.

Piaget, J. The origins of intelligence in children. New York: International Universities Press, Inc. 1952.

Pines, M. *Revolution in learning: the years from birth to six*. New York: Harper and Row, 1967.

U.S. Department of Health, Education, and Welfare, Public Health Service. *Malnutrition and learning*, by M. S. Read. Washington, D.C.: National Institute of Child Health and Human Development, 1969.

U.S. President, 1963–1968 (President Lyndon B. Johnson). Annual message to the Congress on the State of the Union. *Congressional Record Proceedings and Debates of the 89th Congress*, First Session, January 4, 1965, Washington, D.C.: U.S. Government Printing Office, Volume 111, Part 1, 26–29.

U.S. President, 1963–1968 (President Lyndon B. Johnson). Toward full educational opportunity, Message from the President of the United States. *Congressional Record Proceedings and Debates of the 89th Congress*, First Session, January 12, 1965, Washington, D.C.: U.S. Government Printing Office, Volume 111, Part 7, 589–592.

CHAPTER 6

GROWTH OF LANGUAGE AND COGNITIVE ABILITIES

GROWTH OF LANGUAGE ABILITIES

Recent interest and debate over the usefulness of programs of language training for young children, especially those from "disadvantaged" backgrounds, have stimulated a great deal of research. For the most part, effort has been concentrated on the processes by which language is acquired and the sequence and pace of language development.

Much progress has been made in documenting the growth of speech patterns and growth in young children, especially in children from ethnic and low-income backgrounds. A number of educational "myths" have been exposed (such as the notion that black children who come to school speaking black English are "linguistically deprived"), but new questions have been raised and many familiar ones are still not answered. Some of the unanswered questions have to do with the processes through which children acquire speech, the influence of parents, mass media and other adult sources of language upon the child's linguistic development, the long term consequences of teaching preschoolers to read, the optimal time to institute bilingual training for children who come to school speaking a non-standard form of English and in what way socio-economic and cultural differences in speech affect learning and cognitive development.

With so much still unknown, teachers may question the utility of concerning themselves with conflicting viewpoints and spending time trying to learn theories and research results that may be changed or reinterpreted in the near future.

Perhaps the best answer to this is that the teacher who has knowledge about current issues and viewpoints in a developing field is in a better position to make choices and more able to recognize the significance of new findings. She also has a better perspective for evaluating the claims made by "innovative" programs that may be offered her. Obviously, when equipped with this knowledge, she can more adequately assess the language abilities of children and adapt her own teaching to their needs.

Language and Communication

The complex system of speech sounds that we call language is the basic channel for human intellectual and social interaction. Its obvious importance in academic accomplishment and in a broad sweep of human activities outside of school give it particular salience in programs of early education.

The usual description of the role of language, especially speech, in early educational programs is oriented to the view that it is a channel for the communication of ideas, information, and feelings. The way in which language is "taught"—that is, the treatment of the use of language in these programs—assumes that the speaker has the intent to transmit directly and straightforwardly the ideas that are in his mind. This perspective of

FIGURE 6-1 CHILDREN BEGIN TO SPEAK AT APPROXIMATELY THE SAME AGE, REGARDLESS OF THE LANGUAGE SYSTEM THEY ARE LEARNING

language is too narrow; it ignores the additional utility of language as a more subtle strategy having an impact on the listener(s) which may be of a sort not conveyed by the words spoken. Filibustering is an obvious example of using speech as a strategy to achieve a purpose having little to do with communication. The words themselves are not important; the messages they convey are literally beside the point.

The uses of language to disguise meaning, to evade, mislead, impress and arouse are well known. It may be less obvious that language used by teachers in a classroom may unintentionally create an impact quite different from the words which children actually hear. Such an inconsistency in speech can create confusion for both teacher and child.

A teacher who says "Now, we all want to fold our hands and be quiet, don't we?" when she really does not mean to give the children a choice is forcing them to decode (that is, to interpret) the messages that come to them through nonverbal channels (intonation, gesture, timing, modeling, etc.) and abandon in part the meaning of the words for the meaning of the nonverbal signals. Another common example is that children are urged to say "I'm sorry," and "Thank you" and make other ritualistic comments even when they have dubious validity.

When children receive contradictory messages from different channels of communication (verbal messages vs. facial expressions, for example) they tend to discount the more positive information and assume the worst. This also happens with adults, but is more marked with children, who are less accustomed to sorting out and putting in perspective such apparent inconsistencies. They may not understand joking messages, for example, which give approval and disapproval simultaneously (Bugental, et al., 1970).

To an objective observer, perhaps, it might appear that the curricula and programs of language training for young children and the behavior of the teacher (and other adults in the child's life) are not entirely consonant with one another. In the midst of programs which urge the child to "Speak in complete sentences and say what you mean!" the adults around him are often talking to him using words that do not mean what they say. It is interesting to speculate on the logical problems that this poses for the young child and the contribution this discrepancy makes to his understanding of the nonverbal world.

GROWTH OF LANGUAGE AND COGNITIVE ABILITIES

FIGURE 6-2 USES OF LANGUAGE
TO COMMUNICATE INFORMATION   TO EXPRESS EMOTION

Bill Cosby's record "Why Is There Air?" includes a band on which he describes his recollections of how he reinterpreted the teacher's words in order to psych out her meaning—a delightful example of cross-channel "I-don't-mean-what-I-say" messages. That children are likely to use similar tactics against teachers is often suggested in Schulz' inspired comic strip "Peanuts". Recall this exchange between Linus and a classmate at the beginning of the school year. Linus has submitted an essay about the joys of returning to school. Challenged by a classmate, he replies, "Through the years you eventually learn what sells."

Quite apart from the use of language to accomplish things not specifically indicated in the literal meaning of the words used, there is a flow of nonverbal communication which conveys messages without any use of words. Language training programs and curricula do not often include nonverbal communication, but it is nonetheless an important dimension of early learning. While this form of communication is not one that is taught directly, as spoken and written language are, the teacher's own behavior provides a model for the child to acquire techniques and skills in nonverbal exchange.

Acquiring a Language Language is present in every human society, yet no one is born knowing how to speak.[1] In order to acquire and use language, children must first learn a complicated system of sounds. Whether the sounds are those of Chinese, Swahili, Choctaw, or some other system, barring physical or emotional disorder, all children do speak at approximately the same age. They respond to and gradually come to use the speech of their parents and the "important others" with whom they are most closely associated, whether these people are wealthy or poor, educated or uneducated, young or old.

Learning to Speak The first sounds a baby makes are the nasal sounds of discomfort closely followed by the cooing and gurgling associated with comfort and well-being. Around eight weeks of age he characteristically begins to practice vowel sounds and

---

[1] Linguists have identified approximately 3500 languages, many of which contain one or more dialects. About a third of these languages have a written form of some kind.

TO BE SOCIABLE   TO CONTROL BEHAVIOR   TO EXPRESS CONCEPTS

then consonants in a kind of babbling. From five or six months on, he may use his babbling purposefully to get attention and to signal his needs. He also begins to respond with sounds of his own to people who speak directly to him. By eight months his babbling rises and falls in very much the same intonation patterns as the speech around him. He then apparently becomes aware of syllables and other segments of sound distinct from intonation patterns and gradually arranges these into words.

An attempt to understand how children learn to speak must include a consideration of various biological factors. The exact nature of genetic influence on language ability is by no means clear. If there are "genes for language," they have not as yet been identified, although research studies on twins indicate that genetic endowment cannot be wholly discarded in favor of environmental influence.

Studies of twins, (Lenneberg, 1969) show that the onset of speech occurs more nearly at the same time for identical twins than for fraternal twins. Also, if there is a delay in learning, it will be the same for both twins of an identical pair, while fraternal twins may sometimes experience the same delay, but frequently one twin will start later and learn more slowly than the other.

Because of his biological heritage the child responds to speech directed toward him, but how much he continues to respond seems to be highly dependent on environmental factors. During the first three months of their lives, normal babies born to deaf parents obviously do not hear the same kind or amount of verbal discourse as children in families where the mother and father are not deaf. Nor are their normal vocalizations responded to as immediately. Yet it has been shown that their initial cooing and sound production is almost identical to that of babies born to mothers who can hear them and whose sounds the babies hear. As long as children of deaf parents hear language from others, their learning proceeds normally. Communication with their parents takes place through gestures and a repertoire of other nonverbal responses.

Most children who are themselves born deaf may go through the cooing stage but since they do not hear speech, even their own, this behavior is soon extinguished and their introduction to language as a system does not take place until they reach school age unless they have attended a special preschool. Blind children's learning to speak is closely related to physical maturation and follows that of children who have sight.

AGE	ABILITY
2 years	Should be able to follow simple commands without visual clues: *Johnny, get your hat and give it to Daddy* *Debby, bring me your ball* Uses a variety of everyday words heard in his home and neighborhood: *Mommy, milk, ball, hat* Shows he is developing sentence sense by the way he puts words together: *Go bye bye car* *Milk all gone*
3 years	Understands and uses words other than for naming; is able to fit simple verbs, pronouns, prepositions, and adjectives such as *go, me, in,* and *big* more and more into sentences:
4 years	Should be able to give a connected account of some recent experience: Should be able to carry out a sequence of two simple directions: *Bobby, find Susie and tell her dinner's ready*
5 years	Speech should be intelligible although some sounds may still be mispronounced: Can carry on a conversation if vocabulary is within his range

TABLE 6–1 CHILDREN'S PROGRESS IN LANGUAGE ABILITY
adapted from *Learning to Talk,* prepared by the Information Office, U.S. National Institute of Neurological Diseases and Stroke, National Institutes of Health, Public Health Service, U.S. Dept. Health, Education and Welfare, Washington, D.C., 1969, U.S. Govt. Printing Office, pp. 22–24.

Observation of a wide variety of children shows that the acquisition of speech is a natural process which cannot be deterred. Even when children have only minimum resources to aid them, they can and do learn to speak the language they hear.

The teacher's awareness of the social pressure exerted on those whose speech deviates from the forms of standard English often leads her to attempt to "correct" children's pronunciation and grammar. Even though from the standpoint of development a child may not have mastered pronunciation or postulated "rules" that permit his using the forms desired, she will often persist in presenting them, assuming that hearing and acquiring somehow take place simultaneously. But just as research shows that in the matter of grammatical form a child cannot go beyond the "rules" that he has worked out from his understanding of language, his ability to pronounce words is also limited to developmental factors. Some of these are summarized on this page.

The connotation of incompletely developed speech is more true in matters of pronunciation and vocabulary than in grammar, but teachers often assume an obligation to see that children learn to pronounce as well as to use words in approved ways. By so doing they feel they are helping the child avoid later discrimination based on speech differences. The notion of the need for grammatical "correctness" has been so strong as to form the basis for judgment of reading skill. If the printed page shows:

> She goes to school every day and so does her brother.

and the child reads:

> She go to school every day and so do her brother.

he is often held to be a poor reader, when in fact it is his regional or social dialect that is being judged, not his reading skill.

It is not yet known just why young children acquire the language forms they do and not others—why those who spend more hours in a day care center hearing only standard English, or who in their homes listen to more television "talk" than adult conver-

> *During his fourth year the child masters pronunciation of sounds represented by S and Z, of blends like TRain, BLow, faLLS, and of friction sounds requiring muscle coordinations as in Join, fuDGE, CHew, and maTCH.*
>
> *People can usually comprehend all that a five-year-old says even though he may not pronounce every sound exactly as they do. He will use sounds represented by K, G, F, and V fairly consistently. These are difficult to make compared to sounds represented by M, N, P, and B. He may still have some difficulty with them in blends like GRass, CLean, and eLF. Sounds represented by R may not always be said correctly until the eighth year.*

---

sation, still speak as their parents do. Until the reasons are clear, however, teachers should not expect to be able to make changes in the form of a child's language if the change is not one he will regularly hear and use when he is not in school.

Learning the Structure of a Language A child's ability to pronounce sounds and to order them into words does not mean he has learned a language. This kind of imitating is readily taught to various birds, and many kinds of animals can be trained to respond to words or word combinations. Only when a child himself generates and comprehends sentences he has never heard before can it be said he has learned a language.

The various stages a child goes through in learning the structure and use of his own language are similar for all children, but quite different from those experienced by an adult in acquiring a second language. For adults, language learning is likely to be an exercise in reasoning, imitation, and a feat of memory. For a child, it is learning to distinguish and vocalize the sounds of a language and then determining how various elements are put together to express meaning. It is a matter of discovering for himself how a language works. This is not to say that children never imitate sounds as they learn to assemble the elements of a language. Obviously they do. Their choice of speech sounds to express meaning seems to be accounted for by imitation. Likewise, the accumulation of vocabulary is largely a matter of imitation and repetition. But neither of these aspects of learning is the same as sensing the underlying principles of a language, or the ability to arrange combinations of sounds into meaningful patterns according to "rules," even though the rules remain unstated.

As the child acquires tacit knowledge of the structure of language, he is likely to overgeneralize and say "He goed" and "This is mines," even though he never hears these verb and pronoun forms. Apparently he has grasped the regular endings which indicate past tense and possession and has formulated "rules" which he applies to his own utterances.

Despite the widely held opinion that children can be taught to "correct" their usage by hearing and then imitating desired forms, research has not shown this to be true. The following example represents how difficult it is to change behavior by attempted correction. It is a conversation with a four-year-old girl reported by Gleason (1967, p. 1.):

Child My teacher holded the baby rabbits and we patted them.
Gleason Did you say your teacher held the baby rabbits?
Child Yes.

Children . . . can repeat correctly only that which is formed by rules they have already mastered. This is the best indication that language does not come about by simple imitation, but that the child abstracts regularities or relations from the language he hears, which he then applies to building up language for himself as an apparatus of principles.
from E. H. Lenneberg, "On Explaining Language," *Science, 164,* 3880, May 9, 1969, p. 638.

Gleason What did you say she did?
Child She holded the baby rabbits and we patted them.
Gleason Did you say she held them tightly?
Child No, she holded them loosely.

The child clearly heard and comprehended the accepted form "held," but even after repeated "corrections" she continued to speak within her own framework of language understanding. This is an example of evidence that challenges the theory that imitation is the only or primary way language is learned. Other students of language acquisition agree.

Early in their acquisition of knowledge concerning the structure of a language, children will apparently accept corrections of fact and make changes, and they will also substitute a "good" word for a "bad" word. But children gradually learn grammar—the rules of a language—on their own, and are impervious to the type of correction and reinforcement so commonly carried on by adults. Their understanding and application of rules is a developmental behavior, one which all children apparently go through for themselves. The common "errors" in much of children's early speech, therefore, are seen to be overgeneralizations and are subject to adjustment as the child accumulates language experience.

Since language is a learned behavior, children who hear little or no speech, or who attend to only the speech of those who are themselves limited in language development, will be likely to have a language deficit compared with those surrounded by conversation. On the other hand, fairly retarded children who have grown up in various institutions under the care of an older retardate (with limited skill in language) have been known to gain a good deal of language facility. When this has happened, it is thought that their learning might have been influenced by the television that was on all day long in the otherwise bare room where the children played (Lenneberg, 1969).

Children with a language deficit are not necessarily incapable of language learning. To assess *capability,* the teacher should not count vocabulary items and usage errors, nor seek to determine the length and complexity of sentences children use. Results from this kind of evaluation probably measure the adequacy (or inadequacy) of the environment in which the learning took place, rather than a child's ability to learn.

A high correlation exists between chronological age and language development; an even higher one between language development and motor development. The information in Table 6-2 enables us to compare the language behaviors of a particular child with those of other children at the same stage of motor development.

AGE	MOTOR DEVELOPMENT	LANGUAGE DEVELOPMENT
 6 mos.	Sits using hands for support.	Cooing sounds change to babbling with introduction of consonant sounds.
 1 yr.	Stands and walks when held by one hand.	Duplicates syllables. Understands some words. First words used to signify particular objects or persons.
 18 mos.	Creeps downstairs backwards. Walks.	Uses single words not joined in phrases. Understands well. Intonation patterns resemble those of adult conversation.
 2 yrs.	Runs. Mounts steps one foot forward.	About 50 words: two-word combinations common. Interest in verbal communication heightened.
 30 mos.	Jumps with both feet. Can stand on one.	New words every day. Uses three or more words in succession. Many grammatical constructions that are nonstandard. Understands well.
 3 yrs.	Tiptoes, goes up stairs alternating feet.	Fewer "mistakes" in word forms. Most language intelligible. Language is systematic and predictable. 1000+ word vocabulary.
4+ yrs.	 Jumps over rope, hops on one foot, walks line.	Language well established though may have a few unusual constructions and vocabulary choices.

TABLE 6-2 CORRELATION OF MOTOR AND LANGUAGE DEVELOPMENT
adapted from E. H. Lenneberg, I. A. Nichols, and E. F. Rosenberger, "Primitive Stages of Language Development in Mongolism" in *Disorders of Communication*, D. Rioch, and E. A. Weinstein, (eds.). Research Publications of Association for Research in Nervous and Mental Disorders, New York, Baltimore, Williams & Wilkins, 1964, *42*, pp. 128-130.

A LACK OF LANGUAGE?

Recent studies of peer groups in spontaneous interaction in Northern ghetto areas show that there is a rich verbal culture in constant use. Negro children in the vernacular culture cannot be considered "verbally deprived" if one observes them in a favorable environment—on the contrary, their daily life is a pattern of continual verbal stimulation, contest, and imitation. . . . There are many [other] speech events associated with the vernacular culture of the ghetto: jokes, songs, narratives, and of course the hip vocabulary itself. All of these reflect the value system of the vernacular, and because it is opposed in many ways to the standard culture of the school, it does not appear in school contexts.

from J. E. Birren and R. D. Hess, (eds.), "Influences of Biological, Psychological, and Social Deprivation Upon Learning and Performance," from *Perspectives on Human Deprivation: Biological, Psychological, and Sociological,* 1968, pp. 122–23.

The circumstance which seems most conducive to language learning is surrounding the child with what has been called "a sea of language." Exposure to a wide variety of conversation with a chance to enter at his own level from the beginning, listening to stories, hearing books read aloud, and having television, radio and records available, seemingly makes it possible for him to take from what he hears the elements he needs to build language for himself. The fact that no one yet knows exactly how this is done, or how it may be assisted, makes the achievement no less magnificent.

Language Learning and Socio-Economic and Cultural Differences

Many contemporary programs of early education place major emphasis on language training and the development of cognitive skills. This interest is reflected in highly engineered lessons with small groups of children, as well as in arranged environments in which every child is free to follow his own interests. To a great extent, this orientation toward language training comes from two sources: a) the widespread belief that children from poor and ghetto families come to school with inadequate language ability; and b) the theory that language development is a basic prerequisite to successful achievement in school and adult life. These beliefs are undergoing intensive investigation and it appears that both may be exaggerations, yet they have had an impressive influence on the field of early education. Whether or not the particular emphasis on linguistic skills in compensatory education programs is justified, language development is important.

As mentioned earlier, research shows no evidence that socio-economic and cultural differences affect children's capacity to learn a language. Nor do they determine the rate at which this learning takes place. The ability to learn a language at all proves a great deal of conceptual mastery on the part of the learner.

There can be no doubt about the ability of disadvantaged children to learn. In short-term memory skills and rote learning tasks, lower-class children perform at the same levels as middle-class children. But in specific abilities such as vocabulary size, and length of sentences, ghetto children score below middle-class children. What they apparently lack is the kind of language learning needed for success in a school system geared to the prior learning of middle-class children.

STANDARD ENGLISH	BLACK DIALECT
"No one comes here anymore"	"Don't nobody come here no more"
"He works"	"He work"
"Why did you hit me?"	"Why you hit me?"
"Two fights"	"Two fight"
"He's working"	"He be working"
"If you're good"	"If you good"
"He's messing around"	"He messing around"

TABLE 6–3 SOME DIFFERENCES BETWEEN STANDARD ENGLISH AND BLACK DIALECT

Explanations of Cultural Differences in Language Usage In the search for an understanding of the school language problems of disadvantaged children, two explanations form the basis for the emphasis placed on language curricula in preschool programs. If it is thought that children have acquired "less language" than is needed to communicate effectively, then programs seek to provide the children with more language. Since he comes to school with a deficit, he must somehow be given what he lacks as soon as he enters a program of early education.

Nonsense Sentences
Yong tharsled the gringer.
Horbles jonkle zoperly.

But studies show that when tested with nonsense sentences, such as those illustrated, and asked to provide words which can be substituted for the forms underlined, lower-class and middle-class children of comparable ages did equally well in selecting nouns. In other tests, children from differing socio-economic levels showed no significant difference in their ability to generalize from nonsense words standard verb and noun endings to show tense, plurals, and possessives. Only when children were examined from the standpoint of the meaning of words were the middle-class children far ahead of lower-class children.

Some doubt exists as to whether low-income children know and use many words on which they are tested. Perhaps these children recognize and use as many words as middle-class children but not for school-related tasks. Also, little proof exists that simply adding more words used by middle-class children to a child's vocabulary will help his test performance.

Another early basis for emphasis on language development in compensatory programs had to do with the notion of a "different language." Those who subscribe to this philosophy argue that all children acquire the structure of language at about the same age and rate, but that because some children learn a dialect of English which is not "standard English" they have difficulty communicating in school or anywhere that standard English is predominant. Much of the research in this area concerns dialects. A few of the more obvious differences between standard English and black dialect are listed in Table 6–3. Evidence has been growing that despite the differences in the two forms of language, ghetto children understand a great deal of language that they themselves do not use, and black children apparently understand the speech of middle-class teachers.

Situational Setting as a Cause of Difference in Language Apparently the explanation for a language difference that is so severe that it causes marked school difficulties must be sought further. Courtney B. Cazden in a survey of language acquisition (1970, p. 83) suggests that one source may lie in the "effects of situations."

FIGURE 6–3 TEACHERS NEED TO PROVIDE SPECIFIC AND QUALIFIED ANSWERS TO MANY OF THE QUESTIONS A CHILD ASKS

Both the less-language and different-language views of child language are inadequate on two counts. First, they speak only of patterns of structural forms and ignore patterns of use in actual speech events. Second, they speak as if the child learns only one way to speak, which is reflected in the same fashion and to the same extent at all times. On both theoretical and practical grounds, we can no longer accept such limitations.

Cazden makes clear that our understanding of the total range of children's language ability is far from complete and raises the question as to what bearing the situation in which a child speaks has on his ability to use language. A summary of research regarding the influence of situation appears in Table 6–4.

The Teacher's Role in Language Learning

From what is known about language learning, children apparently acquire the grammar on their own as they learn to speak; vocabulary and pronunciation are more a matter of imitation and repetition.

"Teaching" language at the preschool level, then, can best be accomplished by providing as much opportunity as possible for verbal interaction on a one-to-one basis. For example, teachers need to elaborate and qualify their answers to many of the questions a child asks. An instance of how this might be done is shown in the following report of a conversation:

Child What's that?
Teacher It's a pencil sharpener.

If the teacher's goal were "greater use of language," she might better have answered,

"It's a pencil sharpener that Jack's daddy mounted for us. Now we have a way of sharpening pencils. Would you like to sharpen a pencil?"

TEACHERS OF YOUNG CHILDREN

RESEARCHER	CHILDREN	SETTING	FINDINGS
Strandberg (1969)	4- and 5-year-olds with above-average IQ	Children presented with different kinds of pictures.	Talked more about a toy or a 20-second silent film presentation of the toy than about a color photo.
Strandberg & Griffith (1968)	4- and 5-year-olds from laboratory school	Children given simple cameras and shown how to take pictures.	Talked more spontaneously and used longer and more complex utterances discussing pictures they took than those taken under adult direction when learning to use camera.
Cowan et al. (1967)	Elementary school children	Children shown ten magazine covers that were in color.	Length of children's response varied with pictures.
Berlyne & Frommer (1966)	Children in kindergarten and grades 3, 5, and 6 in a laboratory school	Children told stories, shown pictures, and then told stories accompanied by pictures. When finished with each they were invited to ask questions.	Novel, incongruous, and surprising items elicited most questions.
Cazden (in press)	5-year-olds in two English Infant Schools	Setting A: Children given a book that contained blank pages, asked to draw a picture and then dictate story for teacher to write. Setting B: Each child had a word folder with store of basic words plus blanks for his personal choices, and a stand on which words could be set up and arranged as sentences. No pictures.	Setting A: All stories used simple sentences in form "This is a ____." One instance of sentence in another form: "This boy is dead." Setting B: Composed sentences of great variety and length, including questions.
Brent & Katz (1967)	White Head Start children	First asked to tell stories using selected picture – picture was removed and children were to tell story again.	Stories told without picture were superior in logic, explicitness, and length.
Cowe (1967)	Kindergarten children	Recordings were made of children's conversation in nine activities in the classroom.	In maturity and amount of speech, housekeeping activities and group discussions were most conducive to language use. Dance, blocks, and woodworking held least potential.

TABLE 6–4 EFFECTS OF A VARIETY OF SITUATIONS (SETTINGS) ON LANGUAGE USE IN GROUPS OF CHILDREN
adapted from a summary of research by Courtney B. Cazden, "The Neglected Situation in Child Language Research and Education," in Frederick Williams, (ed.), Language and Poverty: Perspectives on a Theme (Chicago: Markham Publishing Company, 1970), pp. 81–101.

PLAIN DISCOURSE	EXPANDED DISCOURSE
It's juice time.	It's juice time and today we're going to have pink juice and big, round crackers.
Bobby, will you help Maria put the blocks away, please?	Bobby, you put all the large blocks away on the bottom shelf. Maria, you can stack all the little blocks on the top shelf.
It's dark in here. Let's turn on the light.	It's much darker in here now than it was a little while ago. I wonder how we can make it lighter.

TABLE 6–5 PROVIDING LANGUAGE EXPERIENCE THROUGH EXPANDED DISCOURSE

If the length of the dialogue children hear makes a difference in their language development, as some researchers believe, classroom routine on a casual, unstructured basis can be a rich resource for language growth. Table 6–5 contains examples of how this technique might be used.

Providing opportunities for children to learn language means reading aloud from a wide variety of sources—nursery tales, folk tales, verses, picture books, and children's dictation. In this way they hear a wide range of sentences and have a chance to think about their own experiences in comparison with those of the characters in the books. It means having formal and informal story telling and discussion sessions. Children can make up their own stories or repeat stories told to them. They enjoy talking about words, rhyming words, and expressing differences between word meanings such as *hit* and *spank, fly* and *soar, walk* and *tiptoe*. Just as children respond to beauty in nature and to elements such as color and line in art and rhythm and melody in music, they also respond to the sounds and imagery of language.

Making records and tapes and books and pictures available to children encourages their interest in language, if there is also time for talking about what they hear and see for themselves. Helping children develop language ability means making sure they have many chances to interact on a verbal level with one another and with adults. Perhaps the best teacher of language is the use of language itself.

GROWTH OF COGNITIVE ABILITIES

Cognitive ability refers to the mental processes which make it possible for human beings to acquire, store, arrange and rearrange information. As the child interacts with the environment, old concepts are constantly modified, and new ones created. Language provides labels for these concepts and furnishes human beings with a means for communicating what they know. Therefore, as concepts develop, the meaning that the child gives to words also changes.

Development of Cognition and Concepts

Because someone hands a child an object saying, "Look, here's a ball," the child doesn't suddenly know what is and what isn't a ball. To be sure, he has a word which

The Object Ball

The Concept Ball

It rolls.
It is usually round.
People expect you to catch, throw, kick and bounce a ball.
Balls come in many sizes, colors, and materials.
People don't eat balls—only food shaped like a ball.
A ball can be solid or hollow.
People play games with balls.
Balls can be light or heavy.

names what he holds. But there is more to a ball than its name. An infant, having learned the word *ball,* and something about the shape of such an object, may point to the moon, to an orange, or to a box turtle and say, "ball," but a school child is expected to know the difference. Before a child can select another object and be correct in calling it a "ball," he must have some notion of what properties balls share (other than roundness) that makes them unique. He needs to have a concept of *ball.*

Through internal cognitive activity a child forms concepts not only of objects he perceives, such as balls, but also abstracts like *up, big, soft, first, good,* and *self.* In short, it is through cognition and the formation of concepts that children make sense of the world. Apparently some of what a child learns takes place by means of direct teaching. He is given labels and taught rules. But much of his knowledge is developmental, not imitative. He constructs on his own; that is, he makes his own sense of his experiences, and cannot be shown otherwise by adult intervention. The evolution of children's use of language is an example of this kind of learning.

The ability to conceptualize begins as a child acts on objects in his environment and builds knowledge through sensory-motor activities and the accompanying modification of cognitive structures. What is learned at one stage is held to be the basis for learning at each successive stage. The age limits are not fixed, and the rate of movement, as well as the scope of development, varies according to individual children. The sequence of stages, however, tends to be consistent. In the development of intellectual functioning children usually go through the various stages in a relatively fixed order regardless of socio-economic or cultural differences. Socio-economic or cultural influences may speed up, slow down or stop development. But they apparently do not greatly change its sequence.

> ...Preschools must build a solid foundation for further development by going back to the sensory-motor period, and making certain that internal stages are not skipped or only partially achieved.
>
> from C. K. Kamii and N. L. Radin, "A Framework for a Preschool Curriculum Based on Some Piagetian Concepts," *The Journal of Creative Behavior,* 1967, *1,* p. 315.

Sensory motor is the name given the first learning stage in Piaget's theory of cognitive development.[2] In this period, which covers approximately the first two years of life, the infant interacts with the physical world through reflexes and perceptual-motor activities to slowly become aware of the physical world in ways that make more complete comprehension possible later. This is followed by the preoperational stage (2 to 7 years) during which the child is perceptually oriented. He makes sense of the world in terms of the way it looks to him, he usually centers on only one variable or dimension (height only rather than height and width) at a time, and he has difficulty realizing that an object can possess more than one property. In the stage of concrete operations (7 to 11 years) the child can use more logical structures and classifications and view things from a perspective outside himself. In the stage of formal operations, he reaches the capacity for symbolic abstractions.

Human knowledge is structured from three principal sources:

Interaction with the physical world: physical knowledge
Interaction with others: social knowledge
Making sense out of experience: logical knowledge

Although the relationships among these sources are not entirely clear, apparently physical and logical knowledge underlie much of what is usually called cognitive development. The acquisition of these types of knowledge is the concern of the rest of this chapter.

The ability to form concepts is developmental; that is, it depends on physical and mental maturation *and* experience. The ability to work at the level of concrete experiences, therefore, isn't automatically assured simply because a child has reached a certain chronological age and is in school. In order to succeed in school tasks he must also have achieved a certain stage of cognitive capability before entering school.

To develop cognitive ability young children need multiple kinds of experiences and the chance to repeat these over and over. Such activities should not be hurried and it is important to make certain that the simpler levels are neither overlooked nor skipped. Constant observation and diagnosis by the teacher will help her set the needed pace and make effective choices.

---

[2] The extraordinary work of Jean Piaget provided the basis for much of the point of view and material of this part of the chapter. Only a small part of his theory of cognitive development is touched on here. Additional references appear in the bibliography of this chapter. Piaget's conceptions of the growth of intellectual capabilities have great appeal for many professionals but are not accepted by others, as the discussion in Chapter 5 indicated.

The activities which follow are examples of materials and procedures which can be used to achieve specific cognitive goals.[3]

ACTIVITIES FOR ACHIEVING COGNITIVE GOALS

Developing Physical Knowledge

COGNITIVE PROCESS
Gaining knowledge of the physical properties of matter

MATERIALS
Half sticks of modeling clay in different colors

Typical Procedure   Give the child a half stick of clay and ask him to tell you what it is. (If he cannot name it, identify it for him.) Then ask, "What is it for?"

Over many, many sessions discuss any or all of the following in whatever order seems appropriate to the circumstances in which the questions are introduced. After each inquiry, give the child ample time to answer, and ask him to show or tell you how he knows.

1. Does modeling clay have more than one color? What are some of its colors? Can you mix the colors together? What happens if you do?
2. Can you change its shape? If you do, can you make it the same shape again? Can you divide clay into separate pieces? Will you be able to put the pieces back again?
3. Have him lick it and ask: What does it taste like?
4. Have him smell it and ask: Does it have a smell? What does it smell like? (He may not be able to tell how it tastes or smells, but he will know from his experience that it has taste and odor.)
5. What will happen if you drop it? Put it in water? Heat it? (Use sunlight, electric bulb, flame.)
6. Does clay move by itself? Can you stretch it? Will it bend? Break?
7. Is modeling clay smooth? Heavy? Cold? Sticky?
(Have other materials available in like quantity for comparison since these qualities are relative.)
8. What happens if you hit clay with your fist? With another piece of clay? With a block?
9. Can you cut clay? Tear it?

The examples offered here simply seek to show the teacher one way she might initiate and maintain motivation for desired learnings. They are in no wise a script and

---

[3] We have drawn significantly from the writings of Constance Kamii for both interpretations of Piaget's theories and for adaptations of his concepts to curricula for preschool programs.

should not be treated as such.[4] Research findings show that tasks too easy for a child bore him; tasks too difficult he rejects.

Also, teachers need to remember that every question should be followed by the child's interaction with the object he holds. If he answers without physical involvement he should be encouraged to explain how he knows. In this way "errors" can be corrected—not by saying, "Oh, no. That's wrong—it's . . . ," but by having him manipulate whatever is involved so that he sees for himself that his answer is not borne out by reality. Dropping clay from a variety of heights allows the child to find out for himself whether clay breaks.

Another way to develop learning about physical properties of matter is to have small groups of children explore together. They might be provided with a collection of objects such as those pictured and encouraged to ask questions of one another.

1. What could we find out if we rolled a ball and a spool at the same time?
2. What could we find out if we put a little water on a paper towel and a paper napkin?

After each question the children raise, they should be given a chance to find the answer. The opportunity to make comparisons of these kinds brings knowledge they can depend on. Children can see the regularity of the physical world regardless of who performs the action, and that objects themselves have certain characteristics no matter who pushes, pulls or drops them.

Learning situations similar to that of exploring the properties of clay can be brought about informally many times during a day, and the child's attention directed to a virtually limitless variety of objects. Teaching sessions do not need to be structured in any way except as the teacher deliberately gives the child a chance to find his own answers. The "lesson" can cease after only a question or two, or can continue as long as a child remains interested.

Children can and should be asked "What will happen if . . . ?" over and over but should not be asked "Why?" From their experiences they can learn to predict that blowing on a candle flame will extinguish it, but why this happens is beyond their ability to understand. When working with preschool level children, it is important to stay within the realm of their experience.

---

[4] Additional tasks based on Piagetian concepts may be found in the language and pre-math sections of *An Activities Handbook for Teachers of Young Children* (D. J. Croft and R. D. Hess, 1972) which accompanies this text.

Developing Logical Knowledge

COGNITIVE PROCESS
Classification
(Grouping only)

MATERIALS
4 sets—each set containing 5 objects identical in size, shape, and color.
Example: nails, bolts, washers, nuts
  or
various kinds of peas and beans
  or
various kinds of shells (snail, conch, scallop, clam)
4 open containers

DESCRIPTION
Classification is the ability to group objects according to similarities and differences[5]

Typical Procedure   (Working with two or three children in a group)

1. Display one object from each set and give its name. (If it is reasonable to expect that children might know, have them name the different objects.) Ask, "What can you tell me about this———?" Wait for answers but probe as to color, size, shape, probable use, where found, etc.
2. Following brief discussion, display all the items in a random mix. Ask, "Do any of these look just the same?" Have child who answers correctly show the choice he made and tell how they are the same.
3. Without using the containers, sort items by kind and include one "mistake." Ask, "Are all the pieces where they belong?" Have a child make the needed change.
4. Ask one of the children to mix the pieces together and set out the containers. Suggest to the child that he put the pieces that are the same in these boxes.
5. When they have finished, have them look to see if the items are correctly grouped. "Are all the pieces where they belong?" ("Is every piece in this box exactly the same?")[6]

The progression suggested above, like that for physical knowledge, is to be thought of as an example, not a curriculum. Children need many individual and group experiences in separating objects according to different criteria before a concept of "class" develops.

Early practice in sorting lends itself to many routine nursery school procedures. Taking out and putting away equipment and materials by size, color, use, material; making sure Ronald has his jacket and not Buddy's; grouping by shape and degree of hardness, finding "five things bigger than this," etc., all provide needed experience. Simple games can be built around teaching similarities and differences based on choosing two of "this kind" and three of "another kind" from an array of highly different items. Putting objects in a bag and sorting by touch instead of visually, gives children experience in sorting by still another dimension. At all times children need to be encouraged to verbalize why they make the choices they do.

The idea of a *consistent criterion* is important and needs to be maintained when working with items that can be sorted in more than one way (by color, shape, size, etc.).

---

[5] This description is limited to the *preoperational stage*. Piaget holds classification to be an ability attained at the stage of *concrete operation*. Before a child can classify objects by both kind *and* number, he needs many opportunities to group them by their qualitative aspect(s) only.

[6] When working with several children, as often as possible have them correct one another—and the teacher! The notion of "correctness" however, holds only for grouping of identical objects. When more than one variable is present, the child's choice should be considered "correct" so long as it remains constant.

Four-year-olds are likely to group a red square with a blue square "because they have the same shape," and then add a blue circle "because they are blue." Maintaining a consistent criterion requires that a child be able to remember why he made his first choice and then make all subsequent choices for the same reason.

Quite complex preoperational exercises in classifying need to be mastered before the child is asked to deal with both qualitative and quantitative properties. If shown a collection of 10 wooden beads, 2 of which are red and 8 green, and asked the question, "Are there more green beads or more wooden beads?" some will be able to consider both qualitative and quantitative aspects, but this ability is not often found in a preschooler. The foundations for classification need to be built early and carefully; the ability to classify both quantitatively and qualitatively is fundamental to many of the demands of schooling and other cognitive activities.

Three types of tasks encountered early in the development of seriation are:

1. Absolute Comparison

Children identify large and small members of different pairs of objects—the biggest block, the smallest doll, etc.

2. Relative Comparison

Children perceive the same object as now large, now small, relative to the size of another object.

3. Additive Seriation

To a series of objects already ordered along a particular dimension, children add other objects and place them correctly.

COGNITIVE PROCESS
Seriation (at preoperational level)

DESCRIPTION
Seriation involves making two or more comparisons and ordering items along some dimension

Materials and Procedures Nursery schools have the variety of materials and the opportunities for sensory-motor activities which make it possible for children to identify differences and order objects in terms of these differences as a part of the daily program. Much of the equipment can be in two sizes (big and little dolls, blocks, plates, cups, paint brushes, etc.) and conversation can frequently be directed toward this relationship. "Kitty, you use the little swing and let Paula have the big one." "Do we need the little wagon or the big wagon for all these blocks?" Size comparisons should also include long or tall/short and narrow/wide.

Dimensions other than size (such as distance, loudness, hardness, amount of heat and amount of color) also lend themselves to comparison and seriation. Questions for diagnosing a child's level of development in seriation are indicated on p. 191.

Comparisons should first be made on the basis of gross differences and then gradually more subtle differences should be noted by matching pairs of elements for precise

Questions for Diagnosing Child's Level for Seriation Exercises

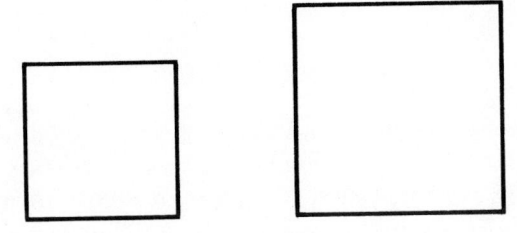

the teacher might first ask, "Are these the same?" If the child answers "yes," she can ask "In what way?" If the child answers "no," she can ask "How are they different?"

If the question regarding size is not productive, she might ask, "Is there one that is bigger than the other? Which one?"

comparison. Dramatic play such as that which relates the size of objects to the needs of Mama, Papa and Baby Bear provides a meaningful base for many comparisons.

Another opportunity a teacher can create to give the child a chance to think about relative size is to have him add an item to an array of three of more ordered objects. For example, you might have him arrange three toy cars in order of size. Then give him a fourth

asking, "Where should this go so it will be in the right place?"

A concept of relative size can be developed by having children learn they are taller than some of their friends, but also shorter than others. This can also be worked out with chairs, books, desks, cups, etc.

Seriation is a concept based on a system of relative dimensions, not just the comparison of two or three objects and their ordering. The ability to place items correctly along some dimension wherein they differ is closely tied to the demands of many school subjects. Its development should be constantly encouraged and sought at the preschool level.

Developing Elementary Number Concepts

Elementary number concepts such as "just enough," "the same number," "more," and "less," are an important part of logical thinking. Their beginnings are a natural part of nursery school activities. The child who holds up four fingers and says, "I'm four," when asked his age, or the child who can correctly count from 1 through 5, may or may not have number concepts. Unless he can also select 4 of something or know that by adding 1 more to 4 he will have 5, he lacks the elementary concepts of "the same number" and "more."

Before children can solve problems involving number—that is, quantity and measurement—they must be able to do more than count. They must be able to comprehend differences between big/little, full/empty, long/short, same/different, etc. Unless a child perceives these contrasts he will not realize there is a problem to solve.

Classification and seriation abilities provide a framework for the kind of knowledge needed, but children must also have experiences leading to the achievement of specific number goals. In Piaget's theory of number, the first of these goals is establishing *numerical equivalence by one-to-one correspondence;* the second is establishing *conservation*.

CONCEPT
Numerical equivalence by one-to-one correspondence

DESCRIPTION
Two sets are equivalent by one-to-one correspondence if each element of one set is exactly duplicated in the other, and vice versa

MATERIALS
Sets of identical small items that can be easily manipulated (bottle caps, checkers, game pieces, slugs, etc.), perhaps 5 or 6 different items per set

Typical Procedure (Practice in linear ordering to make equivalent sets)

1. Make a row of items such as those shown

and ask child to make a row just like it underneath.

TEACHERS OF YOUNG CHILDREN

2. When he has finished ask, "Do we each have the same number of pieces?" Then, "How do you know?" (Even if child can count he should be asked to show his understanding by matching one-to-one.) Repeat this many times with different arrangement of items and also having child arrange a line and check teacher's "wrong" matching.

Children tend to quantify items by the amount of space an array occupies. Consequently, for a situation like the one illustrated, preschool children will probably say there are more in the top row than in the bottom row since they judge from the amount of space occupied rather than by number. Linear ordering and matching one-to-one helps build a logical rather than spatial basis for judging amount. Using dolls and hats and giving children opportunities of "find just enough hats for these dolls and not too many," or "just enough trikes for these children and not too many" (Piaget's *provoked correspondence*), strengthens the notion of one-to-one correspondence qualitatively as well as quantitatively. With mastery of numerical equivalence based on one-to-one correspondence, children are ready for simple addition and subtraction games.

Preschool children do not yet realize that when the shape or location of objects is changed, quantity is conserved since the original condition can be re-established. Although they are unable to consider destruction and re-establishment at the same time (*reversibility*), they can be started toward this kind of cognitive ability by being given practice in arranging, disarranging, and then rearranging. Thus, by proceeding successively in only one direction at a time children begin to understand that objects can be returned to the same spatial relationship and will also retain their original amount. The exercise that follows helps develop this idea:

CONCEPT

Conservation

MATERIALS

16 counters identical in all ways but color; half white and half green

DESCRIPTION

Conservation is the ability to know that the equivalence of two sets *must* remain the same when their spatial arrangement is changed

CONCEPT

Topological content
Transformation

CONCEPT LABEL

Above-below
Over-under
In-out
Behind-in front of
Disassembling object into smaller parts and reassembling to original shape

Typical Procedure

1. Ask child to make a row using all the counters of one color. Then have him make a row of white counters underneath the green without mentioning number. Ask "Are there the same number of green pieces and white pieces?" "How do you know?" "Make the rows so they have the same number."
2. Teacher then removes one counter. "Now are there the same number of green pieces and white pieces?" "How do you know?" She adds two, takes two, takes one from each row, etc., always asking, "Now are they the same number?" "How do you know?" until she is satisfied child has the notion of "same number."

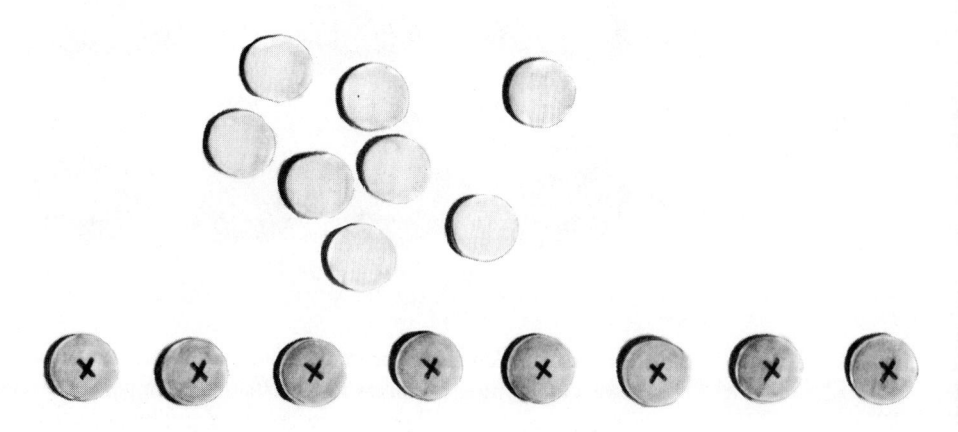

3. Teacher: "Take all the pieces from one row and put them here." (See illustration.) "Now are there the same number of white and green pieces?" "How do you know?" (If he does not answer first question she might ask, "Are there more white pieces than green pieces or are there the same number?")
4. Teacher has child rearrange white pieces in a matching row and asks, "Are there more green pieces than white pieces or are there the same?"

Arranging, disarranging and rearranging can be done first without matching—just by having child "put the pieces in another way" and then back again, over and over, in as many ways as the child can think of for himself or be prompted to do by the teacher. He should have a chance to explore these "exercises" with many kinds and numbers of objects. And he should be permitted to do them over and over but not made to continue beyond the level of his own interest.

Good practice can be achieved by changing plasticene "balls" into "sausages" and back, pouring liquid into different size containers and back, stacking blocks one place or another and then back. From such activities (some of which Piaget used in his classic experiments) children develop experience which enables them to predict results. Children must themselves be involved many times in order to internalize processes of this kind, and so come to perform by thinking instead of empirically. The most fundamental requirement is the child's active participation. At no time should the teacher perform the action and have the child merely observe.

Developing Concepts of Space and Time

At the preschool level developing space concepts includes the concept of *linear ordering*:

> Putting objects in sequence by some
> principle other than numbering

The myriad motoric experiences of children in nursery school build space concepts with topological content: putting objects *in* and taking them *out;* crawling *over, through, around,* and *under;* looking *high* and *low.* From these experiences children learn to recognize that even without their direct manipulation, a cup may be *in* or *on* the sink, a cookie *behind* or *in front of* a glass of juice. A child who has formed concepts of this kind can be expected to say, "The snowman has a hat *on top of* his head," when he sees a representation of this in a picture.

Puzzles, block structures and flannel board stories that return to the first picture at the end of the story, provide a means for children to develop the concept of *transformation*. Further practice in building this idea of space comes when children cut pictures into several large pieces and put them back together.

The space concept of *linear ordering* might begin with the child copying the way a table is set for a tea party. Arranging identical supplies in identical order on different shelves, so that more than one person has the materials needed for a special project, also gives practice in linear ordering.

Young children's questions (such as those listed on p. 197) show their awareness of time. In general, *time concepts* involve:

> Temporal order: first, next, last
> before, after
> sooner, later
> if . . . then (cause and effect)

195   GROWTH OF LANGUAGE AND COGNITIVE ABILITIES

Intervals: minute, hour, day, week, year
sometime ago
in a little while

Studies made by Piaget and his associates indicate that a child's ability to structure uniform intervals comes much later than his ability to deal with temporal order. Therefore, at the preschool level it is desirable to help children develop time concepts based on sequence but not increments.

Many opportunities for children to learn relationships about time come through the teacher's emphasis on what is going on now, what has already been done, and what happens next. Telling a child, "We'll do that in an hour" carries little meaning. Explaining, "That's something for after juice time," relates a forthcoming event to his own experience.

Constant reminders about the regular events of the preschool schedule is one way of making children more aware of time. In addition, teachers convey ideas about time whenever they use expressions such as the following:

As soon as everyone's quiet . . .
When you go home at noon . . .
This morning we'll . . .
Tonight I'm going to . . .
Right now let's . . . then later on we . . .
Before you go out, be sure to . . .
When you come in . . .
First let's finish this and then . . .
Next time, why not . . .
It's Danny's turn first, Maurine is next, and
   Gerry can be last.

Preschoolers can also begin to develop concepts of time related to cause and effect. No special "lessons" need to be prepared since children best understand causal relationships as consequences of their own actions. When a child is using a crayon and it breaks, the teacher can simply ask, "What happens when you press too hard?" Likewise with chalk: "What happens when you drop a piece of chalk?"

Children should have many experiences pouring liquids, stacking blocks, bouncing balls from different heights, shoving, pushing, pulling, fastening. In this way notions of cause and effect can begin to take form. From their own involvement children learn to predict the responses of their teachers, their classmates and the world around them.

**Young Children's Typical
Questions About Time**

*Is today a long time?
Is a year big?   Is my birthday a year?
When will it be tomorrow?
When is it today?
How old will I be when I'm forty?
How much time is 10 o'clock?
What does 4:30 mean?*

Some Issues and Principles of Cognitive Learning at the Preschool Level

The cognitive activity which takes place in the human brain makes it possible to store information received from experience. The structures already present (concepts, labels, patterns of stimuli) determine the way new information is processed. For example, although a big league baseball scout and an interested fan see the same baseball game, each will sort, select and store different details. Information which comes in that does not readily fit the concepts and logic already in use forces whoever is receiving it to examine and perhaps modify his internal structures. *Thus the reality of the external world is at least in part a reality of internal structures.* As these change, the external world is naturally seen in somewhat different ways. This is cognitive growth. The process of changing mental operations in response to externally derived information in turn changes the way the external world is seen and makes additional growth possible.

Although described separately in this text, the acquisition of physical knowledge and logical knowledge are inseparable. A child is not likely to form concepts regarding classification or spatial relationships without at the same time gaining understandings of physical properties. Although they occur simultaneously, acquisition of logical knowledge is more difficult to determine than acquisition of physical knowledge since the former is based on observation and interaction with the external world, the latter on consistency of internal processes. One can be verified, the other only inferred.

Conceptual development raises the basic issue of how much the growth of the mind and its abilities results from teaching and how much of it is an unfolding, maturational process. In other words, does the child best acquire cognitive ability when the teacher presents him with information step by step according to a preconceived curriculum, or when he himself deals with and logically orders changing cognitive structures? As more becomes known about how children learn, these different explanations may eventually converge; they may not be antithetical so much as simply different ways to think about a particular aspect of human growth and development.

For the young child, conceptual operations and cognitive abilities essential for future school success overlap and are less differentiated than they will be later on. Therefore teachers in programs of early education need to provide an environment conducive to a wide range of mental activity, rather than trying to concentrate on developing premath, prescience, or prereading skills. In the early formation of concepts, school-related tasks have common cognitive roots. It is important to recognize that the end points of the mental processes involved in forming concepts cannot be imposed without giving the child an opportunity to build the needed base. Unless the preschooler forms a wide variety of concepts, he is obviously limited in what he can gain from formal education.

The task of the preschool, then, should be to concentrate on the preliminary steps that make further learning more efficient even though the "teaching" may be gradual and undramatic. In these circumstances the importance of the teacher who knows something about how language and cognitive abilities develop cannot be overestimated. In many instances she, more than anyone else, is in a position to help children prepare for success, not failure, in the school years that lie ahead.

REFERENCES

Almy, M. C. *Young childrens' thinking; studies of some aspects of Piaget's theory.* New York: Teachers College Press, Teachers College, Columbia University, 1966.

Birren, J. E. and Hess, R. D. (Eds.) Influences of biological, psychological, and social deprivation upon learning and performance. *Perspectives on human deprivation: biological, psychological, and sociological.* Washington, D.C.: U.S. Department of Health, Education and Welfare, Public Health Service, National Institutes of Health, The National Institute of Child Health and Human Development, 1968, pp. 91–186.

Brearley, M. and Hitchfield, E. *A guide to reading Piaget.* New York: Schoken Books, 1966.

Bugental, D. E. et al. Child versus adult perceptions of evaluative messages in verbal, vocal, and visual channels. *Developmental Psychology,* May, 1970, *2,* No. 3, 367–375.

Cazden, C. B. The neglected situation in child language research and education. In F. Williams, (Ed.), *Language and poverty, perspectives on a theme,* Chicago, Ill.: Markham Publishing Co., 1970, pp. 81–101.

Cazden, C. B. Suggestions from studies of early language acquisition. *Childhood Education,* 1969, *46,* 127–131.

Flavell, J. H. *The developmental psychology of Jean Piaget.* Princeton, N.J.: Van Nostrand Co., 1963.

Gleason, J. B. Do children imitate? Paper read at International Conference on Oral Education of the Deaf, Lexington School for the Deaf. New York City, June 1967.

Inhelder, B. and Piaget, J. *The early growth of logic in the child; classification and seriation.* New York: Harper and Row, 1964.

Kamii, C. K. and Radin, N. L. A framework for a preschool curriculum based on some Piagetian concepts. *The Journal of Creative Behavior,* July 1967, *1,* No. 3, 314–324.

Kamii, C. K. Evaluation of learning in preschool education: socio-emotional, perceptual-motor, cognitive development. In B. S. Bloom, J. T. Hastings, and G. F. Madaus, (Eds.), *Handbook on formative and summative evaluation of student learning.* New York: McGraw-Hill, Inc., 1971.

Kamii, C. An application of Piaget's theory to the conceptualization of a preschool curriculum. In R. K. Parker, (Ed.), *Conceptualizations of preschool curricula.* Boston, Mass.: Allyn and Bacon, Inc., in press.

Lenneberg, E. H., Nichols, I. A., and Rosenberger, E. F. Primitive stages of language development in mongolism. In D. Rioch and E. A. Weinstein, (Eds.), *Disorders of communication.* Research Publication of Association for Research in Nervous and Mental Disorders, New York, Baltimore; Williams and Wilkins, 1964, *42,* 128–130.

Lenneberg, E. H. On explaining language. *Science,* May 9, 1969, *164,* No. 3880, 635–643.

Piaget, J. *The construction of reality in the child.* New York: Basic Books, 1954.

Piaget, J. *The origins of intelligence in children.* New York: International Universities Press, Inc., 1952.

Sinclair, H. and Kamii, C. K. Some implications of Piaget's theory for teaching young children. Paper prepared as part of the Ypsilanti Early Education Program, Ypsilanti, Michigan, March 1969.

Sonquist, H. D. and Kamii, C. K. Applying some Piagetian concepts in the classroom for the disadvantaged. *Young Children,* March 1967, 231–246.

Sonquist, H., Kamii, C. K., and Derman, L. A Piaget-derived preschool curriculum. In I. J. Athey and D. O. Rubadeau, (Eds.), *Educational implications of Piaget's theory,* Waltham, Mass.: Ginn-Blaisdell, 1970, pp. 101–114.

U.S. National Institute of Neurological Diseases and Stroke. *Learning to talk, speech, hearing and language problems in the preschool child.* National Institutes of Health, U.S. Department of Health, Education and Welfare, Washington, D.C.: U.S. Government Printing Office, 1969.

CHAPTER 7

SOCIAL CONCEPTS AND BEHAVIOR

GROWTH OF SELF-KNOWLEDGE

The child gains knowledge about himself in the same way he initially learns about other aspects of the physical world. As an infant he plays with his toes and fingers, explores the contours of his body, pulling, poking, pushing, until he has satisfied his curiosity about where his body leaves off and the external world begins. Later, he can look in a mirror to help him know what he looks like. He needs labels, of course, but he can see for himself the color of his hair, whether he is big or little, what he looks like when he smiles or frowns, and so on.

But such perceptions, important as they are, contribute only partly to the development of self-knowledge. As a child grows, he acquires concepts of himself and his physical features, his worth and an understanding of his place in the society.

The Self

In seeking to understand how to help children develop feelings about themselves, it is important for teachers to distinguish between *self-concept, identity* and *self-esteem.*

Self-concept is a result of cognitive activity. It is the child's awareness of his own characteristics and of the differences and likenesses between himself and others. He learns to think of himself as "tall," "talkative," "red-headed," "strong," "right-handed," and the like. Even though he may not be able to verbalize the differences, he sees himself as separate from the adult members of his family, and distinct from other children. By three he knows whether he is a boy or a girl; his vocabulary includes the words *me, mine, I, you, yours,* and sometimes *we* and *ours.* This aspect of a child's self-knowledge indicates cognitive awareness of his characteristics, but includes no notion of evaluation, nor does it make clear his relationships to others.

Identity has a social connotation. While self-concept gives the child an image of himself as an individual, identity brings awareness of group membership. Understanding that possession of certain physical characteristics means "being a boy" precedes knowledge that there is a group called "boys" and that membership in this group carries with it certain expectations, privileges and restraints. Without necessarily understanding the reasons, the child becomes aware of his membership in such a group. He first finds out he's a boy and then becomes aware of what it is that boys do.

A child's recognition that he has dark skin comes before an understanding that this may also mean he is a Negro, or that Negroes as a group often face discrimination and a set of expectations in white American society. Identity comes when some kind of sociocultural meaning is attached to elements of the self-concept. It is a process through which a child gains knowledge of such matters as his name, race, sex role and social class.

FIGURE 7–1 AS A CHILD GROWS, HE DEVELOPS A SENSE OF SELF-KNOWLEDGE

Self-esteem is the level of regard an individual has for what he is and does. It reflects how a child feels about himself. Almost as soon as self-concepts form, they acquire positive or negative evaluations. For the child, self-concept and self-esteem are highly related since both have their source in feedback from people that are important to him. It is unlikely that children separate fact from evaluation when they hear, "My, aren't you a big boy!" or "Where did you ever get all those freckles?" Self-esteem may be *low* or *high,* self-concepts clear or incomplete, though this distinction is not always made. One is a level of regard, the other a cognitive grasp of characteristics.

Origins of Self-Concept and Self-Esteem The building of self-concept is a cognitive operation carried out in much the same way as children form concepts of the physical world. The source of information for the physical world is much more direct, but the processes are not different. Based on a great deal of information from many different experiences, the child abstracts and generalizes—in one case about an object he perceives, in the other about himself, his behavior, and his feelings.

Self-concept and self-esteem originate from four major sources: 1) the impressions a child receives from others, 2) his own accumulated experiences, 3) his ability to live up to and internalize the goals set for him, and 4) the capacity to evaluate his performance on the basis of his own standards (Coopersmith, 1967). The impressions a child receives from those who are especially significant to him are very important. Their comments about him, their approval or disapproval of what he does, their concern for his welfare, their inclusion or exclusion of him from their activities—all of these influence the way in which a child sees and values himself.

The child comes to know whether he is shy, aggressive, lazy, neat, willing, naughty, or good not from his own analysis, but from remarks made about him. The comments of people important to him are significant whether directly addressed to him or not. Indeed, children are sometimes talked about as though they were not present, as in the following conversation:

SOCIAL CONCEPTS AND BEHAVIOR

Mother   (while Cindy listens) *I just don't know what I'm going to do about Cindy.*
Neighbor   *Why, what's wrong?*
Mother   *Well, she takes forever to eat. And messy! You just can't imagine. By the time she's finished half of what I give her, it's either on the table or on the floor. You know, her father's just the same way. That's why I always use those washable table cloths. Have you ever tried them? They're . . .*

In such instances, a child not only hears the words and ideas of his mother's conversation, but he also receives an underlying message that his mother doesn't care whether he hears her criticism or not.

A second source of the development of a child's self-concept and self-esteem is his accumulation of successful experiences. As a child ventures into a world larger than his immediate family, he competes with others for rewards of many kinds. The child whose appearance and ways make a favorable impression sees himself as quite a different person from the one who meets with indifference or rejection. He may not realize what gives him this advantage, but his history of success in getting approval (even though this may only be sitting on a visitor's lap), forms a basis for high self-esteem. A cumulative effect of this kind is a powerful influence on the development of self-concept.

Success in school-related tasks also plays an important role in the development of both self-concept and self-esteem. Early in the primary grades, children come to see themselves as smart (or not) in the things the teacher requires. The familiar teaching technique of dividing the class into ability groups ("This group is the Redbirds; this one is the Bluebirds") indicating fast and slow learners is an early and dramatic feedback of the teacher's opinion of the child's ability. The teacher also gives individual evaluations of the child's behavior and performance in more individualized, subtle ways.

There is some disagreement among professionals in early education as to whether self-esteem contributes to successful performance or follows from it. One view is that children need to feel good about themselves and their abilities and this sense of confidence will enable them to achieve. The other view is that true self confidence and esteem come from mastery of a task and the clear demonstration of skills. Otherwise the confidence is only a hope. The child who has learned to read or can count (or perform whatever task is set by the teacher) has a firmer sense of his competence because he has shown himself and others that he can perform valued tasks. The route to self-esteem is skill, in this approach, and we mislead the child if he is told he's doing fine when he isn't.

Teachers may find it difficult to take sides on this argument because both positions are appealing. Perhaps the solution may be to let the child know he is valued as a person but move immediately to help him acquire the skills he needs to maintain self-esteem.

The third source which strongly affects the formation of self-concept and self-esteem is the child's ability to live up to the goals set for him and internalized by him. If a child must be "perfect" in order to be content, self-esteem is likely to be very low. Even young children feel obliged to live up to certain expectations and standards, especially those established by a parent. Once this happens, they are often unable to accept what others say, and judge themselves only by this inner value system.

Five-year-old Marshall was such a child. He came from a family that insisted on "excellent" performance at all times and "exemplary manners," including answering "Yes, sir" and "Yes, ma'am" at appropriate times. So strongly had the notion of doing something perfectly or not doing it at all been impressed upon Marshall that he saw himself as a failure in much he attempted on his own. He often went to the art table at school but could not bring himself to draw the dinosaur he really wanted because, he explained, "I can't make them good enough." Instead he contented himself with scribbling as he had when he was much younger.

Marshall and children like him will suffer from lack of confidence and self-esteem until they set realistic standards for themselves and use them to evaluate their performance. This is the fourth source of feelings of esteem and self-concept. Standards which the child has set for himself help him maintain a stable self-esteem even in the face of criticism and other negative feedback. Very young children are unable to do this, but they can be helped to *decide for themselves* what success and good performance mean in the various things they do. Having done so they can recognize for themselves when they have accomplished something satisfactory.

Whatever their origins, a child's self-concept and self-esteem develop continuously. They cannot be "taught" in sessions of ten or fifteen minutes a day. The young child's awareness and evaluation of himself depend largely on the way others talk to him and about him, and how they behave toward him. Teachers aware of the processes involved recognize their part as significant people in the lives of young children.

The Self and the Social System

In infancy a child lacks the ability to distinguish between where his own body ends and where the world that surrounds him begins. The hand whose shape and texture he explores as he might a rattle or toy may be his own or his mother's; at first he does not differentiate or know. Repeated experiences and increasing physical maturation lead him to see himself as an individual, one who shares characteristics with other individuals. He recognizes his membership in a group, and forms not only self-concepts, but concepts of his mother, his father, and the other members of his family. Through interaction with people he enters the social world.

Awareness of Group Membership and Interaction Once he recognizes himself and his immediate family as separate entities, the child becomes aware that there are still other people. Some of these others are like himself. They, too, have mothers and fathers. To his notions of "my mother," and "my father," therefore, he adds the new realization that there are *other* parents and arrives at the general concepts of "mother" and "father." These concepts, based on social knowledge, are developed by the same kinds of cognitive processes used to form concepts from physical knowledge and logical knowledge. Information from which to build social concepts such as "mother" and "father," however, is far more diffuse and difficult to get than information which enables someone to form concepts such as "chair" and "under," yet is apparently processed in the same ways. The child continually receives, arranges, stores and rearranges information as a result of his participation and involvement with humans, objects and relationships.

Generalization about himself and those significant to him leads to an awareness of roles and social groups. The preschooler begins to understand not only that he belongs to a family, but will soon realize that the family itself is part of larger groups. It will be some time before he comprehends the religious, economic or ethnic nature of these, but his awareness is nonetheless real.

The consistency of the relationships he has with others brings about realization that there are not only fathers and mothers, but neighbors, teachers, priests, storekeepers, nurses, bus drivers, dentists, aunts, uncles, grandparents and so on. Until a later stage of his development he will not be able to separate the role from the person. Within the family he may be able to comprehend that his father also has a father and so is both parent and son. But he is usually not able to perceive that his father also fills the role of "mayor" or "clerk." To the child, his father is one or the other but not both simultaneously. Gradually his thinking develops until he is able to grasp the notion of people occupying multiple roles. This same inflexibility pertains to inanimate objects. The only "home" he knows is his own, or perhaps the house of a friend. Abstractions are not part of his mental processes. He deals with only the specific, the concrete, those matters he can know and verify from his own experience.

Gradually the child begins to see that families are composed of fathers, mothers, sons and daughters; a school consists of teachers and children. His participation in groups shows him that the various elements within them depend upon one another and that groups themselves interact with each other to form larger entities—schools, communities, cities, nations. This kind of concept development is like other conceptual growth. It proceeds from personal awareness of repeated events and objects to an abstraction of their common characteristics and the application of a label. It is not something one learns and sets aside or forgets; it is an ongoing, continuous process beginning early in life and developing more completely during the school years.

Because he is likely to perceive the world from only his own viewpoint, the young child's initial role in the social world is that of observer. His inability to comprehend social orientation is analogous to his struggle to deal with spatial orientation; imagining how a person feels and thinks is also difficult for him. Yet effectiveness in social relationships ultimately depends on this ability to imagine how another person feels, to take into account his needs and to communicate with him accordingly.

Role-taking Ability From the work of Piaget and the many who have followed his lead, a great deal is beginning to be known about the development of cognitive operations with respect to the physical environment. The growth of intellectual skills related to social behavior is far less clear. Research undertaken by Flavell and associates (1966) offers clues to understanding these abilities. Flavell concentrated on seeking to determine what role-taking ability children acquire and approximately when it develops.

In two studies he worked with 160 children grades two through 11; in another his subjects were 40 preschool children ages three to six. The ability of preschool children to assume the role of another person was examined by means of the following situations:

1. Subject and experimenter sat facing each other across a table and the child was asked to place a picture so that the experimenter could see it right side up.
2. The sharpened end of an ordinary lead pencil rested in the hand of the experimenter. Its other end (with a cotton ball glued to it) rested in a child's hand. The child was first asked, "Does the pencil feel soft?" Then he was asked to tell if it felt soft to the experimenter.
3. As the child examined an array of objects he was asked to select one he might give to his mother for a birthday present. (Father, teacher, sibling and self were also included in the study.) His ability to choose a gift appropriate to the interest of the person named was held to be indicative of the level of his ability to role play. For example, the child who chose a truck for his mother showed "poor" role-taking performance.

1. What skills does the child acquire, in what order, and at what ages?
2. Does a high level of role-taking performance in one setting mean that use of the same components will result in an equally high level in another setting?
3. What effect does background and experience have on a child's ability to role play?
4. How is social behavior affected by the child's ability to role play?

adapted from J. H. Flavell, "Role Taking and Communication Skills in Children," *Young Children*, No. 3, 1966, p. 176.

From this work and previous studies by others, Flavell speculated that high performance in role-taking requires first an understanding that there is a perspective other than one's own (that not everyone sees, thinks, or feels alike); second, realization that an analysis of the other perspective might be useful; third, possession of the ability to carry out the analysis needed; fourth, a way of keeping in mind what is learned from analysis; and fifth, knowledge of how to translate the results of analysis into effective social behavior—that is, into terms of getting along better with the person whose viewpoint is under consideration.

Of the factors needed for benefiting from role-taking, only the first—the ability to understand that there is more than one viewpoint—is one that the preschooler acquires. Even this awareness depends on "task situations where the experimenter's instructions and the elemental nature of the role attributes in question conspire to facilitate such awareness" (Flavell, 1966, p. 175).

Like Piaget (who finds that until a child is seven or eight his role-taking skills are not sufficiently well developed for him to participate in truly nonegocentric behavior), Flavell (1966, p. 176) reports a lack of role-taking ability in young children:

> Although the data are really not yet ample enough to justify it, one is tempted to predict that middle childhood will turn out to be *the* developmental epoch so far as basic role-taking and allied skills are concerned, with the preschool period contributing the prologue and adolescence the epilogue.

Flavell also points out the need for further knowledge and suggests that answers should be sought to questions such as those listed above.

Racial and Social-Class Awareness

Even as the child becomes conscious of himself as an individual, a member of a family and so a part of society, he develops awareness of racial and social-class differences between himself and others. Children as young as three notice skin color, facial features and hair texture. They look at, touch, and make comparisons regarding one another in much the same way that they explore the physical characteristics of any aspect of the world around them. Judgment is not involved, only a desire to determine what something is like by comparing it with what they already know.

Realization of differences based on race make little change in the children's behavior toward one another. Working with a group of three-year-old Negro and white children, Stevenson (1962, p. 118) found that:

The interaction between children appeared to depend, as it does in most types of social interaction, upon the degree to which the relationship between individuals satisfied each other's needs.

According to various studies it has been found that by age five labels such as "He's black," or "She's Chinese," or "They're Mexican," have discriminatory meanings and children of other groups began to take on negative attitudes and behaviors toward those so labeled. Their prejudice is based for the most part on adult norms.

Children notice skin color differences from pictures before they think of themselves as white or nonwhite. In past studies, identification of others as members of a racial group generally took place earlier for white than nonwhite children. Whereas minority group youngsters rarely saw a white person before starting school, white children came in contact with the minority group members who worked in their neighborhoods. Changing attitudes toward racial identity in both white and ethnic communities and desegregation in schools are stimulating new research in order to understand more completely racial awareness and its meaning for young children.

The preschooler's awareness of social class begins to emerge by noticing the various ways in which people live. Because of these differences he may categorize some people as "poor" and others as "rich" even though he isn't able to explain the meaning of these terms. Also a child may have a notion of status as it accrues to a family because of the father's occupation, but concepts of his own position in the social structure do not form until well along in the elementary school years. The realization that others have more (or fewer) toys than he is likely to be a greater factor in the development of the child's self-concept and self-esteem than the socio-economic status of his family.

CONCEPTS OF SOCIAL RELATIONSHIPS

An essential aspect of a young child's social understanding and behavior involves learning and comprehending rules. From the time he first explores beyond the narrow confines of a particular play area, he is surrounded with verbal and physical constraints: "Don't touch!" "That's a No-No," "Use both hands," "Say, 'please,'" "Stay in your room," "Stop making all that noise." The list is long. Initially, regulations of this kind exist for the child's safety or are intended to "train him in good manners." Many are associated with the comfort and convenience of other family members. All are prohibitive in nature but carry little overtone of right or wrong. Behavior of a very young child is not judged from a moral standpoint. Gradually, he is expected to act in conformity with standards of the family group. He is told it's "wrong" to hit his brother, he's a "bad" boy for pouring his milk on the floor instead of drinking it, or it's "naughty" to

Dimensions of Morality

Moral Knowledge: Information about right and wrong behavior—specific rather than general

Moral Feelings: Inner reactions of guilt or innocence regarding one's behavior

Moral Conduct: Acting according to group standards of behavior

---

play in the mud and get his good clothes dirty. Whether moral behavior is involved, or simply his safety and manners, the child is scolded and punished in the same ways.

At a nursery school he gets new information about how he is expected to behave and what is considered right and wrong. Now he is judged from a much wider context. He must learn rules made by adults whose standards may be quite different from those he has known at home. Right and wrong have taken on a new dimension; however, they are still group standards imposed on the individual.

In turn, both at home and at school, adults respond to the needs of the child. Thus, there exists a contractual relationship between the individual and the social unit of which he is a member.

Development of Concepts about Rules

Children acquire concepts about rules in a more or less predictable sequence but not in well defined stages. Initially, children see themselves as subject to adult authority. Acts which are in accord with the rules made by adults are "right." The rule may not be a formal one in the usual sense; the child who "helps Mother" or "does what Daddy tells him to" is being "good" and doing "right" things. If he is punished, it follows that whatever he did must have been something "wrong."

Rules made by his parents guide his behavior until he accumulates the experience and maturity needed to formulate more sophisticated concepts of right and wrong. Adult authority in the form of rules continues to dominate the child's conception of morality until he is about eight years old. This is the first general phase of moral development. After this time the basis for conduct includes rules based on group agreement and cooperative action. Rules are less often seen as absolutes, but as something that can be changed according to the wishes of the members of the group involved.

Moral Development

Dimensions of Morality In general, morality is the outcome of the dimensions defined above. These are not independent of one another but parts of a whole. Knowledge, feelings and conduct are all involved in the acquisition of morality. For example, suppose a child is told, "Do not steal." Before this ideal of appropriate conduct becomes part of his moral code, he obviously must know what "to steal" means. Is he stealing when he takes a toy from his shelf or only when he takes the same toy from a shelf at a store? Is he stealing when he shuts Mrs. Johnson's cat in his garage? What is stealing? What isn't?

Even though the child has a definition of stealing clearly in mind, if taking possessions that don't belong to him leaves him without a feeling of wrong-doing, morality

Hypothetical Situations Used to Test Moral Judgment of Children

When John is called to dinner, in entering the dining room he inadvertently overturns a tray of fifteen cups and breaks them all.

While his mother is out, Henry goes to a cupboard and helps himself to forbidden jam. In reaching to the shelf where the jam is kept he knocks over and breaks a cup.

adapted from J. Piaget, The Moral Judgment of the Child, 1948, p. 118.

---

is only partially developed. Unless the child feels "guilty" for his theft, or somehow virtuous when he refrains from transgression, he has not yet acquired a sense of morality. The rule must also serve as a guide to conduct. If the child knows he is stealing, feels guilty, but goes right ahead and steals, he has not developed morality. Knowledge, feeling and conduct must all be present before morality is acquired.

At his stage of cognitive development, the preschool child cannot be expected to display morality in this complete sense. He may be made aware of the rules of the teacher and may know what pleases her and what kinds of things will cause her to punish him or withdraw approval. He may also behave accordingly or feel guilt if he does not. Although they are the beginning of a complex process, these are important phases in the development of genuine morality.

Limits of Comprehension Moral development in the sense of understanding, rather than merely acceding to principles associated with moral behavior, begins during the preschool years and continues long after the child embarks on formal education. Obviously understanding is limited at first. However, the child's primitive feeling of inner discomfort which accompanies having broken a rule, may be similar or antecedent to his later orientation toward more sophisticated moral principles. Perhaps the initial learning is the awareness that there *are* rules which one must attend to in social interaction. This early response to underlying moral principles may be analogous to a child's use of grammatical rules. Long before he can define any aspect of syntax, he learns and applies rules which make verbal interaction possible.

Piaget's 1932 study of moral judgment shows that children judge "rightness" and "wrongness" according to how much harm has been done; older children take into consideration the intent of the actor. To confirm his theory, Piaget asked two different age groups of children to tell him which of the boys in the situations summarized at the top of the page had been the naughtier.

The younger children (all under seven years of age) agreed that John was naughtier than Henry because he had broken many more cups. On the other hand, children ages nine and ten were just as certain Henry's intent made him the naughtier child.

Extensive studies by Hartshorne and May as long ago as 1930 show that morality in behavior is not a general trait—that is, it does not apply to all situations. Although their work involved only school-age children (not preschool), it suggests principles with broad applications. Some 11,000 children were given a chance to cheat, lie and steal in many different circumstances without fear of being caught or punished. To their surprise, the investigators found that even in closely related circumstances (a math test and a spelling test, for example), a child would cheat on one and not the other. In other words, there was little relationship from one situation to another between behavior defined as "wrong."

The conclusion that children are not consistently moral in their conduct seems also to apply to the other areas of morality—emotion and knowledge or judgment. Studies of moral knowledge show some individual internal consistency but nothing of the sort of global, unifying concept of conscience and moral principles that is frequently assumed.

Other studies assessing the degree of guilt that accompanies different types of immorality indicate that there may be differences in feelings experienced in immoral conduct from one type of behavior to another and of one type of behavior from one event to the next. The conditions of the specific event, especially the likelihood of punishment or detection appear to be involved in the intensity of feelings of guilt (Brown, 1965, p. 413).

It is important for the teacher of young children to remember that the process of developing moral judgment is not a simple internalization of rules of the adult world or of conditioning through rewards and punishments. The conceptual component of morality continues through adolescence (Kohlberg, 1963) and probably throughout much of adult life as the individual struggles to sort out his own standards and values in the light of his own experience. A valuable part of that experience is having been with adults who made their rules and expectations clear and offered reasons for them. Moral judgment grows through the complex processes involved in other forms of conceptual development but with perhaps more difficulty. The knowledge and subsequent concepts gained from experience with the physical world begin with a firm base of physical tangible information. Social and moral knowledge are based on more ephemeral events and often come from experiences with conflicting evidence or values. The decisions many young men faced in the draft for the war in Vietnam, for example, were struggles between values of loyalty to their country and consequence for themselves and families as opposed to convictions that the war itself was not justified or moral. The development of a moral conceptual framework thus seems to be a matter of absorbing and reflecting upon experience, values of others, knowledge of consequences for oneself and others and beliefs developed in other ways. The preschool child is obviously merely beginning the process of constructing moral concepts and developing appropriate feelings and conduct.

The relationship between overt behavior and other dimensions or morality is not as close as one might think. Moral knowledge does not guarantee moral behavior, nor do feelings of guilt, although both are related to behavior. It appears that the child develops morality through different channels (Brown, 1965, p. 412). Moral judgment and knowledge are cognitive operations. Moral conduct is probably more often a result of reinforcement and imitation, and moral feelings appear to be in part a result of conditioning or association with painful experiences in the past. Feelings about misbehavior (however the act is defined) can be instilled by punishment, praise, approval and disapproval, and especially by withdrawal of love. Within limits these are useful.

A sense that there are "right" behaviors and "wrong" behaviors is a separate learning from what the specific behaviors may be. It is an important phase, but if the child is to be truly moral, he must eventually acquire morality through his own conceptual processes. The moral person is one who is able and willing to regulate his behavior on the basis of his judgments about the rightness or wrongness of his behavior in terms of principles of justice and of conditions in the society in which he is living.

PATTERNS OF SOCIAL BEHAVIOR

Recognizing patterns of social behavior without guidelines of some kind is a little like trying to make sense of a burgeoning, sprawling metropolitan area, such as Los Angeles, without any knowledge of cities and how they grow. Anything so diffuse, so complex, and so seemingly unpredictable as social behavior seems to defy understanding. Nonetheless, there are ways to look at social behavior which help put it in perspective.

Unlike many other aspects of human development, young children's social behavior has thus far failed to attract widespread study. Patterns of physical growth are well documented, and a great deal is beginning to be known about human cognitive development. But the nature, antecedents, and extent of social behavior at this age level are less well known.

Social Interaction

One way to look at social behavior is along dimensions which affect interaction and the way children deal with the issues involved in interpersonal behavior. This view of social behavior avoids some value judgments of whether the interactions are good in some moral sense and concentrates on attempts to understand some of the reasons why children behave as they do.

One of the central concerns of parents and of teachers in early educational programs is whether young children will learn to "get along with others" and develop social skills and competence. This is sometimes accompanied by a belief that a child who is not popular and socially active is not developing properly. The initial question of social interaction, then, is how much a child interacts or wants to interact with other children. As professionals we possibly place too much value upon group activities and social exchange. It is as normal for children to play alone and avoid social contact at times as it is for them to seek companionship. Beatrice de Regniers (1954) recognized this when she wrote:

> But sometimes you just want everyone to leave you alone.
> No children. No grownups.
> You just don't want anyone to bother you.

A child who plays alone frequently is not necessarily antisocial, rejected, lonely or without resources. The teacher who recognizes this aspect of social behavior realizes that her intervention may not be needed and will wait for other signs that something is wrong before interfering.

A central goal of a teacher is to understand the behavior of children in terms that put it in a conceptual context and give meaning to what they do. An identical social act will justify quite different interpretations from different perspectives. One adult may see a child's initiative in leading a group as decisiveness and leadership; another may see the child as bossy and both may be correct. Concepts for viewing and interpreting social behavior thus add perspective and depth, giving the teacher more information on which to decide if a specific act calls for intervention, reinforcement or serious concern.

It may be useful to think of social behavior along dimensions such as these:

1. Territoriality (establishment and maintenance of one's own boundaries)
2. Approach and influence behavior (attempts to obtain resources from others or alter the environment)
3. Alignment and cooperative behavior (joining with others for individual benefit or group goals)

As is true of much of human behavior, its complexity makes it difficult to define pure dimensions of analysis. These dimensions overlap; the same act may apply to more than one.

Territoriality Territoriality is a label given to the attitudes and actions by which humans and other animals establish and maintain both geographic and psychological boundaries (Ardrey, 1966). Just as though he had posted a "Private Property" sign, the young child takes possession of and will defend the physical space which he considers his. The area he chooses for his own may be a corner of a sandbox marked by a finger-swept line or a row of shovels and pails. It may be a bit of floor space outlined by blocks,

FIGURE 7-2 YOUNG CHILDREN OFTEN DISPLAY THE NATURAL INSTINCT OF TERRITORIALITY

a particular chair or place at a table, even just a favorite branch in a tree. He does not always occupy his chosen space alone; others play there with or without him, but they are there only with his consent.

In relationship to social growth, territoriality is not a matter of selfishness—rather it is a means by which children learn to defend their activities, interests, and property. In this sense it is natural and probably healthy behavior. Although it may lead to conflict if others intrude, or are in competition for the same area, it is not in itself a problem. As in all social systems, however, conflict inevitably occurs between individual aims and group goals, and social development is closely tied to the ability to resolve conflict of this kind.

In addition to geographical boundaries, children also seek to establish and maintain psychological space. This leads a child to claim "*my* teacher" and "*my* friend" as though these individuals were his and his alone. Sibling rivalries are of this kind; they, too, express possessiveness and a child's need to be wanted and loved.

Psychological as well as geographical boundaries bring children in conflict with one another. A typical verbal interaction along this dimension of territoriality is given on p. 214.

Approach-and-Influence Behavior Maintaining boundaries of physical and psychological space involves another kind of interaction. As actors within their own "territory," children turn to one another and to the adults for contact, for interaction, and to satisfy their needs. They approach one another with overtures, offers and demands,

> *It is juice time and Sheila says, "Miss Cramer, I get to sit next to you today, don't I? It's my turn."*
>
> *It is Rudy who answers, not Miss Cramer. "No, it's my turn."*
>
> *Sheila disagrees. "No it isn't. You sat by her yesterday."*
>
> *Now Opal joins the conflict. "I never get to sit by her. It's my turn." There is more petulance in her assertion than conviction.*
>
> *With this interference, Rudy and Sheila join forces. "Yes, you do, Opal. You sit by her more than anyone else."*
>
> *"No I don't."*
>
> *"Yes you do!"*
>
> *"No, I don't."*
>
> *The teacher may elect to resolve the conflict in any number of ways, but her solution will invoke a rule the children can understand, such as "We have to take turns," or "Opal can sit next to me because she is new in school," or "I am going to choose a child who never asks to sit by me."*

and requests for assistance, comfort or rewards. Many of these contacts with peers and adults are attempts to influence the behavior of others to one's own ends or are responses to such attempts.

The ability to persuade or influence others in order to get a desired response is an important part of the development of social competence and behavior. In turn, the ability to deal with the demands or overtures of others without surrendering one's own sense of direction or purpose is equally essential. A significant part of adult life involves approach and influence—from political campaigns and other attempts to gain power over large groups of people to the various strategies employed by both boys and girls in more personal and intimate interactions.

This particular phase of development involves inner feelings of assertiveness, guilt, disappointment and gratification. The development of techniques and strategies for dealing with these interactional issues and problems are a significant part of early learning.

The teacher's role in the growth of this kind of social competence may take two forms. First, ways in which she gets children to do things and responds to their requests and demands may provide a model for them (see examples on p. 215). Secondly, she can actively reinforce and support the behavior of children which shows effective styles of approach and influence. She will understand, for example, that there is a difference between attempts to manipulate others to one's own purposes—which she will not reward—and approaches which have goals such as interaction, mutual enjoyment, accomplishment of a task, which she will reinforce.

Alignment A third way to look at social behavior of young children is as a matter of *alignment*—the establishment of linkages and collaboration between and among individuals. Alignment may be the pairing of two children against a third or against a teacher; it may be the derision of boys by a group of girls; it may be the choosing of sides or identification with an ethnic group. It can be a relationship of temporary dependency when it involves a child's need to find someone who will push him on a

> *Jennifer is passing crackers to the other children. She gets to Bobby who takes two large handsful, leaving three crackers in the basket. The expression on Jennifer's face indicates she is disturbed, but does not know what to do. Some of the other children call this to the attention of the teacher, "Look, Miss Cramer, Bobby took all the crackers." The teacher comments "Bobby, you'll need to put some of those crackers back and take just a few so the other children will have some too." The teacher's explanation is effective and Bobby keeps three crackers for himself while all the other children watch carefully.*
>
> *The next day Bobby, who is passing crackers, can be heard saying, "You'll need to put some of those crackers back."*
>
> *The teacher will not always see immediate results of modelling. Sometimes her own style is something a child may not adopt until much later, yet many examples and repeated exposure will have a long time effect.*
>
> *"Teacher, I want you to carry me all day and not play with those other children" wails Susie.*
>
> *"I know you want me all to yourself, Susie, and it will be hard for you to share me, but I need to spend time with the other children, too. I'm not going to carry you. I expect you to walk just like all the other children."*
>
> *While Susie may not have an opportunity to imitate this type of behavior soon, the teacher has provided her with an example of how to say "No," while still accepting the other person's feelings.*

---

swing or pull him in a wagon or perform any number of personal services that he cannot manage for himself, such as tying a shoelace, opening a cabinet door, or unscrewing a widemouth jar top. It is essentially a feeling of affiliation and may involve psychological dependence or mutual satisfaction and support in joint activities. More deliberate grouping and alignment begin in the later stages of the three-to-five period, although temporary alignments and loyalties develop in the classroom and on the playground for specific purposes. Alignment includes acts of friendship and companionship. It encompasses the form of "sharing" displayed when a child breaks off a piece of clay and gives it to the one who has none, or offers to squeeze over so that a friend can occupy the same mat or chair. (When children think and speak in terms of "our school" and "our teacher" and "our guinea pig," however, sharing may be thought of as a redefinition of territory.)

When a group of children play "store" or "house" together, build an elaborate block structure, or engage in dramatizing a story, alignment takes the forms of cooperation and collaboration. Yet children interacting in this way are also involved in approach-influence behavior whenever one of them attempts to persuade another to his way. And cooperation may be closely associated with territoriality since in cooperating, one child may be responding to another's claims regarding space.

Social behaviors are often so subtle, so interrelated, or so transitory as to challenge specific identification. Thinking of them as manifestations of territoriality approach, and influence or alignment, however, gives the teacher a basis for understanding children's attempts to relate to others and helps her find ways to meet their needs. She will also be more effective as she becomes aware of the techniques and strategies children use to achieve these goals through interaction with others.

Techniques and Strategies

Children use a variety of techniques and strategies to pursue goals of territoriality, influencing and alignment. These are rudimentary patterns of social behavior which can be taught and modified. On the whole they fall into two broad groupings: aggressive behaviors and persuasive behaviors.

Aggressive Behaviors Aggressive behaviors are among the most obvious as children interact with one another. They take a number of expressive forms which are often somewhat difficult to distinguish but which are quite different in their motives and consequences.

Assertiveness: The child who insists on turning the pages of the book during story hour, or will use only a certain paint brush, or demands to pour the juice, is behaving assertively. Because he focuses on a particular goal his actions seem self-centered, rude, and often disruptive, although his intention may not be of this nature. Because he knows what he wants, he often achieves his immediate end but to the detriment of social acceptance.

Aggression: Aggression is a familiar response to threats to one's physical and psychological space. The child who "attacks another person, or by word or deed interferes with another, or threatens by word or gesture to do so, or tries by force or spoken demands to direct another's activities or to possess another's things in opposition to the apparent desire of that person" exhibits aggressive behavior (Debus, 1953, p. 95). His intention is to put down, discomfort, or even harm another, while defending himself. Feelings of aggression are as natural to young children as are those of friendliness—and as much a part of their social behavior. It follows, therefore, that the more contacts a child makes with others, the more likelihood there is that he will behave aggressively. In dealing with children's aggression, adults frequently react in terms of their own attitudes and feelings toward this form of behavior rather than by considering the motives and needs of the child.

Hostility: The child who deliberately and knowingly seeks to harm another child by pushing him into a box and closing the lid, by giving him pins or a knife to play with,

FIGURE 7-3

or by doing anything to rid himself of the other child in such a way that the other child is injured, is displaying hostility. The orientation toward destruction of another and the element of deliberateness and forethought make hostility different from either assertiveness or aggression.

True hostility is not often seen in young children; their mental concentration is too transitory to harbor the hatred and vindictiveness involved. However, preschool children frequently use assertiveness and aggression to achieve their ends. These forms of behavior need to be seen as symptoms, not causes. They spring from attempts to protect space, from frustration, rejection and feelings of inadequacy and ineffectiveness—human reactions not always confined to childhood.

Persuasive Behaviors There is a temptation to think of persuasive behaviors as "positive" and "good" and of aggressive behaviors as "negative" and "bad." Persuasive behavior, however, can often be as difficult to handle and as undesirable in terms of the development of social competence as many acts of aggression and assertiveness.

It is true that the most common and most effective forms of persuasion are behaviors such as smiling, hugging, laughing, cheerfulness, cooperation, politeness and acts of friendliness. But whining, persistence, dawdling and arguing are persuasive strategies, too, and as frequently used as the more agreeable methods, if a child finds them to be effective. An observer has only to stand beside a gum ball machine to decide which of the two techniques illustrated in Figure 7-3 children use most frequently to get gum.

The values adults put on different kinds of behavior have little to do with children's techniques and strategies. If a child is concerned with getting a piece of gum or having the first turn on a swing, or finding just the truck he needs for a garage he built, how he reaches his objective is often of little consequence to him. The means will concern him

FIGURE 7–4 SEX AND AGE DIFFERENCES ARE OFTEN NOT OBVIOUS

only when his goal shifts to wanting approval and acceptance *more* than immediate gratification.

Socially active children use many forms of both aggressive and persuasive behaviors in their efforts to establish individuality, develop self-esteem, and yet relate acceptably to adults and other children. The teacher needs to be able to recognize the various techniques and strategies children use so that she can help each child learn ways which will not only meet his needs but also help him become socially competent in long-term as well as immediate situations.

Age and Sex Differences

One can easily observe children's behavior without being aware of age and sex differences. Given a nursery school scene such as the one shown in Figure 7–4, it would be interesting to note if an inexperienced observer would be able to differentiate the youngest from the oldest children. However, it is during the preschool years that the patterning of age and sex-related behavior begins to appear in more obvious forms.

Age Differences in Behavior Patterns A child's age affects the amount of cooperative play he engages in and how much he plays alone, watches others, or contributes to group activity. Older preschoolers not only seek the approval of others more actively, but also do more to avoid disapproval.

During the preschool years, competition increases with age. Two-year-olds show far more interest in the materials they are playing with than in what others are doing. Rivalry exists between three-year-olds, but not really at the level it reaches among those who are four or five. Studies show less frustration among older children and fewer conflicts, but the conflicts that occur last longer.

Twos and threes tend to have preferences among their playmates, but their choices usually last only a short while—perhaps no longer than a day or two, sometimes only a single morning. Older preschoolers often form strong attachments, some of these continuing into elementary school, even though each child also interacts with many other children.

The younger child's lack of motor development and muscular strength obviously limits the activities in which he engages either alone or with others. Yet his smaller size may mean his inclusion in older children's activities even though he does not initiate the contact. When a "baby" is needed for a realistic game of "house," or the firemen need a child to rescue, the two- or three-year-old may be persuaded to become a member of a group. Also, the younger child is sought out as a companion by the older child who finds it difficult to relate to children his own age.

Sex Differences and Behavior Patterns To call a three-year-old boy a girl, or a girl a boy, is to elicit vigorous denial. By this age they know and care. However, it is not so clear how they acquired this knowledge or what their feelings are concerning their sex role and the behavior it requires of them.

Every society differentiates in some way between the sexes. Since the assigned roles often differ so greatly from society to society, many people believe that sex-role development is a purely cultural matter. Adults in Western society transmit expectations for boys and girls in the areas such as those shown on p. 220. Not only are certain characteristics considered feminine (tenderness, emotionality, intuitiveness) and others masculine (dominance, vigor, courage), adults expect children to show these behaviors to demonstrate their sexual identity. They compare and judge children's behavior against such stereotypes, approving appropriate sex-role behaviors and either punishing or withholding approval for opposite sex-role behavior.

Those who hold that sex-role development is innate—that is, biological in a fundamental sense—point out that in addition to obvious anatomical differences, other apparently genetic factors probably exercise control over sex-role behavior. More males are conceived than females, but they have a higher infant mortality rate and a lower life

Areas Involving Sex-Role Expectations

Clothing styles and colors
Hair styles
Kinds of toys
Kinds of games
Roughhousing vs. decorum
Types of emotional expression

---

expectancy. The bone composition of boys changes at a rate different from that of girls, and boys mature physically a year or two years later. These suggest, to some, a strong biological influence upon behavior, as well.

No firm evidence exists to show the ways that biological differences may affect the sex-roles of boys or girls or influence self-concept, although the difference in age at which sexual maturity occurs directly affects behavior patterns during the adolescent years. As far as the early years are concerned, the greater facility of girls in language and reading skills as well as their greater interest in people influence intellectual performance, social behavior, and views regarding sex-roles.

Various studies have been made to determine children's sex-role preferences. Hartup and Zook (1960) found that girls between three and five express a greater preference for being girls than at any later stage. Even during these early years, however, boys' preference for the masculine role is stronger than that of the girls for the feminine role. Likewise, young boys consistently chose sex-appropriate toys more often than girls.

It is well-known that children tend to identify with the parent of like sex, and that as early as three they choose friends of their own sex more often than those of the opposite sex. It is not known, however, what behavior girls would consistently engage in because they are female, and what interests boys would have in the preschool setting because they are male if they were not exposed to cultural expectations. Even for twos and threes, adult expectations are already so strongly operative that the answer is obscured.

REGULATING BEHAVIOR AND DEVELOPING SOCIAL COMPETENCE

The process by which a child gains social competence and acquires acceptable patterns of social behavior depends not only on his energies and efforts but upon the environment which is provided for him by the adult world. If this physical and social environment is confining and restrictive, it may frustrate and irritate the children and induce "discipline problems," or if it is rewarding and open, it may tend to encourage less difficult forms of behavior. Since teachers control the environment of the nursery school to a great extent, it follows that they share responsibility with the child for the behavior which develops as a consequence of his interaction with them and the world they have provided.

Ways to Regulate Behavior

Every teacher has her own particular techniques for regulating classroom as well as individual behavior. Through careful planning and monitoring of activities, she at-

Conversation That Reinforces Rule-Learning

"Good for you, Lennie. You remembered to keep your trike on the pavement, didn't you?"

"Sally, I think you're forgetting you're not supposed to climb on the fence. How about climbing to the top of the jungle gym instead?"

"Marcy, I like the way you used both hands going up the ladder this time."

"I noticed everyone finished juice and crackers without getting up from his seat today."

"It's okay to run, boys, but not inside. There's plenty of space for you outside."

"Vincent, I'm really proud of the way you let Jenny work with your group in the block area today."

---

tempts to anticipate problems, while knowing that the unexpected is as much a part of school life as is daily routine. (This aspect of the teacher's task is more fully described in Chapter 9.)

Children tend to do better as a group if the rules they are expected to follow are the same for everyone, and if everyone knows the rules. Therefore rules need to be specific, concrete, simple and inclusive and part of everyday conversation—rather than an impressive list filled with exceptions and posted on a bulletin board.

Remarks such as those listed above reinforce the rule-learning of not only the children to whom they are directed, but all within hearing. They also provide needed alternatives for the "Don't Do's." As discussed earlier in this chapter, rules inform children what is "right," and preschoolers know well the approval that accompanies doing "right" things.

Just as a well planned room contributes to more orderly "traffic" and helps determine the kinds of activities that go on at the same time, teachers can exercise control by the variety and amount of materials they put out. Plenty of paper, scissors, and paste can mean fewer arguments. Removal of a trike or other piece of equipment that inspires competition does away with a cause of fighting. Drums need not be put out every day and all records don't have to be loud and fast pieces; the number of parties and holiday occasions can be limited. By such means, perhaps unintentionally, teachers regulate the arrangement of stimuli and opportunities, and so control behavior in their classrooms.

When children behave in ways which do not contribute to the objectives the teacher has in mind, she can ask consciously, "What happened to bring this on? What can be done so there won't be a next time?" Whether desirable or undesirable, behavior doesn't take place at random or without cause. Therefore, the teacher who is alert to the situation which brought on a disruption or a peaceful scene is in a better position to regulate the behavior that goes on in her nursery school classroom.

Setting Behavioral Objectives

A child's behavior is in part the responsibility of the teacher. She, with him, is the cause of disruptions and confusions. Surely no teacher needs to be told that unless she has

GOAL	BEHAVIOR INDICATING ACHIEVEMENT OF GOAL
Learning that something can be achieved in more than one way	Child chooses an alternative action if he is unable to solve a problem through his original means
Learning to defend interests and possessions	Child defends himself or his possessions verbally or by force if words are ineffective

TABLE 7-1 EXAMPLES OF GOALS AND BEHAVIOR INDICATING THEIR ACHIEVEMENT

a clear idea of the social behaviors she wants children to display, she isn't likely to know whether her efforts to help them develop these behaviors have been successful. The more uncertain she is in this matter the less she can be sure what needs to be done. Even though a teacher has certain goals in mind—goals such as those listed in Table 7-1—she must have some way of measuring the results in order to know whether she is modifying children's behavior in the desired direction.

Objectives need to be stated in terms of observable behavior; that is, they must specify exactly what behavior is expected. Since a nursery school is concerned with the growth and development of individuals, objectives will be specified differently for each child. Rather than calling for "understanding," or "acceptance," or "initiative," teachers need to define precisely what they want a child to do to show that he has learned what is intended. In this way the teacher can observe the degree to which a child attains the desired behavior. The objectives should concern only behaviors that are within the standards of conduct accepted by the society in which the child is being trained.

Although adults expect children to be responsive to their rules, some are reluctant to set behavioral objectives. The idea of being able to control human behavior in a positive sense somehow introduces a question of ethics. Even though these same people admit they regularly influence and are influenced by others, being in "control" of human behavior makes them uneasy. But knowledge and use of the techniques which most effectively guarantee learning is neither moral nor immoral. It is a matter of necessity if children are to receive the help they need to survive and succeed in a complex world of social and cultural upheaval.

Modifying Behavior

Unlike some aspects of children's growth and development, a good deal is known about ways to modify behavior. Two of the more powerful techniques are: a) imitation and modeling, and b) systematic reinforcement (or withdrawal of reinforcement). The first is especially significant in eliciting desired behaviors, the second in encouraging desired behavior and discouraging undesired behavior.

Imitation and Modeling Most of us would agree with the familiar saying "Actions speak louder than words." Yet it is easy to disregard its validity when involved in training young children. The research and writings of Bandura and his colleagues at Stanford University (1961,1961a) have been particularly effective in showing how much influence models have upon the behavior of young children. Using adults in staged situations, films, and television programs, Bandura has established that children will

> *Young children re-enact everyday experiences over and over as they play "house," "doctor," "store," "welfare visit," and "vacation trip." Much of their conversation and action imitates what they have seen and done themselves or observed others doing.*
>
> *Children frequently repeat the social conversation they hear, imitating both tone of voice and mannerisms as well as exact wordings.*
>
> *As they watch their threes and fours discipline a doll or stuffed toy, some mothers become aware for the first time of the way they sound to their children in the same kind of situation.*

---

imitate and take on the behavior that they have seen in others they respect, admire, or whose behavior has been particularly impressive. In these studies children have imitated aggressive verbal and motor behavior, particularly if they think that the actor they observed was rewarded for his behavior. These studies have given tremendous weight to the old dictum that young children were much more likely to acquire behavior that they see than to take on the behavior they are told to adopt. Teachers of young children can scarcely overestimate how much their own actions, especially aggressive and destructive behavior, are likely to be imitated.

Systematic Reinforcement[1]   Since behavior is learned, it can be strengthened, extinguished or maintained by its consequences. If a child is systematically reinforced (rewarded) for hanging up his sweater when he comes to school, the behavior will likely become habitual. If it is not reinforced, eventually the child will make no attempt to hang up his sweater. Punishing him for failing to do so will have only a temporary effect on his compliance. Since rewards (attention, approval, food, privileges) during the training of young children come from adults, adults must also train their own responses so that they remember to reinforce at appropriate times and in effective ways.

To succeed, reinforcement must be seen as rewarding by the child, and it must be timed correctly. Young children initially respond well to external material rewards such as sweets, toys, stars, and tokens, and to external social rewards like praise, affection, or special privileges. In time, through development of interest and skill, certain behaviors supply effective internal rewards, and the child's pleasure and pride are self-reinforcing.

Internal rewards are especially effective in strengthening behavior when they are occasionally reinforced with external approval of some kind. The young child who waits cheerfully for his turn on the swing should at first be rewarded each time he does this, and then intermittently until the behavior becomes strong enough to be a habit. It should also be rewarded as the child does the waiting and not as a casual afterthought

---

[1] Material in this section draws from the work of Glorianne Wittes and Norma Radin, Ypsilanti Public Schools Early Education Program, Ypsilanti, Michigan, 1968.

FIGURE 7–5 A CLEANUP PROJECT CAN BE TRANSFORMED INTO A SUCCESSFUL LEARNING SITUATION

when he is ready to go home. In this way the child sees the reward as a consequence of his behavior.

Many teachers are faced with the kind of "mess" pictured in Figure 7–5 and children who have no idea they are expected to clean up or how to begin. A teacher will be more successful in teaching them a new behavior if she begins by thinking of the separate tasks involved in restoring order. Then by first rewarding a child for whatever effort he makes, even if it is only to screw a lid back on a paste jar, she will be gradually preparing him to pick up the paper, put away paste, scissors, crayons, etc., and wash off the table top. Rewarding him for each level of effort eventually leads a child to keep trying until he masters the total behavior desired. The child also achieves inner satisfactions from having mastered this kind of skill and contributed to the efficient running of his school.

Behaviors are weakened and eliminated in the following ways:

1. *Providing undesirable consequences,* such as ignoring the behavior (few persons persist in behaviors that do not pay off), or punishing the behavior. Punishment usually just represses behavior, creates anxiety, models aggression (in the case of physical punishment) and sets up a poor relationship between adult and child. Punishment used for quick training, such as for matters of safety, can be effective if it is administered immediately after the behavior occurs and is accompanied by an explanation.

2. *Reasoning* so that a connection can be made between the behavior and its consequences. Explanations provide the child with language that he needs for thinking about why his behavior was unacceptable. This thinking in turn helps him learn to anticipate the consequences of his act and eventually leads to the development of self-control so that he can avoid undesirable consequences.

3. *Providing alternative behaviors* means giving children knowledge of behaviors that meet with approval as well as those that don't. The child should be able to express his anger and exuberance in acceptable ways. Thus, the teacher should see that he has places to climb other than fences, objects to hammer and hit besides his classmates. She can also provide some quiet activities and areas as retreats from the more demanding kinds of interaction. Alternative behaviors also enable him to help make decisions that meet with approval—a step toward the self-reinforcement and self-control he needs for school achievement later on.

Effective modification of behavior based on systematic reinforcement requires clear objectives, determination, and consistency on the part of the teacher. In this way children learn to expect certain consequences as a result of their behavior. By being rewarded and not rewarded for what they *do,* they also learn that it is their behavior and not their person or their feelings that bring about the desired or undesired consequences.

Understanding the Many Messages of Behavior

Not long after a teacher began working in a nursery school she became involved in the following incident:

David had been coming to nursery school for just two weeks and his mother always left him at the door without entering. This morning before going on her way she paused to talk to an acquaintance. As she talked, she saw David drop his jacket and watched as the new teacher hung it in his locker. Angrily, she excused herself and went into the classroom. Before the teacher knew what was happening, David's mother grabbed the jacket, threw it where David had left it and was dragging her son in from the play yard.

Pointing to the jacket, she ordered, "Pick that up and hang it where it's supposed to go. You don't do that at home or here, either."

Except to attempt to wriggle free of his mother's hold, David did nothing. His mother raised her voice. "Didn't you hear me? Pick up your jacket and hang it where it belongs or you're going home. Right now!"

David looked at the jacket and at his teacher but made no move to comply with the order. When his mother started to make good her threat he began to scream. "I don't wanna go, I don't wanna go—o-o-o-o." As they reached the door he jerked loose, raced back, picked up the jacket and slowly went over to hang it up.

Triumphantly the mother turned to the teacher who stood helplessly watching. In a voice that all could hear she announced, "I don't like David to learn lazy habits here at school. From now on see that he hangs up his clothes. Don't you be soft and let him take advantage of you."

The teacher found voice enough to say, "I was going to speak to him but . . ."

David's mother wasn't interested; she had already started to leave. As she reached the door she called back, "If that happens again, you just grab him and spank him so he knows you mean business!" Then she was gone.

Clearly the teacher heard every word and was in no doubt as to the behavior the mother expected her to modify. Yet she heard other messages—messages that appealed just as strongly for other decisions and other behaviors. She suspected that the mother was also saying:

To Her	**To David**
You are weakening my authority.	I want you to respect my authority.
I want you to respect my rules and enforce them.	Do not defy me, test me or threaten me.
I'm having real trouble getting this child to mind.	I want you to be a "well-behaved" child and mind me.
I had hoped you would help me, but I am disappointed.	I want you to be like other children and be socially accepted.

David's failure to hang up his jacket was not the only behavior that needed modifying if good relationships were to be established. Whose need was greatest? The mother's? David's? Her own?

Thoughts raced through her head but the teacher had no idea where to begin. Along with a mounting desperation over being so ineffective in communicating with the mother, and feeling not only her relationship to David threatened but her job as well, the teacher tried to think what to do. Surely she should be doing something, but what?

To help sort out her confusion she began asking herself questions:

Why didn't I say something? How could I let the mother show me up like that? Will I feel more confident, more able to deal with mothers when I have children of my own? Is it because I'm so young that all this happened to me? Would she have treated the other teachers this way?

How much should I discuss with my head teacher? When?

Because she had no answers, asking questions just made matters worse. Then she noticed David. He, too, stood motionless, alone, unable to make decisions. Although he had spoken only once during the whole terrible experience, she sensed his embarrassment, his fear, his doubt.

Suddenly the teacher knew what she wanted to do—what she had to do. She would begin by seeking contact with the child whose confusion and suffering were as great as her own. Perhaps they could work out something together.

"C'mon, David," she called softly as she moved toward him. "Come help me feed the rabbit, he looks hungry and he needs us."

The teacher recognized that unless she could find some way to work with both David and his mother, she would be helpless and ineffective in interacting with them. Some confusion exists as to where the mother's role and responsibility end and the teacher's begins. Both the teacher and mother share the same goal—getting David to pick up his jacket—but their strategies for influencing him are quite different. The teacher must take the initiative in clarifying the roles that she and the mother play in the school setting, trying to make it clear to the mother that as teacher she has her own style and her own ways of relating to the children under her care. It may be possible for the teacher eventually to show the mother by example how she deals with David and do this in a way that gives the mother another alternative without necessarily implying that what she has been doing is inadequate.

In helping children develop social competence, teachers do more than reward and model specific styles and skills. They also help the child learn to confront and resolve conflicts, isolation and rejection as well as to master the social graces. True social competence involves understanding oneself and knowing how to relate to people, not merely being accepted by a group. It involves deeply private communication of interpersonal experience and, perhaps most importantly, the ability to share one's own self with others.

REFERENCES

Ardrey, R. *The territorial imperative; a personal inquiry into the animal origins of property and nations.* New York: Atheneum Publishers, 1966.

Bandura, A. and Huston, A. C. Identification as a process of incidental learning. *Journal of Abnormal and Social Psychology,* 1961, *63,* No. 2, 311–318.

Bandura, A., Ross, D., and Ross, S. A. Transmission of aggression through imitation of aggressive models. *Journal of Abnormal and Social Psychology,* 1961, *63,* No. 3, 575–582.

Brown, R. W. *Social psychology.* New York: The Free Press, 1965.

Coopersmith, S. *The antecedents of self-esteem.* San Francisco, Calif.: W. H. Freeman and Co., 1967.

Debus, R. L. Aggressive behavior in young children. *The Forum of Education,* 1953, *11,* 95–105.

de Regniers, B. S. *A little house of your own.* New York: Harcourt, Brace and World, 1954.

Durkin, D. Children's concepts of justice: a comparison with the Piaget data. *Child Development,* 1959, *30,* 59–67.

Flavell, J. H. Role taking and communication skills in children. *Young Children,* January 1966, *XXI,* No. 3, 164–177.

Hartshorne, H. and May, M. A. *Studies in the organization of character.* New York: The Macmillan Co., 1930.

Hartup, W. W., and Zook, E. A. Sex role preferences in three- and four-year-old children. *Journal of Consulting Psychology,* 1960, *24,* No. 5, 420–426.

Hurlock, E. B. *Child development* (4th edition). New York: McGraw-Hill, 1964.

Kohlberg, L. The development of children's orientations toward a moral order: I. Sequence in the development of moral thought. *Vita Humanae,* 1963, Base 1.

Piaget, J. *The moral judgment of the child.* Glencoe, Ill.: The Free Press, 1948, (1st American edition translated by Marjorie Gabain.)

Stevenson, H. W. Studies of racial awareness in young children. *Journal of Nursery Education,* 1962, *17,* 118–122.

Wittes, G. and Radin, N. *Helping your child to learn: Parent education handbook No. 1, The reinforcement approach.* Ypsilanti, Mich.: Ypsilanti Public Schools, September, 1968.

CHAPTER 8

THE VERSATILITY OF THE ARTS IN A PRESCHOOL PROGRAM

THE PLACE OF THE ARTS IN THE CURRICULUM

The widespread preoccupation in the 1960's with cognitive development of young children and with academically oriented programs reordered the priorities in many preschool classrooms. The academic curricula, with their specific behavioral objectives and well-defined teaching strategies, appealed to a large number of professionals. The apparent relevance of such programs to the educational problems of children from low-income and minority backgrounds enhanced their attractiveness.

The demand for curricula which would prepare the child for success in school and develop his mental abilities also rekindled interest in cognitively oriented programs which had been developed long before. In the midst of the flurry of academically-related activity, those aspects of the preschool program which allowed the child freedom to indulge in dramatic play, finger painting, music and other things referred to as "the arts" lost favor with many professionals and became the target of particular disdain.

Other educators, however, found some of the new academic programs narrow in scope, mechanical, insensitive to the child's feelings and overly concerned with school-related skills which in their view were best taught later in the early elementary grades.

The debate which arose over the place of "the arts" in relation to systematic instruction in preschool classrooms forced many professionals to reexamine the purposes they had in mind, perhaps implicitly, for including these more humanistically oriented elements in the program. This controversy is still lively and is not likely to be settled soon, if at all. Educational priorities, especially at the preschool level, are to a great extent expressions of the philosophy and preference of the school staff and participating community members. It seems unlikely that we will soon achieve consensus.

Although this is not an area in which firm or final answers are available, it is useful for the teacher to become familiar with several disparate points of view. Such familiarity with the issues will put her in a better position to evaluate her own philosophy and to use the arts in a way deliberately intended to accomplish her own purposes without apology or attempts to disguise.

In this chapter the term "the arts" refers to those activities which a teacher uses to help children develop and recognize inner responses to external stimuli and to express these responses in some perceptible or tangible form. In this sense, the teacher's efforts to arouse curiosity, kindle interest, stimulate imagination, stir emotion and otherwise enhance perceptual awareness lie within the arts. Her comment about the color and design of a dress or jacket, her choice of a picture to familiarize children with the work of a famous artist, and her request, "Show me how this kind of music makes you feel," are as much a part of the arts as providing a listening corner with a record player and records, or making available paints, brushes and paper. Each furthers the goal of the

FIGURE 8-1

arts program—that is, it helps children respond and develop artistically. To the degree that producing and responding to music, rhythm, drama and visual art is a part of the human experience, the arts have a legitimate place in programs of early education.

The Purposes of an Arts Program

Teachers often think of the arts as specific activities such as painting, pasting, singing, story acting, dance, etc., without much consideration for the purposes or goals for the use of these tasks (Figure 8-1).

The distinction between the arts as a cluster of pre-selected activities and "the arts" as *any* activity which accomplishes a particular goal of artistic response or expression is an important one. It means that the teacher selects and plans tasks which are oriented toward the effects she wants to achieve and not because these things are done in other nursery schools or as an end in themselves. This emphasis on effects and goals rather than on the activity itself frees a teacher to be more flexible in utilizing the many resources, both planned and spontaneous, at her command.

As an example, imagine a visit to two different nursery schools, both of which use play dough as one of their "art" activities. Ask the teachers why they have play dough. One will say it is an easy activity to supervise; the children like it and play quietly with it for long periods of time.

The other teacher will agree, but in addition will say that the child learns about texture, consistency, color and shape from play dough. She helps to create these experiences by purposely mixing the play dough in different consistencies, textures and colors. She also makes it a point to ask questions as the children are manipulating the dough and helps them to talk about their discoveries.

The scenes in both schools may look alike to an observer, but the expected outcomes of such experiences will be different. The distinction between the casual orientation toward the arts (where the teacher provides an activity because it keeps the children content or is an interesting thing for them to do or because other schools do it) and one in which the teacher uses an activity—any activity—because she has some desired goals in mind, is that in the latter case the teacher will have a clearer idea of what she hopes to achieve and just how she plans to achieve it. This does not detract from the pleasure the children will have, or their spontaneity in play. It in no way suggests that one teacher is necessarily warmer or more child-oriented than the other or that one teacher intervenes or manipulates the child in such a way that he is deprived of spontaneous exploration.

It does mean, however, that one teacher has a more complex, wider range of goals and purposes in mind. She senses, in even the daily routine, more possibilities for developing the child's capabilities. It means that she preplans and selects activities that will entice children to make self-discoveries related to the outcomes she has in mind. It also means that she is sensitive to the child's reactions and responds or questions at appropriate times. The outcome of an activity is more predictable and less likely to be left to chance or come as a lucky surprise to the teacher who knows what she wants and how she intends to achieve it.

The intent of this chapter is to consider some of the ways a teacher may utilize "the arts" to achieve her goals; it is not intended as an enumeration of the activities themselves. There are many sources for "recipes" and suggestions about specific tasks, including the handbook of curriculum activities prepared as a supplement to this text. Those described here are selected to illustrate how a teacher may choose tasks to accomplish specific objectives.

A versatile and imaginative teacher will probably use art activities in several different ways. The most frequent purposes are likely to be these:

1. To develop in the child responses to artistic objects and events and to provide experience and training for artistic expression and judgment.
2. To aid in the teaching of more specifically cognitive, school-related concepts and skills.
3. To give children opportunity to participate in arts for the immediate gratification and "release" they offer.
4. To keep children busy, to occupy time, to soothe and in other ways to help regulate the activities and feelings of the group.

This chapter, then, is oriented toward the issues and purposes that are involved in the use of the arts in a preschool program. The teacher must eventually decide for herself what her own philosophy will be. Once she has her goals established, she can utilize a variety of techniques and activities to achieve them and can also feel free to use the same activities for other purposes.

Teaching Philosophies

One issue is that of priority in the curriculum. Do the arts have a place in an up-to-date, informed, and focused program and, if so, what emphasis should be given them? This is not a new concern. Frederick Froebel (1782–1852), founder of the "kindergarten," created materials which he called "play songs," "gifts," and "occupations" that presented an orderly series of phenomena designed to challenge the children's abilities, stimulate mental activity and produce inner organization and integration (Table 8–1).

Many of Froebel's "occupations" can be found in today's nursery schools, but they do not always serve his educational purposes. The question of how art should be used and what aspects of the arts should be emphasized is of concern to modern day teachers. The issue is illustrated in this informal after-school conversation in which several teachers were discussing their role as instructors in the arts program:

"Frankly, I'm confused," Miss F. announced. "Rich's mother visited today and saw him at the easel. He was painting those figures he's been doing so much of lately. You know, the kind with big heads and enormous eyes but no bodies and just long lines for arms and legs. I was clear across the room but I heard her say, 'Rich, you know better than that! That's not what people look like.' You should have seen his expression. Poor little guy—he was really crushed."

"What did you do?" Bill S. asked.

"I went over and tried to explain that it's quite natural for children to draw people this way at a certain stage, but she wasn't at all impressed. She wanted to know what he was learning from this experience."

"What did you say?"

"Oh, something vague like 'He needs to have lots of opportunities to explore with the materials in order to express himself.' This obviously didn't satisfy her. She complained that we should at least point out to him that people have bodies."

"That's a fairly common complaint," Miss L. remarked. "I've been here five years and I remember how helpless I felt the first time one of the parents confronted me with 'Just what do you teach the children in this school?!'"

"I think Rich's mom is unhappy with us because she can't see the value of an exploratory kind of art activity. I know she is anxious to have him learn to read and write and doesn't want him to 'waste his time' here," commented Bill S.

"I don't want him to waste his time here either," interjected Mrs. A., "but I happen to believe that painting and other art activities are not a waste of time."

"I agree," said Miss L., "but we haven't convinced Rich's mother, and I really think we're doing her a disservice if we ignore her concerns and treat her as if she didn't know anything."

Patsche-Kuchen.

„Mag auch wohl ein höh'rer Sinn
In dem Patsche-Kuchen liegen?—
O, wohl liegt er klar darin:
Willig muß sich Mehres fügen,
Jeder auch zur rechter Zeit
Sein an seinem Theil bereit,
Soll das Werk gelingen
Und uns Freude bringen."

PLAY SONGS	GIFTS	OCCUPATIONS
These were originally prepared for use by the mother but were later employed by teachers in the kindergarten when Froebel observed children spontaneously joining hands in a circle as they played and sang together.	These were a series of play materials which fitted into boxes as units.	Children engaged in each or all of the following activities freely but the materials were presented in a somewhat sequential manner.
He placed chairs in a circle and engaged the children in singing games and stories using his picture song cards.	They were used for creative play but primarily to encourage certain kinds of learning (development of concepts and cognitive skills).	Clay modeling Dot patterns Pricking cards Bead stringing Sewing cards Paper weaving Paper folding Drawing Coloring Tracing Pasting Making gardens Nature study
	The concept of a ball was basic to the understanding of the relationship and form of a unified whole—this unity was basic to all of Froebel's work and philosophy.	

TABLE 8–1 EXAMPLE OF PICTURE SONG CARD AND DESCRIPTION OF FROEBEL'S MATERIALS

picture song card reprinted with the permission of Holt, Rinehart & Winston, Inc., from Cole, Luella, *The History of Education: Socrates to Montessori*, p. 537. Copyright 1950 by Rinehart and Company, Inc.

"Look," Miss F. said. "I have to admit that I often wonder just what the kids are getting out of their experiences, especially when they're splattering paint around in the art area and jingling bells like crazy in the music room."

"What's all this got to do with teaching art?" Bill S. insisted.

"We have to be more clear about our own goals and the ways in which we achieve them," said Mrs. A. "I think the reason we feel threatened by people like Rich's mother is because we aren't sure about what we are doing."

This kind of "shop talk" is fairly common among teachers of young children and represents some of the problems which concern them. The comments of Rich's mother also represent attitudes of some parents who see school achievement and the "3 R's" as essential to success. Unless they are used to develop cognitive abilities, art and art activities have little or no place in a curriculum which is intended to help their child "get ready" for more formal schooling. The early years ought to be spent on the apparently more important skills such as learning letters and numbers. In this view, children are expected to achieve at a faster than normal rate through a highly selective, structured and teacher-directed curriculum. The arts are a luxury.

The teachers in this vignette seem more representative of the view that the curriculum should incorporate activities which develop the "whole child," with the arts being as important as the cognitively oriented tasks. Art along with social activities should be spontaneous and expressive and children should be involved in them in their own individual ways.

These two viewpoints are apparently contradictory and perhaps cannot be reconciled completely even though, as is discussed later in this chapter, art activities can be used to serve *both* cognitive and artistic goals. In planning a program the staff must decide whether activities oriented toward artistic experience and expression are to be given a place in the curriculum and if so, what it will be. If they include art activities they have an additional decision to make about how structured and purposeful they will be in teaching artistic abilities and responses.

The academic aspects of preschool curricula have been given great salience in the recent past; perhaps the arts will soon come into their own. If so, it will be because teachers and other professionals take them seriously, place explicit value upon them and use art and other activities deliberately to develop those dimensions of human capability which are more aesthetic and humanistic.

THE ARTS AS DEVELOPMENT OF ARTISTIC CAPABILITIES

The staff which, having discussed its priorities, wants to give the arts an important place in its program will find nonetheless that there is a diversity of thought as to how the arts should best be implemented. Here again, the teacher faces two different, almost inconsistent, points of view. In one school, the parents and administrators may feel that the child's artistic ability develops best of its own accord in a free environment. This assumes to some extent that the ability is inborn and will, at the early ages, develop naturally through growth processes. The teacher's responsibility is to facilitate the child's efforts; he should be allowed to express himself freely without the imposition of adult standards or direct teaching. This approach sees art as a behavior which can best be developed through providing the child many opportunities for direct interaction with his environment.

Another orientation toward the use of art materials suggests that perceptual skills are more fully trained with instruction than without, and that this training can be effective even with quite young children. The teacher provides specific experiences and directly teaches certain aspects of the arts such as relationships and patterns, and how to begin to use form, line, color and texture. It is argued that some types of instruction are more helpful than others in promoting children's artistic development.

Every teacher needs to consider what she expects to accomplish within a given framework of instructional philosophy. The following description of interaction between a four-year-old and his teacher is an example of what can happen when a teacher either has no specific objectives in mind, or fails to think of ways to achieve those she *has* formulated.

Interaction	Teacher's Thoughts
(Robert stands at an easel, a paint brush in each hand, vigorously stroking heavy, vertical lines on his paper.)	
Robert Look, teacher, look what I'm doing!	
Teacher Mmmmm—you're using both hands, aren't you?	I wonder if it's all right to let him paint that way. Maybe he should have only one brush.
Teacher Robert, why don't you use just one brush?	If I can't stop him he'll make an awful mess. How can I get him to stop?
Robert I don't want to.	
(Robert keeps on dipping and slapping.)	
Teacher But you're making such a mess.	That's not what I should say, but how can I get him to stop?

Robert *I like making a mess, it's fun.*

Maybe I should just let him paint the way he wants to. He really isn't doing any harm. How can I make this a learning situation? Maybe I should talk about circles, or thick and thin lines.

(Robert switches to painting large, drippy circles accompanying each stroke with a loud ZOOM-ZOOM.)

Teacher *I see you're making circles.*

What do I do now?

(As though he hadn't heard, Robert continues to apply paint in rhythm to his ZOOM-ZOOM.)

Teacher *Are you finished now, Robert?*

Thank goodness the paint's almost all gone.

(Without answering, Robert drops his brushes and runs off to play.)

What a relief to have him stop. I don't think I handled this situation in the best way.

Fortunately, this teacher had a supervisor with whom she could talk about the incident. From their discussion and her own reflection she realized:

1. Her feeling of inadequacy was based on the fact that she had no objectives in mind for Robert—only her own desire to have him stop.

2. She had no understanding of Robert's behavior. Why was he painting that way? Why couldn't she control him?

When the supervisor asked her to restate the objectives that had vaguely come to mind, and then to list what she might have done to achieve them, the teacher prepared the following summary:

Possible Objectives
Robert should be allowed to paint without being made to feel guilty.

Possible Ways to Achieve Objectives
Encouragement
  Sometimes it's fun to make a mess, isn't it?
  It's okay to do that but you'll need to keep the paint on the paper.

Robert should have opportunities for being "messy."	Presentation of attractive alternative. *I'll bet you'd like using finger paints even better, Robert. Let's go see.*
Robert should develop concepts about shapes.	Calling attention to and reinforcing specifics *That's great, Robert—you just made some circles. Now, make another circle for me.* *Good work! Now I'd like you to make a square—two lines the same length side by side but with space between them—and two lines to join the ends.*
Robert should be helped to acquire art techniques.	Using questions *(Pointing) First you drew a _____?* *And then you drew a _____?* *Now, tell me, which one is made with straight lines?* *What do we call the shape you drew using a curved line with the ends joined together?* Modeling *Robert, show me if you can hold your brush like this.* *Let's see what a line looks like when you hold a brush this way.* *What do you think a line will look like if you turn your brush this way? Let's try it and see.* Questioning *Can you think of another way you can make a line? Are both lines the same?* *Which one is thicker?* *Draw another thick line.* *Draw another thin line.* *What did you do to make one line thicker than the other?*

As the teacher and her supervisor went over the list, they discussed each of the objectives from the standpoint of Robert's needs. With knowledge of what would most contribute to his development, the teacher's choices became clear. By the time she completed her analysis she realized that having in mind what she wanted for Robert would have helped her use the art activity more effectively.

Ideally, a teacher at any moment in the day should be able to see a stop-action, instant replay of her work and be able to identify what she is doing and for what purpose in any area. Her purpose might be general or specific—that is, she could have in mind "smoother, less noisy transitions from one activity to the next" as her intent, or "getting Marita to use more than one color" as a specific objective. Knowing what she is trying to do alleviates feelings of helplessness, makes decisions easier and provides a way to assess her effectiveness in the use of the arts.

Until a teacher has time to observe the children in her class, she cannot plan for individual needs. She can consider the overall goals of the program in which she is working, however, and gradually prepare objectives for individuals within the framework of those goals. Overall approaches for developing competence in the arts may include the four categories listed on p. 239.

Developing Awareness of Inner Responses to External Stimuli

For all their curiosity and activity, many children have never really looked up at the sky or down at the earth long enough to become aware of what they are seeing or to realize their response to these experiences. They have never run their hands over a stainless steel surface nor touched the bristles of a brush. They haven't thought about the sensations they experience when they put their feet in cool mud or warm sand. Some have smelled their mother's perfume and their father's shaving lotion but may not know the odors of paper, paste, leather, wood, fruit or flowers. They hear noise but have never listened to silence.

Even when they have done such things, experience alone is not enough. Teachers can help them recognize and talk about how these experiences make them feel and become aware of their responses. Children need to know, too, that their responses are important, and that inner feelings can be expressed in many, many ways.

By nature children are curious and eager for knowledge. To help them develop an awareness of their inner responses the teacher should start simply and be willing to take time. No script is necessary, but some general strategies are useful. The teacher may make use of familiar experiences and events and then get the child to focus on

> **Overall Goals for Use of the Arts in Preschool Programs**
>
> 1. Developing awareness of inner responses to external stimuli
> 2. Developing children's competence in the arts
> 3. Developing awareness of cultural heritage
> 4. Developing artistic judgment and standards

some aspect of the experience he may not have noticed before. She may ask if he can see a face or an animal shape in a cloud, or tell him to put his head back and look at the sky while he is swinging. This first strategy is to get the child to view an aesthetic experience in a new way. A follow-up of this is to ask the child how events or experiences make him feel or whether he likes something he has observed and why. This "How-does-that-make-you-feel?" approach has many variations and can be used in many different situations.

Another strategy is to reinforce a child's expression of response to art experiences and to make it clear that such responses are appropriate, welcomed and rewarded.

The following is an example of how a teacher might help a young child develop awareness of inner feelings.[1]

GOAL
To develop awareness of internal response to external stimuli

OBJECTIVE
To get Opal to express in some overt way that she realizes there is a difference in the way two everyday objects feel to the touch

Miss P. watched three-year-old Opal tentatively run a pudgy finger along the edge of a hardwood block. The child picked up another and did the same thing. Then she spread her hand and rubbed it across the top surface of the block as one brushes crumbs from a table. Leaving Opal for a moment, Miss P. went to get a piece of rough bark, slightly curved and not as thick as the block, but about the same size. She put it in the deep pocket of her smock.

When she returned she sat on the floor beside Opal and said, "I like the way you're playing, Opal. What does it feel like when you rub your hand across the top of a block?"

Opal smiled but did not answer.

Miss P. picked up a matching block and held it out. "Rub your hand across the top of this block, Opal."

Opal willingly followed her teacher's instruction.

"Do both of them make you feel the same way when you rub them?"

Opal smiled but did not answer.

Miss P. began swishing her hand like a metronome across the floor. Happily Opal joined in this new game. Swish-swish.

"Does it feel the same when you rub your hand across the floor as it does when you rub your hand across the top of a block?"

Opal answered by rubbing first the block and then the floor but she said nothing. Instead she began stacking pairs of blocks. Every so often she took time to rub one with her hand.

Miss P. watched. Waited. Slowly she took the bark from her pocket and placed it on the floor between them. Opal reached over, picked up the bark, and rubbed her hand

---

[1] For further ideas see Croft, Doreen J. and Hess, Robert D., *An Activities Handbook for Teachers of Young Children.*

Objectives for Developing the Child's Awareness of Inner Responses to External Stimuli

1. Examining the qualities of objects, both natural and man-made
2. Using more than one modality to investigate properties of objects
3. Developing sensitivity to more subtle differences in each of the five senses
4. Learning to notice shapes, colors, textures of natural objects such as flowers, leaves, etc.
5. Seeing and thinking of objects from different perspectives (above, below, inside, outside, etc.)
6. Sharing the child's responses to artistic stimuli and interesting features of the environment

---

across the top. She frowned and rubbed it again. She gave her teacher the bark and picked up a block.

"Do they feel the same, Opal?"

Opal shook her head, her eyes puzzled. "No," she said.

"You're right, Opal. They feel different. The block is SMOOTH. The bark is ROUGH. I'm glad you noticed they were different. Here, feel them again. This block is smooth. The bark is rough."

Opal looked, but put her hands behind her back and said nothing. Miss P. smiled. Then she got up. As she rose she gave Opal an affectionate pat. "Good girl," she said, and walked away. A start had been made; it was all that was needed for now. There would be time enough to engage Opal's interest in the different properties and kinds of wood and bark, in having her find out where bark came from and in getting her to make other comparisons later on. They could also talk about how trees were cut and made into wood and what people did with wood. But for now she felt she had made the right start by gaining Opal's confidence and waiting until she was willing to express her response to the way two different objects felt.

Development of tactile discrimination between "smooth" and "rough" may seem far removed from the arts in the traditional sense. But from such simple beginnings, from a stirring of interest and a conscious realization of differences, come other responses with new experiences. Once children are aware that they have responses, then through music, painting and other art forms they can be helped to find ways to express their inner feelings and the thoughts that accompany them. Using the arts is not just a matter of putting a crayon in a child's hand and saying "Draw a picture," or asking children to clap time to music. The arts are a resource for helping children to develop sensitivity and competence in aesthetic activities.

In the next scene, a teacher uses a wider range of experience and technique to help a boy learn to express his reaction to certain kinds of music.

GOAL
To develop awareness of internal response to external stimuli

Jack, a sturdy five-year-old, sat listening to loud music with a pronounced beat. After the third playing of his record, Mrs. N. joined him.

"You like that record, don't you, Jack?"

"Yeah," Jack answered, ready to drop the needle for a fourth time.

"How does the music make you feel?"

OBJECTIVE

To get Jack to express freely his response to feelings engendered by music, either by body movement or in words, or both

"I like it."

"Does it make you want to do anything?"

"I don't know."

"Does it make you want to get up and march or dance or anything?"

"I don't think so. I just like it."

During the conversation Mrs. N. had sorted through several other records and found one she knew had low tones and a slow rhythm. She handed it to Jack. "Here, play this one. I'd like to listen to it with you."

"Okay." But halfway through the music, Jack stopped the machine. "I like the other one better," he explained. "I'm going to play mine again."

"All right," Mrs. N. agreed. "But tell me, do the two records make you feel the same?"

"I guess so. No. I don't know."

"Look, Jack, let's play the one you like and you show me how it makes you feel. Move around any way you want to."

Mrs. N. could tell from Jack's expression that he wasn't just sure he wanted to follow the suggestion. She smiled and asked David to join them. "David, we're going to play Jack's record and I'm hoping he'll show me how it makes him feel. Will you do that, too?"

David liked the idea. With the first note or two he began to shuffle his feet, wriggle his hips and soon was slapping his thighs calling out, "Man, man!" Clearly David recognized his feelings and found them easy to express.

Jack watched David for a moment and then began to move about. His motions were awkward but the beat caught him up, too, and by the end of the record his response was almost as vigorous as David's. He grinned happily.

"That was fine, boys. Just fine. I could certainly see how happy this kind of music makes you feel. Now I want to play the other record and you show me how that makes you feel." Sensing Jack's hesitancy, she added, "Here, Jack, you put it on for us."

This time several measures went by before either boy responded. David was again first. His shoulders drooped, his head fell forward and slowly he let himself down to the floor where he lay sprawled like a rag doll. Jack watched and imitated. But when both were lying down, it was Jack who got to his knees and began to rock back and forth in time to the slow music. The sounds stopped before he did.

Mrs. N. made no comment. She sat quietly waiting. Jack straightened up and came over to her. "I liked the record better this time," he said.

Mrs. N. put her arm around him. "How did it make you feel, Jack?"

The boy hesitated, uncertain not of his response but of the teacher's. "It was like being in a rocking chair," he said.

Jack's interest in music enabled his teacher to make him aware of his inner response and to encourage him to express how he felt through body movement. In this instance, the arts also included David's response and the teacher's affective behavior. By having in mind what she wanted to do, the teacher was able to take advantage of a combination of resources in order to achieve her objective.

Inner responses to art need not be treated as though they were separate from thought. In fact, a teacher can often help children to feel and think about an object at the same time. The following is an example:

GOAL
To develop awareness of internal response to external stimuli

OBJECTIVE:
To have child use thought and feeling at the same time

Miss B. was standing next to Jerry when she saw him stoop to pick up a leaf. "What a beautiful leaf, Jerry," she commented.

Jerry held his leaf at arm's length, twisting and turning it as though it were a gigantic butterfly whose red and yellow wings flashed in the sun.

"How does it make you feel when you see a leaf like that?" she asked.

"I like to look at it. I think it's pretty."

"I do, too, Jerry. What do you suppose makes it so pretty?"

Jerry looked at the leaf, turning it over and back again, but didn't say anything.

"It's the kind we call a maple leaf, Jerry. What do you notice that makes it different from leaves on that tree over there?"

"It's red and yellow."

"What's different about that?"

Jerry grinned. This was a game he'd played with the teacher before. She knew, but she wanted him to tell her. "You can see that the leaves on the tree are green," he said.

"That's right, Jerry. They have a different color." She stopped and picked up a dry leaf and held it next to Jerry's. "Which of the leaves has brighter colors? Yours or mine?"

"Mine."

"Which leaf is bigger?"

"Mine."

"How do you think the outside edge of your leaf feels?"

Jerry's finger slowly explored the outline of the leaf. "It's bumpy," he said.

"I agree. It's bumpy," his teacher said. "Is the leaf round?"

"No."

"Is it square?"

"No. It has points."

"Hmmmm. Points. How many?"

"One-two-three-four-five."

"That's right, Jerry. We've noticed a good many things about your leaf, haven't we? It has bright colors. Its edges are _____; and there are five _____. Was it a big leaf compared to this one of mine?"

"Yep," Jerry said and ran off for a turn on the swing.

From the thoughts adults express in their interaction with children, the child learns ways to think about and communicate his experiences. He can be shown meanings and

FIGURE 8–2 BY RESPONDING FREELY TO SURROUNDINGS, A CHILD'S AWARENESS IS DEVELOPED

243   THE VERSATILITY OF THE ARTS IN A PRESCHOOL PROGRAM

helped to develop concepts. Not all at once, of course, but from many opportunities to consider his inner responses and to think about the information his senses bring. The information he receives through sensory experience acquires additional meaning from interpretation by adults. For this reason it is important for the teacher to use every opportunity to help a child realize he can both respond and think about his responses at the same time. Providing children with many experiences is important, but unless they are also helped to interpret these experiences, their learning may be limited.

Developing Children's Competence in the Arts

For many children, preschool is their first introduction to a wide variety of materials and equipment. As with anything new and strange, this experience can be puzzling as well as pleasurable. Because they don't know how paint acts, how music is created, or what will happen if they leap, some children are slow to explore and learn to use what is available to them. Some also hesitate to move around and try things until adults assure them that what they are doing meets with approval. Gradually, however, on their own initiative or by watching others, and with suggestions from the teacher, most children begin to experiment with the paints, respond to the rhythms, try out the hammer and saw and use other available materials.

Having plenty of materials is desirable, but simply providing an impressive assortment is not enough. Some publicly funded programs have had money to buy adequate or even fancy equipment, but sometimes much of it was not used or was misused—books torn and thrown around, records damaged, blocks splintered, etc.

Competence in the arts comes through guidance by the teacher, who makes suggestions and gives instructions at appropriate times. Equally important is the fact that she provides him with plenty of time to learn about the properties and uses of materials.

Teaching a child about consistency of materials, e.g., is much more meaningful than giving him thick and thin paint, with appropriate labels. If developing competence in making something thick or thin is the desired effect, the child must first have many opportunities to experience and explore qualities of "thickness and thinness," such as mixing dirt with water to make mud, stirring a thick batter for muffins or a thin batter for crepes, mixing water and flour and oil for thick play dough, or beating cream to make butter.

Teaching competence in the arts does not mean allowing completely free, undirected "messing around," nor does it mean following formal organized units of instruction. The teacher must combine appropriately selected materials, guidance and plenty of time and opportunity for the child to satisfy his curiosity.

A teacher using shapes of faces on a flannel board can give children an opportunity to learn to use lines to indicate feelings; a line curved downward for the mouth and eyes to express sadness, or curved upward for a smile. Artists often use lines to communicate feelings. The soft curved dark lines and three-dimensional effect of Rubens' "Head of a Negro" are used effectively to draw attention to the sad facial features of the subject. Miró creates humorous effects through designs that use straight bright colored lines and dots to represent eyes, nose and mouth. (See pp. 254–257 on aesthetic judgment.)

A seemingly simple skill such as learning how to use a hand punch to make holes in paper can be highly satisfying to a child. Learning how to use scissors to cut in the direction he wants to cut adds to his feeling of competence. A child who knows not only the names of the colors and what color he wants to use, but also how to mix a new color with what he has possesses a greater degree of competence. The teacher might suggest that he mix and stir the primary colors at the easel; or she might choose to give him food colors and test tubes of water and eye droppers with which to experiment under her guidance. His ability to mix colors and create new ones gives him added skills, satisfaction in his own accomplishments, more alternatives for choices, and control over what he wants to express through the arts.

Development of skills aimed at achieving a desired effect can be begun in preschool, through manipulation and conscious selection of materials. These skills need not be achieved at the expense of the child's freedom to explore. A perceptive teacher is cognizant of the child's need to learn through physical interaction with his environment.

Some recent research in art education for young children indicates that children's perceptual abilities are enhanced when they are motivated to look for components of an artistic creation such as color, line, texture and form. Grossman (1970, pp. 421–427) reports a study (Douglas and Schwartz, [1967]) in which professionally-made ceramic pieces were used to illustrate some basic ideas to a group of four-year-olds. Four of the basic ideas were:

1. Art is a means of non-verbal communication.
2. The art product is the result of the artist's idea.
3. The artist uses what he sees, thinks, and feels to create art.
4. There is a great variety of materials available to the contemporary artist.

The children were able to understand these ideas and used them to interpret their own as well as other works of art.

On the basis of studies by Wachowiak and Ramsay (1965, pp. 25–27) and research by Torrance (1963, pp. 110–117), Grossman states (pp. 425–426):

It seems that an effective way of developing young children's artistic expressive abilities is to provide them with real and immediate objects or experiences, and teach them to explore these objects or experiences through all their senses.

Teachers adapt their styles to the type of activity in which they are working. In one school which served predominantly ethnic minority children, the teacher complained that even though the playhouse area was well stocked with a large variety of dress-ups, dolls and puppets, etc. for dramatic play, a small group of children played "cops" all day, arresting other children and putting them in jail. She wondered how she might help them achieve more competence and "skill" even in this area by giving them a less simplistic view of this role.

She invited a policeman to visit. He arrived in a patrol car, let the children take turns getting in and listening to the two-way radio; he let the children wear his badge and hat and gave them a book of tickets similar to the real tickets he had to write. He also told them about the reports he had to fill in and the routine calls he made during the day. After his visit, the children's dramatic play took on new dimensions. They began to incorporate the ideas provided by the policeman's visit. The teacher had helped them gain greater "skill" and competence in dramatic play through additional information about how to portray a single role.

A teacher with five years of experience describes her first attempt to help children learn to use woodworking tools:

"When I first started teaching nursery school, I remember being assigned to supervise the carpentry table. I had no idea what to expect. I got the children to help me push the wood box and tools out and before I knew what had happened, someone ran to the sandbox with a saw and a couple of other children had started hammering on the cement and trikes.

"I was really frightened. I ran after everyone, grabbed the tools from them and put everything away. I went home that night and decided I couldn't avoid potentially dangerous situations like that. I thought a lot about just what the carpentry activity is for, how I can best help the children participate in this activity and how I can help them gain competence in the use of the carpentry materials.

"I learned from experience that I had to start simply. The rules for safety had to be clear for the children and me. For example, I brought out the wood box and suggested that children select a piece of wood first, then I let them select a tool—(sometimes I left the saws in the shed until I was sure the children knew how to use a hammer first). I used to let them bang around on the wood and try to get the nail in as best they could (or I would just end up doing it for them).

Objectives for Developing Competence in the Arts

1. Learning to communicate internal responses graphically (paintings, drawings, etc.) and physically (dance, movement, music)
2. Beginning to be aware of differences of color, line, form, texture and how they are used to create different effects
3. Learning to use variety of tools and equipment and recognize their properties and purposes
4. Acquiring specific skills in music such as responding to rhythm, keeping time, recognizing harmony, tone, etc.
5. Learning how to mix materials to produce new creations (mixing paints to achieve a new color, cooking, etc.)
6. Developing skills in use of materials to facilitate expression of feelings and ideas

---

"I noticed many of the children, especially those who had never had any experience with carpentry before, would take a whack at the wood, fool around with a saw and leave the table; others would get frustrated and complain or wait for help. I gradually began to give more specific supervision. That is, I would hold my hands over the hands of a child and gently guide his movements while he was hammering or sawing. I would help him get the 'feel' of the activity. I tell the children to keep their eyes on the nail when they are hammering and show them how they can remove a nail.

"I remember one little boy who was particularly frustrated one day because he wanted to 'build a barn' by nailing a piece of wood onto the narrow edge of another piece. The wood kept slipping and he couldn't get the nail started while holding the two pieces of wood together with his other hand. I showed him how he could start the nail in one piece of wood and hammer it in until it went through and then nail it onto the other piece which he could attach to a vise. He was so excited when he discovered he could indeed achieve his goal with his newly acquired skills that he went around for days offering to teach the other children how to 'make a barn.' I find that children are more likely to stay with a project and experiment more readily if they feel competent with the tools and materials they have at hand."

As children experiment with materials, the teacher can guide their natural interest and responses in a sequence of activities designed to extend their range of experience and stimulate growth in particular areas.

In the area of music, for example, she might help them learn to listen, to sing, to play simple instruments (tambourine, drum, wood blocks, bells, etc.) and to respond to different kinds of music through body movement. Following is an example of some specific goals in music:

Goal	Activity
Melody	Identify several songs or themes by name
	Indicate by difference in body response that one melody is different from another (high, low, gay, sad, etc.)
	Compose own melodies and sing or play them
Harmony	Signal chord changes they recognize while listening
	Tell whether a piece consists of only a melody or melody plus chord accompaniment

Tone	Identify various instruments by name as they are played
	Tell whether one or more than one instrument is playing
	Recognize loudness and softness in music by clapping or stamping feet in similar volume
Rhythm	Clap, beat time, rock body to different tempos
	Mark out musical accent with hand or foot movement
	Create own rhythm patterns with instruments or clapping
	Draw attention to rhythmic sounds heard in the environment and identify source (clock tick, raindrops, traffic hum, typewriter . . .)
Form	Signal awareness of a repetition of melody or rhythm pattern

By listening to different types of music, children can be taught to distinguish between a waltz and a march, rock music and a symphony, etc. Some children will be interested in hearing about the lives of famous musicians, several of whom were composing and performing at a very early age (Mozart at five). Many children enjoy repeating the sounds of names such as Rachmaninoff, Feliciano, Beethoven and Belafonte. Experiences of this kind accumulate to become part of a rich musical background.

Musical goals are only partially accomplished by having groups of children listen, sing and move about for fifteen or twenty minutes each day. They are also achieved by surrounding the children with a great deal of music and encouraging active response through humming, singing, dancing and moving to sounds. Having a variety of instruments available to play, touch and ask questions about also helps greatly.

It is important for the teacher to know that many aspects of children's artistic responses are based on developmental patterns. Children's expression through the arts follows specific steps which are correlated with growth and development as well as experience. The work of Rhoda Kellogg in the field of children's art has focused attention on this (see p. 250). Her analysis shows that children everywhere scribble before they draw, and draw outline shapes before they reach a representational stage. Even at this level the child draws not from the way things are, but from the way he sees objects and events, or would like to, and concentrates only on what is important to him. In this light children's art can be understood for what it is—spontaneous creation.

Piaget's studies provide information as to why children produce art in the forms they do. He found, for example, that during the sensory motor stage, children explore objects systematically, especially by sight and touch. From this visual and tactile per-

PREOPERATIONAL SUBSTAGE (2 TO 4 YEARS)	INTUITIVE THOUGHT SUBSTAGE (4 TO 7 YEARS)
Up to 3 can only scribble. Between 3 and 4 can indicate open and closed form figures in unorganized attempts at symbolic representation. Makes irregular circles and shapes that enclose other shapes but not straight lines. Forms are drawn only from their topological aspects—no discontinuities.	From 4 to 5 begins to make straight lines, squares, triangles, houses, tables, in his drawings. Figures have little thoughtful organization. From 6 to 7 begins to coordinate mental image of the world. Understands topological relationships of human figure. Spatial relationships of single objects well developed. House will be on a baseline next to other houses, people and trees, yet separate. Proportions are likely to differ from reality and child does not use perspective.

TABLE 8-2 SUMMARY OF PIAGET'S FINDINGS REGARDING CHILDREN'S ABILITY TO DRAW DURING THE FIRST TWO SUBSTAGES OF THE CONCRETE OPERATIONS PERIOD
adapted from Lansing, Kenneth M., "The Research of Jean Piaget and Its Implications for Art Education in the Elementary School," *Studies in Art Education*, Vol. 7, No. 2, 1966, pp. 35–38. Publication of the National Art Education Association.

ception they acquire initial knowledge of geometric forms and space relationships. Although before the age of two a child does not draw, and may not create shapes meaningful to adults before four or five, it is from perceptual learning during his early years that the child eventually produces representational images.

The ability to represent what he has perceived through his senses comes during later stages of development. A brief summary of Piaget's findings regarding children's ability to draw during the first two substages of this period is given in Table 8-2. It is during the preoperational substage that children

> ... make drawings of men by attaching four lines to an irregular circle, and sometimes they put other circles inside a large one to represent eyes and other facial features. But, when the child attempts a complicated human being at this stage, it is clear that his concepts of topological relationships are not *fully* developed, because he may place the mouth over the nose or draw the ears detached from the body. Although his visual concept of proximity, separation, and enclosure is fairly well formed, his mental image of order and continuity is still poor. Thus, he cannot retain in his mind the correct sequence of mouth and nose along a vertical axis, nor can he imagine a man wearing a hat to be a continuous unit. Consequently, he draws the hat above the figure but not on it (Lansing, 1966, pp. 35–38).

Adults frequently urge children to copy rather than to express their own responses and ideas. However kindly and well-intentioned, an adult's saying, "No, dear, you don't have it right. You didn't make the tail long enough. Here, I'll show you," is almost certain to be ineffective in producing a change in a child's work. He may dutifully copy and try to do as he is told, but Piaget's findings show that a child's work in art is not improved by criticism of his visual symbols. During his early development the most effective way to change his work is to help him build additional concepts. In working on aesthetic development, the teacher's goals must be limited because young children can acquire only concepts that deal with actual objects and events. They are less capable of forming concepts of abstracts such as beauty, joy, courage, or pride. However,

Some Characteristics of Children's Art

If left to explore art on their own with no "teaching," children go through the following stages of development

Shape stage	2 to 3	Scribbles
		Draws shapes in outline form
Design stage	3 to 4	Begins to make line formations, such as suns
Pictorial stage	4 to 5	Makes representations of humans, animals, etc.

2's make one scribble after another
3's and 4's generally make a single type of scribble and on one sheet of paper; usually draw an outline first, and later fill it in
5's practice letters and faces; pictures sometimes tell their own story

Mean Ages for Drawing Specific Pictorial Items

Sun	3yrs.7mos.
Human	3yrs.7mos.
Animal	4 yrs.
Vegetation	4yrs.1mos.
Building	4yrs.3mos.
Transportation item	4yrs.3mos.

adapted from R. Kellogg, *Analyzing Children's Art.* National Press Books, Palo Alto, Calif., 1969, p. 193.

Piaget's work and that of others suggests that children can be provided with activities that will increase perceptual knowledge and so add to artistic development.

Dramatic Play Perhaps the most common form of self-expression engaged in by young children is that of dramatic play. Between the ages of three and five children are still in the process of becoming social creatures. They are learning to interact with other human beings. They are finding their own individuality. Dramatic play and other forms of pretending permit children to recreate for themselves what they see all around them. By "trying on" a role, they learn through vicarious experience about themselves and their reactions.

The child of three participates in simple imaginative play. He or she may put a dolly to bed, cover it, kiss it "Night, night" saying, "Baby, go to bed." By four the imaginative aspects are more detailed and complex but they remain within the same framework. Dolls are now fed, elaborately talked to and nurtured. Conversations such as the following are not uncommon: "Now you have to eat all your food and then take a bath and go to bed before Daddy comes home. Tomorrow we will take you on a nice trip and if you're good you'll see Grandma and she'll give you some cookies." Fours may work out aggressions and hostilities through spanking, scolding and even throwing around the dolls they so carefully tend at other times.

At five, make-believe of this kind often involves other children and long processes of "pretend." Typically, several children gather in the housekeeping corner making plans

2 yrs.   3 yrs.   4 yrs.

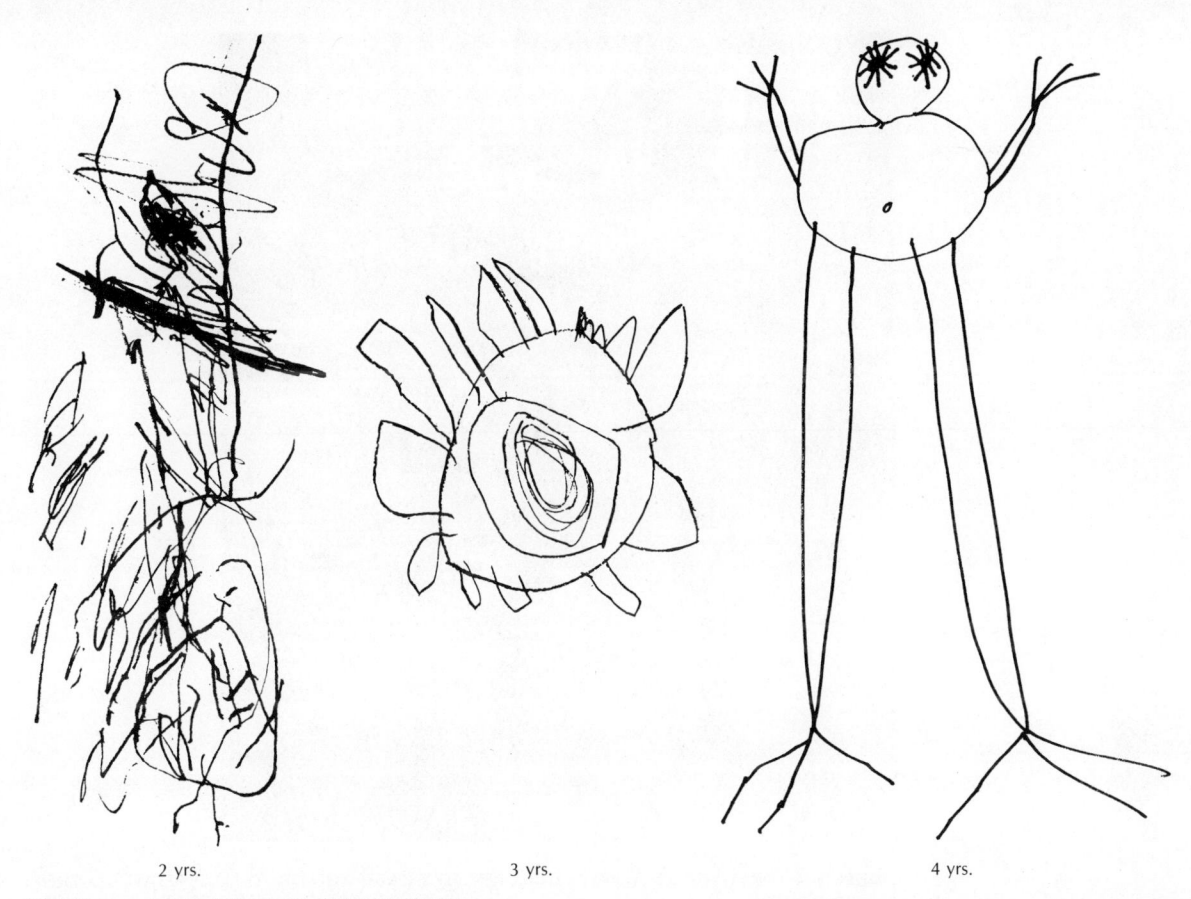

FIGURE 8–3 SOME STAGES IN CHILDREN'S ART

for complex imaginative play involving daddies, mothers, uncles, siblings and friends. All are an extension of the child's real world. Cultural differences are evident in children's imaginative play at this level. Those who see policemen as nonthreatening agents of society create helping roles for them in the scheme of their play. Other children pretend to hide from the "fuzz" and act out being put in jail by "cops" who have caught them. Imaginative play affords children an opportunity to relate to one another and to develop ideas as to how others think and feel. Children learn from one another through the enactments of typical situations.

Children often deal with problems of emotional development by creating imaginary playmates. Three-year-olds who need companionship they are not finding elsewhere, who need someone to look up to, to dominate, or to do things for or with, often create imaginary playmates. By four, many of these needs are closely bound to everyday occurrences in the life of the child. The creature he imagines goes through all the familiar routines with him and has equal rights and needs.

Fours and fives frequently use imaginary people and animals to play out fears and desires which are unacceptable in real life. Beating a doll is permissible, beating one's baby sister is not, no matter what the provocation. Antisocial talk meets little opposition when you are a Badman, whereas a boy or girl is scolded for the same behavior. By five, most imaginative play is closely tied to the world of reality, with children end-

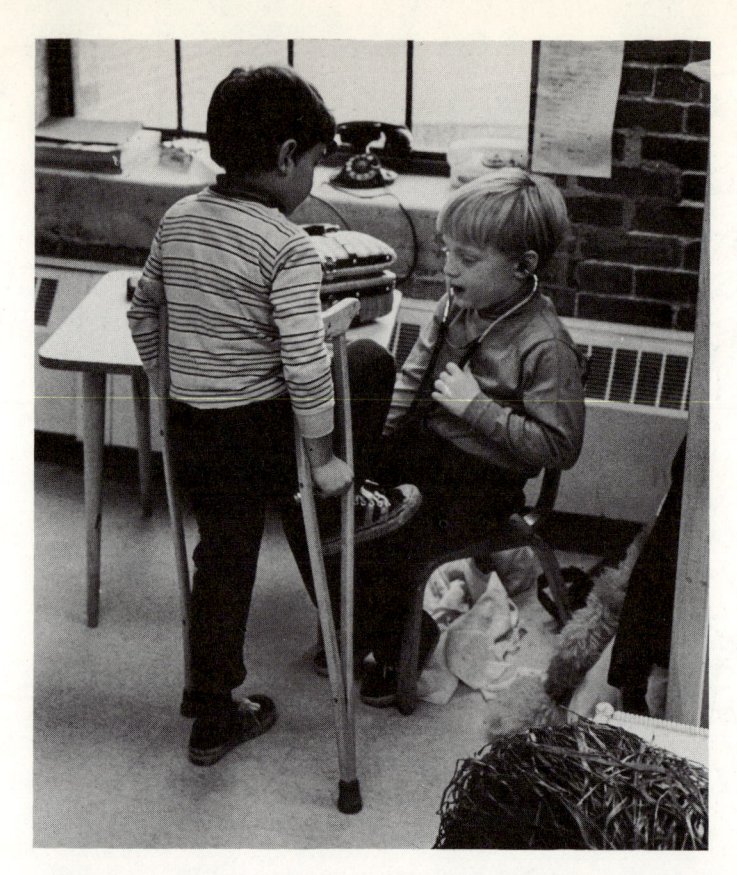

FIGURE 8-4   DRAMATIC PLAY HELPS CHILDREN TO EXPRESS THEMSELVES AND RELATE TO THEIR ENVIRONMENT

lessly re-enacting the events of their daily lives or pretending to be familiar figures, such as family members, firemen, grocers and nurses.

Although little formal study has been made of preschoolers' dramatic play except in the field of therapy, one cannot observe children of three to five very long without realizing that such activity is central to both group and individual behavior. In all its forms, dramatic play is a means by which children come to understand their environment and the people in it. Acting out feelings and impressions externalizes emotions, as does participation in art and music activities. Dramatic play helps children to distinguish between reality and fantasy, and to come to terms with both. It serves as yet another means of socializing the child and teaching him to find his place in the world.

Developing Awareness of Cultural Heritage

Every human society has used the arts to express the hopes and aspirations of its people and to record historic events. The walls of cave dwellers carry a pictorial history of the prowess of their hunters. Trajan's column in Rome continues to tell the story of his military conquests. The temples of Greece reflect a people's love for beauty combined with their worship of many gods. Great works of music reflect man's joy and sorrow, his fear and longing during particular periods of time and reveal how men perceive

> *Jazz music covers more than just one style. It is more than just popular music, though jazz is popular music. It is a distinctive art form that owes much of its popularity to the way it can communicate the human emotions we all understand, and to the way it appeals to a basic love of rhythm which seems instinctive in most humans.*
> from Charles Boeckman, *Cool, Hot, and Blue*, Robert B. Luce, Inc., 1968, p. 4.

---

their world. To the knowing ear, a Gregorian chant has as much to say as an English madrigal, an Italian aria or a modern country ballad. Children are capable of recognizing the differences in these various forms even though they cannot define them.

Even very young children can be given some idea of the forms of art which are the particular products of their culture. American children have an especially rich heritage to draw from since their culture includes music, dance and art from the various ethnic groups who settled the country. In addition to this unique heritage, America has native art and music forms which children should know about. They need to hear and learn to distinguish jazz, soul music, Indian chants, cowboy songs and modern rock music as well as melodies of the classical composers. The work of American artists should become a part of the child's experience, for it has a great deal to tell him about himself and the world he lives in. Artists such as Grant Wood, Winslow Homer, Frank Remington, Mary Cassatt and Andrew Wyeth speak to children as well as to adults.

This is not to suggest that a picture or piece of sculpture should be displayed and the class asked to join in a group discussion about it. Nor that a classroom needs to be turned into an art gallery of Americana. But a teacher bringing in one example at a time on a rotating basis and making a point of engaging children in casual conversation about certain details that are characteristic of the artist, telling a little bit about where the artist lives and when and how he happened to draw the picture, can begin to build a foundation of cultural knowledge. And she should always ask, "What do you see? What do you think this artist has tried to tell you?"

In introducing music and music listening, the teacher need not limit herself to records which are presumably prepared for young children. Using pieces that form a part of children's culture—a well-known aria, folk song, or march—are as likely to elicit responses and at the same time build artistic knowledge. A teacher's choices in such matters are not difficult if she has in mind what she is trying to do.

There is no need to wait until children are old enough to take art appreciation before introducing them to art forms which have won recognition in the adult world. No special time of day or week needs to be set aside for this exposure. Children can be as constantly surrounded by art and music as they are by blocks and swings and sand boxes.

Identification of works of art and music and the names of famous artists and composers is a useful goal in itself. When one picture or piece of music can be recognized as separate from all others, art takes on a new meaning. To give a child the opportunity to be aware of the artistic products of his society and to become acquainted with great art and artists, is to give him access to a wider area of human experience. The teacher will have time to use only a little of the vast amount of material available to her; her

Objectives for Developing Awareness of Cultural Heritage

1. Learning to look at details in a variety of art forms
2. Learning about artists, musicians, sculptors, etc. as occupational roles
3. Beginning to understand how artists contribute to a culture
4. Becoming familiar with some of the social, cultural rituals, celebrations and historical records through works of art (weaving stories into rugs, folk songs and folk tales and their origin, painting, carvings, etc.)
5. Learning that adults and children have been producing art for a long time

---

most difficult task will be to choose exactly what she wants to do and to confine herself to the resources that will be effective for her purpose. A child's recognition that he is part of a particular society, and his resultant interest in learning more about the people in that society, and thus of himself, can begin with a teacher's wise choices.

Developing Aesthetic Judgment and Standards

Helping a child experience and become aware of inner responses and getting him to develop preferences, are first steps toward his acquisition of an ability to judge what is and is not artistically worthwhile. This skill is thus obviously related to an earlier objective. By careful planning and skillful questioning, together with a genuine interest in answers, a teacher can guide a child's initial discriminations. However, it will be quite a while before he builds standards of artistic excellence which will apply whether or not he likes a piece of work.

For example, a teacher's skillful questions about contrasting pictures can teach a child to notice that some pictures are brighter than others; some have people in them, others do not; in one the lines may be mostly straight, in another predominantly curved; some pictures may have many details, others almost none. The teacher will know he has observed the differences and is beginning to make judgments by his answers to questions such as the following:

1. How many colors do you see? Do the colors in this picture make you feel the same as the colors in that picture? Which colors do you like best? How do they make you feel?
2. What do you think the artist is trying to tell you? What does he want you to know about the people (animals, flowers, buildings, etc.) in his picture?
3. Are the people in the different pictures drawn the same way? What are some of the differences? Do they have the same kinds of hands? Of eyes? What are the differences? How are they the same?

At first the child's discriminations may not be very fine, but gradually, after repeated exposure and chances for comparison, he will know that a Van Gogh is not the same as a Rembrandt, nor a Modigliani the same as a Miró. He will also be able to tell which one he prefers though it may take many experiences and conversations with his teacher before this happens. A traveling "gallery" of art reproductions prepared by one school

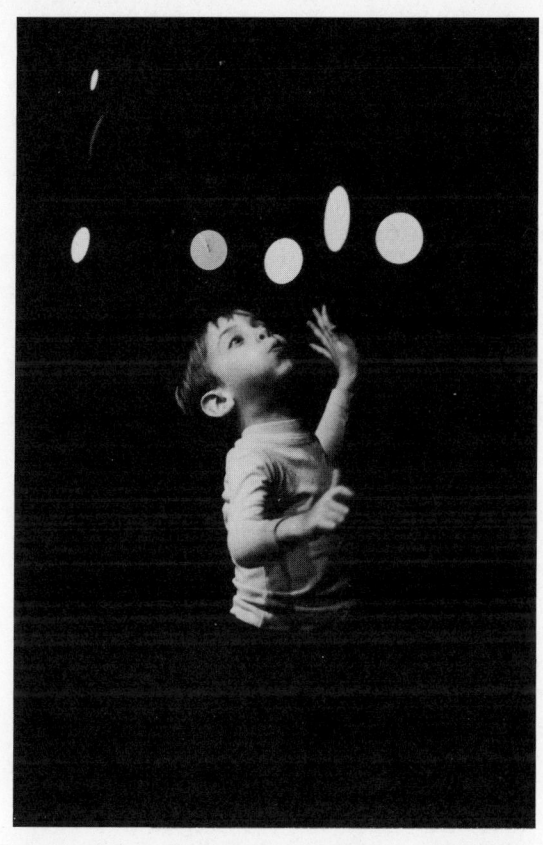

FIGURE 8–5 DEVELOPMENT OF AESTHETIC JUDGMENT BEGINS WITH EXPOSURE TO A VARIETY OF ART FORMS

district[2] consists of portraits of children, along with suggestions for helping children develop artistic awareness and judgment. Some of the objectives suggested are listed below:

Objectives	Commentary
To encourage acceptance of the unfamiliar and unusual	When we look at children we see that they do not always look the same
To develop awareness and sensitivity to feelings reflected in the face	If you are sad your face will look a certain way. (Have children demonstrate and examine expression in paintings)
	If you are feeling especially happy your face might look quite different. (Have children demonstrate and consider expressions in paintings)

[2] Information used by permission of the Palo Alto Unified School District, Palo Alto, California.

255 THE VERSATILITY OF THE ARTS IN A PRESCHOOL PROGRAM

Adults as Subjects

American Gothic	Grant Wood, American
Puppet Show Woman	O. Masara, Japanese
Head of a Negro	Rubens, Belgian
The Postman Roulin	Van Gogh, Dutch
Señora Sabrosa García	Goya, Spanish
People and Dog in the Sun	Miró, Spanish

Children as Subjects

Girl with a Broom	Rembrandt, Dutch
Portrait of a Boy	C. Soutine, Russian
Girl with a Watering Can	Renoir, French
Don Emanuel Osorio de Zúñiga	Goya, Spanish
Girl with Braids	Modigliani, Italian
Head of a Young Boy	Rouault, French

Before they saw the portraits the teachers helped children realize that people perceive the same objects differently, in different settings. For example, it was suggested that teachers have children look at one another in a darkened room and then with bright light; that they look at objects close up and then from a distance; that the size of a person or object be considered relative to various larger and smaller objects nearby. Young children can develop preferences concerning works of art. The two groups of portraits described on this page were displayed in a nursery school where children could see them at any time. At various moments individual children were brought to see them. After talking informally with each child about the first group and then the second, and attracting his attention to various likenesses and differences, the teacher asked:

1. Do you like the pictures?
2. What do you like about them?
3. What don't you like?
4. Which picture do you like best?

All of the children were able to form an opinion; the older children, however, were more unanimous in their preferences than the younger. The choices made were as follows:

Selection	Younger Children (17) (3's and 4's)	Older Children (28) (4's and 5's)
Adult portrait most liked	Miró (7)	Van Gogh (16)
Child portrait most liked	Renoir (7)	Renoir (14)

A child can develop aesthetic responses to things other than recognized works of art. The qualities to which he responds in a Van Gogh or a Renoir exist all around him. An arrangement of flowers, designs on book covers, patterns of sunlight and shadow, the curve of a staircase, can all be viewed and talked about from the standpoint of their effect on the viewer. Asking, "How do they make you feel?" and "Which do you like better," and then accepting the child's answers frees him from fear of being "wrong" or

Objectives for Developing Judgment and Internal Standards

1. Understanding that people respond in personal (unique) ways to the arts
2. Becoming familiar with a variety of art forms and growing in acceptance of different modes of expression
3. Becoming aware of, identifying and responding to some of the specific characteristics which comprise a work of art or expression (color, line, texture, brush strokes, etc. of paintings; timbre, pitch, melody, tempo, etc. of music; gestures, manner, tone of voice, subject matter, etc. of stories; movement, mood, gestures, etc. of dance)
4. Beginning to articulate and justify judgments with some specificity

---

ridiculed. Children can be helped to see details of color, line, texture and form in their surroundings as well as in pictures. They can be asked about their artistic preferences and can gradually build judgments on what they like and dislike and why.

From his response to music a child will show he has learned to recognize not only that there is a difference between the Beatles and Bach, but also between "Skip to My Lou" and "The Blue-Tail Fly." Even quite young children move about very differently to different tempos and rhythms. Once a child demonstrates his realization that not all music is the same, he can be expected to answer questions such as:

1. Which music do you like better?
2. What do you like about it?
3. Which piece goes faster? Is that why you like it (don't like it)?
4. Which one is louder? Is that why you like it (don't like it)?

Helping a child recognize differences in his responses to various stimuli, and asking him to consider whether he likes or dislikes something and why, encourages his making simple judgments about himself and his world. It will be some time before he is able to form an objective evaluation about whether the art he sees or the music he hears is "good" or "bad." But this is not expected of him at the preschool level since he has not had enough experience to permit judgment of this kind.

RELATIONSHIP OF THE ARTS TO COGNITIVE, AFFECTIVE AND SOCIAL DEVELOPMENT

A well-planned arts program brings children in contact with a wide variety of materials and sensory experiences. What the child gets from these experiences is not haphazard; it is up to the teacher to decide how to utilize them in keeping with her educational goals. In some instances she will have in mind the child's artistic development, emphasizing different features and aspects of the arts themselves. In other instances, she may arrange the experience so that it relates to cognitive or affective and social development of the child. At such times the particular form of art she chooses as a resource will be incidental to her objective. She may, of course, wish to keep in mind both purposes at once. On the whole, however, she will tend to emphasize one more than the other during a single instance of instruction.

Teachers as Labelers

The arts offer teachers a wide range of vocabulary to share with children. There are all the terms peculiar to the activities involved—the names of the activities themselves, colors, shapes, instruments, materials, tools, methods and techniques. In addition, she has many ways to describe what is being done. For example, children need not just put objects together. Materials can be made to fit, match, adhere, hold, cleave, cling, or stick to one another. These joinings can be accomplished by using string, nails, pins, dowels, thongs, rubber bands, cement, glue, solder, adhesive, scotch tape and staples as well as paste.

For example, suppose the teacher has decided that a particular child needs help in building concepts about shapes. He likes to draw and often works at the easel. The teacher can help him label and observe the various properties of the shapes that he is drawing, or she may ask him to consider squares, triangles and circles that are apparent in other pictures. She may or may not at the same time seek to interest him in color, brush technique or the characteristics of an artist's work.

Contribution of the Arts to Cognitive Growth

There are various ways in which the teacher can use the arts to encourage cognitive development. She can use the arts to increase vocabulary, to give the child many new opportunities for gaining physical and logical knowledge. She can help him realize he may both affectively respond to something and think about it at the same time.

Increasing Vocabulary and Developing Concepts When interacting with children, the teacher provides many labels to help them increase their vocabulary and make it possible for them to reflect upon and communicate their experiences. The remarks listed below are typical of the kind teachers make in order to point out similarities and differences and to increase vocabulary:

1. I see you're using a *wide brush* today, Laura.
2. What *bright tempera colors* you chose to paint your picture with, Charles.
3. Do you want me to help you move that *heavy easel*, John?
4. That's certainly *lively* music, isn't it?

A child doesn't have to know he's using a wide *brush* filled with *bright tempera color* in order to paint a picture on a piece of paper that's mounted on an *easel*. Nor does he need to be told that music is *lively* before he will start hopping or dancing to its rhythm. However, by labeling, the teacher makes it possible for children to acquire the vocabulary which helps them sort, organize, classify and keep track of the vast amounts of information they accumulate as they participate in art activities. The vocabulary she provides also aids in the gradual development of a store of concepts by which children order new experiences.

Gaining Physical and Logical Knowledge The child's approach to painting and clay modeling, to using musical instruments and record players, to the "props" for dramatic

Gaining Physical Knowledge from Clay

If you hand a young child a piece of clay, it will be a long while before he makes a pot or figure with it that you will recognize if this is his first experience with clay.

He will explore its properties. That clay will be rolled, squeezed, slapped, smelled, and perhaps tasted. He will pull it, drop it, throw it, take tiny pieces from it and then put it all back together again.

Once satisfied as to how clay feels and what he can do with it, he may use it to make "balls" or "cakes" or perhaps simply roll out an endless supply of rope-like pieces for which he has no use. He is unlikely to seek labels for what he does or to talk about his activities.

Later, he may use clay to represent objects, though what he depicts may or may not be recognizable to anyone else. Only after many experiences of this kind he is ready to create something of his own choosing.

---

play—in short, to any of the materials provided in the arts program—is initially one of investigation, not expression. The description above summarizes the way in which children typically acquire physical knowledge from their experiences with an art form.

In addition to deriving a great deal of physical knowledge from the materials that are part of an arts program in a nursery school, the arts lend themselves to the acquisition of logical knowledge. Many drawings involve shape and space relationships, music and finger games bring understanding of counting, adding, subtracting and seriation; dramatic play encourages categorizing and transfer; and, as mentioned earlier, all of the arts help children acquire labels and develop concepts about in-on-under-around-over, fast-slow, loud-soft, happy-sad, up-down, etc.

Miriam Stecher reports the following example as one of the ways she and her associates have used free movement as a means for children's acquisition of logical knowledge:

The kindergarten was exploring the concept of *lightness* and *looseness* through movement experience with tension and relaxation.

Teacher Hug yourself real hard. Harder. That's very tight. Let go! That's not tight at all now, is it?

Katy It's loose.

Teacher Do it with your hands. Can you make a fist like this? Make it so tight that I can't open it. (She tried to pry open Peter's fist.)

Pete It's like a knot in my shoelace.

Tony B-o-i-i-n-g. (He fell down and remained there limp.)

Teacher What's that?

Tony The knot busted.

Both teacher and children were delighted with the image and together proceeded to develop it, first with isolated parts of the body, then the whole body, and finally "tying up" with a partner. At a signal (a glissando on the piano) all shouted "Boiing!" then, falling suddenly, they lay quietly and limply loose. Later, when

Questions for Encouraging Physical Activity

1. Can you walk quickly?
2. Can you walk less (more) quickly than that?
3. Can you walk quietly?
4. Can you walk less (more) quietly than that?
5. How would you walk to show you're happy? (angry, frightened, sad, tired, in a hurry, afraid of getting wet in the rain, being blown by the wind?)
6. Are there ways to move without moving your feet? Show me

---

the teacher wished them to relax again after vigorous galloping, she asked them to lie down and "be loose like a busted shoelace" (Stecher, 1970, p. 148).

Relationship of the Arts to Affective and Social Development

The nursery school has traditionally emphasized the affective and social development of children, with the arts considered as one means for achieving this purpose. The use of music, art, drama and other artistic activities is often initiated by individual children with development left to their own imaginations. Thus, the use of the arts is frequently unsystematic even though there may be an established daily routine. As more is known about the value of a more structured approach to furthering affective and social development, hopefully the arts will assume the place of importance that is rightfully theirs in programs of early education.

Physical and Emotional Release The arts provide many opportunities for children to release energy, and teachers make use of them for this purpose. It is natural for a child to want to wriggle and jump and run and climb and move about. Children can be encouraged to march, skip, clap and dance to music; to beat and stomp to the sound of drums, to recreate the gait of animals in dramatic play, to manipulate clay and other modeling materials freely, and to draw and finger paint with broad movements.

In addition they can release physical drives by experimenting with the use of balance beams, obstacle courses, hula hoops, ladders, climbing ropes and other playground equipment. When appropriate to the child's interest, the teacher might ask questions such as those listed above. From these and many other experiences involving movement, children can become more and more aware of themselves as human beings with bodies that can be controlled and used the way they wish. Through physical experiences they can develop skills that lead to self-confidence and ways of expressing themselves through movement.

The arts also provide channels for emotional release. Young children are not always aware of their emotions, do not always know why they cry, strike out at others, are restless or feel good-to-bursting at times. Few have the ability to recognize feelings of these kinds or the verbal skills to express them in words. But they do have emotions. Yet almost from infancy pressure is often placed on children to conceal their emotions, especially those expressed loudly or accompanied by tears. Adults are intolerant of

> *If I had influence . . . I should ask that the gift to each child in the world be a sense of wonder so indestructible that it would last throughout life, as an unfailing antidote against the boredom and disenchantment of later years, the sterile preoccupation with things that are artificial, the alienation from the source of our strength.*
>
> from Rachel Carson, *The Sense of Wonder,* Harper and Row, 1965, pp. 42–43.

what they consider "too much noise," and unable to control their own reactions to the sight and sound of crying.

Thus children repeatedly hear instructions such as "Be quiet," "Don't cry," "He won't hurt you" or "You don't have to worry." As can be noted, sometimes he is even told not to have an emotion. Yet how should he respond to experiences such as confrontation with a large animal, being left alone in the dark or having to stay with strangers?

The child's affective development needs to include opportunity for him to recognize and express feelings. Psychologist Arthur T. Jersild of Columbia University states:

> If an older person wishes to understand a child's emotions and to help him cope with the conditions that arouse emotion, it is necessary to encourage the child to face feelings rather than to falsify them or run away from them. But to do this requires courage on the adult's part, the courage to permit the child to allow his feelings to show and the courage to face feelings that are aroused within himself when the emotions of someone else appear in raw form (Jersild, 1968, p. 312).

It is clear that the arts give children a means to express emotion outwardly. An angry child who paints a picture and covers it with masses of dark color, or stomps his feet as he marches to music, is often finding a way to vent his frustration. But he is not engaging in art experiences or artistic expression and development. Realizing that emotions can be released and expressed through the arts, the teacher needs to be careful not to misinterpret behavior. Masses of dark paint do not always signify hate and anger; some children simply like these colors; others use them liberally to represent rain or night. A child who stamps his feet and clenches his fists as he marches may be imagining himself a giant, not reacting to hurt or disappointment. It is up to the teacher to be sure she knows the difference before she decides whether to help a child control his emotions or provide encouragement to further his artistic development.

Social Experiences In discussing music as a universal language, Florence Foster said:

> Music has an integrating power on the individual and the group. The withdrawn child tends to relax his guard and is more ready to participate with the others, while the hostile child seems to be less aggressive, so that each is helped to become a contributing member of the group. Here is one task in which all can cooperate to produce something mutually pleasing (Foster, 1965, p. 375).

Singing and listening to music, participating in finger games, acting out "The Wheels of the Bus Go Round and Round," or some other action song, and playing in a rhythm band are often the first, and for some time the only, group activities in which young children join. Until three or four they engage in most experiences, including those of the arts, as individuals, or with an older person.

Gradually, however, the arts provide many opportunities for interaction. Talking about stories or poems and pictures, dramatic play (even though some children act out their role alone and say nothing), a construction project, and planning and making decorations for a "party," lend themselves to a good deal of conversation and social experience.

Not all children in a preschool are ready for group experiences, and the teacher will help decide which part of the arts program best meets his social needs. Using the child's experiences as a medium for her own interaction with him may be all that is required. In time he can be encouraged to make more and more contacts through interests in the arts, and through the universal appeal of music.

By her understanding of their potential, the teacher can use the arts as a means to further children's total development. However, to use them most effectively she must have goals in mind and know the needs of individual children. Her responsibility in the arts program is both to impart knowledge and to further children's response to the world about them. Rather than seeking to make children into artists, musicians or craftsmen, she should strive to help them develop as social beings with capacity to observe, to respond and to communicate.

REFERENCES

Boeckman, C. *Cool, hot, and blue*. Washington, D.C.: Robert B. Luce, Inc., 1968.

Carson, R. L. *The sense of wonder*. New York: Harper and Row, 1965.

Cole, L. *A history of education: Socrates to Montessori*. New York: Rinehart and Co., Inc., 1955.

Croft, D. J. and Hess, R. D. *An activities handbook for teachers of young children*, Boston, Mass.: Houghton Mifflin Co., 1972.

Douglas, N. K. and Schwartz, J. B. Increasing awareness of art ideas of young children through guided experiences with ceramics. *Studies in Art Education,* 1967, *8*, No. 2, 2–9.

Foster, F. P. The song within: music and the disadvantaged preschool child. *Young Children,* September 1965, *20*.

Grossman, M. Art education for the young child. *Review of Educational Research,* June 1970, *40*, No. 3, 421–427.

Hartley, R., Frank, L. K., and Goldenson, R. M. *Understanding children's play*. New York: Columbia University Press, 1952.

Jersild, A. T. *Child psychology*, (6th edition), Englewood Cliffs, N.J.: Prentice-Hall, Inc., 1968.

Kellogg, R. *Analyzing children's art*. Palo Alto, Calif.: National Press Books, 1969.

Lansing, K. M. The research of Jean Piaget and its implications for art education in the elementary school. *Studies in Art Education,* 1966, 7, No. 2, 33–42.

Lewis, H. P. (Ed.). *Child art, the beginnings of self-affirmation.* Berkeley, Calif.: Diablo Press, 1966.

Stecher, M. B. Concept learning through movement improvisation: the teacher's role as catalyst. *Young Children,* January 1970, 25, 148.

Torrance, E. P. *Education and the creative potential.* Minneapolis, Minn.: University of Minnesota Press, 1963.

Wachowiak, F. and Ramsay, T. *Emphasis: Art.* Scranton, Pa.: International Textbook, 1965.

CHAPTER 9

CRISIS IN THE PRESCHOOL

CRISIS DOESN'T MEAN FAILURE

Inevitability of Crisis

Janet Fong had been an assistant teacher for almost six months. Today she was assigned to supervise outdoor activities, one of her favorite duties. She moved leisurely about the playground, stopping to admire Sally's sand cake, then over to the swings to push Kevin. Even though he might not rise high enough to see "rivers and trees and cattle and all," at least with a little help he'd be able to glimpse that busy part of the world which lay just over the fence of the Lincoln Street Nursery School.

Between Kevin's regular ups-and-downs she caught sight of the new boy maneuvering a wagon under the jungle gym to use as a mounting block. Giving Kevin a final push, she started over to move the wagon and explain the rule of "nothing under the jungle gym," noting as she went how quickly the child had climbed to the top. But she was too late; even as she approached him the boy failed to gain a handhold, and tumbled to the ground.

An outstretched arm slapped against the wagon with such force that Janet never understood how the fall resulted only in a bad bruise. As she hastened to help him, the stunned child struggled to his feet and began to scream. Anxious to reassure him without alarming others, Janet gently but firmly lifted him into her arms and carried him to the office. The crisis was not over, but for the time being, at least, the situation was under control.

Crisis and stress are part of the routine of a preschool as surely as they are part of the life of a family with young children. No matter how experienced and competent a teacher may be, or how carefully she plans and works, she will frequently have to deal with crisis and may herself occasionally be its cause.

Several features of the preschool make it virtually inevitable that such tension will be a normal, though unplanned, element in the schedule. First, for both educational and developmental reasons, the child obviously needs an environment in which he can freely explore and manipulate a variety of materials. Given such opportunity, he often shows remarkable ingenuity for arranging things in ways that physically endanger himself and/or others. In addition, situations arising from coincidence, equipment breaking, falls and other accidents, mean that children will be hurt despite all precautions. A second potential source for crisis at the preschool level is illness. Illness presents a physical hazard not only for the child directly affected, but also in the case of infectious or communicable disease for others.

The responsibility of the teacher to be custodian, both on school grounds and during trips or outings, is a third source of potential crisis, bound as it is to legal liability. Other potential sources include psychological and social pressures arising from value differences between teacher and parents, problems which parents or children bring to the school from family interaction, as well as personal difficulties and staff tensions. Individually or collectively, these features, all of which will be discussed in more detail later in the chapter, are not entirely avoidable. Indeed, the only certain way to avoid crisis in a preschool is to close the school down.

The teacher who is experienced and prepared sees such situations as part of her job. Since they pose specific threats to her, she obviously has an interest in learning how to deal with them and in knowing what the possible consequences will be and how they can be avoided. She has a legal responsibility and will feel severe psychological distress if a child is hurt or not properly taken care of and she is at fault, especially if she faces court action. She also has an investment in her reputation as a teacher, which affects both her own self-esteem and her career.

The teacher's primary interest, of course, is the care and education of the children for whom she is responsible. In order to meet her responsibilities, she will orient herself toward crisis by learning to diagnose a stressful situation immediately to identify whether a crisis exists and how severe it can become; by familiarizing herself with the major types of critical incidents and situations that can arise; and learning how to avoid crisis, minimize it and deal with its effects. In short, she must recognize the presence of a crisis, the type of situation it is, learn how to deal with it and respond to its effects.

Difficulties in Identifying Crisis Situations

Crisis is not an "all or nothing" matter. Stressful situations and events range in severity from the obvious one of severe physical injury, through subtle signs of a child's or parent's inner turmoil, fear or depression; in addition there are the normal stresses of social interaction and socialization. While one can define crisis in a general way as an event or condition which interrupts the routine of the school and demands a shift in plans and resources, a comprehensive definition of crisis which would be useful to different teachers in many differing situations is probably not possible.

Some elements can, of course, be identified. There is an element of threat to someone or something; there is usually some urgency for immediate action to keep conditions from getting worse; and there are likely to be other, more serious consequences if no action is taken. The teacher as a diagnostician is the judge of the nature and seriousness of the circumstances; her competence and effectiveness as a professional are reflected in her ability to deal with the unexpected and difficult.

The task of evaluating the seriousness of a situation is complicated by the fact that the symptoms of distress—crying, hysteria, accusations, threats, pleas for help and complaints of various kinds—do not always mean there is a crisis and, conversely, one may exist without these cues. While these indicate that something is wrong, they do not

FIGURE 9-1 STRESS IS PART OF THE ROUTINE OF A PRESCHOOL

clearly signal a crisis or reveal the nature or extent of the problem. A crying child may be one who is frightened by a fall; a child who acts subdued after a tumble may be more seriously hurt. Noise and emotion may easily distract the teacher from her task of assessing a situation accurately. A mother who gets upset when a child throws sand in the sandbox can create the impression that a) the child is the only one creating the problem and b) the problem and danger are severe. Actually, it is also the mother who creates the stress by making an unnecessary emotional fuss, threatening or accusing a child and overestimating the physical dangers involved. The experienced teacher recognizes that the mother is herself part of the problem and avoids turning against the child as a way to deal with the minor uproar.

The analysis of crisis takes into account the different interests of those involved and the fact that they see the problem and its seriousness from their own perspective. To a degree, this implies that particular events present crises to the child, others to the parents, still others to the teachers, staff and administrators of a preschool. All involved recognize and share concern about the difficulties that others have, but initial reactions most often reflect their individual viewpoint. The lists on pp. 270, 271, and 272 present some common crises as seen from differing points of view.

Although the teacher cannot entirely avoid defining a particular crisis in terms of who will be affected by it, her role is to assess a situation both from the viewpoint of the child and other participants. Her action, however, is necessarily based on her responsibility to the child, even though this may mean that she gives a parent, aide or volunteer less attention and support than they feel they deserve. In addition, she has the task of keeping her own response from contributing to the crisis.

Dimensions for Analyzing Crisis

A preschool is a complex organization and many different kinds of crises can occur. General questions or guidelines may be useful in sizing up a crisis or potential problem. Suppose, for example, a group of mothers hears that a school plans to bus in children from a minority neighborhood and they let the teacher know that they oppose this change in policy. What threat, if any, does this represent to the teacher? To the school? Will the consequences of the new policy be severe or minimal in economic or other terms? Are there obvious solutions to decrease community resistance? What are the consequences for all the children involved? How soon must a decision be made? These questions can be summarized in the four general groups listed on p. 268.

It may be useful to apply these dimensions of analysis to several hypothetical situations. As you study each one, consider whether it is a genuine crisis and how it should be assessed in terms of these questions:

Situation One Leon strides boldly to the sandbox where Jeff is busy digging a "tunnel." Grabbing Jeff's shovel from him he raises the tool threateningly, stomps on the tunnel and loudly orders "Move over, stupid, so I can build a battlefield."

A teacher quickly walks over to the boys and puts her hand on the shovel saying, "Give it back, Leon. Jeff had it first. You'll have to wait your turn."

Rather than doing as he has been told, Leon snatches the shovel from the teacher, very nearly striking another child in the eye as he does so. "Get away from me," he shouts. "You're not gonna boss me." To emphasize his remark he spits at her, then runs away, shovel in hand.

Checklist for Dimensions of Crisis

1. Who or what is threatened? The child? The teacher? The parent? The school?
2. How severe are the consequences likely to be for each one involved?
3. How obvious is the solution (or solutions)?
4. How urgent is it that a decision be reached?

Situation Two   It is almost the end of nap time in a small, private nursery school. The owner has not returned from a series of errands and the assistant teacher is busy helping children put on shoes and sweaters so they can go out to play. The older children are already at the far end of the yard on a nature "hike" with Brad, who comes in two afternoons a week. The teacher looks up to see a well-dressed man walk in and hears him say, "How do you do. I'm Jennifer Hamilton's father. I realize it's a bit early, but I've come to take her home."

Hearing his voice, Jenny runs to him crying, "Oh, Daddy, come look. I did a painting today." At her urging, Mr. Hamilton accompanies Jenny to see her work and all the areas of special interest to Jenny. The teacher hastens to get Jennifer's coat and mittens and to speed the girl and her father on their way.

Within moments of their departure Jennifer's mother arrives. She is horrified when told that Jenny's father has already taken the child. She becomes upset, cries, and then threatens to sue the teacher and the school for releasing the child to her former husband, who has been denied custody and visitation rights. She knew he might "kidnap" Jennifer, because he'd threatened to do so unless she would agree to what he considered a more reasonable settlement. All of this had been explained to the owner. By the way, where was the owner?

Situation Three   One morning when Pam, aged three and a half, is brought to school, her mother stays to visit. In honor of the occasion, Pam's mother has dressed herself and her daughter in matching new outfits. Eager to show her mother what she has learned to do, and before any of the teachers can help her into a smock, Pam rushes to the finger paint table and immerses both hands in the colorful "goo."

At her mother's shout she withdraws her hands and hastily wipes them down the front of her dress. "You naughty, naughty girl," her mother scolds as she drags the cowed child toward the washroom. "You know you're not to get your clothes dirty."

The mother's anger continues all through the clean-up process. When she has finished berating her daughter she starts in on the teacher who has been trying to help by supplying extra towels. "You spoil the children here. It's easy for you; you don't have to wash and iron their clothes. Believe me, I'm not paying good money for my child to learn how to make a mess!"

These situations are obviously of varying degrees of severity, with quite different consequences and involve the teacher and other participants in different ways. Are they all genuine crises? How urgent are they? After evaluating them by the basic dimensions for assessing crisis, how would you react to each situation if you were the teacher involved?

Some critical situations seem to combine all the elements of crisis—physical injury, psychological and social stress and possibility of legal action. Consider one such incident and how it was handled. This involved a young college student hired as an aide.

FIGURE 9-2   A POTENTIAL CRISIS MUST BE QUICKLY ASSESSED

Ted lived in the neighborhood of the nursery school where he worked and knew many of the children and their families personally. He enjoyed the children's affection for him and willingly joined in playground supervision, pleased that so many of the children seemed to like being with him.

He initiated games, roughhoused with the children, organized "races," and was the center of one project after another. The head teacher suggested he do more guiding and less directing, but Ted felt he wouldn't be doing his job if he "just stood around and watched." Besides, when he tried to follow her advice, the kids spent a lot more time arguing and fighting, and he couldn't stand that. Kids should have fun together.

One day, while pushing Lester and Ellie on the swings, he noticed how much hitting and shoving went on as the other children waited their turns. He felt he had a good solution to the problem when he thought of putting one of the climbing boards across the swings so that as many kids as could hang on to the board or each other could have a turn.

The children responded enthusiastically, eight of them finding places for the first turn. "Higher! Higher!" they shrieked, their excitement matching the request. Amidst the screaming and shouting Ted suddenly heard another sound, a thud. Susie had somehow been hit by the end of the board. A moment ago she had been walking around the swing; now she lay motionless.

"Stop! Stop pumping!" Ted shouted. "Susie's hurt!" His fright communicated more quickly than the command. As the board slowed the children slid off to cluster around the limp form. Rufus spoke Ted's question. "Is she dead?" he asked.

In answer, Ted stooped and took Susie in his arms. Too confused to think what was best, too frightened to remember what to do, oblivious to the others, he knew only his own fault, his own guilt. Her parents would never forgive him; he would never forgive himself.

The two children closest to him began to cry. Several of the boys shoved forward demanding to see. Attracted by the noise and confusion, the director came to determine its cause. As she took in the situation she spoke quietly.

269   CRISIS IN THE PRESCHOOL

Teachers' View of Crisis

1. *Inability to reach parents when child ill or hurt*
2. *A bleeding or badly injured child*
3. *Sand or soap in a child's eye; choking, nosebleeds*
4. *Children running out of the room and refusing to return*
5. *Child who loses control of himself*
6. *Wrong person taking child home*
7. *Volunteers who don't show up when expected*
8. *Child's work discarded by mistake*
9. *Children arguing adamantly over toys or equipment*
10. *Mother upset about a classroom situation as reported by her child*
11. *Supplies and materials not available when needed*
12. *Collapse of play equipment*
13. *Small child bullied by larger child*

"Ted, put Susie down carefully, then go call the doctor. Everyone else, inside, quickly, and Miss Lewis will read you a story."

Dutifully the children moved toward the classroom, only to turn back as they heard Ted remonstrating with the director. "Susie needs help bad . . . her parents won't ever . . . to the hospital. I'll drive her myself. I'll take care of her. I'll . . ."

Realizing his desperation, and noticing that Susie had begun to stir, the director again gave instructions. "Ted, put her down carefully. Keep her quiet until the doctor comes," she said. Then calling Miss Lewis to take the children in for a story, she went to summon both doctor and parent.

A director's calmness and positive course of action had restored order, but a crisis may not be over once order is restored. There are other things to be done. The children should have a chance to talk about and to learn from the accident. The concern of the parents and their attitude toward the school must be considered. Any fears that Susie might have about being hurt again after she returned to school would need to be overcome.

The person who brings on the crisis is also its victim. Ted would need help. His poor judgment had contributed to the crisis, as had his inability to put aside his own feelings in reacting to the emergency. Once the extent of Susie's injury was known and her care assured, the director and Ted would talk about what had happened. They would also talk about his feelings and what he had learned about his own reactions in emergencies and how to improve his work with the children.

One of the features of crisis is that it often represents a mingling of several types of potential damage to the people and institution involved. The incident brought about by Ted included physical injury, danger of lawsuit over carelessness or incompetence, psychological trauma to Ted as well as others, and created a particular stress within the staff, as well as between the parents and the school.

These four types—psychological, social, medical and legal—thus constitute different kinds of stress, each with its own consequences. They often overlap, but it is useful to consider them as different components of a stressful situation when trying to decide how to cope with a possible emergency.

Parents' View of Crisis

1. Severe illness or injury
2. Children fighting, hitting, biting one another
3. Child striking a teacher or parent
4. Re-adjustment due to teacher change during the school year
5. Temper tantrums
6. Child released to unauthorized person
7. Not enough supervisory staff due to absence of teacher
8. Other parents not doing their part in co-op program

THE MAJOR AREAS OF CRISIS

Psychological and Social Crisis

The difficulties that arise in psychological and social types of stress are often closely related. In a general sense, *psychological* stress refers to subjective strain or tension, fear, extreme anxiety and other internally traumatic conditions. The *social* aspects of stress include straining of social ties, morale of staff, and community pressures such as protests from parents or groups of parents. The problem extends beyond the internal feelings of individuals involved to possible changes in relationships, reputation, income and the like. Because they are often intimately related however, they will be discussed together.

Psychological and social situations are not easily categorized into positive and negative instances. When a child gashes his chin or complains, "I don't feel well" and his temperature reads 102°, the teacher has fairly clear evidence of a problem that should be alleviated, although she may not know how serious it is and what measures to take. Broken equipment left unrepaired, or failure to report an injury clearly invite charges of negligence. Where there is doubt, professional advice is available to give the staff or teacher expert consultation about the seriousness of the crisis and the probable consequences of different courses of action.

Unlike medical and legal problems, various kinds of psychological stress are not only inevitable but may be a necessary part of human development. Interaction with others almost necessarily involves frustration of a wish or need, and the learning of ways to deal with disappointment, frustration and failure may well be a part of normal growth. Internal stress in a psychological sense may not be a crisis if it is within limits although it can obviously also reach traumatic proportions.

In similar fashion, social interaction within the staff and between the staff and parents cannot always be smooth and satisfying. There may be instances in which parents need to be told something less than pleasant about a child or face disappointment if they have expected too much from the teacher and the school. In short, unlike the stress inherent in medical and legal situations, the stress resulting from social and psychological problems may not require a positive action. Emotional responses which are natural for one child, for example, may create a psychological crisis for another. Psychological situations call for an on-the-spot evaluation in order to decide whether there *is* a crisis or whether the stress may have positive consequences. The decision

Children's View of Crisis

1. Separation from parents
2. Loss of bladder or bowel control
3. Arbitrary attack by other children
4. Being called "names"
5. Parents forgetting to pick them up at going-home time
6. Deviation from usual routine

---

with respect to medical matters is less complex in that it is, in most instances, a matter of deciding how *severe* the problem is.

In all types of crisis situations, the teacher is called on to make prompt decisions which usually require an evaluation of the circumstance and what action if any should be taken. Much as she would occasionally like to let things settle themselves, she cannot avoid a decision of some kind.

It isn't enough to get busy and start tying shoe laces, or help a child put a book on the shelf as though nothing had happened. In a psychological crisis, *not* doing something about a situation is just as much a decision as taking positive action. Although a teacher may have little time to weigh the appropriateness of what she does, or to assess the consequences of adopting one procedure over another, the choice is hers. The decision she makes may later be overruled, but its effect cannot be changed.

In dealing with social and psychological crises it is difficult to assess whether a decision was "right" or "wrong." For example, a teacher who had been concerned about Lyn, an unusually dependent four-year-old who had recently enrolled in the school, decided it was time to help Lyn gain some experience and confidence on her own with the other children. Despite Lyn's clinging, she put her with a group of children at the play dough table. Lyn was obviously even more upset and sat quietly not playing and scarcely moving. Even though the teacher returned to her after a few moments, Lyn seemed more shy and dependent than before. Had she done the right thing, she wondered, or made the situation worse?

In psychological crises, the teacher's own feelings may be part of the problem. Obviously, if she gets upset about what the situation may mean to her and her job she is not in a position to make the necessary decisions. Personal feelings of resentment against a child or mother may make her more sensitive and less objective in response to a crisis involving that particular family. Her own response to attack by a child or parent, or to criticism by other staff members may contribute to a crisis and affect her ability to deal effectively with tension.

For the teacher, psychological crisis is frequently based on a conflict in values. No matter how well-trained she may be, or how objectively she approaches her work, the actions or words of children that clash with her sense of values will distress her. A teacher who has grown up believing that swearing, name calling, defiance of authority and various sex and toilet behaviors are taboo, won't find them easy to accept or ignore in the classroom.

One of the most distinctive features of psychological crisis is the ripple effect—the way one situation brings about another or spreads until a chain reaction is set in motion. The examples given earlier in the chapter illustrate how this may occur. The chain reaction may not be immediate. Suppose Miss C., a teacher, intervenes when Frank and Andrew start hitting each other over the head with wooden blocks. She may feel a satisfactory solution has been reached if she gets the boys separated—Frank in with a group of children in the housekeeping corner and Andrew outside kicking a ball. However, that night a phone call from the head teacher makes her realize the parents are anything but calm. They want to know why their son was told he had to play house with the girls; they aren't about to let anyone make a sissy of Frank.

Naturally their attitude has upset the head teacher but she listens without comment to the explanation. Even though she says she feels the situation was properly handled and that the parents are being unreasonable, Miss C. finds herself worrying about how she will react to Frank the next time he loses control of himself, and whether the head teacher really still has confidence in her. Next day, in her anxiety to keep everyone under control, she is on edge and so are the children. The crisis has gone full circle—from child to parent to school to teacher and back into the classroom.

Medical Crises[1]

Illness and Injury A teacher must learn to deal with children's physical problems—ranging from minor bruises to traumatic injury. The demands that these make on the teacher, and the possible dangers to the child, vary enormously. Every wound, sniffle, exposure to measles or mumps does not constitute a crisis. There are, of course, potentially severe consequences, and part of the teacher's role is to judge the severity of the situation and know when to soothe and when to call for professional aid. The familiar medical situations are described below.

Eye, Ear, Nose and Throat Infections To some parents, nursery schools are breeding grounds for colds, coughs, sore throats, and all the familiar childhood diseases. Parents are probably right in thinking that a young child does get more colds and illnesses when he first goes to nursery school. The reason for this is his exposure to so many children in a confined area, rather than the school program itself. Also, whether or not mothers realize it, the child isn't getting the *same* cold over and over. Each time he has been infected by a new virus, he gets a new illness. As he builds up antibodies to these, he also builds up immunity and eventually cuts down on the number of illnesses he contracts.

Most colds are not communicable after the first three days. The child's nose may be

---

[1] Information in this section is based largely on lectures by Dr. Birt Harvey, assistant clinical professor of pediatrics, Stanford University School of Medicine, Stanford, California.

running, his throat sore, his spirits low, and he may be more susceptible to other illness, but he is not likely to infect another person.

Colds are a problem in the classroom only if a child's sniffling and sneezing interfere with his activities or make the teacher uneasy about parents' reactions to allowing children with cold symptoms to be in school. Response to the concerns of parents often guides school procedure. In addition to the rule "Keep a child home the first three days of a cold," some schools have a uniformed nurse on duty each morning to check the children's throats as a precaution. Even though nurses are not required by state or local health regulations, and cold symptoms are not very visible in the throat, having a nurse on hand means that the parent is more likely to keep a child home another day rather than risk his not being admitted. The nurse can also give professional answers to parents' questions about health and encourage good habits on the part of the children.

Tonsillitis (inflammation of the tonsils), however, is highly contagious when a child coughs. Many cases, particularly in the winter and spring, are produced by bacteria called hemolytic streptococcus—hence the more familiar term *strep throat* (see scarlet fever, Table 9–1). These and other bacteria can be quickly controlled by penicillin or other antibiotic drugs. Tonsillitis is usually accompanied by a fever, and as with any fever, the child should be isolated until an authorized person can take him home. He should not return to school until at least 24 hours after his temperature returns to normal.

The most common types of eye infection in young children are *conjunctivitis* (pink eye) and *sties*. Pink eye is highly contagious and is almost always accompanied by discharge and crusty matter around the eyes. In general, as long as there is a discharge the mother should be requested to keep the child at home while the infection is being treated by a doctor. With antibiotics it can usually be cleared up very rapidly.

Allergies may also cause children's eyes to tear and redden and itch, but they are not infectious. Even though noncontagious and generally harmless, allergies do have a potential for crisis: Some children develop acute allergic reactions to insect (especially bee) stings, react adversely to certain foods (including chocolate), and suffer from contact with animal fur, etc. These circumstances should be noted on the child's records together with whatever emergency treatment is prescribed. Naturally every effort should be made to keep the child away from exposure of this kind, but if it occurs, the parent should be notified and the instructions on the child's record followed. Obviously, the school staff should not administer medicine, either prescription or nonprescription, *without written* authorization from parents or legal guardians.

Earaches occur frequently in young children. They are almost always secondary to a common cold. A child may not be able to locate the point of his distress but can be

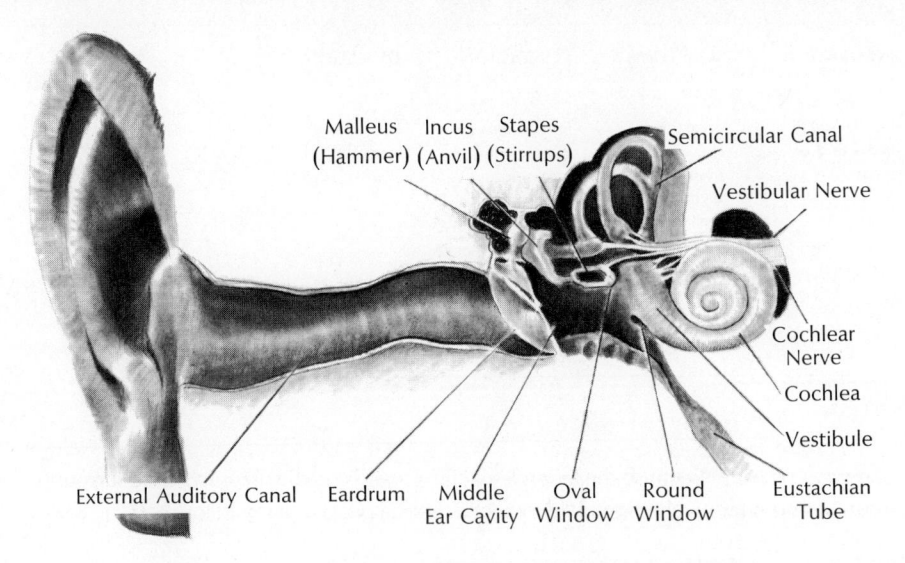

FIGURE 9-3 DIAGRAM OF THE HUMAN EAR SHOWING LOCATION OF INFECTION

observed tipping his head to the side that hurts, rubbing the area and exhibiting general fussiness. Ear infections are not contagious, but the child is generally more comfortable at home. The common belief that the infection will be prevented by having children wear hats or turn up their collars to cover the ears is incorrect. The medical cause of earaches is an infection that travels from the back of the eustachian tube and lodges in the middle ear (Figure 9-3).

Communicable Disease Teachers should be aware of communicable disease symptoms and immediately send notices home when children have been exposed to an illness known to be infectious. Although there is little else a teacher can do in the school setting, teacher and parental awareness may enable them to avert the disease or lessen its consequences if the child becomes ill. These are diseases for which notices should be sent:

German Measles: Mothers should be notified because those who contact German measles during the early months of a pregnancy may give birth to babies who have defects of the brain, eyes, ears, heart, or other body systems.

Measles: This is a dangerous disease in the first two years and the death rate can be high. Complications can be drastically reduced if gamma globulin is given early after known exposure.

Scarlet Fever: When suitable drugs are administered at the onset of illness, kidney involvement and rheumatic fever are usually avoided.

A chart giving essential information about common communicable diseases will be found in Table 9-2. Tuberculosis (TB) deserves special attention in the nursery school for two reasons: 1) Adults are known to be carriers and even though they may not act or feel ill, they can easily communicate it to the children in their care. A measure of control can be gained by requiring yearly chest x-rays or tuberculin skin tests of *all* persons who interact with children at school, including volunteers serving on any kind

CAUSE	AVERAGE OCCURRENCE	INCUBATION	SYMPTOMS	CONTAGION	DURATION
Various viruses	In young children, 4 to 6 per year—usually in winter	From several hours to 2 or 3 days	Sneezing, runny nose, eyes tearing, fever, letdown feeling	Spread through droplets from nose and throat to those nearby. Uncovered cough or sneeze extends radius of infection to 12 feet	Few days to several weeks

TABLE 9–2 THE COMMON COLD

of regular basis. 2) Because the tubercle bacillus breeds readily in unhygienic surroundings, there is a relatively high incidence rate among people living in low-income areas.

Broken Bones and Head Injuries Those who work with young children must be cognizant of the constant threat of serious injury to youngsters. Because motor control, balance and physical strength are undergoing rapid change, falls are common. Children have little understanding of "safety" for themselves or others, and are therefore careless about leaving equipment in hazardous places or throwing toys and tools without thought of the consequences. The wonder is that there are so few accidents in school resulting in serious injury to children. Proper precautions and knowledge of procedural steps can alleviate many of the anxieties of both child and teacher in the event of an accident.

Broken bones are not always readily detectable, unless there is a compound fracture—i.e., a breaking of the skin. When a child falls it is best not to be too eager to pick him up. If he is out of danger, let him lie still until he attempts to rise on his own. Breaking one of the many foot bones other than the big toe won't affect him very much. Serious injury to an ankle, a knee, or a leg means the child won't be able to stand up. Breaking a collar bone, rib, arm or wrist usually means too much pain for the child to want to move this part of his body.

Directing a child to "point to where it hurts," gives some idea of what may have happened. If after a few minutes everything seems to be all right, it is probably safe to let the child get up and continue whatever he was doing when the interruption occurred. He should be watched carefully until the teacher is sure his activity seems "normal." Whatever type of accident report is required by the school should be filled in (example Figure 9–4) and a copy given to the parent when the child is dismissed for the day. Time should be taken to tell the parent what happened, too.

When the consequences are more serious—a bone broken or a child obviously in pain or distress—the child should be made as comfortable as possible and the instructions on the child's emergency card followed immediately. No matter how well-trained the teacher is in first aid or how many similar experiences she has had, she should not try to diagnose or minister to the child beyond doing whatever might be needed to preserve life (as in the case of serious bleeding, or asphyxiation).

Inexperienced teachers often misinterpret the seriousness of head injuries. Because the scalp has more blood vessels than any other part of the body of similar size, even

	CHICKEN POX	GERMAN MEASLES	MEASLES	MUMPS	SCARLET FEVER	TUBERCULOSIS	WHOOPING COUGH
CAUSE	Virus	Virus	Virus	Virus	bacterium Hemolytic streptococcus	Tubercle bacillus	Pertussis bacterium
HOW SPREAD	Droplets in air from sneezing, coughing, or from rash	Droplets from nose and throat of infected person	Droplets from talking, breathing, sneezing, coughing	Droplets from infected person's throat	Droplets, and direct contact with contaminated food and milk	Cough	Droplets and direct contact with discharge
INCUBATION PERIOD	Usually 14–16 days; maximum 21 days	Usually 17–18 days; can be 13–21	Usually 11 days; can be 7–14	Usually 18 days; can be 11–26	Usually 2–4 days; can be 1–7	Usually 6–8 weeks; can be 2–10 weeks	Usually 5–7; can be 5–14 days
SYMPTOMS	Fever, rash, itching; bite-like eruptions starting on face and trunk	Usually mild: swollen lymph nodes, low-grade fever, rash, cold or merely a stiff neck	Red eyes, runny nose, cough and high fever for 3–4 days, then rash.	Swollen, tender glands in front of and below ear, fever, general discomfort	Headache, vomiting, sore throat, rash, fever, flaking skin	Persistent cough, low-grade fever, weight loss, or no symptoms	Mild hacking cough or cold followed by spells of heavy coughing; maybe vomiting
POSSIBLE COMPLICATIONS	Skin infection	If pregnant, injury to fetus	Many, including pneumonia and encephalitis	Injury to testes and ovaries and (rarely) encephalitis or deafness	Inflamed glands, sinuses, pneumonia, kidney disease, Rheumatic fever	Damage to brain, liver, kidney, intestines	Pneumonia, bronchitis
COMMUNICABILITY	1 day before rash until last lesion crusted	Usually 3–7 days	Especially during first few days of "cold" symptoms; 7–8 days total	2 days before swelling starts until swelling gone; 5–7 days	7 days unless penicillin given; then 1 day thereafter	At any time by active case, especially during coughing	5–6 weeks

TABLE 9-1 COMMUNICABLE DISEASES COMMON AMONG PRESCHOOL CHILDREN

a minor blow to the head may easily form a "goose egg." *Where* the child is hit, and the amount of swelling have relatively little bearing on the degree of injury. What needs to be known is whether internal bleeding is taking place.

When a child has had a fall or been struck on the head, he may suffer a concussion. After any head blow, three significant signs should be watched for:

1. Initial unconsciousness   2. Progressive lethargy   3. Recurrent vomiting

Even if a child is unconscious for only ten or fifteen seconds from a fall or blow on his head, this fact needs to be reported. Normally the family should be notified immediately and their instructions followed. If the child must be kept for a time, however, and he

GREENMEADOW NURSERY SCHOOL

Accident Report

DATE _____ APPROX. TIME OF ACCIDENT _____

NAME OF CHILD _____

ADDRESS _____ PHONE _____

ACCIDENT REPORTED BY _____

NATURE OF INJURY: _____

    Location _____

    Type: Bump__; Bruise__; Scratch__; Blister__; Abrasion__; Cut__; Laceration__; Suspected Strain or Sprain__; Suspected Fracture__; Burn__; Bite__; Other _____

    Extent of bleeding _____

    Estimate of extent and severity _____

_____

DESCRIPTION OF CHILD's OVERT REACTION TO INJURY:

DESCRIPTION OF FIRST-AID MEASURES:

                      First-Aid Given By: _____

DESCRIPTION OF ACCIDENT:

DISPOSITION OF CASE:

    Parent or doctor not notified__. Reason _____

    Parent notified__. Parent's Instructions _____

_____

    Family Physician Notified__. Name _____

    Other Physician Notified__. Name _____

        Reason _____

        Physician's Instructions _____

_____

    Child remained at school__; was taken home__; was taken to _____

    for medical attention by _____ (Name of Person Transporting Child).

    Other disposition _____

                      Head Teacher _____

                      Director _____

USE REVERSE SIDE FOR ADDITIONAL INFORMATION PERTINENT TO CASE AND DISPOSITION.

FIGURE 9-4 EXAMPLE OF AN ACCIDENT FORM REPORT

DO'S and DON'TS in Cases of Severe Injury

1. DO keep the child quiet and someone with him until his parent or a doctor takes over

2. DON'T try to diagnose or repair damage

3. DO follow the procedure given on his emergency card

4. DON'T neglect the other children in the class

5. DO make a complete report to the parent and for the school records

---

becomes lethargic, call the doctor and follow his suggestions. The teacher needs to keep an exact record of what she does and when. This should be given to the parent or the person taking over the treatment of the child.

Vomiting immediately following a head (or any other) injury is frequently an emotional reaction and may have little significance, but it should be recorded. Vomiting that occurs after half an hour later is considered significant.

What seemed to a teacher to be an inconsequential head injury brought untold consequences to a three-and-a-half year old girl, her family, and the owners of a nursery school. The details of this event are described fully in the section on crisis and the law (p. 283).

Minor Injuries Many common emergencies in nursery schools present little threat to an experienced teacher even though she knows the consequences could be serious for the child and herself depending on how she handles each situation. Wherever there are children, there will be a certain number of cuts, scrapes, bruises, eyes with sand in them, nose bleeds, abdominal pains, etc. Every school provides first aid supplies and has them readily available. However, the head teacher, or the teacher most likely to see the parent after school, should have knowledge of even the most minor bumps or bruises so she can enter them in the school record and inform the parent. It is advisable to inform the parents of every "accident" lest they discover even a small injury later and be disturbed both by the accident and by the teacher's failure to notify them. Of course, in the case of serious injury, the parent or indicated guardian should be called immediately.

The following are descriptions of common minor injuries and remedies with which the teacher should be familiar:

CUTS
(knife, glass, paper)

If there is any possibility that stitches are needed (to avoid scar when healed), parent should be notified. Otherwise clean with soap and water and protect with band aid. (For any washing following injury, soap with a high content of hexachlorophene should be used.)

SCRAPES

If gravel, sand, or any foreign substance is deeply imbedded, call parent. (The injury may need a doctor's attention in order to avoid infection or scarring.) Otherwise, clean *thoroughly* with soap and water and perhaps apply an antibiotic ointment. It is important to remove all foreign matter. Cover lightly.

BURNS If burn blister is very deep, call parent. While waiting, keep area under cold water or wrapped in clean cloth. Do not apply any ointments. If burn is minor and small in area, soothe with cool water. Area is already bacteria-free from the burn itself.

SAND-IN-EYE Not harmful but quite irritating to child. Wash eye(s) with plenty of cool water.

NOSE BLEED Can usually be stopped by keeping child quiet for a few minutes and squeezing nostrils together. If bleeding persists or recurs, call parent.

ABDOMINAL PAIN Pains in the abdominal area are often related to infectious diseases, in which case there will be other symptoms present. If the pain is connected with appendicitis, child won't want to move and he'll probably have fever and vomiting. Abdomen will remain rigid and painful when touched, particularly low on the right side. Parent should be called in either of above circumstances. Common "tummy ache," which often accompanies anxiety, comes and goes but while present is very real to child. Can be alleviated with judicious amount of reassurance. Report to parent.

CHOKING Can be very serious if foreign matter gets into lungs or air passage is completely blocked. Enforce simple rules in the nursery school:

1. Sit to eat
2. Avoid giving foods such as raw carrots, peanuts, bacon, popcorn (exceedingly difficult to remove once in the windpipe)

If child is choking, try to hook finger into mouth and around whatever is caught in throat. Pull forward. When this is ineffective or impossible, sit down, place child face down across lap and give sharp "whack" across his shoulder blades. If still gagging, get medical help immediately. Notify parent.

Miscellaneous Medical Problems Teachers hear about the following group of medical problems far more than they encounter them. Yet because these conditions sometimes represent serious problems for young children, teachers understandably want to know how they can identify them, and in what way they should attempt to help.

SKIN DISEASES Children suffer from a wide variety of skin diseases. Those caused by fungi are probably the most widespread, including athlete's foot (tiny, itchy blisters between the toes) and ringworm (circular, scaly lesions on the body and in the scalp). They are difficult to cure and a physician's advice is needed in determining whether an infected child should be in school. Impetigo, a germ-caused infection, is characterized by yellowish crusted sores anywhere on the body, but especially at nostril openings. It is highly contagious and if not cured may occasionally lead to erysipelas or kidney diseases. Until all infected areas are healed and the skin is clear, children should probably remain at home, although a day or two after proper treatment the disease is not communicable. Boils, an infection at the root of a hair, are caused by the same germs responsible for impetigo. They start as a red swelling, fill with pus, and are quite painful. Their treatment should be left up to the child's family and agreement reached with them as to whether the child should be in school.

LICE   Infestation with lice is not uncommon whenever there is a shortage of soap and laundering. Unwashed hair, unwashed bodies, and unwashed clothes furnish perfect breeding places for head and body lice. They usually are found in a child's hair or the seams of his clothing, where they cause severe itching and irritation. Although lice rarely carry disease, they need to be removed. This can best be done by disinfection—a task not usually handled by the school.

BITES   The bite of any sharp-toothed animal can be quite painful, may become infected, and generally brings discomfort to the person bitten. When the skin is broken, whether by guinea pigs, rats, or any other animal, including a human being, tetanus or other infections may result and make the victim quite ill. Bites require the attention of a physician. Wash the area thoroughly with soap and water and check the child's health record for date of latest tetanus injection.

CONVULSIONS   Convulsions are spasmodic muscular contractions which come without warning and cannot be stopped. When having a convulsion the child falls unconscious, his muscles stiffen and then relax and start a series of somewhat rhythmical contractions. When the attack is over, the child sleeps from a few moments up to an hour or more. The attacks themselves may be brief or prolonged. During an attack the child needs to be protected so that his breathing is not impaired (by vomit or the tongue being swallowed) and so that he does not bruise himself by his movements. Until help comes he should be placed face down on a soft surface with his head to one side and a rolled-up cloth between his teeth. Seizures of this kind accompany certain sudden high fevers and are also associated with epilepsy.

CHILD BEATING   Occasionally a teacher suspects that a child is the victim of brutal punishment. She may notice welts and bruises, find him crying for no apparent reason, or hear his innocent remark, "They hit me all the time." If tactful questioning and further observation confirm her suspicion, she should immediately see that the proper authorities are notified. Usually this means a call to the Department of Dependent Children of the local welfare office. Many of these groups are now in a position to take over with no further involvement on the part of the teacher. Some states have laws which protect the teacher from lawsuit.

Seeking help from an outside agency is considerably facilitated if the school and agency personnel have already met and are familiar with one another's work and

Safety For You

1. Sit down to eat or drink
2. Keep sticks, balls, and all foreign objects out of your mouth
3. Keep wheeled equipment on the paved areas or in the sheds
4. Walk around swings
5. Use both hands when climbing
6. Use tools properly and keep them where they belong

---

jurisdiction. Prior introduction of this kind, whether formal or informal, makes it possible to give maximum help to children if and when it is needed.[2] Additional references on this important topic are listed in the bibliography.

Teacher Responsibility Prevention is perhaps a teacher's best strategy as far as medical crisis is concerned. She probably can do little beforehand about the illnesses children bring to school, but is in a position to do a great deal about injuries at school. Careful maintenance of equipment, strict enforcement of safety rules (such as those listed above) and consideration for the rights and comforts of others are effective ways to eliminate many of the accidents which all too often bring on crisis.

When the teacher must deal with illness or injury, she needs first of all to remember that she is neither parent nor doctor. Other than providing simple first aid and large quantities of reassurance, her primary responsibility to the child is to notify the parent and follow the instructions on the emergency card. She should also make the child as comfortable as possible until someone who is responsible arrives and can take over.

Neither during the time of crisis, nor in the normal routine of the day, should the teacher administer medication (including aspirin) without written permission and instructions from a parent. Some children, such as those with certain allergies, are on a schedule which requires dosage during the time the child is in school. When this is the case, the teacher should act only upon explicit, written procedures worked out with the parent and kept on file at the school. Teachers should not make medical decisions regarding the kind of care a child is to receive when he is ill or injured. Both the child and the school are best served by following instructions exactly as they are given in the child's records.

Fortunately, real medical crisis is rare in a nursery school compared to the number of hours and the number of children involved in routine procedures. When a child is hurt or ill, the time it takes to decide what to do, and how the decision is to be implemented, are not likely to be the critical factors. The crisis is far more likely to rest in the psychological effect on the staff, the child and the parent. This aspect of crisis is discussed later on in this chapter.

---

[2] A good source for materials on this subject is Children's Division, The American Humane Association, P.O. Box 1266, Denver, Colorado.

Crisis and the Law[3]

Suppose that in the nursery school where you work a child is injured:

1. By a child who has previously been cooperative, pleasant, and quiet
2. By a child whom you know is destructive and physically aggressive
3. Because of a defective piece of equipment (a slide that has a sharp edge, a jungle gym that collapses, etc.)
4. Through his own carelessness and in violation of school rules that have been explained to him
5. Because of your carelessness or that of another teacher

Who is liable? When the owners of a nursery school occupy a facility and enroll students, they establish a relationship recognized by law. The owners automatically assume certain responsibilities, whether or not these are written into the school records. The same is true for a person who agrees to teach in a nursery school. By law, in many instances a teacher may also share in the responsibility for what takes place during school hours even if she is not directly involved. In essence, the administration and staff become liable for the health and safety of the students and, if legally challenged, must provide suitable explanation for the way they met this responsibility.

General Principles of the Law Nursery school liability is essentially different from that of other schools, because when a young child is injured, there is deemed to be no contributory negligence on his part. If older children are injured, lost, kidnapped or in some way harmed while at school, the courts hold that they may conceivably have contributed to their condition. In cases involving nursery schools, however, the law is clear that young children are not expected to be able to take care of themselves. Because caretaking, not education, is interpreted to be the primary purpose of a nursery school, a special burden is placed on the school and its teachers. Although a given situation may not in any sense be an emergency, the threat of a lawsuit constitutes a crisis for many teachers. The anxiety resulting from the prospect of court proceedings is very real not only for the teacher but for the child, the parents and the school as well.

The case of Fowler vs. Seaton, involving action against a nursery school, brings out the broad range of responsibility that lies with the school. The plaintiff, Jenny Gene Fowler, at the age of three years and ten months was a student in a private school that provided day care for children of working mothers. Mrs. Seaton, the defendant, was its owner.

---

[3] Information in this section is based on lectures by Richard G. Mansfield, Attorney at Law, Palo Alto, California.

When picking Jenny Gene up one evening, the mother was told there had been an "accident"—Jenny Gene had wet her pants. This was unusual but not alarming as far as the mother was concerned. What was alarming was the fact that at supper an hour later the parents noticed that Jenny Gene's eyes were crossed and that there was a large lump on her forehead. The mother immediately called Mrs. Seaton, asking what had happened. The owner then explained that another child "who had nothing in his hands" had struck Jenny Gene in the forehead.

Jenny Gene eventually had three operations to correct the crossing of her eyes, and the parents sued the school, alleging negligence resulting in personal injuries to their child. At the time of the proceedings the child's eyes were still crossing. After a judgment by a lower court, in favor of the owner of the school, a higher court reversed the verdict in an opinion that included these points:

> Thus, it appears that the school was a preschool nursery operated for profit. We know, as a matter of common knowledge, that such schools are primarily intended to give the children an opportunity to engage in supervised group play and other supervised activities. Such schools hold themselves out as furnishing supervision for the children. Furnishing supervision is the basic service for which these schools charge. It is their main function.[4] The duty owed by the operator of such a school to the students in attendance is substantially different in degree from that owed by schools whose primary function is education, where the children are much older, and where supervision is incidental. The supervision required must be commensurate with the age of the children and with their activities. Thus the several cases cited by respondent relating to the duties owed to grammar and high school students are not in point. (61 C. 2d 681; 39 Cal. Rptr. 881, 394 P. 2d 697, p. 688).
>
> Certainly it is true that this was an unusual occurrence. While it may be common knowledge, as contended by defendant, that in the normal course of play children suffer bumps, bruises, and scratches, it certainly is not a matter of common knowledge that children normally come home from a nursery school with concussion of the brain and crossed eyes. If that were "normal" or "usual," nursery schools would not stay in business very long. Such a school, as already pointed out, by its very nature, holds itself out as a place where children can be safely left and carefully supervised.
>
> Of course, in most *res ipsa* cases, it is incumbent on the plaintiff to show that the actions of the plaintiff did not contribute to the injuries. Here it was shown

---

[4] Underlining ours.

that plaintiff is of an age that, as a matter of law, she could not be guilty of contributory negligence, and also that, as a result of shock caused by the accident she cannot remember or communicate the cause of the accident. Under such circumstances, of course, she is entitled to the presumption that she exercised due care for her own safety. (61 C. 2d 681; 39 Cal. Rptr. 881, 394 P. 2d 697, p. 690).

In Fowler vs. Seaton the California Supreme Court found that the facts justified application of the doctrine of *res ipsa loquitur* to require the Happy Day Nursery School to produce evidence that it was not careless. This doctrine includes three central conditions:

1. That the plaintiff for some good reason really does not know or cannot say how he was injured and cannot produce witnesses of his own to tell what happened
2. That the plaintiff's injuries are of the sort which are usually caused by carelessness or negligence
3. That if anyone was careless, it was probably the defendant

The teacher or nursery school director or owner should understand that in the event a situation analogous to Fowler vs. Seaton should occur, and the three elements of the doctrine of *res ipsa loquitur* apply, the school will have to prove its innocence. If, on the other hand, the doctrine does not apply, the burden will remain upon the child and his or her parents to demonstrate that the school staff was careless.

In general, the following principles of law apply to nursery schools:

1. Children in the nursery school age group are too young to be required to take care of themselves, therefore no doctrine for contributory negligence exists because nursery school children cannot be negligent
2. Care is the predominant principle. The law views the nursery school as a place that cares for children primarily and only secondarily educates them
3. The employer is liable for the acts of his employee. If a teacher or other employee is involved in harming a child, either negligently or intentionally, the owner is usually also liable if the employee was in the scope of his employment. It does not, however, release the employee from liability
4. The standard of care that must be exercised in providing for the safety of a child increases as the child's capacity to take care of himself decreases
5. Waivers signed by parents or guardians do not release the teacher or nursery school operator from liability. The child is considered a ward of society through the courts and

even the parents cannot waive a child's rights. However, from a psychological standpoint, it is always a good idea to require signed permission slips or detailed releases for field trips and emergency treatment. A release prepared by the school with details of every field trip should be signed each time; a general release for all trips is not adequate.

The Teacher's Responsibility Since the courts have established that nursery school owners and teachers are responsible (and therefore liable under the law) for the health and safety of their students during school hours, the staff of a school must be able to show they have consistently done all that is reasonably required to maintain the health and safety of the children in their school.

Teachers need not simply "wait until something happens" before meeting their responsibility. A great many practical steps can be taken to protect those in charge, should they become involved in legal action, steps that often discourage the initiation of such action. Even though the final decision of the courts may be favorable to the school, the inconvenience, expense and emotional strain of a suit can be very great.

In order to lessen the dimensions of a potential legal crisis, a school should constantly observe the following measures:

1. Adequate and consistent recording and reporting
2. Comprehensive safety measures
3. Realistic insurance coverage

Many errors can be avoided in a nursery school if its records for every child are complete and up to date. A teacher needs to have information available regarding whom to call in case of an emergency, who is responsible for each child when he is not in school, and who is authorized to pick the child up. The school should also have on file any limitations on the child's diet or physical activity and a record of any family beliefs which take precedence over usual school procedures.

Written reports made at the time of illness or injury at school and filed as a matter of record can be an important resource if a teacher's actions are questioned later on. Regularly reporting to parents any unusual occurrence or any emergency action taken, and involving them as much as possible in the affairs of the school, build support rather than suspicion, and show good faith on the part of the school and the teachers.

A school's safety program indicates as much as anything, the extent to which it meets its responsibility for the children in its care. In addition to establishing simple rules which are easy to remember (see p. 282), enforcement should be carried out in such a way as to make the staff and children safety-minded.

Who Is Liable?

1. If a child whose temperament is generally pleasant injures another child, and the teacher is exercising proper supervision, the teacher is not liable because the event is completely unforeseen
2. If the teacher knows that a child has a tendency to hurt others, she is liable for not protecting other children from him. A school (and/or teacher) is liable for accidents caused by defective equipment
3. The teacher is probably not liable for the child's carelessness if reasonable precautions have been taken such as providing soft surface under climbing equipment, having play equipment suited to age of children, and so on
4. The teacher is liable for injury to another due to her own carelessness. The owner or administrator of a school is also liable for the negligence of an employee

---

Whatever equipment is provided should be sturdy and bought or built with consideration for safety features as well as economy. Because of the danger of children being hit in the mouth or face, swing seats should be made of canvas or soft material, never of wood or metal. Teeter-totters are a poor choice of equipment for similar reasons. Raised sandboxes are more likely to cause tripping than sunken ones (see Chapter 2, on impact of physical environment). All permanent supplies and equipment should undergo regular inspection and constant upkeep rather than allowed to break or wear out.

A realistic insurance program must cover teachers as well as the owners of a school in a variety of ways and for many contingencies. It lessens the fear of the consequences of unavoidable accidents such as loss by fire, or injury in a car accident while on a field trip. When a teacher is hired, she should determine what insurance coverage a school has and in what way, if any, it protects her.

The consequences of critical situations can, of course, be tragic for all involved, including the teacher. She need not be apprehensive; with good training, reasonable precautions and sensible reactions, she will be able to deal effectively with crisis.

How To Deal With Crisis

Crisis is an unscheduled part of a preschool program and the alert and prepared teacher will have several strategies for dealing with it. The consequences are, to a degree, within the capability of the staff to control.

Avoiding and Minimizing Crisis Even though some stress and an occasional emergency will be inevitable, this does not mean that they are to be awaited with a passive philosophy of "Accidents will happen." Crisis is not only accidental, it may come from carelessness, neglect and lack of foresight or experience. An apparently smooth, safe, well run school is never accidental.

The basic rules of safe equipment and procedures were discussed in the sections on legal and medical crisis. In addition to these elementary principles covering physical injury or illness and liability, the teacher can avoid crisis and stress by *creating an environment in which accumulated frustration is minimized*. The teacher can provide many safe places for play, many acceptable outlets for aggression. Trees to climb, dirt to dig in, clay to thump, nails to pound, drums to beat, balls to kick, dolls to spank, mattresses to jump on, paint and paste to smear and water for washing, splashing and bubbling provide opportunity to work off a great many aggressions without extra help.

The teacher who praises and spends time with children when they are engaged in approved behaviors is likely to minimize stress in her classroom. This may be especially important for those children who come to school with fears and basic frustrations. These children often need more help than those who have been allowed to explore and share a variety of experiences with other children their age.

In a program of early education there are many experiences which are naturally frustrating to children. Someone else wants what they want; the teacher expects them to pick up after themselves, to wait until later, to take turns; they aren't strong enough or skilled enough to pursue many of their interests; they ask questions that no one answers; they want to read but the book they're looking for isn't on the shelf where it belongs; when they need a red crayon the only ones left are black, blue or green. Just when it's their turn on the slide, it's time to go home. Even an environment that is designed to meet the needs of children seems to induce frustration. Anything that can be done to help reduce frustration can help deal with crisis.

Psychological and other stress in the classroom, while often not severe, is a persistent source of potential crisis. It is more readily avoided or resolved if the teacher understands children's natural eagerness in pursuit of what they want and recognizes that aggression and passivity, anger and withdrawal may be brought on by frustration. She needs to accept children as they are and lend her support, at the same time working to give them an understanding of more acceptable behavior.

One teacher may find it helpful to concentrate on relating a goal or rule to the child's true feelings and needs. Using a comment such as "I'm sure you won't mind letting Julie have a turn" is less mindful of the child's feelings than "I know you don't want to give up the swing, but it is time to let Julie have a turn now."

The latter statement recognizes and accepts a natural response on the child's part, yet is firm about letting the child know what is expected of him. The teacher may still have to remove the child from the swing, but her technique will be based on an understanding of needs and expectations and confident follow through. Sometimes the best solution to a fight or an act of defiance is to find a compromise and go on from there; at other times it may seem best to ignore it or to direct the children's attention to a new activity.

SITUATION	ALTERNATIVES	EXAMPLES
Three children who are playing store refuse to let a fourth join them	Suggesting a solution	"Maybe Billy can deliver groceries for you?"
	Diverting	"It's almost juice time. Billy, you go call everyone and the rest of you can come help get out the juice and crackers."
Two boys claim the same post in the tree house and start pushing one another	Explaining property rights	"Kenny, Steve was there first. It'll be your turn next."
	Enforcing rule	"No pushing when you're up high."
Jane is sweeping and Margie grabs the broom from her. Jane complains to teacher	Encourage experimentation in coping with problems	"What are some of the things you can do to get it back? What do you think will happen? Let's try it."
	Offering a substitute	"Maybe you would like to use this mop until Jane can trade with you."
A group of children are acting out the song, "Row, row, row your boat." Much to Lisa's annoyance, Danny insists on holding her hands to do the rowing	Interpreting	"Danny, I think Lisa wants to do her rowing alone."
	Separating	"Danny, you move over on this side, please."
Wendy has carefully collected all the plastic tiles and sorted them into two piles. Paul approaches, eyeing the piles longingly. He is not a patient child	Encouraging sharing	"You've done a fine job, Wendy. Which pile may Paul play with?"
	Restraining, should Paul start to grab	"Wendy is playing with these, Paul, and I can't let you take them." (Teacher would probably also suggest a solution or divert Paul to another activity.)
Child falls while running down grassy slope—breath knocked out and frightened—but otherwise okay	Child's feelings recognized	"That was pretty scary, wasn't it? Let's try it again. I'll hold your hand so you won't fall."
	Warning	"You're okay. Try not to run so fast next time—you don't want to get hurt."
About an hour before closing time, both Gloria and Helen want to wash a large rubber doll. In their determination, the water is spilled and the doll's arm is pulled off. As the teacher attempts to restore order, Helen kicks and shouts obscenities	Making acceptable behavior clear	"I know you're angry, Helen, but I can't let you kick and use words like that." (Teacher is prepared to remove Helen from the situation.)
	Ignoring unacceptable behavior	"Let's mop up the water and decide how you both can wash the doll."

TABLE 9-3 EXAMPLES OF TECHNIQUES FOR DEALING WITH POTENTIAL PROBLEMS

Each of the examples in Table 9-3 illustrates procedures teachers find useful in dealing with potential problems. Some are teaching techniques; others are simply ways of terminating a situation and going on to something else. They represent how some teachers handle various aspects of "crisis" resulting from children's behavior.

Some Principles in Dealing With Crises

When a genuine crisis cannot be avoided, the teacher's response to it may be more effective if she acts on the basis of two general principles. The first of these is that a crisis has a number of consequences that follow the event itself—the ripple effect described earlier. In dealing with a stressful event the *attention* should be paid to *other persons* who may not be the central focus but who are affected in various ways. The incident involving Ted, for example, illustrated how the director or head teacher needed to attend to his reaction and those of the other children as well as the injury to the girl. A child who hits another may also need help in dealing with his own reactions as he sees the response of other children and adults to what he had done. Parents whose children have been involved in a crisis may need reassurance and information.

Another general principle in dealing with social and psychological stress is to *follow up* in a day or two—and perhaps again later—by contacting persons outside the immediate staff with information about how a crisis turned out. Word of how an injured child is doing, comments about whether safeguards have been taken to avoid future accidents, or sharing the resolution of a problem can give people a much needed opportunity to express their concerns, which they may not otherwise have had occasion to voice.

The teacher's skill in coping with crisis may in itself be useful in dealing with the effects of stress. Studies of disaster, for example, show that adults who remain calm instill similar behavior in children; when they become openly frightened, children also react in frightened ways. In the classroom, children obviously imitate their teachers. In times of stress they are especially in need of models as to how to respond.

Dealing with crisis is partly a matter of experience, and the teacher will find it useful to find time to reflect on what has happened once the situation has passed. She needs to review the circumstances that led to the event and her own response to it. She may then consider alternatives, and decide whether she handled their feelings and those of the others involved as effectively as possible. Every crisis should become a learning situation and provide a background for sound action in the future.

REFERENCES

Child Welfare League of America, Inc. *Child welfare league of America, standards for child protective service.* New York: Child Welfare League of America, Inc., 1960.

De Francis, V. *Child abuse—preview of a nationwide survey.* Denver, Col.: Children's Division, The American Humane Association, May, 1963.

De Francis, V. *Interpreting child protective services to your community.* Denver, Col.: Children's Division, The American Humane Association, nd.

Fowler vs. Seaton. (61 C 2d 681; 39 Cal. Rptr. 881, 394 P. 2d 697) San Francisco, Calif.: Bancroft-Whitney, August, 1964.

Karelitz, S. *When your child is ill: a guide to infectious diseases in childhood,* (revised edition) New York: Random House, 1969.

CHAPTER 10

THE CHALLENGE OF EVALUATION

THE INEVITABILITY OF EVALUATION

Attitudes and Apprehensions

Whether by formal procedure or informal conversation, preschool programs and teachers are evaluated by staff, parents, colleagues, teams of evaluation experts and others. Evaluation is essentially a judgment of staff quality and accomplishment or a comparison between different programs or individual performances. Although often threatening, evaluation may be useful to the teacher who understands the basic issues and procedures involved.

Evaluation done in a benign fashion and without threat to self-esteem rarely meets objection. Newspaper and magazine editors well know the attraction of popular quizzes which claim to reveal personality or talent. People respond eagerly to them; their consequences are minimal, and lives and behavior change little no matter what the results may indicate. The response to this form of self evaluation is an indication of a mild kind of competition such as wanting to know how one compares with some presumed norm of desirable behavior.

Self evaluation, however, is in sharp contrast to evaluation by others, especially by others whose judgment is respected or who are in a position of influence and power. Suppose, for example, that you are teaching in a nursery school program and your director has just said, "Tomorrow Mrs. G. from the superintendent's office is coming in. She's making the annual checkup. I'll post a copy of the evaluation form on the bulletin board." (See Figure 10-1.) How would you feel? What would you think?

Many teachers, even experienced ones, become apprehensive when they know that their professional skills and personal qualifications are being assessed. This is a natural response—perhaps one conditioned by years of school grading, selection procedures, entrance tests, verbal recommendations and the like. In such a situation it is easy to raise questions about the legitimacy of the evaluation.

For example, is it fair for an outsider to make judgments when a visit lasts only an hour or two, and each part of the program is observed only a few minutes? What kind of person is Mrs. G. and what are her feelings about a particular type of program? Is she really up to date on the new trends in the field or will she reject innovation? Has she ever taught kids like these? Who will read her report, and what effect will her comments have on someone else's job?

Many people find the prospect of evaluation disturbing, regardless of how well they may be doing. When they feel they are being judged by a particular standard, no amount of reassurance puts them at ease. Nonetheless, evaluation of some form is a part of every profession. The teacher's task is to become aware of the kinds of evaluation which will be made of her and her school, to prepare herself to deal with them and to use the information she gains as a means of improving her teaching.

Program No._____

Date_____

Time Observed_____   Name of teacher_____

Observer_____

PERFORMANCE

Efficient

Excellent	Good	Fair	Poor

Imaginative

Excellent	Good	Fair	Poor

Maintains good control

Excellent	Good	Fair	Poor

Dependable

Excellent	Good	Fair	Poor

ATTITUDE

Responds well to suggestions

Excellent	Good	Fair	Poor

Happy, warm personality

Excellent	Good	Fair	Poor

Sympathetic, sensitive

Excellent	Good	Fair	Poor

Relates well to children

Excellent	Good	Fair	Poor

Relates well to staff

Excellent	Good	Fair	Poor

PERSONAL QUALITIES

Sense of humor

Excellent	Good	Fair	Poor

Self confident

Excellent	Good	Fair	Poor

Appropriately dressed

Excellent	Good	Fair	Poor

Well modulated voice

Excellent	Good	Fair	Poor

FIGURE 10-1 EXAMPLE OF A TEACHER EVALUATION SHEET

Evaluation ranges from informal and even casual comments about the behavior, performance and characteristics of another, to formal testing and assessment programs carried out by teams of experts. The major distinction between formal and informal assessment is in the methods by which comparisons are made and how data or impressions are gathered and processed. One parent informally asking another, "How do you like the new teacher?" is essentially the same kind of inquiry as a formal rating made by an official observer from the State Department of Education on the item:

Overall effectiveness of teacher _____
                                            Excellent   Good   Fair

Other differences between formal and informal assessments lie in the way the evaluation is used, how it is processed and reported, whether it is made public, how much confidence is placed in it and the consequences it will have.

Informal Evaluation

Although this discussion deals for the most part with formal evaluation, the informal evaluation system also deserves attention. Teachers and school staff members make informal evaluations of themselves and one another. These, too, can create anxiety. For example, shortly after starting to work on a new job, Alice H. overheard a group of teachers casually discussing the problem of a child to whom she'd been giving extra attention.

> *"You know," one of the teachers said, "I can't decide whether Harry has a speech impediment, doesn't hear well, or what's happening. He seems happy here at school, but something's wrong."*
>
> *"What do you mean?" another asked.*
>
> *"Well, I noticed Alice spending extra time with him, but he still doesn't talk very much. When he does speak, you can hardly understand what he's trying to say."*
>
> *"Maybe Alice should have the kid tested by the speech consultant. That's probably the only way we'll be able to find out what's wrong."*

In this kind of situation, the teacher may feel that the staff is actually talking about her, as well as about a particular child. In effect she hears: "The new teacher really

How Do You Evaluate a Teacher?	What Makes a Good Teacher?
I watch to see if she hears the children and gives her undivided attention when she listens to a child or speaks to him.	*She attends to the needs of the children.*
	She is firm without being mean.
	She doesn't hold a grudge or play favorites.
I depend on the judgment of my friends if I am not able to observe for myself.	*She gives of herself to every child equally.*
I notice whether or not she treats children as individuals or always as members of a group.	*She is able to handle unexpected situations smoothly and doesn't let herself get excited in emergencies.*
I expect her to talk to me as an equal and not to make me feel she knows much more than I do.	*She makes learning situations out of every "problem."*
	She watches and listens and concentrates on the children.
I wait to see if she stoops down to put her arm around a child and look him in the eyes when she talks to him.	*She gives me specific information about my child and helps me learn how to teach him what she wants him to know.*
I don't want her to tell me everything is "just fine" when I know it isn't.	
I keep track of how often she touches and holds them and lets them be near.	*She reinforces what I think is important for my child to know.*
I look to see what she does with quiet children.	*She is warm and friendly and smiles sincerely.*
I count how often she tells the kids what to do.	
I think she should punish children and not let them get away with things.	

TABLE 10-1 PARENTS' ANSWERS TO QUESTIONS REGARDING TEACHER EVALUATION

isn't doing a very good job." Or she senses that her work is likely to be criticized when a consultant comes to make a diagnosis. Even though the comments are impersonal and casual, some teachers may be upset by implications they imagine.

Many informal evaluations are carried out by supervisors. Directors assess teachers and staff, head teachers assess assistants, aides and volunteers. Part of the job of each person in any hierarchy is a continuous appraisal of the performance and personal qualities of those for whose work they are responsible. The consequences of this kind of evaluation are, of course, related to the person who is making the evaluation and the resources for change that he commands.

Parents evaluate the program, the teacher and the school. The comments they make among themselves and to others about what the school offers, the way a teacher looks and what the program is or isn't doing for their children, have consequences for the reputation and image of the school. These consequences are reflected in increased (or decreased) enrollment, changes in staff and program, offers of help and cooperation and requests for parent conferences and meetings. Table 10-1 contains information indicating what parents notice and expect of teachers based on informal answers to two questions.

Although their appraisal may not be as clearly defined as the examples given in Table 10-1, children also informally evaluate their teachers and one another. Whether expressed in words or actions (such as acceptance or rejection), evaluation of this kind usually brings about at least subtle changes in the behavior of the person assessed.

A Good Teacher:

Holds you and reads to you

Sings songs to you

Doesn't slap you

Pushes you high on a swing

Goes to meetings

When you have a hurt finger she puts a band aid on it right away

Smiles at you

Doesn't make you sit still or be quiet

Wears pretty beads

Lets you play with her hair

Helps you

Fixes bikes

Doesn't get mad

Works hard

Builds with us

Makes you laugh

TABLE 10-2 CHILDREN'S ASSESSMENTS OF WHAT MAKES A GOOD TEACHER

Another type of informal evaluation which preschool teachers frequently face is an appraisal by outsiders who come to visit or to do research. The effect on a teacher may be more readily understood by considering what each of the following persons might find of interest if he were to come into a nursery school some morning and observe the program as it is shown in Figure 10-2.

1. Owner of the school
2. Mother who has not yet enrolled her child
3. Mother whose child is smallest in the class
4. Visitor from a low-income area
5. State Welfare Department representative
6. Doctoral candidate doing research for his thesis on the effects of school discipline on children's curiosity

Informal evaluation goes on all the time and cannot be ignored by the teacher who wants to become competent in her field. The fact that it frequently poses a threat signifies, of course, that the teacher has a sense of standards and quality and that she wants to think of herself as doing a good job.

Formal Evaluation

Formal evaluation of a school program or of the teachers and children in a school is based on data obtained by various kinds of tests and techniques. The teacher should become familiar with these, their purposes, uses and limitations, so that she can recognize what resources are available to her and how she can best use them.

FIGURE 10–2 TYPICAL SCENES IN A PRESCHOOL PROGRAM

297 THE CHALLENGE OF EVALUATION

OBSERVATIONS OF SCHOOL STAFF

School:_____

Staff Member:_____

Observer:_____

Date:_____

Circle the number on each line that describes most accurately the behavior and performance of the staff members in carrying out their assigned tasks and duties.

1. In working with the group, the staff member is:

   strict   1 2 3 4 5 6   permissive, easy going

2. With respect to racial and ethnic history and customs of children and parents, the staff member:

   promotes ethnic pride and awareness   1 2 3 4 5 6   ignores or puts down ethnic background and behavior

3. When the staff member is together with the children, in a relatively free and unstructured situation, she is:

   warm and outgoing to the children and other staff members   1 2 3 4 5 6   distant, detached, stiff

4. In the daily curricular routine schedule, the staff member:

   selects and directs most activities   1 2 3 4 5 6   lets the children pick their activities

FIGURE 10-3 EXAMPLES OF SCALES FOR RATING STAFF PERFORMANCE

Techniques of Assessment One popular method for obtaining data is to ask staff members to make *ratings* of the performance and behavior of individuals. This rating is usually done with the assistance of a scale of some type, descriptions of the behavior to be rated and the kinds of cues or acts which indicate where the individual being rated falls on the scale (Figure 10-3 and Figure 10-4). The judgments called for by this method are summaries of observations, impressions and interpretations of specific acts that have accumulated over a period of time.

Thus, a teacher may be asked to rate a child on the extent to which he works independently or depends on her or others for assistance. She can make a general judgment on such a global cluster of behaviors only if she has seen the child in many different

BEHAVIOR RATING FORM

Instructions: Please rate the way this child behaves by circling one of the numbers on each line.

		Very much	Quite a bit	Slightly	Not at all
1.	Talks easily to adults about what he thinks and feels.	1	2	3	4
2.	Attempts to work out things for himself rather than ask for help	1	2	3	4
3.	Has little respect for others' rights: takes toys, tries to get to head of line, etc.	1	2	3	4
4.	Reacts to frustration by becoming aggressive or angry	1	2	3	4
5.	Shows creativity in his use of materials and toys	1	2	3	4

Etc.

FIGURE 10-4 EXAMPLES OF SCALES FOR RATING CHILDREN'S BEHAVIOR

situations and can average out in her own mind the different expressions of independence and dependence that she has observed. Ratings are judgments of typical, modal or average behavior and always depend on the objectivity and opportunity to observe that the rater has had in the past. This is why many rating scales include an alternative response such as: "Insufficient opportunity to observe," or "No information." The choices on rating scales vary considerably, ranging from a simple Yes/No type of response to brief descriptions of behavior on more elaborate forms.

Recording data about behavior from direct and immediate *observation* is another formal method for evaluation of early educational programs and their specific activities. Where ratings are based on information accumulated over a period of time, observation as an evaluation technique is a way to record data in certain categories immediately as it occurs. One general approach to observation is to have in mind a specific kind of behavior or activity which is to be recorded and to note only those instances which fit predetermined categories.

One might, for example, look for all acts which indicate cooperation between children, noting who initiates them, what the response is and whether they lead to cooperative activities. Or, the observer might watch the teacher to see what her response is to acts of aggression in the group. Does she respond (reward) with attention? Is her attention a punishment of some kind, an attempt to distract or some other behavior?

Children's Pre-Math Skill By Rank
(From Highest to Lowest)

1. Halle
2. Mary Lou
3. Isadore
4. Ellen
5. Alice
6. Karl
7. Paula
8. Willie
9. Carlotta
10. Michele

An alternative approach is to record all the "significant" types of behavior that occur in a particular time span, or in successive time spans. One pattern would be to observe a given child during a 30-second period once every five minutes in order to get cross sections of his behavior during an hour, day, week or even longer period. As an evaluation technique, observation is a more flexible approach than the use of rating scales, useful to teacher, researcher and parent as well.

A third procedure for evaluation is *ranking*. An example of ranking children by pre-math skill is given above. Rank does not need to involve an entire group, nor must it be confined to people. A director might ask her staff to pick out what they consider "the two best ways to help children learn to ask questions," or "the most and least successful means of teaching a song." Factors to consider in making choices may or may not be defined, although ranking of particular skills is often carried out using scores on formal tests.

Each of the techniques frequently used for formal evaluation—that is, rating, observation and ranking—poses certain limitations. To be useful all three must overcome the influence of what is called "halo effect." Halo effect refers to the tendency to give higher or lower ranking to one behavior than might otherwise be deserved because of a favorable or unfavorable impression made by another behavior or characteristic. Short-term assessment of a child's behavior may not always be distinct from the impression made by his physical appearance. The performance (especially in affective areas) of children who evoke the response "What a darling child!" is likely to be judged more positively than that of children less well-endowed physically. Likewise, the evaluation of a program may be colored by the fact that the teacher running it possesses unusual charm and good looks, or is especially skillful as a hostess with the result that the program is viewed as positively as the teacher.

In general, the major difficulty with using rating scales for formal evaluation is that the judgment is a summary of impressions which may not accurately reflect the behavior of the child or the teacher. It is especially subject to halo effect from one scale item to another, and raters often need training in order to understand what the person who constructed the scale had in mind. Ratings on autonomy, for example, may evoke quite different definitions and specific behavioral examples in the mind of the teacher than in that of the evaluator. Also, the specific behaviors that indicate "autonomy" vary from one age to another, between boys and girls and from one ethnic community to the next. It is essential to know the reliability of ratings, in the sense that two or more people rating the same child will rate him in somewhat similar fashion. If not, the rating may reveal more about the rater than about the teacher or child rated. The rating scale gives considerable opportunity for rater bias to operate.

A major limitation of observation as a rating method is that the large amount of data collected may be difficult to process and summarize. It is easily adaptable to a case study, however, where the object is to study in depth and detail the behavior of a particular child. The problem of dealing with excessive amounts of information can be solved in part by selective observation, that is, by observing for intervals of a few minutes each and by choosing particular types of behavior to observe before information is recorded.

The use of ranking as a means of evaluation also presents difficulties. Ranking leaves completely open the question of whether the person lowest in a particular group needs special help. Suppose pre-math skills are at issue. In some schools the child ranked "low" might have scores that would be "high" in another school. The same is true when ranking items in a program. What might be judged inadequate in one environment could conceivably be highly useful in another.

Ranking ignores absolute values and orders those individuals or items under consideration in relation to one another. Individuals or items may, of course, be ranked on the basis of any quality the evaluator chooses to judge. The difficulties in this method are those involved in getting data to make a valid ranking. If the ranking is based on accumulated impressions ("Rank the children on the basis of their creativity"), the difficulties involved in rating or observation also apply.

Unobtrusive Measures Assessment may include measures which are less immediate and direct, sometimes called unobtrusive measures. These are measures of one type of behavior from which fairly clear inferences may be made about some other area of attitude or behavior. They can be as useful as ratings, rankings and observations. The morale of a project staff, for example, may be indicated by turnover rate among the teachers. The eagerness of teachers to sign contracts, as shown by the time it takes to get all staff positions filled for the coming year, is another example.

Parent interest and involvement may be shown by the number of offers for volunteer work, the number of times parents keep their children from school to involve them in other activities, and the like.

Another example of an indirect measure of evaluation is the keeping of records showing absences or lateness. Although perhaps not critical in a preschool program, student attendance has a bearing on the effectiveness of a total program and on staff performance and may therefore indicate a need for change of some kind if it does not meet certain standards.

Unobtrusive measures are handicapped by the fact that the behavior observed or recorded is connected with other behavior only by inference. High teacher turnover rate *may* indicate low morale but may also indicate other conditions, such as a well-trained staff which is motivated to go on for additional training or is hired away for promotions which the school itself could not provide. This type of measure is useful but should be interpreted cautiously with alternative interpretations kept in mind.

Instruments for Testing

Educational and performance tests, as we know them today, were introduced in Europe early in the 1900's. They received great attention in the United States where they were further developed and widely used for the evaluation and selection of recruits during World War I and subsequently for the evaluation of student achievement and ability in the schools. At the present time, testing and the sale of a wide variety of tests are major industries, whose growth was accelerated by the development of the IBM punch card and scoring sheet.

Tests and test scores are typically based on the principle of comparing individuals to group norms. That is, a child is considered not on an absolute standard of mastery, but in relation to what has been found to be typical for an age or sex group. This is not true of all tests, but it is the premise on which a large part of the testing movement has been developed.

Some evaluations of performance, however, are based on the concept of mastery of a given subject matter. For example, there are tests which indicate whether a child has learned to count and/or how far he has learned to count, whether he can identify colors, how many objects he can name, etc. Standards of this kind apply to a child without regard to where he stands in relation to other children. Subsequent interpretation of such data, however, is almost inevitably made in terms of the performance typically expected of children his age.

Literally thousands of tests are on the educational market, hundreds of which apply to evaluation of preschoolers and programs of early education. Probably the best known and most controversial in the United States are those developed to measure intelligence. Even though there have been numerous attempts to put IQ into reasonable perspective, many parents and teachers still regard this measure as having finality and permanence.

Tests designed to show academic achievement at all school levels, and various

**Representative Organizations
Active in Evaluation and
Testing in the United States**

*Educational Testing Service,
Princeton, New Jersey*

*Stanford Research Institute
Menlo Park, California*

*American Institutes of Research,
Palo Alto, California*

---

personnel tests, have also captivated the public. Unfortunately they have sometimes been misused and misinterpreted. It is particularly tragic when they are used early in a child's educational experience to put him in a "track" or otherwise label him as "slow" or educationally retarded in some way. These reputations may influence the child's learning and achievement all his life. This is especially true when the teacher represents a test score as indicating an inherent disability when it may actually indicate the quality of the education provided and the experience offered by the society.

In recent years, institutes devoted to the development of tests have grown up rapidly in the country, several of them large research organizations. (See above listing of representative groups.) In the field of education, some handle much of the testing program that determines college entrance, others work closely with reading readiness, the evaluation of math skills and subject matter testing of all kinds.

Bias in Testing Traditionally, achievement and IQ tests have been constructed by professionals who come from academic, white middle-class society. Their beliefs of what children should know are in part a product of their middle-class environment, status and experiences. Results of efforts at the state and local levels to force a more equitable means of assessing children's ability are shown in Figure 10-5, pp. 304-305.

A child's IQ may change considerably as he grows older and there is no justification for discrimination, for example, between children with an IQ of 96 and those with an IQ of 102. Placing children into ranks or streams within a grade on the assumption that a given IQ test score represents an absolute and total potential may adversely affect a child's self-esteem and consequently his motivation to learn. A child so labeled may be given a significantly false impression of his talents which will be difficult to overcome. It should be remembered that tests, to some extent at least, inevitably reflect the values, life style and experiences of the group that has created them, and of those who administer and evaluate them.

Tests in Programs of Early Education Teachers in preschool programs should become familiar with the tests commonly used for evaluating young children and with the kinds of goals and behavioral objectives considered to be relevant criteria for evaluation. The use of tests assumes the existence of standards of measurement—that is, behavioral objectives. Goals inherent in the test may not coincide with those the teacher has established and those the program tends to foster. A nursery school program that encourages children to play, to build with blocks and to get along well together, should obviously be evaluated in terms of how well the children engage in play activities, build with blocks and accept one another.

SF Schools Halt Negro IQ Testing

SAN FRANCISCO (UPI) —Board of Education members voted unanimously today to stop administering intelligence tests to students by groups.

Also voted was a moratorium on individual intelligence tests for Negro children unless their parents requested them.

Those actions came after repeated demands by Negro organizations which asked moratoriums on both intelligence tests and achievement tests, contending they were culturally biased against black students.

The board decided, however, to continue achievement tests.

It also decided to employ consultants "who have expertise in test development and knowledge of ethnic minority backgrounds" to find means of testing the intelligence quotients of black and other minority students.

Among the organizations that objected to standard intelligence tests were the Association of Black Psychologists, the Urban League, the National Association for the Advancement of Colored People and the Neighborhood Legal Assistance Foundation.

School administrators were ordered not to put the results of either group or individual IQ tests in a child's permanent record folder and a committee was appointed to find ways of getting existing test scores out of such folders. (Palo Alto *Times,* July 17, 1970, p. 2.)

FIGURE 10–5 EFFORTS TO FORCE MORE EQUITABLE ASSESSMENT SOMETIMES HAVE DRAMATIC RESULTS

There is little justification in measuring such a program with a test that scores the ability to recognize letters of the alphabet and to count. Tests are usually designed to measure cognitive performance because affective performance does not easily lend itself to testing. This doesn't mean that affective behaviors or goals are any less important. There is simply a temptation to find situations which call for the instruments on hand, much as the small child armed with a hammer goes around looking for some-

UNITED STATES DISTRICT COURT
NORTHERN DISTRICT OF CALIFORNIA

DIANA, et al., Plaintiffs,
vs.
STATE BOARD OF
EDUCATION, et al., Defendants

C-70 37 RFP
STIPULATION AND ORDER

Dated Feb. 5, 1970

(Excerpt from Agreement) . . . The State Department of Education . . . shall require districts to get statistics sufficient to enable a determination to be made of the numbers and percentages of the various racial and ethnic groups in each Educable Mentally Retarded class in the district . . .

(Excerpt from Exhibit A) . . . If the primary language used in the home of the minor is a language other than English, the minor shall be tested by a school psychologist or other qualified person. . . . in both English and the primary language used in his home and shall be permitted to respond in either language during the testing session. . . . The school psychologist or other qualified person giving a test . . . shall be competent in speaking and reading the language used by the minor in his speaking and cognitive activity.

(Excerpt from Exhibit B) . . . It is the intent, of the State Board of Education that all children who come from homes in which the primary spoken language is other than English shall be interviewed, and examined, both in English and in the primary language used in his home. The examiner should take cognizance of the child's differential language facility. Any assessment of the child's intellectual functioning should be made on the basis of the spoken language most familiar to the child. In determining the intellectual functioning of a child whose primary language is other than English, it is recommended that the examiner utilize more than one instrument and include tests with performance scales.

---

thing to hammer. Characteristics and qualities for which measures have not been devised can easily be ignored despite their importance.. Thus ignored, they tend to lose value in the mind of the professional and fail to be built into future program objectives and evaluation procedures.

Table 10-3 contains examples of typical kinds of items used at this time in the evaluation of preschoolers and preschool programs. These are adapted from many different types of tests and are shown for illustration only.

SKILL AND LEVEL	SETTING	PROCEDURE	RESPONSE EXPECTED
Naming Objects from Memory 3- and 4-year-olds	Child and teacher are seated across from one another at small table In a concealed location teacher has six different items commonly used by child and whose names he knows 　　Example: doll, book, ball, spoon, car, crayon	For a total of six different trials, teacher places any two of the objects in front of the child, side by side Teacher: "This is a game where I'm going to take one of these away while your eyes are closed" "Look at the objects and think what they are" "Now, close your eyes and don't look while I take one away" "Open your eyes. What did I take away?"	Child should *name* the object that the teacher removed If he simply points to where the missing object was located, teacher should rephrase question so that he understands he is to *tell* her *what* she took away 　　Example: "What was here a moment ago that isn't here now?" Score: 　　1 point for each name correctly given
Simultaneous Voluntary Movement 5-year-olds	Child seated at table has box approximately half the size of a shoe box in front of him; at either side of box there are ten small items such as bottle caps, checkers, scrabble-type squares (total of 20)	Teacher: "Pick up a checker in each hand and put them in the box at the same time until all the checkers are in the box"	Two by two, child should put all pieces in the box using both hands simultaneously He is successful if he can do this in one out of two trials
Digit Span Preschool	Teacher and child in conversation together Teacher has list of number sets which vary according to quantity of numbers; three examples of each set—sets to go as high as 7 numerals | 4 | 2, 5 | 8, 1, 6 | 4, 7, 2, 1 | | 9 | 6, 3 | 7, 8, 2 | 9, 6, 8, 3 | | 1 | 4, 8 | 5, 9, 4 | 5, 8, 1, 4 |	Teacher: "Whatever numbers I say, you say them, too" She then says, "4" or whatever number is first on her list. She gives all numbers in the set with just 1 number, then all in the 2-set, the 3-set, etc. until child fails all items of any set	Child is to repeat the numbers after the teacher in the same serial order Score: 　　1 point for each correct repetition

TABLE 10–3 EXAMPLES OF TESTING METHODS USED IN EVALUATION OF PRESCHOOLERS AND PRESCHOOL PROGRAMS

SKILL AND LEVEL	SETTING	PROCEDURE	RESPONSE EXPECTED
Visual Perception Preschool	Teacher and child sit facing one another across small table Teacher has nine different cards with four pictures each The pictures are geometric figures, letters, words, numbers, shapes, and/or colors; one of the pictures on each card is the same as the first one in its row	Teacher places the cards in front of the child one by one Pointing to the first picture in the row (to the left for the child) she asks, "Which picture in the row is most nearly like the one I am pointing to?" If child has had training in matching she can say, "Which picture matches the one I am pointing to?"	Child is to point to his choice. *Score:* 2 points for each item matched without hesitation; 1 point if child was unsure or simply guessing
Visual Discrimination 3 to 6 years	Teacher and child sit facing one another across small table Teacher has 33 different cards each containing four pictures of the same object; picture at top of each set serves as model The objects are identical but differ in position	Teacher places the cards in front of the child one by one For each card she points to the model picture saying, "Which of the other pictures is most like this one?"	Child is to point to or in some way select picture of his choice *Score:* 1 point for each correct identification
Letter Recognition 5-year-olds	Teacher and child sit facing one another across a small table Teacher has 3 cards, each containing 6 lines of letters with 4 letters per line Letters are both upper and lower case Child has cardboard strip big enough to cover one row of 4 letters and a pencil for marking answers	Teacher puts cards in front of child one at a time She shows child how to use the cardboard strip he has to cover line *below* the one he will be working on Then she says, "Put a mark on the letter I name. If you are not sure, mark the one you think it might be." As child finishes one line he goes to next below in each column	Child is expected to put a mark (or cross out) his choices *Score:* 1 point is given for each correct choice

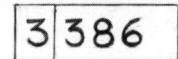

TABLE 10–3 (CONTINUED)

SKILL AND LEVEL	SETTING	PROCEDURE	RESPONSE EXPECTED
Stimuli Recognition (Vocabulary) 3½ up	Teacher and child face one another standing or seated From different items in 20 specific areas such as parts of body, classroom objects, foods, sounds, amounts, occupations, household items, teacher asks a total of 100 questions (number of questions during any testing time varies with maturity of child; each area has 5 items) Half of items are directly visible, the other half of a general nature	Teacher calls child by name or talks to him so she knows she has his attention, then asks a series of questions waiting for child to answer one before going on to next Examples: "What is a man who fixes teeth called?" (Touching knee) "What part of my body am I touching?" (Holding up picture of girl roller-skating) "What is this girl doing?"	Following each question, child is expected to name the object or activity indicated Score: 1 point for each correct answer
Self-Concept Preschool and primary	Child and teacher are seated together side by side Teacher has photograph of child. She also has a written list of questions designed to test child's concept of himself, and how he thinks his mother, teacher, and peers perceive him The questions consider pairs of bi-polar adjectives—one of which describes a socially approved quality Self-referent questions are used first	Photograph is shown to child and teacher asks him to tell her whose picture is shown ("Who is this a picture of?") Before going further, teacher makes sure child recognizes that what he sees is a picture of himself Pointing to the photo she asks questions such as the following, using child's name—he is here identified as Tom "Is Tom sad or happy?" "Does Tom's mother think he is neat or messy?" "Does Tom's teacher think he's quiet or noisy?" "Do Tom's friends like to play with him or dislike to play with him?"	Child is to respond verbally choosing one of the paired adjectives as criteria Score: 1 point for each answer in which he uses the positive adjective to represent how he sees himself, and how he thinks others see him N.B. Keeping track of the number of times child is unable to respond helps make total evaluation more realistic

TABLE 10–3 (CONTINUED)

SKILL AND LEVEL	SETTING	PROCEDURE	RESPONSE EXPECTED
Concept of Social Relationship Preschool	Teacher and child seated beside one another Teacher has 8 cards each with 6 identical circles except first which contains a picture representing a stimulus person—mother, father, teacher, friend; each stimulus person is used twice	Teacher shows child one card at a time As she does she says, "Pretend this circle is your mother (pointing to circle on left and naming stimulus person) "Show me which circle would be you" When child chooses she says, "I'll write your name in the circle you chose" 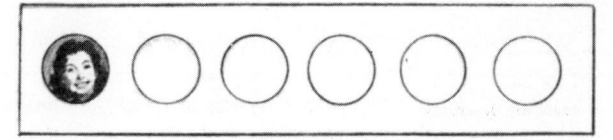	Child points to or in some way indicates his choice. *Score:* 1 to 5 points from nearest to farthest away from stimulus picture High score shows least identification.

Ordering-Sequencing
 	
5-year-olds
	Teacher and child seated across from one another at small table
	
	Teacher has sets of pictures of recognizable objects, varying in size, shape and number
	
	Child will be asked to order them by
	  shape
	  size
	  number
	or a combination of these factors
		Depending on skill to be tested, teacher gives child an appropriate set of items or shows him pictures
		
		Example: "Here are four pictures of trucks; put the pictures in a line so that the one with the most red trucks comes first, and the one with the fewest red trucks comes last"
			Child should order, or attempt to order items as directed.
			
			In example given, scoring would be as follows:
			
			3 points for correct ordering
			2 points if end sets correct but middle reversed
			1 point for attempt but no success
			0 points for no attempt

TABLE 10–3 (CONTINUED)

309   THE CHALLENGE OF EVALUATION

SKILL AND LEVEL	SETTING	PROCEDURE	RESPONSE EXPECTED
Recognizing Ordinal Numbers Preschool	Teacher and child at table or on floor together Teacher has 5 open containers (trucks, boxes, cups, dishes, etc.) lined up in a row She also has a checker or marble or object that can easily be placed in any of the containers	Teacher hands the checker (or whatever item) to child saying, "Put this in the fifth dish" (or whatever container used) Teacher removes checker from whichever container child put it in and hands it to him again asking that he place it in the following ordering: 5th, 4th, 1st, last, 2nd	Child is expected to place the marble in the location asked for Score: 1 point for each correct placement
Matching Quantities 5-year-olds	Teacher and child sit facing one another across small table Teacher has 4 cards, each with 5 sets in the arrangement shown. Center picture used as model	Placing a card in front of the child teacher says, "I will point to a picture; put your finger on another picture that has the same number of objects"	Child is to put his finger on the matching picture. Score: 1 point for each correct answer

Parallel Sentence Production
 	
Preschool
	Teacher and child seated together in any comfortable arrangement
	
	Teacher has 22 cards—two of which are samples. Each card has two drawings on it. One drawing illustrates a clue sentence, one the sentence desired
	
	Some require only simple word substitution, others require more elaborate word substitution
		Teacher shows one of the sample cards to the child and gives the clue sentence; she then points to other picture and gives parallel sentence; repeats but asks child to give parallel sentence; if child's answer is incorrect, she uses second sample card; she does not begin until child has responded correctly
		
		She then shows each of the 20 cards gives clue sentence, and waits for parallel sentence response before going on
			Child should give sentence called for with whatever word substitutions are needed
			
			Score:
			    1 point for each parallel sentence
			
			Teacher is to record any deviation from sentence expected
			
			    Example:
			    The boy is standing still
			    The girl is running

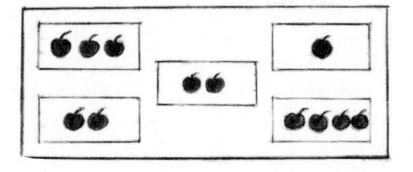

TABLE 10–3 (CONTINUED)

SKILL AND LEVEL	SETTING	PROCEDURE	RESPONSE EXPECTED
Verbal Facility Using Parts of Speech 5-year-olds	Teacher and child seated comfortably together Teacher has list of 40 questions—one for each of 40 pictures which are designed to elicit word responses containing various parts of speech	While child looks at a picture teacher asks question associated with it and calling for answer that contains desired parts of speech Example: What is the girl shown doing? (crying) What is different about these two circles? (one is bigger)	Child is to give verbal answer in appropriate word form Score: 1 point each correct answer

Knowledge of Word Meaning
 	
Preschool
	Teacher and child seated facing one another across small table
	
	Teacher has 10 cards each of which contains four pictures—all elements essentially alike in each set of pictures but arranged in different relationships
	
	    Examples: over, on, under, with, beside, around, in through. . . .
		Teacher asks child to look at each card, one by one; as he does she reads a sentence describing one of the pictures
		
		Example: The cat is in the barrel
		
		Then she says, "Put your finger on the picture that shows what I said about the cat"
			Child is expected to put his finger on picture asked for (or to point to it)
			
			Score:
			    1 point for each correct answer
			
			(If child does not respond, sentence and instruction may be repeated)

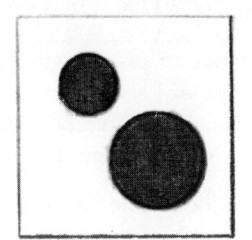

TABLE 10–3 (CONTINUED)

THE PURPOSE OF EVALUATION

Although an assessment usually carries with it the possibility that some change in program or behavior may be indicated, the specific purpose of each evaluation depends upon the persons responsible for the assessment plans and procedures. Many of the reasons for evaluations fall in these three categories:

1. To determine the effectiveness of the program or some of its elements
2. To obtain research data
3. To diagnose behavior and performance of an individual child and set objectives and goals for him

In the recent past, there has been a growing resistance to research in low-income and minority communities. Arguments against research include accusations that the information gained has not been used to assist the community or change the educational opportunities of children from poverty areas. Other objections have been raised to the use of test data in debates about differences in performance between ethnic groups and children from white communities. Additional arguments are raised against the use of scarce funds for research when there is insufficient money for improving the educational programs. The role of research and that of evaluation are made somewhat ambiguous by these objections.

Evaluating Program Effectiveness

One of the most prominent types of evaluation of early educational programs is oriented toward an assessment of the success of different approaches and major programs. These evaluations are inspired by pressures from political sources and desires to determine program efficiency. They fall into the following somewhat overlapping categories.

1. Desire to Know What Has Been Done and How Well One response to increased educational costs and higher taxes is that voters are more likely to ask, "What are we getting for our money?" And many are following up this question with another: "Are we getting what we want?" School bonds and higher taxes have been justified by school officials on the presumption that educational benefits would result from increases in expenditures. There have been many public attacks on the school in the mass media and books, and the questions that have been raised have given school communities a sense of caution and skepticism. They are now beginning to ask for an accounting, at least in the sense that they want more evidence that additional funds or new programs have some chance of accomplishing their aims. Questions regarding the problems of

SACRAMENTO (AP) —The state's superintendent of public instruction says he is setting up a special evaluation unit to determine if new school programs are doing what they're supposed to do.

"If they're not, we'll cut them off," said Wilson Riles in an interview. "Funds are scarce."

Riles commented Tuesday on a report by Legislative Analyst A. Alan Post that said California public schools are wasting large amounts of money through misguided efforts to improve education.

Post mentioned such programs, as smaller classes, hiring more consultants and higher teacher pay.

Post said there has been no indication that all these special programs—some of them federally financed—have improved the pupils' performance in school.

The problem, he said, is a lack of yardsticks to measure the effectiveness of the programs.

Riles commented, "Accountability is what we have to have to get the job done."

Riles had no quarrel with the study, conducted while the State Department of Education was under his predecessor, Max Rafferty.

Evaluation and approval unit he is setting up for special programs will have authority to "determine whether the new projects are coordinated with anything else," Riles said. "If not, we'll disapprove them."

"We should put all our funds together in some kind of comprehensive thrust so that we're dealing with something you can handle, not in bits and pieces," Riles said.

Post has been a frequent critic of the State Department of Education's organization and handling of projects such as the special federal programs. (Associated Press, June 23, 1971)

FIGURE 10-6

preparing youth for a complex society, and the increased political activity and new behavior codes among young people (as reflected in attitudes toward protests, sex, drugs, etc.) stimulate many taxpayers to call for evaluation of the schools to determine whether they are doing an effective job in this society.

2. Demand for Cost-Benefit Analysis Staff members of governmental and other fund-granting agencies are particularly interested in the economic side of education and are inclined to see the need for evaluation from an additional viewpoint. They are concerned with students' achievement, the efficiency of the schools and the cost of increasing their effectiveness. They want to compare results from alternative ways for accomplishing the same end to see which method gives the greatest return for the money spent. In effect, they ask, "It has cost x number of dollars to obtain these results, how much more will it cost to increase achievement even more? What would a different way cost?" The unit of measure may be IQ points, the number of children reading at grade level, or the proportion completing high school. In any event, their reason for assessing a program is closely tied to an analysis of cost-effectiveness.

3. Guarantee of Contract Performance   Evaluation is obviously a part of the philosophy of *performance contracting*. Within the last few years, education has come to be looked upon by some groups as a commodity—as something that can be bought and delivered on a guaranteed basis. For example, various private organizations are now advertising that for a given number of dollars and within such an amount of time they will teach a child to read. Parents who respond to this kind of promise are paying money for which they expect certain guarantees in return. An obvious reason for evaluation, therefore, is to determine whether a child has learned what the agency has contracted to teach him.

4. Follow-Up of Large-Scale Programs   Large-scale, publicly financed, innovative projects have brought pressure for evaluation to determine whether they have achieved their intended goals. Quite logically, researchers and administrators responsible for these undertakings want to know how well they are going. Funding is generally year-to-year, and at renewal time legislators and their constituents are naturally curious to know what has been accomplished. In appropriating money to launch efforts such as Head Start, Follow Through and Sesame Street, Congress said in effect, "We're convinced the need is great. Here's the money to get started on a solution to our problems. Be sure to let us know what happens." Accordingly, programs of this magnitude have evaluation provisions incorporated into the original proposals—evaluation that is to be carried on by outside agencies and not the people receiving the funds. In this way innovators recognized the need for objective assessment.

The results of an evaluation of a program mean different things to different audiences. They do not interpret themselves but are given meaning by those who write the report, by mass media and by informal discussions. The interpretations that can be placed on an evaluation must be assessed against the objectives that the program staff had established. In this case, the instruments used and the criteria of performance applied are limited to those agreed upon in advance. This is perhaps the most "fair" type of evaluation, but rarely is a program director or teacher given sole authority to say in what terms his or her results will be measured. Programs designed to raise self-esteem will probably be assessed by pre-academic measures, such as pre-math skills and pre-reading skills. The interpretation of results does not always make this clear, especially if there is publicity through mass media.

An essential principle in interpreting evaluation results, then, is to consider the criteria used and the standards against which the quality of the program is described. In other instances, the reader might want to take into account the length of time the program had been underway and the opportunity that had been provided for staff training and curriculum development. It is wise to be skeptical and withhold judgment about a program's effectiveness until opportunity has been given for the results to stabilize and to discover if gains can be obtained by more than one program staff or teacher.

Evaluation of the Side Effects of Programs

Evaluation of national educational efforts typically takes into account the success of a program in terms of its own goals. However, large-scale programs such as Head Start may have unexpected side benefits incidental to the original intent itself. An example is the wealth of research data that has come and is still coming from Head Start and Follow Through. In 1965, when Head Start began, relatively little was known about poor children in the United States. Since that time, knowledge has been tremendously increased in areas such as language development, family interaction and physical, cognitive and emotional growth of children from ghetto areas.

Another example is the impact of highly visible programs upon the attitudes and expectations of the general public in a neighborhood, state or nation. The publicity accompanying Head Start in its early years and the orientation of much of this publicity toward ghetto neighborhoods aroused increased concern among adults about the educational opportunities available to their children and a greater desire to participate in this sort of effort. The long range effects of this sort of community interest are difficult to measure but are nonetheless significant. The teacher who has as her goal "to involve mothers in the school program" can evaluate whether or not this is being accomplished in her particular situation. Without the teacher's knowledge, however, a mother may continue to participate in school-related concerns throughout her child's educational development because of having become involved at the preschool level. The teacher may learn of the mother's involvement if the family continues to live in the same neighborhood and has younger children who are subsequently enrolled at the preschool level. But she may never be able to assess the total results of her plan "to involve the mother" once she loses contact with the family.

Another unanticipated result of Head Start which did not appear during the formal evaluations of the program was the considerable increase in the number of professional men and women both interested and active in the field of preschool education. Within a short period sociologists, psychologists, linguists, anthropologists and people highly trained in related fields brought considerable talent and experience to bear on the problems associated with early education.

Evaluation for Research Purposes

Evaluation procedures are also utilized in research studies and in projects developing materials and programs on an experimental basis. A great many experimental programs and new procedures have been introduced into preschools in the past few years, and one of the principal aims of researchers has been to discover which types of programs are most efficient in achieving specific kinds of objectives. Such data may also be used to gain a more complete understanding about the effectiveness of teaching as well as information about learning patterns and processes. In addition, these techniques may be used to aid consultants in recommending new programs or procedures. Evaluations of innovation in preschool programs provide a basis for discussion with staff about program decisions and their consequences.

DIAGNOSING PROGRESS AND SETTING GOALS

From the teacher's point of view, the most significant functions of evaluation procedures are to diagnose growth patterns and achievement levels of her class and establish learning objectives for both individual children and the group.

Evaluation not only makes it possible to obtain information about performance but offers opportunities for diagnosis. At any time, a teacher is able to see how a child or an entire procedure is meeting her objectives. This is also true for group performance or program items. The use of simple records such as the one in Figure 10–6 enables a teacher to determine instantly what has happened and what still needs to be done in order to achieve a particular objective.

Such an observation might be made once a week for three weeks. The sample information shown in the figure clearly indicates that there would be little point to sitting quietly and reading a story to the group as a whole since nearly all of the children have met the criterion she has in mind. Naturally, the teacher will concentrate her efforts in helping Orlando and Judy to achieve this particular objective. Or she may decide that this objective does not meet the needs of these two children and adjust her efforts

OBJECTIVE: CHILD'S ORIENTATION TO AND PERSISTENCE AT A TASK

Number Key to Diagnostic Chart

a = Sept 20   b = Sept 27   c = Oct 4

	1	2	3	4	5	6
Mark				a		b,c
Bobby					a,c	b
Mary Anne						a,b,c
Bunny					a,b	c
Orlando	a	c		b		
Judy		b,c	a			
Juanita	a			b		c
Peter					c	a,b
Sherrill			b			a,c

1. Short attention span; easily distracted
2. Relies heavily on adult help to begin a task
3. Initiates a project but easily distracted
4. Initiates project but completes it only with help
5. Initiates project and completes it most of the time
6. Initiates a project and persists until complete

FIGURE 10-7 DIAGNOSTIC CHART MEASURING PROGRESS TOWARD A SPECIFIC GOAL

accordingly. The data simply make it possible for the teacher to diagnose where she stands in relation to where she wants to be.

Diagnosis can also be especially helpful in two other situations: 1) when it is used to keep students and parents informed as to individual progress; and 2) when the teacher diagnoses her own performance and applies the knowledge she gains toward her professional growth.

Evaluation can be a kind of constant diagnosis of what works, where a program stands and how procedures can be improved. Used in this way, tests and assessment devices are valuable tools for identifying areas of programs where growth is needed and change is possible. When teachers understand this, they will no longer see evaluation as a threat, but as a valuable resource for better teaching.

Developing Objectives

The use of evaluation techniques to assist a teacher in her primary task of education requires that some clear and specific goals be established for her, for the group and for the children as individual learners. Without such specific statements of educational objectives it is impossible for a staff to assess in a systematic way the effectiveness of their program and of themselves as teachers.

There have been many attempts to plan and describe preschool programs in such individually specific terms. Perhaps the most familiar of the recent approaches to identifying aims of a program is called "setting behavioral objectives." Although there is some controversy about the philosophy on which this approach is based (often on the argument that it is too mechanical, artificial and confining for the child and that it ignores important areas of behavior that are not easily specified in overt behavioral terms), the approach has had a significant impact on early educational programming and may, by virtue of its presence in the field, influence professionals to think more carefully about their programs and the implicit as well as the explicit goals they have in mind.

Behavioral Objectives Typically Used as Criteria for Language Competence of Four-Year Olds

1. As the teacher names three objects shown in a picture, the child will be able to point to each in turn without error; for two of them he will tell something about their use or characteristics (examples: tricycle, door, teacher).

2. Upon being shown ten different objects (or pictures of them), the child will be able to articulate the names of eight; (examples: apron, clock, elephant, knife, boat, butterfly, ladder, envelope, wall, plug, guitar).

3. When asked three questions such as the following examples, the child will be able to answer all of them using standard verb forms for bring, run *and* see.
a. "What did your teacher bring to school today?"
b. "How far did the dog run?"
c. "Which did you and your friend see—an airplane or a helicopter?"

4. To a small group of listeners the child will be able to repeat from memory a nursery rhyme or verse containing at least four lines.

The method of the behavioral objectives approach is most relevant, it is argued, for programs which state their goals in very broad terms, such as "We want children to develop language competence," or "Children should develop strong positive self-concepts" or "Children should learn respect for one another." Sweeping statements of this kind are usually so obviously desirable as to preclude any opposition by teachers or parents. They may indicate the general orientation of a program, but they are so vague as to defy evaluation. When have they been achieved? How can the teacher or parent tell what progress has been made? They offer no measurable standard.

Characteristics of Behavioral Objectives

Behavioral objectives such as the examples listed in Table 10–5 shows that they have three factors in common. A behavioral objective:

1. States what the learner is expected to do
2. Specifies in what context the desired behavior will occur
3. Gives a standard of achievement for acceptable performance

A behavioral objective must state what the learner is expected to *do* in terms of specific behavior.

Consider the desire of many parents and teachers to have a child "know his alphabet." To know one's alphabet is part of readiness for reading, but stated in this fashion, it doesn't indicate how to determine whether a learner has indeed achieved the goal set for him. Is he simply to say, "I know my alphabet," or will he be expected to name letters as they are pointed out, perhaps even to recite the names himself with or without any special order? Or will it be considered he "knows" his alphabet when he can copy the letters in some fashion, or perhaps draw pictures of objects whose names begin with certain letters? Must he identify all twenty-six letters or are twenty-four enough? When can it be said that a child "knows" his alphabet?

TABLE 10-4 INEFFECTIVE BEHAVIORAL TERMS CONTRASTED WITH EFFECTIVE BEHAVIORAL TERMS

AMBIGUOUS PERFORMANCE TERMS	SPECIFIC PERFORMANCE TERMS
know	give a reason
know how to	construct (build)
appreciate	select (choose, pick out)
understand	describe (tell)
show	mark
enjoy	name
comprehend	draw a line (circle, X)
realize	match (pair)
see	copy
learn	define
	count
	place
	touch

Obviously the evaluator must specify how a child should demonstrate whether he has learned what he was expected to learn. It takes words of a more specific nature than "know" or "develop" in order to formulate behavioral objectives. It takes performance terms such as "describe," "point to," "articulate," "repeat from memory" and "answer." Table 10-4 lists some commonly used words which are subject to a wide range of interpretation (and therefore misinterpretation), and some which make fairly specific statements of behaviors or products that can be expected of a student as evidence of learning.

Examples of behavioral objectives which clearly specify what a child might be expected to do to show competence in a variety of cognitive skills are given in Table 10-5, together with the characteristics of each objective. The second column isolates the performance expected of the child, while the third column specifies the context in which the behavior is to occur. A final essential in the formulating of behavioral objectives is that each shall give a standard of achievement for acceptable performance. Such standards are demonstrated in the last column of Table 10-5. Whenever possible, it is preferable for the specified behavior to take place in a context of meaningful activity. Many children tend to perform better and more willingly if they are asked to set a table using three pieces of silverware at each place or to construct a base for a square house, rather than simply being asked to "pick out three" of something or to "make a square."

Some Difficulties in Establishing Behavioral Objectives

Thus far the examples given have related to learning skills that are primarily cognitive or academic in nature. In these areas it is usually possible to be explicit because behaviors of this kind lend themselves to observation and measurement and often there is only one standard of performance. However, social and emotional behaviors present certain difficulties. Take the matter of cooperation. Many schools have as a goal "teaching children to cooperate." But there are many possible evidences of this kind of behavior. There's nothing really vague about cooperation—most people observing a child have a fairly good idea whether he is being cooperative. But each situation may involve different ways to exhibit cooperation and unless the teacher is willing (or able) to list all the examples of cooperation/noncooperation she can think of, she has no specific guidelines to use for comparison.

EXAMPLE	PERFORMANCE TERM	CONTEXT	ACCEPTED STANDARD
When asked by the teacher he can construct a base for a square house using 4 blocks.	construct	when asked by the teacher	using 4 blocks
From an assortment of 12 picture cards he can turn over all that represent an animal.	turn over	from an assortment	recognizing all that represent animals
He can touch 6 different parts of his body as the teacher names the different parts.	touch	as teacher names them	6 different parts
Without hesitation he can count out 10 chips from a handful held by the teacher.	count	from handful held by teacher	10 chips
When looking at 30 objects of different sizes and shapes (4 blue, 4 red, and 4 green; 3 yellow, 3 purple, 3 pink and 3 orange; 2 brown, 2 white and 2 black), he can select 3 green.	select	when looking at 30 objects of varying sizes and shapes	3 green
Upon request he can draw without lifting his pen or pencil a circle whose circumference at no point varies more than a ratio of 1:10 from a perfect circle.	draw a circle	upon request	circle as specified
From 10 different sized balls placed in front of him, with no errors he can point to: the largest ball the smallest ball the 2 balls closest together the nearest ball the farthest ball	point to	from 10 different sized balls placed in front of him	no errors

TABLE 10–5 BEHAVIORAL OBJECTIVES USED AS CRITERIA OF COMPETENCE

In other words, there is no single standard for social performance, because a child's behavior may take many different forms and still demonstrate that he is "cooperative." There are many different ways to show empathy, interest, friendliness and so on. Also, the particular situation itself determines whether the child *should* be cooperative or friendly or interested. Unlike knowledge of language, numbers, properties of the physical world and other specific skills, social and affective behavior are responsive to the conditions and demands of the context in which the behavior occurs. It may be most

Examples of Behavioral Objectives Related to Affective Areas

When faced with a problem he cannot handle himself:
1. The child will ask the teacher for help in a matter-of-fact manner
2. The child will not react in a manner which results in physical harm to himself or others
3. The child will not have a tantrum.

If a toy he considers "his" is taken from him by another child:
1. He will verbalize his feelings.
2. He will not use physical aggression.
3. He will persist in his efforts to regain the toy.
4. He will not withdraw from the situation.

---

appropriate for a child to be uncooperative, for example, when the demands are unreasonable:

Five-year-old Emily spent most of the day directing four-year-old Maria to do the "dirty work" of rejecting and hitting other children whom Emily disliked. "Tell them to get out of our kitchen. We don't want them here. Go hit him and throw water on his head."

Maria's compliance caused her much discomfort, unhappiness and confusion, especially when the children hit her back. The teachers continually sought to interpret the consequences of her behavior to Maria and to suggest alternatives, so they were delighted and approving when Maria finally exhibited some "appropriately uncooperative behavior" by saying "No!" to Emily's demands.

Judgments of appropriateness are fluid, complex and unique, so the evaluation of the response is also complicated. In areas involving skills or specific knowledge, performance is evaluated by positive indications of achievement—the specific desired behavior, the right answer. In social and affective areas, however, the goal may also include the discarding of undesirable behavior. The child should *not* do certain things when faced with frustration, such as another child beating him to a favorite swing, for example. He should not attack the other child; he should not stand in front of the swing so as to get hurt; he should not lie down and whine and cry, etc. In other words, there are behaviors desirable for him to *avoid* as well as socially acceptable alternatives. In competition with other children the child can avoid certain displays of temper and envy which are disruptive to the group and to himself; a desirable goal, then, may be the elimination or discarding of certain behaviors.

Suppose a program has as one of its goals "to develop clear self-concepts." Teachers need to observe children and record enough examples so that they can say, "These behaviors are indications (criteria) of clear self-concepts, these others are not." Unless they reach agreement of this kind, they have little basis for evaluation and no standard against which to measure performance.

It is possible to do a great deal more than has been done to specify behavioral objectives related to affective areas. Some examples are shown above.

Areas of affective and humanistic behavior and feelings are delicate and complex, and progress that a teacher may see in a child may elude the more formal evaluation procedures. A teacher will come to have confidence in her own sensitivity in these important kinds of growth and remember that evaluation is a tool which must serve her own purposes and ultimately contribute to the development of children in the society.

REFERENCES

Association for Supervision and Curriculum Development Yearbook. *Evaluation as feedback and guide.* Wilhelms, F. T. (Ed.) Washington, D.C.: National Education Association, 1967.

Bloom, B. S., Hastings, J. T. & Madaus, G. F. *Handbook on formative and summative evaluation of student learning.* New York: McGraw-Hill Book Company, 1971.

Mager, R. F. *Preparing instructional objectives.* Palo Alto, Calif.: Fearon Publishers, 1962.

Paulson, C. *Strategies for evaluation design.* Monmouth: Teaching Research Division, Oregon State System of Higher Education, 1970.

Popham, W. J. & Baker, E. L. *Establishing instructional goals.* Englewood Cliffs, N.J.: Prentice-Hall, 1970.

ILLUSTRATION CREDITS

All drawings by George Eisenberg

47	both, Office of Economic Opportunity
50	Lucia Woods
51	Office of Economic Opportunity, photo by James Foote
56	Mel Malinowski
57	Lucia Woods
58	Richard Penton
59	A. J. Sullivan
60	Office of Economic Opportunity
61	top, Mel Malinowski; bottom, A. J. Sullivan
62	Nancy Rudolph
63	Lucia Woods
64	Nancy Rudolph
65	Katrina Thomas
66	Mel Malinowski
67	Nancy Rudolph
68	Lucia Woods
69	Nancy Rudolph
70	Lynn McLaren
71	left, Elsa Dorfman; right, Office of Economic Opportunity, photo by Michael Sullivan
80	Lucia Woods
89	Mel Malinowski
92	A. J. Sullivan
94	Lucia Woods
95	Theodore & Jacqueline Bridges
101	Mel Malinowski
107	Black Star, photo by Mike Mauney
108	Black Star, photo by Dennis Brack
109	Black Star, photo by Michael Hayman
110	Magnum, photo by Charles Harbutt
111	Black Star, photo by Mike Mauney
112	Katrina Thomas
113	Katrina Thomas
114	Black Star, photo by Dan McCoy
118	Culver Pictures
136	left, Office of Economic Opportunity; right, Magnum, photo by Charles Harbutt
137	left, Office of Economic Opportunity; right, Time-Life, photo by Margaret Bourke-White
142	Black Star, photo by Werner Wolff
162	both, Office of Economic Opportunity
213	Monkmeyer, photo by Dorothy Reed
243	top, Lucia Woods; bottom, A. J. Sullivan
252	Lynn McLaren
255	Sam Unger
266	A. J. Sullivan
267	both, A. J. Sullivan
269	both, Lynn McLaren
296	Lucia Woods
297	left, Office of Economic Opportunity, photo by James Foote; right, Lynn McLaren

INDEX

Abdominal pain, 280

Ability grouping, 202

Academic achievement: influence of parental behavior upon, 91–103; intellectual interaction between parent and child, 91–93; effect of affective relationships, 93; patterns of maternal regulation and control, 93–95; of low-income and minority group children, 136–44; deficit model, 136–39; cultural disparity model, 139–41; miseducation model, 141–42; destructive system model, 142–44; testing, 302–3. See also Educational achievement; School performance

Accident form report, 278

Administrators: importance to success of preschool programs, 27, 38–39

Aesthetic judgment and standards: development of, 254–57

Affective behavior: judgment of appropriateness, 319–21

Affective development: relationship of arts to, 260–62

Affective relationships: influence on school achievement, 93

Affective skills: programs emphasizing, 165

Age: correlation with language development, 178–79; correlation with behavior patterns, 218–29

Aggression: transmission to children through imitation, 11–12, 216–17, 223

Aggressive behaviors: assertiveness, 216; aggression, 216; hostility, 216–17

Aides: employment in private schools, 34–35; guidelines for employment in compensatory programs, 35–36

Alignment, 214–16

Allergies, 274

Alternative behaviors, provision of: as means of weakening and eliminating undesirable behaviors, 224–25

American Indians, 118, 140

Animal behavior: research on, 4–5; investigations of imprinting, 5–6; investigations of critical periods of learning, 6

Apache children: study of, 139

Apathy: as a result of malnutrition in children, 9

Approach-and-influence behavior, 213–14

Arguing: as persuasive strategy, 217

Art: helping children to feel and think about objects at the same time, 242–44; motivating children to look for components of artistic creations, 245; characteristics of children's art, 250; role in developing awareness of cultural heritage, 252–54; development of artistic judgment and standards, 254–57

Artistic capabilities, development of: overall approaches for, 224–38, 239; developing awareness of inner responses to external stimuli, 238–44; developing children's competence, 244–50; dramatic play, 250–52; developing awareness of cultural heritage, 252–54; developing aesthetic judgment and standards, 254–57

Arts: place in preschool curriculum, 229–30; purposes of an arts program, 230–31; teaching philosophies, 232–34; as development of artistic capabilities, 234–57; relationship to cognitive, affective, and social development, 257–62

Assertiveness, 216

Assistant teacher: role of, 31–32

Bandura, A., 11, 222

Bank Street Approach, 157

Becker, Wesley C., 156

Behavior: influence of socio-cultural factors on, 104; effects of hunger and malnutrition on, 139; relationship to other dimensions of morality, 210–11. See also Behavior patterns; Classroom behavior; Social behavior

Behavioral objectives: as criteria for evaluation, 303; development of, 317–18; characteristics of, 318–19; difficulties in establishing, 319–21

Behavior Analysis Model, 152

Behavior patterns: persistence of earliest learnings, 5; imprinting, 5–6; critical periods of learning, 7–8; influence of genetic factors, 8–9; influence of environmental factors, 9–12; effects of formal education, 12–15

Bereiter, C., 145

Bereiter-Engelmann Programs, 156

Bias: in raters, 300–301; in testing, 303

Binet, A., 127

Birren, J. E., 180

Bites, 281

Blacks: discrimination against, 118, 120; strata within black community, 120; preparation of children for first school experience, 125–26; study of patterns of ability, 129–30; myth of "linguistic deprivation," 172, 180, 181; differences between dialect and standard English, 181; children's recognition of identity, 200; efforts to force more equitable assessment of pupils' ability, 304, 305, 312

Blind children: onset of speech, 175

Bloom, B. S., 12

Boeckman, C., 253

Broken bones: treatment of injured children, 276

Brown, R. W., 210, 211

Bugental, D. E., 173

Burns: treatment of, 280

Bushell, D., Jr., 151

California: state aid for day care programs, 23; teacher certification requirements, 42; establishment of school evaluation unit, 313

Casler, L., 9

Cazden, C. B., 181–82

Certification requirements, 42–43

Child beating, 281–82

Children's center: organizational structure, 28

Chinese-Americans; discrimination against, 118, 120; study of patterns of ability, 129–30

Choking, 280

Church: traditional role in personality development and morality training, 19; enrollment policy for preschool programs, 46; funding of preschools, 49

Classification: activities to develop, 189–90

Classroom behavior: ways to regulate, 220–21; setting behavioral objectives, 221–22; modifying behavior, 222–25; imitation and modeling, 222–23; systematic reinforcement, 223–25; recognizing the messages underlying behavior, 225–27

Cloward, R. A., 124

Cognitive abilities: growth of, 184–98; development of cognition and concepts, 184–87; activities for achieving cognitive goals, 187–98; developing physical knowledge, 187–88, 258; developing logical knowledge, 189–90, 259–60; developing seriation, 190–91; developing elementary number concepts, 192–94; developing concepts of space and time, 195–96; issues in cognitive learning at preschool level, 197–98; relationship to arts, 257–60. See also Cognitive skills

Cognitive goals: activities for achieving, 187–98

Cognitively Oriented Model, 154

Cognitive skills: as component of educability, 79; programs emphasizing, 165

Colds, 273–74, 276

Coleman, J. S., 129

Colleges: night and home study offerings in preschool education, 42

Comenius, J. A., 4, 137, 163, 166

Commercial or franchise schools: determination of purpose, 45

Communicable disease, 275–76, 277

Communication: of deaf children and children of deaf parents, 175. See also Language abilities; Nonverbal communication

Community adviser: teacher's role as, 20
Community colleges: two-year programs for preschool and nursery teachers, 42
Community Controlled School Model, 158
Community control of schools: growing demands for, 72-73, 131-32, 146-47
Community Coordinated Child Care (4 C's), 131
Compensatory education programs: role in socializing children, 18-20; potential conflict between family and school, 18-20; use of aides, 35-36; purpose, 45; enrollment policy, 46; early hopes for, 131; notion of "different language," 140; emphasis on linguistic skills, 180. *See also* Follow Through; Head Start
Competition: increase with age of preschoolers, 219
Concepts: development of, 184-85, 197, 258
Conditioning: as element in moral feelings, 211
Conflicts among preschoolers, 219
Conservation: exercise to develop, 193-94
Consistent criterion: necessity of maintaining, 189-90
Content-oriented programs, 165
Convulsions, 281
Coopersmith, S., 201
Cosby, Bill, 174
Cost-benefit analysis: of educational programs, 213-14
Crisis in the preschool: inevitability of, 264-65; difficulties in identifying crisis situations, 265-66; dimensions for analysis of, 267-70; teacher's view of, 270; parents' view of, 271; children's view of, 272; psychological and social crisis, 271-72; medical crises, 273-82; and the law, 283-86; the teacher's responsibility, 286-87; how to deal with, 287-90
Critical periods of learning: research on animal behavior, 5-6; comparison of nursing home and orphanage children, 7
Croft, D., 43

Crowding: effect on academic achievement, 95
Cultural differences: and language learning, 140, 180-32; effect on development, 185
Cultural disparity model: as explanation of school performance of poor children, 139-41; cultural pluralism, 139-40; acquisition of behavior not rewarded at school, 140-41
Cultural enrichment programs, 126, 139, 144
Cultural heritage: development of awareness of, 252-54
Culturally Deprived Child, 137
Cultural pluralism, 139-40
Cumulative deficit concept, 144
Curriculum: structured vs. unstructured, 161, 163-65
Cuts, 279

Dawdling: as persuasive strategy, 217
Day care: facilities provided by industry, 23-24; hospital and university provisions for, 24; federally funded parent-child centers, 24, 147; lack of facilities for children of the poor, 24; projected needs, 40
Deaf children: introduction to language, 175
Debus, R. L., 216
Deficit concept of school program design, 126. *See also* Cultural enrichment programs
Deficit model: as explanation of failure to achieve in school, 136-39
Dennis, M. G., 8
Dennis, W., 8
de Regniers, B., 212
Destructive system model: as explanation of school failures of poor and minority group children, 142-44
Developmental patterns: as basis for children's artistic patterns, 248-50
Diet: effect on IQ scores, 9

Digit span: testing of, 306

DiLorenzo, L. T., 13, 14

Direct observation: as technique for formal evaluation, 299–300, 301

Disadvantaged children: "early training" project in Tennessee, 13; New York State Education Department program, 13–14; short-term effects of early intervention programs, 14–15; defined, 22; increase in programs for, 22–23; concentration of federal programs in metropolitan areas, 22–23; percentage of preschoolers in early education programs, 24; teachers' problems in dealing with, 104; description of "poor" families, 104–6; poor school performance, 136–44; deficit model, 136–39; cultural disparity model, 139–41; miseducation model, 141–42; destructive system model, 142–44; ability to learn, 161, 180–81. See also Disadvantaged groups; Low-income groups

Disadvantaged groups: defined, 115; poverty as result of socio-economic inequalities and ethnic discrimination, 115; socio-economic basis of inequality in industrialized society, 115–16; racial and ethnic discrimination, 116–21; features common to, 121–24; consequences of disadvantage, 124–26

Discrimination. See Racial-ethnic discrimination; Social class discrimination

Disease. See Communicable disease; Medical crises in preschool

Discipline: benefits of consistent enforcement, 93, 94

Douglas, N. K., 245

Dramatic play, 246, 250–52

Drawing ability: development of, 248–49

Dropout rates, 128, 129

Earaches, 274–75

Early education: as a career, 1–25; motivation to teach young children, 1–3; importance of early experience, 3–15; critical periods of learning, 5–8; influence of genetic endowment and environmental factors, 8–12; effects on behavior of young children, 12–15; social relevance of, 15–20; role in maintaining the system, 15–16; during times of social change, 16–17; as social opportunity, 17–18; as intervention, 18–20, 144–47; career opportunities, 20–25; public commitment to, 20–21; rise in preschool enrollment, 22–23; range of programs, 23–25; choice of employment, 24–25; need for teachers, 40; school licensing requirements, 42; launching of Head Start, 134–35. See also Early education programs

Early education programs: parent demands for control of, 73–74; Head Start, 134–35; controversies over, 135; impact of poverty and discrimination on school achievement, 136–44; recent developments in, 147–49; Tucson Early Education Model, 150; Behavior Analysis Model, 151; Responsive Model, 152; Florida Parent Education Model, 153; Cognitively Oriented Model, 154; Instructional Games-Independent Learner Approach (NYU Model), 155; Engelmann-Becker Program, 156; Bank Street Approach, 157; Community Controlled School, 158; Primary Education Project, 159; underlying assumptions, 160–61; structured vs. unstructured curriculum, 161, 163–65; cognitive vs. affective skills, 165; content vs. process, 165; planned instruction vs. self discovery, 166–67; extrinsic vs. intrinsic motivation, 167–68; evaluation of, 303–5, 312–15; evaluating side effects of, 315–16; evaluation for research purposes, 316. See also Follow Through; Head Start

Educability: family influences on, 79–80

Education: as traditional agent of socialization, 16; during times of social change, 16–17; improvement of educational opportunities for poor and minority groups, 17–18; as intervention, 18–20. See also Early education

Educational achievement: and social opportunity, 104–32; influence of sociocultural factors on behavior, 104, 126–29; bias in intelligence tests, 127–28; dropout rate of pupils from low-income areas, 129; relative effects of social class and ethnic-racial differences on, 129–30. See also Academic achievement

Educational intervention: short term effects, 13–15; approaches to, 144–47; enriching cultural and educational environment, 144; engineering an instructional program, 144–45; involving parents in educational process, 145–46; increasing community control over schools, 146–47; beginning instruction at earlier ages, 147

Educational Policies Commission (NEA), 21

Educational research: as purpose of preschool programs, 46; growing resistance of low-income groups to, 312; evaluation procedures, 316

Educational Research and Development, Panel on, 141

Educational Testing Service, 303

Elman, R. M., 124

Emotional climate: influence of light and noise, 52

Emotional release: through the arts, 260–61

Employment patterns: of white and nonwhite women, 120–21, 122

Engelmann, S., 145, 156

Engineered programs of instruction, 144–45

Enrollment: See Kindergarten enrollment; Preschool enrollment

Enrollment policy: as function of school sponsors, 46

Environment: influence on behavior, 8, 9–12; and differences on intelligence test scores, 127; influence on continuation of child's responses to speech, 175. See also Physical environment

Equipment safety, 286–87

Evaluation: attitudes and apprehensions of teachers, 291–93; informal, 293–95; formal evaluation, 295–302; techniques of assessment, 298–301; unobtrusive measures, 301–2; instruments for testing, 302–11; test bias, 303; tests in programs of early education, 303–11; of program effectiveness, 312–15; of program side effects, 315–16; for research purposes, 316; diagnosing progress and setting goals, 316–21

Expanded discourse: as means of providing language experience, 184

Experience: as factor in increasing teacher competence, 43–44

Extrinsic motivation, 167–68

Eye infections, 274

Facilities: as factor differentiating preschools, 47–48

Family: traditional responsibility for transmission of society's values, 16, 17–18, 72; potential competition with teacher in transmitting values to children, 18–20; growing separation from school, 72–74; rationale for parent involvement in preschools, 72–80; stresses in interaction with school, 74–76; benefits of parental participation in preschools, 76–79; influences on educability, 79–80; getting parents involved, 80–90; influence of parental behavior upon academic achievement, 91–103; training programs for, 96–103. See also Mother-child interaction; Parent involvement

Family size: and poverty, 106

Fantini, M. D., 119, 142

Fathers: techniques for encouraging participation in school affairs, 87–90

Fear: as factor influencing growth, 9

Federal government: creation of Head Start, 21; increase in funding for experimental and operational purposes, 21; concentration of preschool programs in metropolitan areas, 22–23; Follow Through, 24, 314; parent-child centers,

24; funding of preschool programs, 49. *See also* Head Start

Financial control: function of school owners and boards of directors, 39

Flavell, J. H., 205–6

Florida Parent Education Model, 153

Follow Through, 24, 314

Follow-up: importance in reducing psychological stress after injuries, 290

Formal evaluation: rating scales, 298, 301; direct observation, 299–300, 301; ranking, 300, 301, unobtrusive measures, 301–2

Foster, F., 261

Fowler vs. Seaton, 283–85

Free movement: as means for children to acquire logical knowledge, 259–60

Freedman, D., 8

Froebel, F., 5, 166, 232–33

Frustration among preschoolers, 219

Funding: as factor differentiating preschools, 48–49

Genetic influence: on behavior, 8–9; and differences on intelligence test scores, 127; on language ability, 175

Geographic boundaries: establishment by children, 212–13, 216–18

German measles, 275

Ghetto children. *See* Disadvantaged children; Minority groups; Negroes

Gilkeson, Elizabeth C., 157

Glass, D., 9

Gleason, J. B., 177–78

Gonzalez, Congressman H. B., 105

Gordon, I., 153

Gotkin, L. G., 155

Gray, S., 13

Grossman, M., 245

Group behavior. *See* Social behavior

Group membership and interaction: child's awareness of, 204–5

Guilt, 210, 211

Halo effect, 300

Harlem: description of child's life, 138

Harlow, H. F., 6

Harlow, M., 6

Hartshorne, H., 209

Hartup, W. W., 220

Harvey, Dr. Birt, 273n

Head injuries, 276, 278

Head Start: launching of, 21, 134–35; effect on enrollment of nonwhite children in preschool programs, 22–23; early literature of, 138; recognition of importance of learning in preschool years, 147; innovation in developing programs, 148; evaluation programs, 314; side benefits of, 315–16

Heinroth, O., 5

Henderson, R. E., 150

Hesburgh, Rev. Theodore M., 11

Hess, E., 6

Hess, R. D., 6, 43, 76, 80, 91, 96, 125, 180

Home visits: as technique for involving parents from low-income families in schools, 85–86; as means of involving fathers in school affairs, 90; occasions for teaching by modeling, 99–103

Hopi children: study of, 8

Hostility, 216–17

Hughes, M., 150

Human knowledge; three principal sources, 186*

Hunger: effects on behavior of children, 139

Hunt, J. McV., 12

Identification: and transmission of aggression to children, 11–12

Identity, 200

Imaginary playmates: child's means of dealing with emotional problems, 251

Imprinting, 5–6

Imitation: of filmed examples of aggression, 11–12; role in moral conduct, 211; as means of eliciting desired behaviors, 222

Income: differences between white and non-white workers, 120–21, 122*
Industrialized society: socio-economic inequalities, 115–16
Infancy: as prime time for establishing base for later learning, 147
Informal evaluation, 293–95
Informational meetings: as means of involving parents, 81–83
Instructional Games-Independent Learner Approach (NYU Model), 155
Insurance coverage of preschools, 287
Intelligence tests: bias in, 127–28
Interpersonal behavior. See Social behavior
Intervention: education's role in socializing children for change, 18; potential competition between teacher and family in transmitting values, 18–20
Intrinsic motivation, 167–68
IQ tests, 302, 303

Japanese-Americans: discrimination against, 118, 120
Jazz, 253
Jensen, A. R., 8
Jersild, A. T., 261
Jewish children: study of patterns of ability, 129–30
Job selection procedures: hidden bias in, 119
Johnson, President Lyndon B., 134, 143
Junior colleges: programs for nursery and preschool teachers, 42
Justice: different treatment of rich and poor, 123

Kamii, C. K., 186, 187n
Kellogg, R., 248, 250
Kindergarten enrollment: rise in, 21, 22–23
King, Coretta Scott, 123
King, Dr. Martin Luther, Jr., 123
Klaus, R. A., 13
Kohlberg, L., 210

Krech, D., 9
Kugelmass, I. M., 9

Language abilities: growth of, 172–84; myth of "linguistic deprivation" among black children, 172, 180, 181; language as basic channel of human interaction, 172–74; language as a subtle strategy to disguise meaning, 173; acquiring a language, 174; learning to speak, 175–77; learning structure of a language, 177–80; language learning and socio-economic and cultural differences, 180–82; teacher's role in language learning, 182–84
Lansing, K. M., 249
Learning: critical periods of, 5–7. See also Cognitive abilities
Legal responsibility: of school owners and boards of directors, 39
Lenneberg, E. H., 175, 178
Lesser, G. S., 129, 130
Letter recognition: testing of, 307
Liability of nursery schools, 283–86
Lice, 281
Licensing requirements for nursery schools, 42, 48
Light: influence on emotional climate of preschool, 52
Linear ordering: developing concept of, 195
Lindsley, 9
Locke, J., 5, 137
Logical knowledge: activities for developing, 189–91, 197; acquisition of, 197
Lorenz, K., 5
Low-income groups: subordination of mother's role to teacher's role, 19–20; problems in communication with teachers, 76; techniques for involving parents in schools, 84–87; training programs for, 96–103; strategies for encouraging parents' sense of competence, 96–97; teaching strategies in the home, 97–98; teaching parents to teach, 98; contact-

ing parents, 98–99; teaching by modeling, 99–103; studies of school performance, 129–30, 136–44; growing resistance to educational research, 312. *See also* Disadvantaged children; Poor people

Lyford, J. P., 138, 143

Make-believe. *See* Dramatic play

Malnutrition: effect on physical development, 9; effects on behavior of children, 139

Mansfield, R. G., 283n

Matching quantities: testing of, 310

Maternal behavior: effect on children's early cognitive and academic development, 93, 145

May, M. A., 209

Measles, 275

Medical crises in preschool: illness and injury, 273; eye, ear, nose and throat infections, 273–75; communicable disease, 275–76, 277; broken bones and head injuries, 276, 278; minor injuries, 279–80; miscellaneous problems, 280–82; teacher responsibility, 282

Melting pot tradition, 117–18

Metropolitan areas: concentration of federal programs in, 22–23; growing demand for community control of schools, 72–73, 131–32, 146–47

Mexican-Americans: Texas Conference for, 105; discrimination against, 118; achievements of, 120; cultural patterns for children, 139–40; Tucson Early Education program, 150

Miller, J. O., 15, 21

Minor injuries: treatment of, 279–82

Minority groups: improvement of educational opportunities, 17–18; effect of compensatory programs on values of children, 18–20; growing demands for community control of schools, 73, 131–32, 146–47; need for teachers to understand influence of socio-cultural factors on children's behavior, 104; racial and ethnic discrimination, 116–21; study of academic performance of children, 129–30; efforts to force more equitable assessment of pupils' ability, 304, 305, 312. *See also* Blacks; Disadvantaged children; Mexican-Americans; Racial-ethnic discrimination

Miseducation model, 141–42

Modeling: as means of teaching parents how to teach, 99–103; as means of eliciting desired behaviors, 222–23

Models: imitation by children, 11–12

Modifying behavior, 222–25

Moral development: dimensions of morality, 208–9; limits of comprehension, 209–11

Morality: dimensions of, 208

Montessori, M., 135, 147, 160

Montessori schools, 91

Mother-child interaction: effect on academic achievement, 93–95; encouragement of self-reliance and independence, 93–94; consistency in enforcing discipline, 94; use of control strategies, 94–95; resources available for, 95, 96. *See also* Mothers

Mothers: competition with teachers, 18–19, 75; teachers as confidantes, 76–77; preparation of black children for first school experience, 125–26; sharing of responsibility for child with teachers, 225–27. *See also* Family; Mother-child interaction; Parent involvement

Mothers' meetings: as techniques for involving parents in school, 86–87

Motivation: to teach young children, 1–3; as component of educability, 79, 160; extrinsic vs. intrinsic, 167–68

Motor and language development, correlation of, 179

Music: as resource for developing children's competence in aesthetic activities, 240–42; goals of a preschool program, 247–48; as integrating factor between individuals and groups, 261–62; as reflection of man's perception of his world, 252–

53; identification of specific works, 253–54; development of aesthetic judgment and standards, 257

Naming objects from memory: testing of, 306
National Education Association: recommendation regarding early education, 20
National Laboratory on Early Childhood, 15
National Nutrition Survey, 139
Negroes: discrimination against, 118, 120; strata within black community, 120; preparation of children for first school experience, 125–26; study of patterns of ability, 129–30; myth of "linguistic deprivation," 172, 180, 181; differences between black dialect and standard English, 181; children's recognition of identity, 200
New York State Education Department: prekindergarten program, 13
Nichols, I. A., 178
Nimnicht, G., 152
Noise: influence on emotional climate of preschool, 52–53
Nonverbal communication, 174, 175
Nonwhites: enrollment in preschool programs, 22–23; employment patterns, 120–21, 122. See also Blacks; Minority groups
Number concepts: activities for developing, 192–93
Nursery schools: liability in case of injury to children, 286. See also Early education; Preschools

Observation. See Direct observation
Open House meetings: as means of involving parents, 83
Operation Head Start. See Head Start
Ordering-sequencing: testing of, 309
Ordinal number recognition: testing of, 310*
Ornati, O., 106

Orphanages: characteristics of institutionalized children, 7; effect of fear on growth, 9; effect of enriched environmental opportunities, 9–11
Outdoor play areas: impact on goals of preschool programs, 51–52
Owen, R., 5

Parallel sentence production: testing of, 310
Parent-Child Centers, 24, 147
Parent conferences: as strategy for involving parents, 81
Parent cooperatives: role of owner-directors, 39; enrollment policy, 46; funding of, 49; direct parent involvement, 74
Parent involvement: rationale for, 72–80; separation between family and school, 72–74; required in parent coops, 74; stresses in family-school interaction, 74–76; benefits of, 76–79; family influences on educability, 79–80, 145; getting parents involved, 80–90; strategies and techniques, 80–90; involving low-income families, 84–87; involving fathers, 87–90; parents as teachers, 91–103; influence of parental behavior on academic achievement, 91–103, 145; training programs for families, 96–103; teaching parents to teach, 98; contacting parents, 98–99; teaching by modeling, 99–103. See also Academic achievement; Educational achievement
Parents: view of crisis, 271
Parks, G., 122
Perceptual skills: training with instruction, 235
Performance contracting, 314
Persistence: as persuasive strategy, 217
Persuasive behaviors, 217–18
Pestalozzi, J. H., 4, 163
Physical activity: questions for encouraging, 260
Physical environment: as factor differentiating schools, 46–47; impact on goals of preschool program, 49–52; influence on emotional climate, 52–53

Physical knowledge: activities for developing, 187–88; acquisition of, 197
Physical release: through the arts, 260–61
Piaget, J., 82, 166, 167, 186, 187n, 189n, 192, 193, 196, 205, 206, 209, 248–49
Planned instruction method, 166–67
Plato, 4
Play areas. See Outdoor play areas; Space requirements
Police: children's views of, 246, 250
Poor people: improvement of educational opportunities, 17–18; effect of compensatory education programs on values of children, 18–20; as targets of federal programs, 46; Social Security Administration definition of, 104–5; institutional exploitation of, 105–6. See also Disadvantaged children; Poverty
Poull, L. E., 9
Poverty: defined, 104–5; institutional exploitation of poor people, 105–6; education as avenue of upward mobility, 106; and family size, 106; depicted, 107–14; as consequence of socio-economic inequalities and racial-ethnic discrimination, 115–21; impact on school performance, 136–44. See also Academic achievement; Educational achievement; Low-income groups; Poor people
Prejudice: meaning of, 119. See also Racial-ethnic discrimination
Preschool: duties and responsibilities of personnel, 30; dimensions that differentiate schools, 44–49; differences in purpose and sponsorship, 44–46; types of, 45; other factors of differentiation, 46–49; impact of physical environment, 49–53; handling crisis in, 264–90; psychological and social crisis, 271–73; medical crises, 273–82; liability in case of injury, 283–86; how to deal with crisis, 287–90. See also Early education
Preschool enrollment: rise in, 21, 22–23; projection, 40
Pretending. See Dramatic play
Primary Education Project, 159

Private schools: enrollment policy, 46; funding of, 49; parent involvement and control, 73
Process-oriented programs, 165
Professional training of teachers: need for teachers, 40; programs of, 40–42; certification and licensing requirements, 42; training through experience, 43–44
Project Follow Through. See Follow Through
Psychological crisis, 271–73, 288–90
Psychological space, 213
Public school programs: funding of, 49
Puerto Ricans: discrimination against, 118; study of patterns of ability, 129–30; cultural patterns for children, 139–40
Punishment, 224
Pupil role: acceptance of as component of educability, 79

Racial and ethnic discrimination: melting pot tradition, 117–18; persisting legal restrictions, 119; ways to determine existence of, 119–20; strata within various ethnic groups, 120; impact on earnings of nonwhites, 120–21; effects on learning and cognition, 143. See also Blacks; Disadvantaged children; Minority groups
Racial awareness, 206–7
Radin, N. L., 186, 223
Rafferty, M., 313
Ramsay, T., 245
Ranking: as technique for formal evaluation, 300, 301
Rating scales: for programs of early education, 164
Read, M. S., 139
Reasoning: as means of weakening and eliminating undesirable behaviors, 224
Reinforcement, 211, 223–24, 224–25
Relative size: developing concept of, 191
Reliability of ratings, 301
Research. See Educational research
Res ipsa loquitur, doctrine of, 285

Resnick, L. B., 159
Responsive Model, 152
Reversibility, 193
Rewards, use of: as motivation for learning, 168, 169
Riles, W., 313
Ripple effect, 272–73, 290
Rivalry among preschoolers, 219
Role-taking ability, 205–6
Rosenberger, E. F., 178
Rosenzweig, M. R., 9
Ross, D., 11
Ross, S., 11
Rousseau, J. J., 4, 163, 166
Rules: development of concepts about, 208; learning of, 221
Rural areas: low preschool enrollments, 23

Safety programs in preschools, 286–87
Samuel, E. L., 9
Sand-in-eye, 280
School of the Mother's Knee, 137
School performance: relation to self-esteem, 202–3. See also Academic achievement; Educational achievement
Schools: as agent of socialization, 16; changing responsibility of teachers in technological age, 17; formal and informal structure, 27–31; assistant teachers, 31–32; teacher's perspective, 32–34; aides, 34–36; volunteers, 36–38; role of administrators, 38–39; increasing separation from family, 72–74; viewpoint of low-income mothers, 125–26; administrative organization chart, 117*
Schwartz, J. B., 245
Scott, J. P., 5–6
Scrapes, 279
Scarlet fever, 275
Self-concept: defined, 200; origins of, 201–3; testing of, 308
Self discovery method, 166–67

Self-esteem: defined, 201; origins of, 201–3
Self-knowledge: growth of, 200–207; self-concept, 200–203; identity, 200; self-esteem, 200–203; awareness of group membership and interaction, 204–5; role-taking ability, 205–6; racial and social class awareness, 206–7
Self-reliance and independence: strategies to encourage, 93–95
Sensory motor stage, 185, 186, 248–49
Seriation: activities for developing, 190–91
Sesame Street, 15, 314
Sex differences: and behavior patterns, 219–20
Sex-role expectations, 220
Shipman, V.C., 76, 80, 125, 126
Simultaneous voluntary movement, 306
Site selection: responsibility of school owners and boards of directors, 39
Situational setting: as cause of difference in language, 181–82, 183
Skeels, H., 9–11
Skin diseases, 280–81
Skinner, B. F., 166, 167
Social behavior: patterns of, 211–20; social interaction, 211–12; territoriality, 212–13; approach-and-influence behavior, 213–14; alignment, 214–15; aggressive behaviors, 216–17; persuasive behaviors, 217–18; age differences in behavior patterns, 218–19; sex differences and behavior patterns, 219–20; judgments of appropriateness, 319–21. See also Classroom behavior
Social change: effects of conflicts on role of schools, 16–17; education for, 18
Social-class awareness, 207
Social class discrimination: influence on behavior, 104; reinforcement by institutions, 105–6; rooted in industrialized society, 115–16; myth of equality, 115–16; features of lower-class life, 121–24; consequences of, 124–26; effects on educational achievement, 126–29; implications for program planning, 136–69;

failure of slum schools to teach effectively, 141–42; and destruction of children, 142–44; preschoolers' awareness of, 207; reflected in achievement and IQ tests, 303, 304, 305

Social competence: approach-and-influence behavior, 214; teacher's role in growth of, 214; aggressive behaviors, 216–17; persuasive behaviors, 217–18; development of, 220–27; relation of arts to, 260–62

Social crisis: in preschool, 271–73

Social-developmental schools, 45

Social experiences: through the arts, 261–62

Social interaction: territoriality, 212–13; approach-and-influence behavior, 213–14; alignment, 214–16; aggressive behaviors, 216–17; persuasive behaviors, 217–18; inevitability of stress, 271. See also Social behavior

Socialization: as joint burden of school and family, 15–16, 72

Social opportunity: and educational achievement, 104–32; influence of socio-cultural factors on behavior, 104; poverty in the United States, 104–14; socio-economic basis of inequality, 115–16; racial and ethnic discrimination, 116–21; features common to disadvantaged groups, 121–24; consequences of disadvantage, 124–26; relation of socio-economic level to performance, 126–29; cultural and ethnic differences, 129–30; implications for the classroom, 131–32

Social relationships: concepts of, 207–11; development of concepts about rules, 208; moral development, 208–11; testing concept of, 209*

Social stress: ways of avoiding, 288–90

Society: effect of social conflicts on traditional role of schools, 16–18

Socio-economic differences: relation to educational achievement, 126–29; effects on language learning, 180–81; influence on development, 185; in industrialized societies, 115–16

Sorting, 189–90

Space: developing concept of, 195

Space requirements: effect on goals of preschool program, 49–52

Speech, onset of, 174–77

Spitz, R. A., 7

Sponsorship of schools: different forms, 46

Staff-child ratios, 49*

Staff competence and training, 48

Standard English: use of different language at home, 140; and black dialect, 181

Standards of performance: importance to self-esteem, 203

Stanford Research Institute, 303

State aid: for preschool programs and day care, 23

Stecher, M., 259, 260

Stevenson, H. W., 206

Stimuli recognition (vocabulary), 308

Stimulus deprivation, 137–38

Strep throat, 274

Structured vs. unstructured curriculum, 161, 163–65

Success: as source of development of self-concept and self-esteem, 202–3

Systematic reinforcement: 223–24, 224–25

Teacher evaluation sheet, 292

Teachers: as potential competitors of mothers, 18–19, 75, 225–27; as community advisers, 20; perception of formal and informal structure of school, 27–31; an assistant teacher's concerns, 31–32; perspective of, 32–34; need for, 40; programs of training, 40–42; certification and licensing requirements, 42–43; training through experience, 43–44; as confidantes of mothers, 76–77; benefits of close contact with parents, 77–78; parental roles as teachers, 91–103; attempts to "correct" children's pronunciation and grammar, 176; role in language learning, 182, 184; need to understand behavior of children in conceptual context, 212–16; role in growth of approach-and-influence behavior, 214; need to recognize children's strategies, 216–18; ways of regulating classroom behavior, 220; setting behavioral objectives, 221–22; imitation and modeling, 222–23; systematic reinforcement, 223–24; weakening and eliminating undesirable behaviors, 224–25; understanding messages of behavior, 225–27; as labelers, 258; role in crisis situations, 265–66; view of crisis, 270; responsibility in medical crisis, 282; ways to deal with crisis, 287–90; attitudes toward evaluation, 291; informal evaluation, 293–95; formal evaluation, 295–302; use of evaluation procedures, 316–17; setting behavioral objectives, 317–19; 319–21

Television: imitation of aggressive behaviors portrayed, 11–12, 216–17, 223

Territoriality, 212–13, 215, 216–18

Test bias, 127, 303

Test instruments, 302–5, 306–11*

Texas Conference for Mexican-Americans, 105

Time: developing concept of, 195–96

Tokens, use of, 168, 169

Tonsillitis, 274

Torrance, E. P., 245

"Tracking," 303

Traffic patterns: importance in nursery school functioning, 50–52

Transformation: developing concept of, 195

Truth-in-Lending, 123

Tuberculosis, 275–76

Tucson Early Education Model, 150

Twins: influence of genetic factors, 8; studies of onset of speech, 175–77

Tyack, D., 119, 120

United States: number of poor people, 104–5; education as traditional route to escape poverty, 106; unequal distribution of privileges and resources resulting from industrialized society, 115–16; racial and ethnic prejudice as source of poverty and disadvantage, 116–21

University extension courses in preschool education, 42

Unobtrusive measures: as means of assessment, 301–2

Upward mobility: education as a principal avenue, 106

Urban areas. See Metropolitan areas

Values: role of school in transmitting, 16; conflicts, 16, 272

Verbal facility: testing of, 311

Visual discrimination: testing of, 307

Visual perception: testing of, 307

Vocabular development: as effect of arts program, 258

Volunteers: as source of enrichment in preschool programs, 36–38

Wachowiak, F., 245

Weikart, D. P., 154

Weinstein, G., 119, 142

Whining: as persuasive strategy, 217

White House Conference (1950), 20

Widdowson, E. M., 9

Wittes, G., 223

Wolff, D., 155

Woodworking: helping children to use tools, 246–47

Word meaning, knowledge of: testing of, 311

Workshop meetings: as means of involving parents, 83–84

Zimiles, H., 157

Zook, E. A., 220